Anne Moody

COMING *of* AGE IN MISSISSIPPI

"Soul is an elusive, overworked, often misapplied term . . . but it fits this powerful autobiography." —*Library Journal*

"Anne Moody recounts the horror and shame of what growing up in Mississippi really means if you are black. Poverty, knives, threats, arson, miscegenation, illegitimacy, domestic service, police brutality, Uncle Toms, lynchings, the works. Miraculously, out of the quagmire the personal excellence of this extraordinary woman and writer emerges. . . . Her later involvement with NAACP, CORE, summer projects, rights demonstrations, ugliness, violence, she describes without a trace of see-what-a-martyr-am-I. . . . A lovely and true book that gives you what good writing is supposed to: catharsis." —*Publishers Weekly*

"Supremely involving . . . written with stripped simplicity . . . not a single false high note." —*Kirkus Reviews*

"The most moving and honest account of what life is like for the negro in Mississippi that one is apt to find . . . a far better story (and certainly far better told) than most fiction being published today. . . . One of the most (possibly *the* most) engrossing, sensitive, beautiful books of nonfiction which has been published for years and years." —*San Francisco Sun-Reporter*

ANNE MOODY

COMING *of* AGE IN MISSISSIPPI

Delta Trade Paperbacks

COMING OF AGE IN MISSISSIPPI
A Delta Book

PUBLISHING HISTORY
Doubleday edition published 1968
Laurel paperback edition published 1976
Delta trade paperback edition / February 2004

Published by
Bantam Dell
A Division of Random House, Inc.
New York, New York

The quotation from the song "Danger Zone" on page 351 reprinted by
permission of Tangerine Music Corp., Copyright 1965.

Book design by Laurie Jewell

ISBN 0-385-33781-7

Manufactured in the United States of America
Published simultaneously in Canada

BVG   10

CONTENTS

part one

CHILDHOOD

chapter

| ONE |

I'm still haunted by dreams of the time we lived on Mr. Carter's plantation. Lots of Negroes lived on his place. Like Mama and Daddy they were all farmers. We all lived in rotten wood two-room shacks. But ours stood out from the others because it was up on the hill with Mr. Carter's big white house, overlooking the farms and the other shacks below. It looked just like the Carters' barn with a chimney and a porch, but Mama and Daddy did what they could to make it livable. Since we had only one big room and a kitchen, we all slept in the same room. It was like three rooms in one. Mama them slept in one corner and I had my little bed in another corner next to one of the big wooden windows. Around the fireplace a rocking chair and a couple of straight chairs formed a sitting area. This big room had a plain, dull-colored wallpaper tacked loosely to the walls with large thumbtacks. Under each tack was a piece of cardboard which had been taken from shoeboxes and cut into little squares to hold the paper and keep the tacks from tearing through. Because there were not enough tacks, the paper bulged in places. The kitchen didn't have any wallpaper and the only furniture in it was a wood stove, an old table and a safe.

Mama and Daddy had two girls. I was almost four and Adline was a crying baby about six or seven months. We rarely saw Mama and Daddy because they were in the field every day except Sunday. They would get up early in the morning and leave the house just before daylight. It was six o'clock in the evening when they returned, just before dark.

George Lee, Mama's eight-year-old brother, kept us during the day. He loved to roam the woods and taking care of us prevented him from enjoying his favorite pastime. He had to be at the house before Mama and Daddy left for the field, so he was still groggy when he got there. As soon as Mama them left the house, he would sit up in the rocking chair and fall asleep. Because of the solid wooden door and windows, it was dark in the house even though it was nearing daybreak. After sleeping for a couple of hours, George Lee would jump up suddenly, as if he was awakened from a nightmare, run to the front door, and sling it open. If the sun was shining and it was a beautiful day, he would get all excited and start slinging open all the big wooden windows, making them rock on their hinges. Whenever he started banging the windows and looking out at the woods longingly, I got scared.

Once he took us to the woods and left us sitting in the grass while he chased birds. That night Mama discovered we were full of ticks so he was forbidden to take us there any more. Now every time he got the itch to be in the woods, he'd beat me.

One day he said, "I'm goin' huntin'." I could tell he meant to go by himself. I was scared he was going to leave us alone but I didn't say anything. I never said anything to him when he was in that mood.

"You heard me!" he said, shaking me.

I still didn't say anything.

Wap! He hit me hard against the head; I started to boo-hoo as usual and Adline began to cry too.

"Shut up," he said, running over to the bed and slapping a bottle of sweetening water into her mouth.

"You stay here, right here," he said, forcing me into a chair at the foot of the bed. "And watch her," pointing to Adline in the bed. "And you better not move." Then he left the house.

A few minutes later he came running back into the house like he forgot something. He ran over to Adline in the bed and snatched the bottle of sweetening water from her mouth. He knew I was so afraid of him I might have sat in the chair and watched Adline choke to death on the bottle. Again he beat me up. Then he carried us on the porch. I was still crying so he slapped me, knocking me clean off the porch. As I fell I hit my head on the side of the steps and blood came gushing out. He got some scared and cleaned away all traces of the blood. He even tried to push down the big knot that had popped up on my forehead.

That evening we sat on the porch waiting, as we did every evening, for Mama them to come up the hill. The electric lights were coming on in Mr. Carter's big white house as all the Negro shacks down in the bottom began to fade with the darkness. Once it was completely dark, the lights in Mr. Carter's house looked even brighter, like a big lighted castle. It seemed like the only house on the whole plantation.

Most evenings, after the Negroes had come from the fields, washed and eaten, they would sit on their porches, look up toward Mr. Carter's house and talk. Sometimes as we sat on our porch Mama told me stories about what was going on in that big white house. She would point out all the brightly lit rooms, saying that Old Lady Carter was baking tea cakes in the kitchen, Mrs. Carter was reading in the living room, the children were studying upstairs, and Mr. Carter was sitting up counting all the money he made off Negroes.

I was sitting there thinking about Old Lady Carter's tea cakes when I heard Mama's voice: "Essie Mae! Essie Mae!"

Suddenly I remembered the knot on my head and I jumped off the porch and ran toward her. She was now running up the hill with her hoe in one hand and straw hat in the other. Unlike the other farmhands, who came up the hill dragging their hoes behind them, puffing and blowing, Mama usually ran all the way up the hill laughing and singing. When I got within a few feet of her I started crying and pointing to the big swollen wound on my forehead. She reached out for me. I could see she was feeling too good to beat George Lee so I ran right past her and headed for Daddy, who was puffing up the hill with the rest of the field hands. I was still crying when he reached down and swept me up against his broad sweaty chest. He didn't say anything about the wound but I could tell he was angry, so I cried even harder. He waved goodnight to the others as they cut across the hill toward their shacks.

As we approached the porch, Daddy spotted George Lee headed down the hill for home.

"Come here boy!" Daddy shouted, but George Lee kept walking.

"Hey boy, didn't you hear me call you? If you don't get up that hill I'll beat the daylights outta you!" Trembling, George Lee slowly made his way back up the hill.

"What happen to Essie Mae here? What happen?" Daddy demanded.

"Uh...uh...she fell offa d' porch 'n hit her head on d' step..." George Lee mumbled.

"Where were you when she fell?"

"Uhm...ah was puttin' a diaper on Adline."

"If anything else happen to one o' these chaps, I'm goin' to try my best to *kill* you. Get yo'self on home fo' I..."

The next morning George Lee didn't show up. Mama and Daddy waited for him a long time.

"I wonder where in the hell could that damn boy be," Daddy said once or twice, pacing the floor. It was well past daylight when they decided to go on to the field and leave Adline and me at home alone.

"I'm gonna leave y'all here by yo'self, Essie Mae," said Mama. "If Adline wake up crying, give her the bottle. I'll come back and see about y'all and see if George Lee's here."

She left some beans on the table and told me to eat them when I was hungry. As soon as she and Daddy slammed the back door I was hungry. I went in the kitchen and got the beans. Then I climbed in to the rocking chair and began to eat them. I was some scared. Mama had never left us at home alone before. I hoped George Lee would come even though I knew he would beat me.

All of a sudden George Lee walked in the front door. He stood there for a while grinning and looking at me, without saying a word. I could tell what he had on his mind and the beans began to shake in my hands.

"Put them beans in that kitchen," he said, slapping me hard on the face.

"I'm hungry," I cried with a mouth full of beans.

He slapped me against the head again and took the beans and carried them into the kitchen. When he came back he had the kitchen matches in his hand.

"I'm goin' to burn you two cryin' fools up. Then I won't have to come here and keep yo' asses every day."

As I looked at that stupid George Lee standing in the kitchen door with that funny grin on his face, I thought that he might really burn us up. He walked over to the wall near the fireplace and began setting fire to the bulging wallpaper. I started crying. I was so scared I was peeing all down my legs. George Lee laughed at me for peeing and put the fire out with his bare hands before it burned very much. Then he carried me and Adline on to the porch and left us there. He went out in the yard to crack nuts and play.

We were on the porch only a short time when I heard a lot of hollering coming from toward the field. The hollering and crying got louder and louder. I could hear Mama's voice over all the rest. It seemed like all the people in the field were running to our house. I ran to the edge of the porch to watch them top the hill. Daddy was leading the running crowd and Mama was right behind him.

"Lord have mercy, my children is in that house!" Mama was screaming. "Hurry, Diddly!" she cried to Daddy. I turned around and saw big clouds of smoke booming out of the front door and shooting out of cracks everywhere. "There, Essie Mae is on the porch," Mama said. "Hurry, Diddly! Get Adline outta that house!" I looked back at Adline. I couldn't hardly see her for the smoke.

George Lee was standing in the yard like he didn't know what to do. As Mama them got closer, he ran into the house. My first thought was that he would be burned up. I'd often hoped he would get killed, but I guess I didn't really want him to die after all. I ran inside after him but he came running out again, knocking me down as he passed and leaving me lying face down in the burning room. I jumped up quickly and scrambled out after him. He had the water bucket in his hands. I thought he was going to try to put out the fire. Instead he placed the bucket on the edge of the porch and picked up Adline in his arms.

Moments later Daddy was on the porch. He ran straight into the burning house with three other men right behind him. They opened the large wooden windows to let some of the smoke out and began ripping the paper from the walls before the wood caught on fire. Mama and two other women raked it into the fireplace with sticks, broom handles, and anything else available. Everyone was coughing because of all the smoke.

Soon it was all over. Nothing had been lost but the paper on the wall, although some of the wood had burned slightly in places. Now that Daddy and Mama had put out the fire, they came onto the porch. George Lee still had Adline in his arms and I was standing with them on the steps.

"Take Essie Mae them out in that yard, George Lee," Daddy snapped.

George Lee hurried out in the yard with Adline on his hip, dragging me by the arm. Daddy and the farmers who came to help sat on the edge of the porch taking in the fresh air and coughing. After they had talked for a while, the men and women wanted to help clean up the house but Mama and Daddy refused any more help from them and they soon left.

We were playing, rather pretending to play, because I knew what was next and so did George Lee. Before I could finish thinking it, Daddy called George Lee to the porch.

"Come here, boy," he said. "What happened?" he asked angrily. George Lee stood before him trembling.

"Ah-ah-ah-went tuh th' well—tuh get a bucketa water, 'n when ah come back ah seen the house on fire. Essie Mae musta did it."

As he stood there lying, he pointed to the bucket he had placed on the edge of the porch. That seemed proof enough for Daddy. He glanced at me for a few seconds that seemed like hours. I stood there crying, "I didn't, I didn't, I didn't," but Daddy didn't believe me. He snatched me from the porch into the house.

Inside he looked for something to whip me with, but all the clothes had been taken off the nails of the walls and were piled up on the bed. It would have taken hours for him to find a belt. So he didn't even try. He felt his waist to discover he was wearing overalls. Nothing was in his reach. He was getting angrier by the second. He looked over at the wood stacked near the fireplace. "Oh my God," I thought, "he's goin' to kill me." He searched through the wood for a small piece. There was not one to be found. Moving backward, he stumbled over a chair. As it hit the floor a board fell out. He picked it up and I began to cry. He threw me across his lap, pulled down my drawers, and beat me on my naked behind. The licks came hard one after the other.

Screaming, kicking, and yelling, all I could think of was George

Lee. I would kill him myself after this, I thought. Daddy must have beaten me a good ten minutes before Mama realized he had lost his senses and came to rescue me. I was burning like it was on fire back there when he finally let go of me. I tried to sit down once. It was impossible. It was hurting so bad even standing was painful. An hour or so later, it was so knotty and swollen I looked as if I had been stung by a hive of bees.

This was the first time Daddy beat me. But I didn't speak to him or let him come near me, as long as my behind was sore and hurting. Mama told me that he didn't mean to beat me that hard and that he wasn't angry at me for setting the fire. When I kept crying and telling her that George Lee started the fire, she told Daddy that she thought George Lee did it. He didn't say anything. But the next morning when George Lee came he sent him back home. Mama stayed with us the rest of the week. Then the following week Mama's twelve-year-old brother Ed came to keep us.

A week or so after the fire, every little thing began to get on Daddy's nerves. Now he was always yelling at me and snapping at Mama. The crop wasn't coming along as he had expected. Every evening when he came from the field he was terribly depressed. He was running around the house grumbling all the time.

"Shit, it was justa waste o' time. Didn't getta nuff rain for nuthin'. We ain't gonna even get two bales o' cotton this year. That corn ain't no good and them sweet potatoes jus' burning up in that hard-ass ground. Goddamn, ah'd a did better on a job than this. Ain't gonna have nuthin' left when Mr. Carter take out his share." We had to hear this sermon almost every night and he was always snapping at Mama like it was all her fault.

During the harvest, Daddy's best friend, Bush, was killed. Bush was driving his wagon when his horses went wild, turning the wagon over in the big ditch alongside the road. It landed on his neck and broke it. His death made Daddy even sadder.

The only times I saw him happy any more were when he was on the floor rolling dice. He used to practice shooting them at home before every big game and I would sit and watch him. He would even play with me then, and every time he won that money he would bring me lots of candy or some kind of present. He was good with a pair of dice and used to win the money all the time. He and most of the other men gambled every Saturday night through Sunday morning. One weekend he came home without a cent. He told Mama that he had lost every penny. He came home broke a few more times. Then one Sunday morning before he got home one of the women on the farm came by the house to tell Mama that he was spending his weekends with Florence, Bush's beautiful widow. I remember he and Mama had a real knockdown dragout session when he finally did come home. Mama fist-fought him like a man, but this didn't stop him from going by Florence's place. He even got bolder about it and soon went as often as he liked.

Florence was a mulatto, high yellow with straight black hair. She was the envy of all the women on the plantation. After Bush's death they got very particular about where their men were going. And they watched Florence like a bunch of hawks. She couldn't even go outdoors without some woman peeping at her and reporting that she was now coming out of the house.

Mama had never considered Florence or any of the other women a threat because she was so beautiful herself. She was slim, tall, and tawny-skinned, with high cheekbones and long dark hair. She was by and far the liveliest woman on the plantation and Daddy used to delight in her. When she played with me she was just like a child herself. Daddy used to call her an overgrown wild-child and tease her that she had too much Indian blood in her.

Meantime, Mama had begun to get very fat. Her belly kept getting bigger and bigger. Soon she acted as if she was fat and ugly. Every weekend, when she thought Daddy was with Florence she didn't do a thing but cry. Then one of those red-hot summer days, she sent me and Adline to one of the neighbors nearest to us. We were there all day. I didn't like the people so I was glad when we finally went home. When we returned I discovered why Mama had gotten so fat. She called me to the bed and said, "Look what Santa sent you." I was upset. Santa never brought live dolls before. It was a little baldheaded boy. He was some small and looked as soft as one of our little pigs when it was born.

"His name is Junior," Mama said. "He was named for your daddy."

My daddy's name was Fred so I didn't understand why she said the baby's name was Junior. Adline was a year old and walking good. She cried like crazy at the sight of the little baby.

While I stood by the bed looking at Mama, I realized her belly had gone down. I was glad of that. I had often wondered if Daddy was always gone because her belly had gotten so big. But that wasn't it, because after it went down, he was gone just as much as before, even more.

Next thing I knew, we were being thrown into a wagon with all our things. I really didn't know what was going on. But I knew something was wrong because Mama and Daddy barely spoke to each other and whenever they did exchange words, they snapped and cursed. Later in the night when we arrived at my Great-Aunt Cindy's place, all of our things were taken from the wagon and Daddy left.

"Where is Daddy goin'?" I cried to Mama.

"By his business," she answered.

Aunt Cindy and all the children stood around the porch looking at him drive the wagon away.

"That dog! That no-good dog!" I heard Mama mumble. I knew then that he was gone for good.

"Ain't he gonna stay with us?" I asked.

"No he ain't gonna stay with us! Shut up!" she yelled at me with her eyes full of water. She cried all that night.

We were allowed to stay with Aunt Cindy until Mama found a job. Aunt Cindy had six children of her own, all in a four-room house. The house was so crowded, the four of us had to share a bed together. Adline and I slept at the foot of the bed and Mama and the baby at the head. Aunt Cindy had a mean husband and our presence made him even meaner. He was always grumbling about us being there. "I ain't got enough food for my own chillun," he was always saying. Mama would cry at night after he had said such things.

Mama soon got a job working up the road from Aunt Cindy at the Cooks' house. Mrs. Cook didn't pay Mama much money at all, but she would give her the dinner leftovers to bring home for us at night. This was all we had to eat. Mama worked for the Cooks for only two weeks. Then she got a better job at a Negro café in town. She was making twelve dollars a week, more than she had ever earned.

About a week after she got the new job she got a place for us from the Cooks. Mrs. Cook let Mama have the house for four dollars a month on the condition that Mama would continue to help her around the house on her off day from the café.

The Cooks lived right on a long rock road that ran parallel to Highway 24, the major highway for Negroes and whites living between Woodville and Centreville, the nearest towns.

To get to our house from the road you entered a big wooden gate. A little dirt road ran from the gate through the Cooks' cattle pasture and continued past our house to a big cornfield. The Cooks planted the corn for their cattle. But often when Mama didn't have enough money for food she would sneak out at night and take enough to last us a week. Once Mrs. Cook came out there and put up a scarecrow. She said that the crows were eating all the corn. When Mama came home from the café that evening and saw the scarecrow, she laughed like crazy. Then she started taking even more corn. She had a special way of stealing the corn that made it look just like the crows had taken it. She would knock down a few ears and leave them hanging on the stalks. Then she'd drop a few between the rows and pick on a few others. I don't remember everything she did, but before that season was over, Mrs. Cook had three more scarecrows standing.

Right below the cornfield, at the base of the hill, was a swampy area with lots of trees. The trees were so thick that even during the day the swamp was dark and mysterious looking. It looked like an entirely different world to us, but Mama never let us go near it because she said it was full of big snakes, and people hunted down there and we might get killed.

Our little house had two rooms and a porch. The front room next to the porch was larger than the little boxed-in kitchen you could barely turn around in. Its furniture consisted of two small beds. Adline and I slept in one and Mama and Junior in the other. There was also a bench to sit on and a small tin heater. Our few clothes hung on a nail on the wall. In the kitchen there was a wood stove with lots of wood stacked behind it, and a table. The only chair we had was a large rocking chair that was kept on the porch because there was no room in the house for it. We didn't have a toilet. Mama would carry us out in back of the house each night before we went to bed to empty us.

Shortly after we moved in I turned five years old and Mama started me at Mount Pleasant School. Now I had to walk four miles each day up and down that long rock road. Mount Pleasant was a big white stone church, the biggest Baptist church in the area.

The school was a little one-room rotten wood building located right next to it. There were about fifteen of us who went there. We sat on big wooden benches just like the ones in the church, pulled up close to the heater. But we were cold all day. That little rotten building had big cracks in it, and the heater was just too small.

Reverend Cason, the minister of the church, taught us in school. He was a tall yellow man with horn-rimmed glasses that sat on the edge of his big nose. He had the largest feet I had ever seen. He was so big, he towered over us in the little classroom like a giant. In church he preached loud and in school he talked loud. We would sit in class with his sounds ringing in our ears. I thought of putting cotton in my ears but a boy had tried that and the Reverend caught him and beat him three times that day with the big switch he kept behind his desk. I remember once he caught a boy lifting up a girl's dress with his foot. He called him up to his desk and whipped him in his hands with that big switch until the boy cried and peed all over himself. He never did whip me. I was so scared of him I never did anything. I hardly ever opened my mouth. I don't even remember a word he said in class. I was too scared to listen to him. Instead, I sat there all day and looked out the window at the graveyard and counted the tombstones.

One day he caught me.

"Moody, gal! If you don't stop lookin' out that window, I'll make you go out in that graveyard and sit on the biggest tombstone out there all day." Nobody laughed because they were all as scared of him as I was.

We used the toilets in back of the church. The boys' toilet was on one side and girls' on the other. The day after Reverend Cason yelled at me, I asked to be excused. While in the toilet I thought to myself, "I can stay out here all day and he won't even know I'm out here." I began to spend three and four hours a day in the toilet and he didn't even miss me, until a lot of other kids caught on and started doing the same thing. About three weeks or so later about five of us girls were in the toilet at the same time. We had been out there almost an hour. We were standing behind the partition in front of the toilet giggling and making fun of Reverend Cason when all of a sudden we heard him right outside.

"If y'all don't come outta that toilet right this second, I'll come in there and drown you!"

We peeped from behind the partition and saw Reverend Cason standing there with that big switch in his hand.

"Didn't I say come outta there! If I have to come in there and getcha, I'm goin' to beat yo' brains out!"

"Reverend Cason, I ain't finished yet," I said in a trembling voice.

"You ain't finished? You been in there over three hours! If y'all don't get outta there—" Then he was silent. I peeped out again. He was coming toward the door.

I ran out and headed for the classroom, followed by the rest of the girls. When we got around in front of the church we met up with a bunch of boys running from the boys' toilet. We all scrambled in the door. There were only two students sitting in class. I sat in my seat and didn't even breathe until I heard Reverend Cason's big feet hit the bottom step. He came through the door puffing and shouting, but he was so tired from yelling and chasing us that he didn't even beat us. After that he wouldn't excuse us until recess. And then he would have to round us up and bring us back to class.

Every morning before Mama left for the café, she would take us across the road to Grandfather Moody. I would leave for school from there and he would keep Adline and Junior until I came home. My grandfather lived with one of my aunts. He was a very old man and he was sick all the time. I don't ever remember seeing him out of his bed. My aunt them would leave for the field at daybreak, so whenever we were there, my grandfather was alone.

He really cared a lot for us and he liked Mama very much too, because Mama was real good to him. Sometimes my aunt them would go off and wouldn't even fix food for him. Mama would always look to see if there was any food left for him in the kitchen. If there wasn't, she would fix some batty cakes or something for him and he would eat them with syrup.

Often when Mama didn't have money for food, he gave her some. I think he felt guilty for what his son, my daddy, had done to us. He kept his money in a little sack tied around his waist. I think that was his life savings because he never took it off.

Some mornings when Mama would bring us over she would be looking real depressed.

"Toosweet, what's wrong with you?" Grandfather would ask in a weak voice. "You need a little money or something? Do Diddly ever send you any money to help you with these children? It's a shame the way that boy run around gambling and spending all his money on women."

"Uncle Moody, I ain't heard nothin' from him and I don't want to. The Lord'll help me take care o' my children."

"I sure wish he'd do right by these chaps," Grandfather would mumble to himself.

Soon after school was over for the year, Grandfather got a lot sicker than he was before. Mama stopped carrying us by his place. She left us at home alone, and she would bake a pone of bread to last us the whole day.

One evening she came in from work looking real sad.

"Essie Mae, put yo' shoes on. I want you to come go say good-bye to Uncle Moody. He's real sick. Adline, I'm gonna leave you and Junior by Miss Cook. I'm gonna come right back and y'all better mind Miss Cook, you hear?"

"Mama, why I gotta say good-bye to Uncle Moody? Where he's goin'?" I asked her.

"He's goin' somewhere he's gonna be treated much better than he's treated now. And he won't ever be sick again," she answered sadly.

I didn't understand why Mama was so sad if Uncle Moody wasn't going to be sick any more. I wanted to ask her but I didn't. All the way to see Uncle Moody, I kept wondering where he was going.

It was almost dark when we walked up in my aunt's yard. A

whole bunch of people were standing around on the porch and in the yard. Some of them looked even sadder than Mama. I had never seen that many people there before and everything seemed so strange to me. I looked around at the faces to see if I knew anyone. Suddenly I recognized Daddy, squatting in the yard in front of the house. He had a knife in his hand. As Mama and I walked toward him, he began to pick in the dirt. He glanced up at Mama and he had that funny funny look in his eyes. I had seen it before. He looked like he wanted us back so bad, but Mama was mean. She had vowed that she would never see him again. As they stood there staring at each other, I was reminded of the first time I saw him after he left us, when we lived with my Great-Aunt Cindy. It was Easter Sunday morning. Mama, Aunt Cindy, and all the children were sitting on the porch. We were all having a beautiful time. It was just after the Easter egg hunt and we were eating the eggs we had found in the grass. Mama was playing with us. She had found more eggs than all of us and she was teasing and throwing eggshells at us.

As I was dodging eggshells and giggling at Mama, I saw Daddy coming down the road. I jumped off the porch and ran to meet him, followed by the rest of the children. He gave me lots of candy in a big bag and told me to share it with the others. As we walked back to the porch, I could see Mama's changing expression. Daddy was grinning broadly. He had something for Mama in a big bag he carried with care in his arms.

I don't remember what they said to each other after that. But I remember what was in the big bag for Mama. It was a hat, a big beautiful hat made out of flowers of all colors. When she saw the hat, Mama got real mad. She took the hat and picked every flower from it, petal by petal. She threw them out in the yard and watched the wind blow them away. Daddy looked at her as if he hated her, but there was more than hate in it all. This was just how he looked out in the yard now as he sat picking in the dirt.

I was very frightened. I thought at first he would kill Mama with the knife. Mama stared at him for a while, then went straight past him into the house, leaving me in the yard with him.

"Come here, Essie Mae," he said sadly. I walked to him, shaking. "They say you is in school now. Do you need anything?" he asked. I was so afraid I couldn't answer him. He felt in his pocket. Out of it came a roll of money. He gave it to me, smiling. I took it and was about to smile back when I saw Mama. She came out of the house and snatched the money from me and threw it at him. Then Daddy got up. This time I was sure he would hit Mama. But he didn't. He only walked away with that hurt look in his eyes. Mama grabbed me by the arm and headed out of the yard, pulling me behind her.

"Ain't ah'm gonna say good-bye to Uncle Moody?" I whined.

"He told me to tell you good-bye," she snapped. "He's sleeping now."

That night we had beans for supper, as usual. And all night I wondered why Mama threw back the money Daddy gave me. I was mad with her because we ate beans all the time. Had she taken the money, I thought, we could have meat too.

chapter

| **T W O** |

Now that school was out and there was no one for us to stay with, we would sit on the porch and rock in the rocking chair most of the day. We were scared to go out and play because of the snakes. Often as we sat on the porch we saw them coming up the hill from the swamp. Sometimes they would just go to the other side of the swamp. But other times they went under the house and we didn't see them come out. When this happened, we wouldn't eat all day because we were scared to go inside. The snakes often came into the house. Once as I was putting wood in the stove for Mama, I almost put my hands on one curled up under the wood. I never touched the woodpile again.

One day we heard Mrs. Cook's dog barking down beside the swamp at the base of the cornfield. We ran out to see what had happened. When we got there, the dog was standing still with his tail straight up in the air barking hysterically. There, lying beside a log, was a big old snake with fishy scales all over his body. Adline, Junior, and I stood there in a trance looking at it, too scared to move. We had never seen one like this. It was so big it didn't even look like a snake. It looked like it was big enough to swallow us whole. Finally the snake slowly made its way back into the swamp, leaving a trail of mashed-down grass behind it.

When Mama came home that evening from the café, we told her all about the snake. At first, she didn't believe us, but we were shaking so that she had us go out back and show her where we had seen it. After she saw the place next to the log where it had been lying and the trail it left going to the swamp, she went and got Mr. Cook. For days Mr. Cook and some other men looked in the swamp for that snake, but they never did find it. After that Mama was scared for us to stay at home alone, and she began looking for a house in town closer to where she worked. "Shit, snakes that damn big might come up here and eat y'all up while I'm at work," she said.

In the meantime, she got our Uncle Ed, whom we liked so much, to come over and look after us every day. Sometimes he would take us hunting. Then we wouldn't have to sit on the porch and watch those snakes in that boiling hot summer sun. Ed made us a "niggershooter" each. This was a little slingshot made out of a piece of leather connected to a forked stick by a thin slab of rubber. We would take rocks and shoot them at birds and anything else we saw. Ed was the only one who ever killed anything. He always carried salt and matches in his pockets and whenever he'd kill a bird he'd pick and roast it right there in the woods. Sometimes Ed took us fishing too. He knew every creek in the whole area and we'd roam for miles. Whenever we caught fish we'd scrape and cook them right on the bank of the creek. On those days we didn't have to eat that hard cold pone of bread Mama left for us.

Sometimes Ed would keep us in the woods all day, and we wouldn't hunt birds or fish or anything. We just walked, listening to the birds and watching the squirrels leap from tree to tree and the rabbits jumping behind the little stumps. Ed had a way of making you feel so much a part of everything about the woods. He used to point out all the trees to us, telling us which was an oak, and which was a pine and which bore fruit. He'd even give us quizzes to see if we could remember one tree from another. I thought he was the smartest person in the whole world.

One day Ed was late coming and we had resigned ourselves to spending the whole day on the porch. We rocked for hours in the sun and finally fell asleep. Eventually Ed came. He locked the house up immediately and rushed us off the porch. He told us he was going to surprise us. I thought we were going to a new creek or something so I begged him to tell me. He saw that I was upset so finally he told me that he was taking us home with him.

As we were walking down the rock road, it occurred to me that I had never been home with Ed and I was dying to see where he lived. I could only remember seeing Grandma Winnie once, when she came to our house just after Junior was born. Mama never visited Grandma because they didn't get along that well. Grandma had talked Mama into marrying my daddy when Mama wanted to marry someone else. Now that Mama and Daddy had separated, she didn't want anything to do with Grandma, especially when she learned that her old boyfriend was married and living in Chicago.

Ed told us that he didn't live very far from us, but walking barefooted on the rock road in the boiling hot sun, I began to wonder how far was "not very far."

"Ed, how much more longer we gotta go? These rocks is burning my foots," I said.

"Ain't much further. Just right around that bend," Ed yelled back at me. "Why didn't you put them shoes on? I told you them rocks was hot." He waited on me now. "Oughter make you go all the way back to that house and put them shoes on. You gonna be laggin' behind comin' back and we ain't never gonna make it 'fore Toosweet get off o' work!"

"Mama told us we ain't supposed to wear our shoes out round the house. You know we ain't got but one pair and them my school shoes."

"Here it is, right here," Ed said at last. "Essie Mae, run up front and open that gate." By this time he was carrying Junior on his back and Adline half asleep on his hip.

I ran to the gate and opened it and rode on it as it swung open. We entered a green pasture with lots of cows.

"Is that where you stay?" I asked Ed as I pointed to an old wooden house on the side of a hill.

"Is any more houses down there?" Ed said, laughing at me. "See that pond over there, Essie Mae!" he called as I ran down the hill. "I'm gonna bring y'all fishing over here one day. Boy, they got some big fishes in there! You shoulda seen what Sam and Walter caught yesterday."

I glanced at the pond but ran right past it. I didn't have my mind on fishing at all. I was dying to see Grandma Winnie's house and Sam and Walter, Ed's younger brothers, and his sister Alberta whom I had never met. Ed had told me that George Lee was now living with his daddy and stepmother. I was glad because I didn't want to run into him there.

Alberta was standing in the yard at the side of the house feeding the big fire around the washpot with kindling. Two white boys about my size stood at her side. I looked around for Sam and Walter. But I didn't see them.

"Ed, what took you so long? I oughta made you tote that water fo' you left here," Alberta shouted at Ed as she turned and saw us.

"I had to tote Adline and Junior all the way here. You must think um superman or something," Ed answered angrily.

"I ain't asked you what you is! You just git that bucket and fill that rinse tub up fulla water!" Alberta shouted. "Sam, yo'n Essie Mae help Ed with that water. And, Walter, take Adline and Junior on that porch outta the way."

I stood dead in my tracks with my mouth wide open as the two white boys jumped when Alberta yelled Sam's and Walter's names. One boy ran to the wash bench against the house and got a bucket and the other picked up Junior, took Adline by the hand, and carried them on the porch.

"Essie Mae! Didn't I tell you to help Sam and Ed with that water?" Alberta yelled at me.

"Where is Sam and Walter?" I asked with my eyes focused on the white boy on the porch with Adline and Junior.

"Is you blind or somethin'? Get that bucket and help tote that water," Alberta yelled.

I turned my head to look for Ed. He was headed for the pond in front of the house with a bucket in his hand. "Ed!" I shouted, still in a state of shock. He turned and looked at me. I stood there looking from Ed to the white boys and back to Ed again, without saying anything. Ed opened his mouth to speak but no words came. A deep expression of hurt crossed his face. For a second he dropped his head to avoid my eyes. Then he walked toward me. He picked up another bucket and handed it to me. Then he took me by the hand and led me to the pond.

As we walked toward the pond, one of the white boys ran ahead of us. He climbed through the barbed-wire fence right below the levee of the pond. Then he turned and pushed the bottom strand of the wire down to the ground with his foot and held the middle strand up with his hands, so Ed and I could walk through. I began to pull back from Ed but he clutched my hand even harder and led me toward the fence. As we ducked under, I brushed against the white boy. Jerking back, I caught my hair in the barbed-wire overhead.

"Essie Mae, watch yo' head 'for you git cut! Wait, wait, you got your hair caught," the white boy said as he quickly and gently untangled my hair from the wire. Then he picked up the bucket I had dropped and handed it to me. Ed didn't say one word as he stood beside the fence watching us.

The white boy caught me by the hand and attempted to pull me up the levee of the pond. I pulled back. Still holding my hand, he stopped and stared at me puzzled. "Come on, Essie Mae!" yelled Ed, giving me an "it's O.K., stupid" look as he ran up the levee past us. Then the white boy and I followed Ed up the hill holding hands.

As we toted water from the pond, I kept watching the white boys and listening to Alberta and Ed call them Sam and Walter. I noticed that they treated them just like they treated me, and the white boy called Sam was nice to me just like Ed. He kept telling me about the fish he and Walter had caught and that I should come and fish with them sometimes.

After we finished toting the water, we went on the porch where Adline, Junior, and Walter sat. Adline had a funny look on her face. I could tell that she was thinking about Sam and Walter too. Before the evening was over, I finally realized that the two boys actually were Ed's brothers. But how Ed got two white brothers worried me.

On our way back home, Ed carried us through the woods. As we walked, he talked and talked about the birds, the trees, and everything else he could think of, without letting me say a word. I knew he didn't want to talk about Sam and Walter, so I didn't say anything. I just walked and listened.

I thought about Sam and Walter so much that night, it gave me a headache. Then I finally asked Mama:

"Mama, them two boys over at Winnie's. Ed say they is his brothers. Is they your brothers?"

"What boys?" Mama asked.

"Over at Winnie's. They got two boys living with her about my size and they is the same color as Miss Cook...."

"What did y'all do over at Winnie's today? Was Winnie home?" Mama asked as if she hadn't heard me.

"No, she was at work. Wasn't nobody there but Alberta and those two boys...."

"What was Alberta doing?" Mama asked.

"She was washing and we toted water from the pond for her. Them boys is some nice and they say they is kin to us. Ain't they your brothers, Mama?"

"Look, don't you be so stupid! If they's Winnie's children and I'm Winnie's too, don't that make us sisters and brothers?" Mama shouted at me.

"But how come they look like Miss Cook and Winnie ain't that color and Alberta ain't that color and you . . ."

"'Cause us daddy ain't that color! Now you shut up! Why you gotta know so much all the time? I told Ed not to take y'all to Winnie's," she shouted.

Mama was so mad that I was scared if I asked her anything else she might hit me, so I shut up. But she hadn't nearly satisfied my curiosity at all.

While Mama was working at the café in town, she began to get fat. She often told us how much she could eat while she was working. So I didn't think anything of her slowly growing "little pot." But one day after taking a good look, I noticed it wasn't a little pot any more. And I knew she was going to have a baby. She cried just about every night, then she would get up sick every morning. She didn't stop working until a week before the baby was born, and she was out of work only three weeks. She went right back to the café.

Mama called the baby James. His daddy was a soldier. One day the soldier and his mother came to get him. They were real yellow people. The only Negro near their color I had ever seen was Florence, the lady my daddy was now living with. The soldier's mother was a stout lady with long thin straight black hair and very thin lips. She looked like a slightly tanned white woman. Mama called her "Miss Pearl." All the time they were in our house, Mama acted as though she was scared of them. She smiled a couple of times when they made general comments about the baby. But I could tell she didn't mean it.

Just before the soldier and Miss Pearl left, Miss Pearl turned to Mama and said, "You can't work and feed them other children and keep this baby too." I guess Mama did want to keep the little boy. She looked so sad I thought she was going to cry, but she didn't say anything. Miss Pearl must have seen how Mama looked too. "You can stop in to see the baby when you are in town sometimes," she said. Then she and the soldier took him and drove away in their car. Mama cried all night. And she kept saying bad things about some Raymond. I figured that was the name of the soldier who gave her the baby.

At the end of that summer Mama found it necessary for us to move into town, in Centreville, where she worked. This time we moved into a two-room house that was twice the size of the other one. It was next to where a very poor white family lived in a large green frame house. It was also located on one of the main roads branching off Highway 24 running into Centreville. We were now a little less than a mile from the school that I was to attend, which was on the same road as our house. Here we had a sidewalk for the first time. It extended from town all the way to school where it ended. I was glad we lived on the sidewalk side of the road. Between the sidewalk and our house the top soil was sand about two feet deep. We were the only ones with clean white sand in our yard and it seemed beautiful and special. There was even more sand for us to play in in a large vacant lot on the other side of our house. The white people living next to us only had green grass in their yard just like everybody else.

A few weeks after we moved there, I was in school again. I was now six years old and in the second grade. At first, it was like being in heaven to have less than a mile to walk to school. And having a sidewalk from our house all the way there made things even better.

I was going to Willis High, the only Negro school in Centreville. It was named for Mr. C. H. Willis, its principal and founder, and had only been expanded into a high school the year before I started there. Before Mr. Willis came to town, the eighth grade had been the limit of schooling for Negro children in Centreville.

For the first month that I was in school a Negro family across the street kept Adline and Junior. But after that Mama had them stay at home alone and, every hour or so until I came home, the lady across the street would come down and look in on them. One day when I came home from school, Adline and Junior were naked playing in the sand in front of our house. All the children who lived in town used that sidewalk that passed our house. When they saw Adline and Junior sitting in the sand naked they started laughing and making fun of them. I was ashamed to go in the house or recognize Adline and Junior as my little sister and brother. I had never felt that way before. I got mad at Mama because she had to work and couldn't take care of Adline and Junior herself. Every day after that I hated the sand in front of the house.

Before school was out we moved again and I was glad. It seemed as though we were always moving. Every time it was to a house on some white man's place and every time it was a room and a kitchen. The new place was much smaller than the last one, but it was nicer. Here we had a large pasture to play in that was dry, flat, and always closely cropped because of the cattle. Mama still worked at the café. But now she had someone to keep Adline and Junior until I came home from school.

One day shortly after Christmas, Junior set the house on fire. He was playing in the front room. We had a small round tin heater in there and Junior raked red-hot coals out of it onto the floor and pushed them against the wall. I was washing dishes in the kitchen when I looked up and saw flames leaping toward the ceiling. I ran to get Junior. The house had loose newspaper tacked to the walls and was built out of old dry lumber. It was burning fast.

After I had carried Junior outside, I took him and Adline up on a hill a little distance away. The whole house was blazing now. I stood there with Junior on my hip and holding Adline by the hand and suddenly I thought about the new clothes Mama had bought us for Christmas. These were the first she had ever bought us. All our other clothes had been given to us. I had to get them. I left Adline and Junior on the hill and ran back to the house. I opened the kitchen door and was about to crawl into the flames and smoke when a neighbor grabbed me and jerked me out. Just as she pulled me away, the roof fell in. I stood there beside her with tears running down my face and watched the house burn to the ground. All our new Christmas clothes were gone, burned to ashes.

We had only lived there for a few months and now we moved again to another two-room house off a long rock road. This time Mama quit the job at the café to do domestic work for a white family. We lived in their maid's quarters. Since Mama made only five dollars a week, the white woman she worked for let us live in the house free. Mama's job was now close to home and she could watch Adline and Junior herself.

Sometimes Mama would bring us the white family's leftovers. It was the best food I had ever eaten. That was when I discovered that white folks ate different from us. They had all kinds of different food with meat and all. We always had just beans and bread. One Saturday the white lady let Mama bring us to her house. We sat on the back porch until the white family finished eating. Then Mama brought us in the house and sat us at the table and we finished up the food. It was the first time I had seen the inside of a white family's kitchen. That kitchen was pretty, all white and shiny. Mama had cooked that food we were eating too. "If Mama only had a kitchen like this of her own," I thought, "she would cook better food for us."

Mama was still seeing Raymond, the soldier she had the baby for. Now we were living right up the road, about a mile from Miss Pearl. Raymond started coming to our house every weekend. Often he would bring us candy or something to eat when he came. Some Sundays, Mama would take us out to his house to see the baby, James, who was now two years old and looked a lot like his daddy. Mama seemed to like the baby very much. But she was always so uncomfortable around Miss Pearl and the rest of Raymond's people. They didn't like Mama at all. Sometimes when Mama was there she looked as if she would cry any minute. After we had come home from their place, she would cry and fuss all evening. She would say things like, "They can't keep me from seeing my baby. They must be crazy. If I can't go see him there I'll bring him home." But she only said those things. She knew she couldn't possibly take the baby home and work and take care of the four of us. Once when we went out there to see the baby, he was filthy from head to toe. Mama gave him a bath and washed all of his clothes. Then every Sunday after that Mama would go there just to wash his clothes and bathe him.

Raymond was going with a yellow woman at the same time he was going with Mama. All of his people wanted him to marry her. They didn't want him to marry Mama, who wasn't yellow and who was stuck with the three of us. Things began to get so tense when we would go to see the baby that we'd only stay long enough for Mama to give him a bath. Then one day Raymond went back to the service and that ended some of the tension. But Mama got scared to go to Miss Pearl's without Raymond there, so she stopped going and we didn't see the baby for a long time.

chapter

| THREE |

That white lady Mama was working for worked her so hard that she always came home griping about backaches. Every night she'd have to put a red rubber bottle filled with hot water under her back. It got so bad that she finally quit. The white lady was so mad she couldn't get Mama to stay that the next day she told Mama to leave to make room for the new maid.

This time we moved two miles up the same road. Mama had another domestic job. Now she worked from breakfast to supper and still made five dollars a week. But these people didn't work Mama too hard and she wasn't as tired as before when she came home. The people she worked for were nice to us. Mrs. Johnson was a schoolteacher. Mr. Johnson was a rancher who bought and sold cattle. Mr. Johnson's mother, an old lady named Miss Ola, lived with them.

Our house, which was separated from the Johnsons' by a field of clover, was the best two-room house we had been in yet. It was made out of big new planks and it even had a new toilet. We were also once again on paved streets. We just did make those paved streets, though. A few yards past the Johnsons' house was the beginning of the old rock road we had just moved off.

We were the only Negroes in that section, which seemed like some sort of honor. All the whites living around there were well-to-do. They ranged from schoolteachers to doctors and prosperous businessmen. The white family living across the street from us owned a funeral home and the only furniture store in Centreville. They had two children, a boy and a girl. There was another white family living about a quarter of a mile in back of the Johnsons who also had a boy and a girl. The two white girls were about my age and the boys a bit younger. They often rode their bikes or skated down the little hill just in front of our house. Adline, Junior and I would sit and watch them. How we wished Mama could buy us a bike or even a pair of skates to share.

There was a wide trench running from the street alongside our house. It separated our house and the Johnsons' place from a big two-story house up on the hill. A big pecan tree grew on our side of the trench, and we made our playhouse under it so we could sit in the trench and watch those white children without their knowing we were actually out there staring at them. Our playhouse consisted of two apple crates and a tin can that we sat on.

One day when the white children were riding up and down the street on their bikes, we were sitting on the apple crates making Indian noises and beating the tin can with sticks. We sounded so much like Indians that they came over to ask if that was what we were. This was the beginning of our friendship. We taught them how to make sounds and dance like Indians and they showed us how to ride their bikes and skate. Actually, I was the only one who learned. Adline and Junior were too small and too scared, although they got a kick out of watching us. I was seven, Adline five, and Junior three, and this was the first time we had ever had other children to play with. Sometimes, they would take us over to their playhouse. Katie and Bill, the children of the whites that owned the furniture store, had a model playhouse at the side of their parents' house. That little house was just like the big house, painted snow white on the outside, with real furniture in it. I envied their playhouse more than I did their bikes and skates. Here they were playing in a house that was nicer than any house I could have dreamed of living in. They had all this to offer me and I had nothing to offer them but the field of clover in summer and the apple crates under the pecan tree.

The Christmas after we moved there, I thought sure Mama would get us some skates. But she didn't. We didn't get anything but a couple of apples and oranges. I cried a week for those skates, I remember.

Every Saturday evening Mama would take us to the movies. The Negroes sat upstairs in the balcony and the whites sat downstairs. One Saturday we arrived at the movies at the same time as the white children. When we saw each other, we ran and met. Katie walked straight into the downstairs lobby and Adline, Junior, and I followed. Mama was talking to one of the white women and didn't notice that we had walked into the white lobby. I think she thought we were at the side entrance we had always used which led to the balcony. We were standing in the white lobby with our friends, when Mama came in and saw us. "C'mon! C'mon!" she yelled, pushing Adline's face on into the door. "Essie Mae, um gonna try my best to kill you when I get you home. I told you 'bout running up in these stores and things like you own 'em!" she shouted, dragging me through the door. When we got outside, we stood there crying, and we could hear the white children crying inside the white lobby. After that, Mama didn't even let us stay at the movies. She carried us right home.

All the way back to our house, Mama kept telling us that we couldn't sit downstairs, we couldn't do this or that with white children. Up until that time I had never really thought about it. After all, we were playing together. I knew that we were going to separate schools and all, but I never knew why.

After the movie incident, the white children stopped playing in front of our house. For about two weeks we didn't see them at all. Then one day they were there again and we started playing. But things were not the same. I had never really thought of them as white before. Now all of a sudden they were white, and their whiteness made them better than me. I now realized that not only were they better than me because they were white, but everything they owned and everything connected with them was better than what was available to me. I hadn't realized before that downstairs in the movies was any better than upstairs. But now I saw that it was. Their whiteness provided them with a pass to downstairs in that nice section and my blackness sent me to the balcony.

Now that I was thinking about it, their schools, homes, and streets were better than mine. They had a large red brick school with nice sidewalks connecting the buildings. Their homes were large and beautiful with indoor toilets and every other convenience that I knew of at the time. Every house I had ever lived in was a one- or two-room shack with an outdoor toilet. It really bothered me that they had all these nice things and we had nothing. "There is a secret to it besides being white," I thought. Then my mind got all wrapped up in trying to uncover that secret.

One day when we were all playing in our playhouse in the ditch under the pecan tree, I got a crazy idea. I thought the secret was their "privates." I had seen everything they had but their privates and it wasn't any different than mine. So I made up a game called "The Doctor." I had never been to a doctor myself. However, Mama had told us that a doctor was the only person that could look at children's naked bodies besides their parents. Then I remembered the time my Grandma Winnie was sick. When I asked her what the doctor had done to her she said, "He examined me." Then I asked her about "examined" and she told me he looked at her teeth, in her ears, checked her heart, blood and privates. Now I was going to be the doctor. I had all of them, Katie, Bill, Sandra, and Paul plus Adline and Junior take off their clothes and stand in line as I sat on one of the apple crates and examined them. I looked in their mouths and ears, put my ear to their hearts to listen for their heartbeats. Then I had them lie down on the leaves and I looked at their privates. I examined each of them about three times, but I didn't see any differences. I still hadn't found that secret.

That night when I was taking my bath, soaping myself all over, I thought about it again. I remembered the day I had seen my two uncles Sam and Walter. They were just as white as Katie them. But Grandma Winnie was darker than Mama, so how could Sam and Walter be white? I must have been thinking about it for a long time because Mama finally called out, "'Essie Mae! Stop using up all that soap! And hurry up so Adline and Junior can bathe 'fore that water gits cold."

"Mama," I said, "why ain't Sam and Walter white?"

"'Cause they mama ain't white," she answered.

"But you say a long time ago they daddy is white."

"If the daddy is white and the mama is colored, then that don't make the children white."

"But they got the same hair and color like Bill and Katie them got," I said.

"That still don't make them white! Now git out of that tub!" she snapped.

Every time I tried to talk to Mama about white people she got mad. Now I was more confused than before. If it wasn't the straight hair and the white skin that made you white, then what was it?

In the summer Mr. Johnson would drive down to Florida in a big trailer truck and bring it back running over with watermelons. Then he would sell them to the stores and markets in Centreville and nearby towns. Often Mrs. Johnson would go with him now that school was out and she wasn't teaching. When she went, I would stay with Miss Ola.

Miss Ola was a very nice old lady. She would bake cookies, candy or something for us every Saturday. She had a little bell that she used to ring for us to come over when she had cooked us something or wanted one of us to help her in the yard. We always sat out in the clover on Saturdays and listened for that little bell. I learned to like Miss Ola even more when I started staying with her at night. She liked me very much too and we had lots of fun together when I was there.

Mrs. Johnson had a shaky little rollaway bed that I was supposed to sleep on in the dining room which was right next to Miss Ola's room. I never did sleep much on it, though. Before going to bed I had a hundred chores to do for Miss Ola. First, I had to scratch her white hair and brush it. Then I cleaned her false teeth, got water in a foot tub for her to soak her feet in, and a thousand other little things. It would be about twelve o'clock at night before I got in that little shaky bed. But as soon as I got in, Miss Ola would call me into her room and read to me. She slept in one of those old ante-bellum beds with big posts covered with a flowered canopy. It was high with big soft feather mattresses. I had to use a stool to get up in it. Most of the time, as soon as Miss Ola started reading, I was so tired that I fell asleep. I would just look up at that flowered canopy, close my eyes and I was out cold, sleeping down. I guess I never heard a single story she read to me.

During those nights with Miss Ola, I had access to the first bathroom I had ever used. I had never had such a privilege before. I used to go in that bathroom and sit on the stool even if I didn't have to use it. I would just sit there and look at that big beautiful white tub, the pink curtain that hung over it, the pink washing powder in the big beautiful glass container, the sink with pink soap in the soap tray. It all looked so good to me. There was a small round pink rug in front of the stool. I would take my shoes off as I sat on the stool and just run my feet all over that soft rug. Sometimes I would stay in there so long Miss Ola would come in to see what I was doing. After taking my first bath in that beautiful white tub, I hated our round tin tub every time I bathed in it.

I liked everything about the Johnsons' house. There was always soft music playing on the radio as I did my little chores. The house was large and spacious with beautiful furniture all the way through it. It was everything ours wasn't.

I kept trying to learn the white folks' secret from Miss Ola. When I asked her questions about it, she didn't get mad like Mama. But she still didn't tell it to me. However, there was one secret I learned. That was why all white women had colored women working for them. Because they were lazy. Mama would clean that house up for those white folks every single day. She would make the beds, dust the furniture, run the vacuum, and clean the bath. Then she would cook three meals a day too. After eating the food Miss Ola made I could see Mama had to do the cooking because white women didn't know how.

Miss Ola had a cold one night when I was staying with her, and I saw her make some soup. She was coughing and mucus was running out of her nose and dripping right into the pot. Miss Ola was so old she had lost control of her bladder. Every time she coughed pee ran down her legs. Then she would wipe it off the floor with the dish towel. When she set some of that snotty-pee soup in front of me my stomach turned inside out. Now when she would ring that little bell for us on Saturday, Adline and Junior ran over there but I didn't. I finally realized what Mama meant when she said, "Miss Ola is gonna kill y'all with that shit she cooks."

Adline and Junior started school the second year we lived on the Johnsons' place. Now that they were in school, I had a problem on my hands. Junior was only four and a half and Adline six. Mama started him early because she didn't have anyone to keep him or for him to play with while Adline and I were in school. He wouldn't stay in his classroom because he thought he belonged with me and Adline. I was now nine years old and in the fourth grade. Junior would follow Adline everywhere she went. Sometimes I would look up and he was standing outside my classroom door peeping in. I think I must have taken him to his classroom at least ten times a day. During the lunch hour, he would follow me all over the campus holding onto my skirttail. I would send him to play with the other boys. Then a few minutes later, he came running around a corner telling me some boy was chasing him.

Mama was seeing the soldier again. He was out of the army now and he didn't wear his uniform any more. So now we called him "Raymond" instead of "the soldier." He was coming to the house every other night now. When he was there he would help us with our lessons. Mama never did help us. She said she had only finished sixth grade, and she could barely read my fourth grade reader. But Raymond had almost finished high school. He could read and work arithmetic better than my teacher. I didn't need much help from Raymond because Miss Ola helped me a lot when I stayed with her. She had taught me lots of words and showed me how to spell and write them too. Because of Miss Ola's help, I made all A's in reading and spelling. In arithmetic, with a little help from Raymond, I made B's. In no time at all I was doing my homework without any help from anyone. Adline and Junior were the big problems. Raymond had to work so hard with them. He would take Junior over his lesson eight or nine times but Junior wouldn't remember a single word afterward. He was a dumb little thing. Adline wasn't as dumb as Junior, but she didn't do much better. She thought it was funny to learn words. She would laugh the whole time Raymond was helping her. They never did learn their 1-2-3's.

When I was the only one going to school, Mama would buy one loaf of bread a week and a jar of peanut butter and jelly for lunch. I had a peanut butter sandwich every day. Now that all three of us were in school, she couldn't afford the loaf of bread. So she bought ten pounds of flour instead of the five she had always bought. Each night she would make biscuits and fix two biscuits with peanut butter for each of us. I kept the lunch bag and Adline and Junior would come to me for their lunch at twelve. I remember that once when I was eating with some of my classmates, I pulled my peanut butter biscuits out of that lunch bag and they laughed at me all day.

After that embarrassment, I never took those biscuits to school again. We ate our lunch on our way to school every morning. All day long I was hungry but it was better than being laughed at by my classmates. Sometimes during the lunch hour Adline and Junior would tell me they were hungry and I would send them to the water fountain to fill up on water.

Times really got hard at home. Mama was trying to buy clothes for the three of us, feed us, and keep us in school. She just couldn't do it on five dollars a week. Food began to get even scarcer. Mama discovered that the old white lady living in the big white two-story house on the hill sold clabber milk to Negroes for twenty-five cents a gallon. Mama started buying two or three gallons a week from her. Now we ate milk-and-bread all the time (milk with crumbled cornbread in it). Then Mrs. Johnson started giving her the dinner leftovers and we ate those. Things got so bad that Mama started crying again. And she cried until school was out.

One Saturday I went to get some clabber milk and the old white lady asked me to sweep her porch and sidewalks. After I had finished she gave me a quarter and didn't take the quarter Mama had given me for the milk. When I got home and told Mama, she laughed until she cried. Then she sent me up there every day to see if the old lady wanted her porch swept. I was nine years old and I had my first job. I earned seventy-five cents and two gallons of milk a week.

Soon after I started working for that old lady, I stopped drinking her milk. One evening, I was cleaning the back porch where she kept it, when a little Negro boy came to buy two gallons. She came in to get them while he waited out in the backyard. She kept the milk in three old safes with screen doors. I saw her open one of them and pour some milk out of a big dishpan. Then she went out to the yard, leaving the safe door open. Now this old lady had eight cats that also lived on the back porch. About five of them scrambled into the open safe and began lapping up the milk in the dishpan. She was fussy about her cats so I didn't yell at them or shoo them away. I just let them eat. "She'll run them out and pour that milk out when she come back in," I thought.

But when she came back, she just let those cats help themselves. When they had had enough, she pushed them away from the milk and closed the safe door. I stood there looking at all of this and I thought of how many times I had drunk that milk. "I'll starve before I eat any more of it," I thought.

I could hardly wait to tell Mama, but when I did she didn't believe me. "She probably is gonna give the rest of that milk to them cats too. I don't think that woman would sell us milk she let cats eat out of," Mama said. I didn't argue with her. "I will still bring the milk home," I thought. "Y'all can eat it but not me."

I didn't keep that job long. That big old white house had the biggest porches I had ever seen. It had a porch on the bottom and top floors circling the entire house, which gave the house a rounded look. Pretty soon the old lady even had me sweeping the inside of the house downstairs where she lived and dusting the furniture. She started keeping me up there all day. Mama didn't like that. One day she kept me up there until after dark. Mama came up there and got me.

"What she got you doing she have you up there all day?" Mama asked me when we got home.

"I sweep the porches and dust the furniture and sweep the bottom house. I was washing out some stockings for her today," I told her.

"You go up there tomorrow and you tell her you ain't gonna

come back no more, you heah. She been trying to kill you for seventy-five cent and that little shittin' milk she gives you. Tell her you gotta stay at home with Adline and Junior."

The next morning I went and swept the porches and cleaned the house and stayed up there all day. When I had finished, I told her what Mama told me to tell her. I didn't really want to quit working for her. I got a good feeling out of earning three quarters and two gallons of milk a week. It made me feel good to be able to give Adline and Junior each a quarter and then have one for myself.

When school started again things were still pretty rough, so Mrs. Johnson got one of her friends, Mrs. Claiborne, to give me a job. Mrs. Claiborne taught Home Economics at the white school. I worked for her every evening after school and all day Saturdays. I really liked this job because I made almost as much as Mama. Mrs. Claiborne paid me three dollars a week and the work was easy compared to what I had been doing for seventy-five cents. Now I could pay our way to the movies every Saturday and then give Mama two dollars to buy bread and peanut butter for our lunch. Besides that I was learning a lot from Mrs. Claiborne. She taught me what a balanced meal was and how to set a table and how to cook foods we never ate at home. I'd never known anything about having meat, vegetables, and a salad. I enjoyed learning these things, not that they were helpful at our house. For instance, we never set a table because we never had but one fork or spoon each; we didn't have knives and didn't need them because we never had meat.

Mrs. Claiborne was in charge of selling candy, peanuts, and hot dogs during the Friday night football and basketball games at her school. On Saturdays when I went to work she would give me the leftover wieners and some of the peanuts and candy. Now, when I got off work on Saturdays, I'd run all the way home with what she had given me. Adline and Junior would be sitting out in the street waiting on me. I'd give them some of the peanuts and candy and take the wieners to Mama. On Sunday she'd make them for us. The wieners and the three dollars a week that I earned kept us from being hungry at school and at home.

Mrs. Claiborne's husband was a businessman. The only thing I knew about businessmen at the time was that they carried brief cases, smoked cigars, and wore suits every day. Mr. Claiborne was nice, so I thought all businessmen were nice. One Saturday I was setting the table for them and he asked me to set up a place for myself. I sat down with them—the first white people I had ever eaten at the same table with. I was so nervous. We sat in silence eating. Dessert was served and then they started talking to me.

"Essie, how do you like school?" Mr. Claiborne asked.

"Oh, it's all right," I answered.

"What kind of grades you make?" he asked.

"I make A's in everything but arithmetic and I make B's in that," I said.

"See, I told you she's very smart," Mrs. Claiborne said.

"What would you like to do after you finish school, Essie?" he asked.

"I don't know. Mama say I could be a teacher like Mrs. Claiborne and Mrs. Johnson," I said. Mr. Claiborne just nodded his head.

When I was doing the dishes Mrs. Claiborne came to help me and she told me that Mr. Claiborne thought that I was very smart. She said that she didn't know many ten-year-old girls who worked to keep herself and her sister and brother in school. After that Saturday, I ate with them every time I was there for a meal. They started treating me like I was their own child. They would correct me when I spoke wrong, and Mrs. Claiborne would tell me about places she had traveled and people she met while traveling. I was learning so much from them. Sick or well, I went to work. I was afraid if I stayed home I would miss out on something.

I came home from work one day and it seemed as though Mama's belly had gotten big overnight. I knew she was going to have another baby. And I also knew it was for Raymond. Now that she had gotten fat he wasn't coming by any more. He hadn't been to the house in almost a month. Again Mama started crying every night, like she did when Junior was a baby and my daddy was staying with Florence all the time. Then I thought Raymond had left her for that yellow woman his people wanted him to marry. When I heard Mama crying at night, I felt so bad. She wouldn't cry until we were all in bed and she thought we were sleeping. Every night I would lie awake for hours listening to her sobbing quietly in her pillow. The bigger she got the more she cried, and I did too. I cried because I thought she would make me quit school and work full time for Mrs. Claiborne to take care of all of us. It seemed as though any day she would have to quit work.

I had worked late for Mrs. Claiborne one evening and when I got off work, it was raining. I didn't have an umbrella or anything. By the time I got home, I was soaking wet. I was so mad because I had on my first new dress in almost two years. Mama had bought five yards of beautiful pink flowered material for a dollar at the bargain store. She had a lady make dresses for me and Adline. We had both worn our dresses to school that day. Now mine was all wet and had lost its newness. All the way home, I was thinking about my wet sagging dress and Adline's new dress hanging against the wall still looking new.

When I walked in the door, Mama was singing. I forgot about my wet dress. Instead of looking depressed and sick as usual, she seemed so happy. Dripping wet, I stood in the door a long time just looking at her. I didn't know why she was happy and I didn't really care. I was just glad to see her like this. She was walking around carrying her big belly like it was as light as a feather.

"Take that wet dress off before you git a cold!" she said as she noticed me standing in the door. Any other time she would have said something like, "Look how wet you is. Why didn't you wait till it stopped raining!" That night I listened to see if she would cry and she didn't. So I didn't have anything to cry for that night, either.

She walked around in that spell of happiness for three or four days. Then one evening I came home after work and found Raymond there. When I walked in the door he was rubbing her belly and she was blushing down. I got so mad standing in that door, I started trembling with anger. I felt like going up to him and slapping his hand off her belly. Mama was laughing now, I thought, but I knew she would be crying again as soon as her belly went down and he made it big again. When they noticed me standing in the door looking at him disapprovingly he jerked his hand away. Mama stopped blushing. They both could tell that I didn't like it at all. In fact when he left, I didn't say anything to Mama. I just went about the house doing anything I could find to do to keep from talking to her. Raymond had brought some candy for us. Adline and Junior were eating theirs and grinning, but I didn't touch the candy Mama had left for me. If Adline and Junior knew Raymond had made Mama cry every night like I did they wouldn't be eating that candy either, I thought.

Later that evening when I was taking my bath in the tin tub, Mama came in the kitchen. Without saying a word, she got down on her knees with her belly touching the tub and washed my back. She was still happy, but she knew I wasn't. She was putting lots of soap on my back and scratching it and rubbing it good. Usually she fussed at us for using so much soap.

"We gonna be moving pretty soon," she said.

I sat there stiff and didn't say anything. "The Johnsons probably is asking her to move because she is too big to work," I thought. She kept rubbing my back.

"Ray done built us a new house," she said.

"What!" I yelled, almost jumping out of the tub.

"And you can quit working for Mrs. Claiborne as soon as we move," she said.

"Mrs. Claiborne treat me good and I don't want to stop working for her," I said.

"O.K., you can go on working for her if you want to. But Ray will be able to take care of us now," she said.

I cried that night because I was so happy. I no longer hated Raymond for feeling Mama's belly. All night I lay awake thinking of how Mama must be feeling to have someone build a house for her after she had been killing herself for more than seven years working on one job after another trying to feed us and keep us in school and all. We had moved six times since she and Daddy separated. Now she would have a place of her own. And we were going to be moving off white people's places probably for good.

chapter

FOUR

We stayed at the Johnsons' until the end of the summer. Then one day we moved. Raymond had built the house at the bottom of the Ash Quarters right off Highway 24. We were now living next door to Raymond's mother, Miss Pearl, and all the rest of Raymond's people. Somehow, by hook or by crook, Raymond and his entire family had bought land there, along the gravel road that formed the main street. On the very first day we moved there Mama already showed signs of nervousness.

Raymond, with help from his brothers, had built the house for us with his own hands. It was a green frame house with a gray front porch. There were five rooms, more than we had ever lived in—a living room, three bedrooms, and a kitchen. The only thing wrong was that we still had an outdoor toilet. Raymond and his brothers had also built Miss Pearl's house and she had a bathroom. Raymond said that later on he would build a bathroom for our house too. We didn't have running water in the house either but the water line had been run to our house and a water faucet had been put up in the front yard. At least we had plenty of water to fill that tin tub.

The inside of the house had not been finished when we moved in. Raymond and his brothers worked on it daily, sealing it with sheet rock. When all the sheet rock was up, Mama and I went to town and bought some beautiful flowered wallpaper for each room, except the kitchen. Then it was time to buy the new furniture. Mama always took me with her to buy things for the house.

"Mama, let's get the beds first," I said as we walked in to the only furniture store in Centreville.

"O.K.," she said, "but don't let me forget the icebox." I think Mama was a little scared, because this was the first time she had ever bought furniture. Before, we had always been given old discarded furniture by other people. We looked over all the beds and Mama picked her bed in no time. She selected one with a solid mahogany headboard that was part of a mahogany bedroom set. But I still didn't see my bed, the one I wanted for my room.

"Have you got a bed with big tall brown posts?" I asked the saleslady.

"Yes, we have one with posts," she said. "Here, don't you like this one?" she asked, pointing to a little mahogany bed with little straight posts.

"That's not what I want," I told her. "I want one with big tall posts and a cover over the top."

"Where did you see that kind of bed?" she asked, looking at me as if I were crazy.

"The lady I used to work for had a bed like that," Mama answered quickly.

"You got one like that?" I asked the saleslady again.

"No, we don't carry them and it would cost too much for you. How old are you?" she asked me coldly.

"Eleven. I'll be twelve next week," I answered.

The saleslady acted as if she was mad and so did Mama. So I

took the bed with the little brown posts. Then Mama picked out a green three-piece sofa set for the living room. Mama asked for an icebox and they didn't have one. I was glad because then I hoped she would buy one of those nice big refrigerators like the Johnsons and the Claibornes had. But she didn't. She gave the lady a down payment on the furniture and we left. On the way home she kept telling me I shouldn't want everything white folks had. She said that Miss Ola's bed cost more money than our house had cost. "Miss Claiborne and Miss Ola done ruined you," she said. I often got the feeling that Mama didn't like Mrs. Claiborne acting like I was her daughter. The way she said they had "ruined me" I knew for a fact that she didn't like them treating me like their equal. I remember once I had told her that I ate at the same table with the Claibornes and she asked me, "What they say to you when y'all be eatin'?" So I told her, "We *just* eat and *talk!*" "*Eat* and *talk!*" she said. "What you gotta talk about with them white folks?"

After the furniture was delivered, we settled down. There were only a few things that kept us from being middle class—the outdoor toilet, the wood stove, and the tin bathtub. However, we did have mahogany furniture and Raymond had a small bank account from the service and a car.

Now that we had moved into Raymond's house, he brought James to live with us. James was now four years old. He had gotten used to living with Miss Pearl, and he wouldn't stay with us in the beginning. Every night he would cry until Mama and Raymond sent him over to Miss Pearl's to spend the night.

When we went back to old Willis High that September, I was twelve years old and in sixth grade. Adline was in third grade and Junior in second. We no longer carried one sandwich apiece to school, we were now able to carry two, and they weren't always peanut butter either. Sometimes we had bologna. Everything at school seemed to take on a different look. I got a big kick out of showing off my bologna sandwich and drinking the cola I bought from the snack bar each day.

But my new happiness didn't last very long. We had been living in the midst of Raymond's people for about three months and none of them had befriended Mama. Adline, Junior, and I had been accepted, at least by the children. All of us had become friends in school. Raymond's sister Darlene was my age and in the same grade and his sister Cherie was the same age and grade as Adline; then Raymond had five or six little nephews that Junior played with. But the adults hardly spoke to Mama. Miss Pearl and Raymond's older sisters would pass right by her without saying anything, and Mama would be so hurt. Sometimes she would sit on the porch and stare over at their house as if she wished she could just go over there and talk to them. I think Mama thought she could somehow make the adults accept her through us. So she began to make us study our lessons at home twice as hard as before. I was still doing my homework alone, but every night now Raymond would drill Adline and Junior again and again over the same lessons. "Little man, where is your book?" he would say to Junior, or "Come on, Junior, you ain't got time to be playing." After he had finished with Junior, he was often too disgusted with him to go on to Adline and he would tell me to help Adline with her lesson before I started mine. Within a month I was helping both of them, because no matter how Raymond drilled Junior he just didn't learn anything. Now I had very little time for my own homework. But I still managed to keep my grades among the highest in my class.

After Raymond had given Adline and Junior up and told Mama, "They are the dumbest little things I ever saw," Mama started in on me. She was always telling me things like, "Y'all gotta do good in school. Y'all can't let Darlene and Cherie be smarter than y'all. They already think they is better than y'all 'cause they is yellow."

When she said this to me I knew she didn't mean "y'all," she meant me. She had given Adline and Junior up just as Raymond had.

I was already making better grades than Darlene. However, now that I realized Mama was depending upon me to keep my grades higher, I tried even harder. Soon a visible strain of competition developed between us. I remember in class we would try to outdo each other in answering more questions, working more problems, and even trying to outread each other. Cherie and Adline got along well together. Neither one of them was the competing kind. But after a while Darlene and I didn't get along very well at all. She worked twice as hard as me and she hated like hell that I still made better grades.

Because my grades were going so well, I decided I could afford to go out for the junior high basketball team, the only extracurricular activity offered for sixth graders. Mrs. Willis, the principal's wife and one of the most active teachers at Willis High, was my coach. She was the eighth grade homeroom teacher, she managed the snack bar at noon, and now she had organized a junior high basketball team. Because I was the tallest girl on the team, she worked with me more than with the others, drilling me mostly in jumping and rebounding. I would practice an extra hour each day after school plus the two evenings a week that I wasn't working for Mrs. Claiborne. By the time we got ready for our first game, I was the best player on the team. I was also the most scared player because Mrs. Willis expected so much of me.

Our first game was to be played on a Thursday in November at some little country school I had never heard of. I kept hoping it would be called off. It rained that Wednesday and on Thursday morning it was cold and cloudy—I remember I got out of bed and prayed that the outdoor court at the other school would be too wet for us to play. But it wasn't. In fact, when Mrs. Willis called up to ask about the court, the coach told her that it was in good shape and that he was still expecting us.

We arrived late. The other team was already warming up. Once I looked at those girls out there, all the little courage I had managed to muster up was completely gone. These were the biggest girls I had ever seen. They were even larger than the girls that played on our high school team. They looked like grown women.

"These are some mighty big girls," Mrs. Willis commented to us as if we hadn't already noticed them. And I felt my blood stop circulating. "What you all gotta do," she advised us, "is guard them close and if possible get them to foul a lot. Try to keep them from that goal too." Then she looked at me and started to say something but changed her mind when she saw how I was shaking.

The referee blew his whistle, and the girls from both teams went to the center of the court and surrounded him. I found myself standing there too. "All you girls know the rules of the game?" he asked and we nodded yes. "Well, remember you have only five fouls and you are then taken out of the game and you can only bounce the ball three times before it's passed on to the next girl." When the game started, the referee blew his whistle again and passed the ball to one of the girls on my team. She passed the ball to the other forward opposite her and the forward passed it on to me. I was supposed to pass the ball back to her and fall back to play the pivot. But I didn't. I just looked up at the big girl that was guarding me and froze. "Play that ball, Moody!" I heard Mrs. Willis yell. I held the ball up as though I was going to pass it. But again I froze. "If you don't play that ball . . ." I heard Mrs. Willis say. I looked toward the goal and the only thing I could remember was that I was supposed to shoot. I didn't bounce or pass. I ran straight to the goal with the ball held high above my head, and shot it. All the time I was running, the referee was blowing his whistle and the spectators standing around the court were laughing like crazy. Mrs. Willis took me out of the game in the first quarter. We lost. And everyone blamed me and made fun of me all the way back to school. I had enough embarrassment from that game to last me a year.

Every day after that I would sit in my classroom after the lunch hour and watch the other girls on the team practice. Once or twice Mrs. Willis asked me to come back to the team. But I wouldn't. It was one thing to play ball among people you knew but I didn't like playing outsiders.

Just before Christmas, I came home from Mrs. Claiborne's one evening and found Mama's sister Alberta at the house. As I walked in, she was running around like she was lost. Mama was in bed. I looked at Mama and she had big drops of sweat dropping off her face. Her eyes were closed and she was biting her lips as though she was in great pain. I stood there looking at her for a long time before Alberta saw me standing there.

"Essie Mae, come here and help me find some clean rags," she said to me.

"What's wrong with Mama, Alberta?" I asked her.

"She is about to have the baby," she answered, plowing her way through the clothes in the dresser drawers.

"Look in that big box behind the door in Junior's room," I said. "Mama's got a lot of rags in there."

"I hope Raymond hurry up," she said. "Toosweet is going to have this baby and I don't know what to do," she continued, almost crying.

When she said that, I ran back in the room to look at Mama. Her eyes were still closed and she was lying flat on her back clutching the sides of the bed. I looked at her belly and saw it move. I thought sure the baby was coming. I opened my mouth to call Alberta but the words wouldn't come, I was so scared. "Essie Mae! Come out of there! Go outside and see if that water is getting hot!" Alberta yelled to me. But I couldn't move. "What is she going to do with hot water?" I thought. "Get to the yard and look at that water, Essie Mae!" Alberta pushed me all the way through Junior's room to the kitchen door. I walked outside and found a big fire burning around the washpot. It was now dark and the fire lit up the whole yard. I just stood there staring at the pot full of water and the big blaze leaping up around it. The whole scene was like killing a hog at night.

As I was standing out there Raymond drove up, hitting the brakes so hard he sent rocks sailing into the air. He ran around to the side of the car and opened the door to help some old woman get out. She was carrying a ragged-looking black medicine bag, and looked so dried up she could hardly walk. Raymond was leading her to the front porch when he noticed me standing in the yard. "Essie Mae," he called to me, "what are you doing here? Go on over to Pearl's where Adline and Junior is."

I walked out of the yard and headed down the road toward Miss Pearl's, but halfway there I turned around and went back. I stood behind Raymond's car for a long time looking and listening. At first it was real quiet. They had cut out all the lights but the one in Mama's room. I couldn't see anyone moving around inside. A little while later I heard Mama screaming and hollering and carrying on. Raymond came running out in the backyard and got a bucket of hot water from the washpot. All I could hear was Mama holler ing from the house. Except for her yells everything else was still.

I stood out there thinking how bad it must hurt to have a baby. I would never have a baby if I had to holler and carry on like Mama, I thought. And that old lady. What did she know about de-livering babies? Suppose she did something wrong and Mama died from it? I would kill Raymond if she died. "He should have taken Mama to the hospital," I thought. "Instead he went out in the country and got that old woman to deliver Mama's baby."

When Mama finally stopped yelling, I went over to Miss Pearl's. Well past midnight Raymond came over there and told us we could come home. As soon as he said that, Adline, Junior and I ran all the way home to see the little baby. For the first time we weren't scared to run down that dark road that late at night.

I was the first one to make it home. When I walked in the door, that old lady was sitting beside the bed with her little black bag at her feet. She looked up and smiled at me when I walked over to see the baby, and something started crawling all over me and I started to shake. "Why is she still here?" I thought. "Something must be wrong with Mama." But then I saw that Mama was asleep.

"Is the baby here?" Adline asked as she came in the door with Junior following her.

"Stop all that noise!" Alberta said from the kitchen. Why was Alberta still here too, I wondered.

Adline, Junior, and I were all standing at the foot of Mama's bed and the old lady just sat there smiling. "Mama *must* be sick," I thought.

"Alberta, is Mama sick?" I asked as she walked into Mama's room.

"Is you crazy? Sho' she's sick after just having a baby."

Then Mama opened her eyes and saw all of us, me, Adline, Junior, and Alberta standing at the foot of her bed. "Show them the baby, Toosweet," Alberta said, "so they can go to bed." There it was lying right next to Mama. She lifted the cover back and Adline, Junior, and I walked to the head of the bed and peeped at it. It was a girl. She didn't look like she was just born like most babies. She looked like she was already four or five months old.

"She is some big!" I said.

"She is big," Mama said. "She weigh ten pounds and three ounces."

"That's as much as I weigh, huh, Mama?" that little stupid Junior asked.

"Your belly weigh that much," Mama said to him.

"You weigh that much, Essie Mae, when you came," the old lady said to me.

I didn't know how she knew I weighed that much. I wanted to ask her but I was scared. Something about her gave me the creeps. "Your mama brings big babies," the old lady said. "Every one of her babies weighed from eight to ten pounds." I looked at her shocked this time and I figured she must have delivered all of us. "No wonder she looks so old," I thought.

"Aunt Caroline, you ready to go?" Raymond asked her as he walked in the door.

"Yes, I guess so, and Toosweet is going to be all right," the old lady said.

"Y'all go to bed!" Raymond said to us, and he and the old lady left.

I got up early the next morning because I wanted to talk to Mama and get a good look at the baby before I went to work. Mama was asleep when I went into her room. Her face looked different, I thought—so calm and young. She hadn't looked young for a long time. Maybe it was because she was happy now. She had never been happy before to have a baby. I remembered how she had cried all the time after Junior and James were born. I thought she'd gotten to the point where she hated babies.

For a long time I stood there looking at her. I didn't want to wake her up. I wanted to enjoy and preserve that calm, peaceful look on her face, I wanted to think she would always be that happy, so I would never be unhappy again either. Adline and Junior were too young to feel the things I felt and know the things I knew about Mama. They couldn't remember when she and Daddy separated. They had never heard her cry at night as I had or worked and helped as I had done when we were starving. No they didn't know the misery Mama suffered. Not even Raymond knew. Mama loved him too much to fight with him or have him see her cry.

But even while I was standing there with all those dreams about the eternal happiness I wanted for Mama, I knew deep down in my heart that it wouldn't last. Deep down, I knew that she wasn't really happy now and that she hadn't been since we'd moved. I had seen her sit on the porch too many times and look over at Miss Pearl's with hate in her eyes. I also knew that

Raymond's people hadn't really accepted Adline, Junior, and me either, even though we went to their houses often and played with their children. But the biggest worry I had was the fact that Raymond still hadn't married Mama. Now she would have two babies for him and three for my daddy and still no husband. Mama didn't think I knew this but I did. I knew that even though she was living in the same house with Raymond and even though he supported us, she still wasn't safe without being married to him.

Some Sundays, Raymond would go over to Miss Pearl's and spend the afternoon. Mama would be so uneasy every minute he was over there. And if Raymond came home in a bad mood, I would hear Mama mumble to herself, "I know they don't do nothing but sit over there and talk about me." I was always afraid that any day Raymond could be taken away from Mama. I didn't think she could take it if that happened. She had waited for him so long.

I got myself all flustered standing there thinking about Mama and all we had been through. Now I didn't even feel like seeing the baby or talking with Mama. We were out of school for the Christmas holidays and I was helping Mrs. Claiborne do her Christmas cleaning, so I just left Mama sleeping and went to work.

That evening as I was coming home a little early from Mrs. Claiborne's, I saw Raymond and Miss Pearl walking down the road toward our house. "She can't be coming to see us," I thought. "After all she doesn't even speak to Mama." But she certainly looked as if she was coming. When I reached our front walk, I hurried inside. Mama was sitting up in bed when I walked in.

"Raymond and Miss Pearl is coming down the road," I said. "She look like she is coming here."

"What?" Mama asked me as if she didn't believe me. She got all nervous. Her face went through a million different changes as she started patting her hair, straightening the covers on the bed, and looking at the baby to see if she was wet.

In what seemed like seconds Raymond and his mother were walking through the door. I just stood at the foot of Mama's bed, waiting to see what was going to happen.

"Come on in," I heard Raymond say to Miss Pearl.

"Where is my little girl?" Miss Pearl cooed as she entered Mama's room.

Mama looked at me and then pulled the covers off the baby.

Miss Pearl didn't come all the way into Mama's room. She stood in the doorway and didn't move one step from there. She acted as if Mama wasn't even in the house. Raymond walked over to the bed and picked up the baby and carried it to her.

"She does look like her grandmother," Miss Pearl said, shaking the baby and carrying on over her.

"I told you she looked just like you," said Raymond. Then he pulled in a chair from the living room for her to sit on.

All this time Mama looked like she was so anxious for Miss Pearl to just speak to her. The least Miss Pearl could have done was ask Mama how she felt even if she didn't mean it. But Miss Pearl wasn't even about to do that.

"I ain't got time to sit down, Ray. I gotta go cook dinner," she said quickly, and gave Raymond back the baby. He took the baby over to the bed and handed it to Mama. Then he and Miss Pearl left the house.

As soon as they walked out, Mama starting fussing. "She got some nerve coming in my house and not even speaking to me. How dare Ray bring her in here and run over me." I looked at Mama and now tears were running down her face. I didn't say a word to her, I just turned and walked out of the room onto the front porch. Miss Pearl and Raymond were standing in the road talking. I sat down on the front steps and stared at them.

I thought of the calm, peaceful face Mama had had that morning before I went to work. After seeing her tears again so soon I knew that, as long as Raymond's people could make her cry, they would. "Raymond is just a fool," I thought. "He is not a man at all. He could easily put a stop to this. No, he's too scared of hurting their feelings." I sat there on the steps wishing that Mama had never moved with him. Looking at him now, I could see he would never break with his family for Mama and they would never accept her, no matter how hard she tried to make them like her.

A few days later Aunt Caroline came by to check on Mama, and see if she was ready to name the baby. She brought some papers for Mama to fill out and send off to get the baby's birth certificate. I had heard Raymond and Mama talk of naming the baby after Miss Pearl. But I knew Mama wouldn't do that now. Mama named the baby Virginia after Mrs. Johnson and called her Jennie Ann, same as Mrs. Johnson is called.

After Aunt Caroline left, Mama told me that she had also delivered Adline and Junior, and all my grandmother's children. She and Aunt Mary Green, who had delivered me and James, had been midwives for every Negro baby between Woodville and Centreville for the past forty years. Aunt Caroline even delivered babies for families who had moved out of the county. When Mama told me Aunt Caroline only charged her ten dollars, I figured she must have had to deliver a lot of babies to keep alive. After I had heard all this about Aunt Caroline, the thought of her didn't give me the creeps any more. In fact, now I thought of her as a great old lady. She must have really enjoyed bringing babies to bring them for so little and to continue doing it at such an old age.

A week later we had our first Christmas in our new house. When I got off work Christmas Eve, Mrs. Claiborne gave me five dollars for a present and paid me seven dollars for helping her do her Christmas cleaning. In addition to that she gave me something that was wrapped so prettily I was tempted not to open it. Twelve dollars was more money than I had ever had at one time. When

Mrs. Claiborne first gave it to me I felt like hugging and kissing her. The Claibornes and the Johnsons were the nicest white people I had ever known.

All the way home I thought of how nice these people were to us. Mrs. Claiborne was white but she and Mr. Claiborne treated me like I was their own daughter. They were always giving me things and encouraging me to study hard and learn as much as I could. Mr. Johnson's mother, Miss Ola, had done the same. She taught me how to read when I was in school and helped me with my homework when my own mother was unable to do it. Then I began to think about Miss Pearl and Raymond's people and how they hated Mama and for no reason at all than the fact that she was a couple of shades darker than the other members of their family. Yet they were Negroes and we were also Negroes. I just didn't see Negroes hating each other so much.

When I got home, Alberta was there baking cakes and Mama was sitting in the kitchen with her. Alberta and Mama got along very well. Alberta was married now and had just moved to the neighborhood about two weeks before. I was glad that Mama would finally have someone to talk to. Now she wouldn't have to sit out on the front porch and look over at Miss Pearl's. She and Alberta could visit each other.

The following morning I got up and smelled apples and oranges all over the house. The kitchen was scented with freshly baked cakes and I heard carols playing on the new radio. I thought of the past and what all the other Christmases had been like. For the first time this seemed to me like a real Christmas.

FIVE

Even though Mama stopped going to Mount Pleasant when we moved from the country, she continued to pay her membership dues. Raymond and Miss Pearl them belonged to Centreville Baptist, the largest Negro church in town. Now that we were living with Raymond Mama started thinking about joining Raymond's church. She figured that maybe she could get in with Miss Pearl them by going to their church regularly.

One Saturday in early spring she went to town and bought a new dress and hat for herself. That night, before we went to bed, she told us that we'd have to get up early the next morning because we were going to Centreville Baptist. I couldn't fall asleep for a long time, thinking about going there. Raymond had once taken us for a ride and showed it to us. It was a big white frame building on a brick base with cement steps all the way across the front. It had great big windows painted in different shades of blue and green. I wondered as I fell asleep what it was like inside.

Next morning when Mama woke us up, she was already dressed and our breakfast was on the table. She rushed us through eating and all and then helped us dress in our best Sunday clothes. "They can't say we came to church half dressed or lookin' any kinda way," she said. All the way to church she kept looking at us in the back seat of the car. "Stop messin' with that ribbon fo' you untie it!" she said to Adline, who was playing with the ribbon on one of her three plaits. Mama was so nervous. Once she looked back and Junior had his hand in his mouth and she slapped him. Raymond drove along smiling and acting like he wasn't nervous but I could tell he was.

When we got there we were late. Everyone was already inside and we could hear them singing. As we walked in the door, two ushers met us. One directed Raymond down the right aisle to the men's section. The other led us down the left aisle where a group of ladies and children sat. About halfway down, I spotted Miss Pearl, sitting with Cherie and Darlene and their older sisters, Betty and Vera, in the center pews. When they saw us, they started hunching and whispering and I knew they were saying things about us. The usher directed us to seats in the right pews somewhat behind them. I could see them easily now and I was glad the usher had seated us there. I kept looking at them and every now and then they would look back to where we sat. "Stop looking over there at them!" Mama said as she caught me smiling at Cherie and Darlene. I was sorry that I had looked and smiled at them, since they didn't smile back. Now that they were out in public with Miss Pearl and Betty, they were acting like they didn't even know us. "After this, I'll never play with them again," I thought.

After we were seated for a while, I forgot about them and I began looking around. Since it was pastoral Sunday, Reverend Polk's regular preaching Sunday, the church was crowded. Just like at Mount Pleasant every member showed up to pay his dues and put on a good front for the pastor. I tried to notice every little thing that happened to see if things were different in a big town church.

First, a couple of deacons began the service by offering two long, boring prayers. As each one finished, he hummed a song and the congregation hummed along with him. At Mount Pleasant the men sang through their noses, and here the deacons were doing the same thing, singing through their noses and hollering and going on. At Mount Pleasant I had even seen men cry in church like women, when they finished praying. At least these men weren't crying, I thought, but they were hollering just the same. And just like at Mount Pleasant, I couldn't understand one word of any song. All the old ladies did, though. They were humming right along with them.

While the collection for the sick was being taken up, the choir sang a few songs. This was the first time I had been in a church that had a choir. I used to listen to choirs on the radio sometimes, and this one sounded just as good. They sang "Rock of Ages" and "Stand by Me." There were young girls among the singers. Some of them didn't look any older than me. I sat there listening to them and hoping Mama would change her membership to here. "Then I could sing in the choir too," I thought. "Yes, I am going to join this church, I don't like Mount Pleasant anyway."

When the choir finished the songs, one of the deacons announced the amount taken up for the sick. Then Reverend Polk, who had been sitting in the pulpit in the big comfortable pastor's chair with two deacons at his side, rose to his feet. He raised his hands and everybody stood. The choir then sang "Sweet Jesus," joined by the congregation. When the song was over Reverend Polk stepped up to the lectern that contained a big open Bible. That Bible was the biggest I had ever seen.

Reverend Polk was a middle-aged minister with snow-white hair. I didn't understand his hair being that white. The only other person I had seen with hair that white was Miss Ola. Her hair was white because she was very old, but Reverend Polk didn't look half as old as she was. As soon as he opened his mouth the women in the church started fainting, shouting, hollering, and carrying on. One large lady jumped straight up out of her seat and fell out stiff as a stick. It took about five deacons to carry her outside. It seemed as though almost every woman in the church was crying. I looked over at Miss Pearl them again and saw tears in the corner of Miss Pearl's eyes. "She should cry," I thought. "She shouldn't even *be* in church and she doesn't even speak to Mama and she lives right next door to her." I looked at Mama now and she wasn't crying but she looked like she would any minute.

I didn't understand why all these women were crying. I hadn't heard a word Reverend Polk had said. He looked as though he was mouthing a sermon for a movie or something and the soundtrack wasn't working. Once or twice he raised his hands and the women hollered even louder. They went on hollering at least fifteen minutes after he stopped working his mouth and sat down, so then I knew they weren't crying because of anything he said. "They are all probably crying because they are doing somebody wrong," I thought. "Maybe they don't speak to their neighbors, just like Miss Pearl, and *she* is crying. They must have done something bad and they think God is going to slap the breath out of them while they are in church."

Within an hour or so we were out of church and this was another thing I liked about Centreville Baptist. Mount Pleasant and the other country churches I had attended held services that lasted all day. They also kept taking up collections in the country and here at Centreville Baptist, they took up collection only twice. As usual when church was out a lot of people stood on the church grounds talking for a while. I felt so funny standing there. It seemed as though everyone had someone to talk to but us. Mama, Adline, Junior and I stood near the car all by ourselves. I noticed that Miss Pearl and Betty them seemed to be popular with the other church members. As Mama stood looking at them she had tears in her eyes. She had hoped that they would at least speak to her. But they pretended they didn't even see us. Their car was parked right next to ours. They got in and drove off without even looking in our direction. Raymond had been talking with Betty's husband and one of the deacons. Now he came to our car and we left.

"How did y'all like Reverend Polk?" he said to no one in particular since he realized Mama was in no mood for conversation.

"Why is his hair that white?" I asked.

"It's been like that ever since he got out of prison," Raymond said.

"Prison! A preacher! What did he do?"

"He killed a man. Then when he was in prison he worried so his hair turned white. He was called to preach while in prison."

"The Bible say thou shall not kill! How can he kill a man and preach what the Bible say to people?" I asked Raymond.

"Why you gotta know everything! Always asking questions all the time?" Mama said to me. I could tell she was real mad so I hushed.

I didn't say anything else all the way home, but that didn't stop me from thinking about Reverend Polk. He had killed a man and all he had to do was raise his hand in church and women fainted all over the place. It seemed to me, at the time, that we were going to church to listen to a killer preach the gospel of Christ. Then you sit next to your neighbors and playmates and they don't even speak to you. This didn't seem like church at all. Not the way of Christ anyway. Not the Christ Mama was always telling us all those good things about.

Mama never did go back to Centreville Baptist again. But Adline, Junior, and I went back the very next Sunday and every Sunday after that. It seemed as though Mama had completely resigned herself to not being accepted, yet she was determined to make Raymond's people accept us, even in their church. Every Sunday now she made us study our Sunday school lesson just as hard as our regular homework for school each day. Within a month or so we were not only going to Sunday school but to the eleven o'clock church services and B.T.U. (Baptist Training Union).

Later on Mama was not satisfied with us just going to Centreville Baptist, but now at every church-celebrated holiday we had to say speeches or participate in every program offered for children and teen-agers. It wasn't always "we" that took part in the programs but it *was* always "me." Mama gave up on Adline and Junior in the church too. They were worse in church than in school. They were always given speeches but they never did learn them in time to say them. Within a few days after I received mine, I would know it by heart. And when I said it on the program, unlike most of the other participants, I didn't forget a word or stumble.

While we were doing all this at Centreville Baptist and winning the approval of all the church members there, Mama decided to go back to Mount Pleasant. Raymond really wanted her to join Centreville Baptist but Mama just couldn't bring herself to sit up in the same church with Miss Pearl them. When they argued about it she would say, "You think I'm gonna join church with them *hypocrites* jus' because *you* belong over there? Shit, they don't even *speak* to me. Why should I go over there and give 'em sumptin' to talk about? Be sittin' up there lookin' at me, rollin' their eyes and hunchin' and whisperin' to each other, make me so mad I can't even think 'bout what the preacher's sayin'." Raymond had no defense against what Mama said about Miss Pearl them so he'd just say, "You go on, you join church where you wanna join, go on, if you will be happier out there at Mount Pleasant then go back out there!"

Even though Mama kept hinting that she was going back to Mount Pleasant, months and months passed and she still didn't go. I understood her feelings about Miss Pearl them, but I still wanted her to join Centreville Baptist. Since we *were* living in Centreville and Adline, Junior, and I were going to church and Sunday school there, I thought it was crazy for Mama to go all the way back to the country to attend church. She should have gone back to Centreville Baptist *in spite* of Miss Pearl them, instead of running to Mount Pleasant and letting them know that they were getting next to her. Besides, I had gotten to the place I was really enjoying Centreville Baptist, for there, at Darlene's own church, I was outdoing her.

Sometimes I would come in from Sunday school raving about how well I had explained the lesson and Mama wouldn't say anything. She would just look at me. I got the feeling that she wanted me to outdo Darlene, but she still didn't want me to enjoy Centreville Baptist too much. From the way she was acting I could tell that she wanted Adline, Junior, and me to go back to Mount Pleasant with her. So whenever I said something nice about Centreville Baptist she would say something nicer about Mount Pleasant.

Finally, that August, Mama resumed her church activities at Mount Pleasant. By this time I was so involved in Centreville Baptist that I had made up my mind that I definitely would not join her church no matter what. So when Mama told us to get ready to go to Mount Pleasant one Sunday morning, I didn't say a word. Since she had told me that we'd go out to Aunt Cindy's after church, and had got me thinking of all the fun we had always had playing in the woods out there, I figured it would be worth it even if I had to sit up in church half the day. "Besides," I thought, "she can't *make* me join church out there."

As Raymond drove up to Mount Pleasant, I saw that just as I expected things hadn't changed much. It was a gloomy day and the graveyard looked just like it did when I used to sit up in school and count the tombstones. Automatically my eyes were drawn from the tombstones to that little raggly school building. The cracks in the wood seemed even larger now and the whole school looked like it was about to collapse. I was sure it was no longer used, but as Raymond parked the car in front of the church, I saw through the open door that they still had Sunday school for the smaller children there. Mama, Adline, Junior, and I got out of the car. As I watched Raymond drive off with Jennie Ann in his lap and James on the seat beside him, I was more aware than ever that we were two families living under the same roof.

We went inside the church and sat on the back seats. Sunday school classes for teen-agers and adults were being conducted up front. I watched the teen-ager class for a while and noticed that none of them said anything. Their minds seemed to be far away. The old lady who was teaching them kept mumbling the lesson as if she was talking to herself. "And Mama want me to come to Sunday school out here!" I thought, remembering our lively discussions at Centreville Baptist.

In a little while, Sunday school ended, and the church began to fill up with adults. Mama knew nearly everybody who walked in. She smiled and waved like she had come home from a long vacation or something. When the adults were all seated, church started. The new minister, Reverend Tyson, was short, dark, and soft-spoken, just the opposite of Reverend Cason. He gave a brief sermon and then talked about revival which would be starting in a week. The look Mama gave me when he mentioned "revival" made me suspicious of why she came back to church the month before baptism.

As soon as the sermon was over, came the first collection. I sat through two collections but when they started a third, I decided that it was time for me to take a break. Since Reverend Tyson's sermon was only about twenty minutes long, I had thought that Mount Pleasant had gotten "modern," like Centreville Baptist, and would let us out early. Now I saw that I was wrong, so I went out back of the church to the same old toilet I used to escape to when I was in school there. I discovered that some of the carvings I had made of Reverend Cason over six years ago were still on the walls. On my way back I met one of Aunt Cindy's daughters and we stayed outside talking for two hours or so, standing under the oak tree near the toilet. When I thought they were almost through taking up collections, I went back inside the church.

As I entered, Deacon Brown was just beginning still another collection, this time for the "sick and invalid." I stood in the back of the church, trying to decide whether to stay or not.

"Sisters and brothers, we've heard the good minister preach here today," Deacon Brown was shouting, "and it was a good sermon, wasn't it?"

"Yes...Sure was...Thank the Lord," several old sisters answered.

"Well now, we should be glad and thankful to the Lord that we're *able* to come out and hear Brother Tyson today."

"Yes, Lord...Yes, Lord."

"And you all know that we're much more fortunate than those brothers and sisters of ours who are lyin' in their beds sick today."

"Yes, Lord."

"And you all know of our beloved Sister Turner who's been on her sickbed for many many months now...."

"Yes."

"Let us dig into our pockets and show Sister Turner that we're thinkin' of her. I'm gonna start this collection with a dollar. I want all y'all out there to match this dollar. Come on now, let's show Sister Turner how we feel about her."

"Here's my dollar, brother," someone called.

"And mine...Fifty cents over here."

In a few minutes Deacon Brown had raised about twelve dollars. Now he was calling for fifteen dollars. When he got fifteen dollars and thirty-six cents he tried to make it twenty dollars. Just as I was leaving to go back outside I saw Mama having a serious conversation with old Sister Jones who was now sitting beside her. I knew that she was trying to get Mama to get me to join Mount Pleasant.

Usually during revival season older sisters of the church recruited candidates for baptism and Sister Jones always outdid the others. During revival she went from house to house, hopping on her stick, trying to get members with unbaptized teen-agers to have them join the church. A lot of parents got their children to join by telling them that Sister Jones would put the "bad mouth" on them if they didn't. Now there was Mama nodding her head to everything Sister Jones was saying.

"I just bet Mama's gonna tell me Sister Jones say I oughta join church," I thought. "Well, I'm not! I ain't scared of that old witch! I'm goin' to join Centreville Baptist."

I went back outside, trying to convince myself that Sister Jones didn't have any power to put a "bad mouth" on people. I was walking back toward the big tree over by the toilet. As I came up to it I felt sick. I told myself that it was only hunger. I didn't want to believe that I was scared.

About four-thirty church finally let out. Unlike Centreville Baptist, Mama had lots of friends to talk to here. She had been born in the Mount Pleasant vicinity and had been a member of Mount Pleasant Church since she was fourteen. She had attended church regularly until we moved to Centreville. "She belongs here," I thought to myself, "and rightfully so, but not me."

Before Raymond came, Mama pointed out about fifty people who she said were our "cousins" or something. It seemed like just about everybody out there was kin to us one way or another. I knew she was introducing me to all of them to try and make me feel like I belonged out there too. But I didn't know anybody but Aunt Cindy them and I didn't want to know the rest.

All that following week leading up to revival, I tried to avoid Mama. Everytime I came within hearing distance she'd start nagging me to join Mount Pleasant. To get out of her way, I went to pick cotton for one of the neighboring farmers. But she always managed to corner me somehow.

"Looka there! Looka there! Walkin' round here *pokin'* your mouth out. Can't nobody say *nothin'* to you. You better go *join* church!" Mama would scold.

"I'm goin' to join church, but I'm not goin' to join Mount Pleasant! Shoot, why should we go out there, we go to Centreville Baptist every Sunday, we go to Sunday school, church, and everything. Why don't you change *your* membership?" I said angrily.

"Don't you tell *me* where to join church. When you 'spect to join Centreville Baptist? They don't baptize till way next year. You be thirteen years old next month! I ain't responsible for your sins after you reach twelve. Sister Jones was just tellin' me 'bout some girl who . . ."

"Sister Jones! What *she* got to do with this? She's always tryin' to run everybody's life."

"Don't you sass that old woman! God'll put a curse on you this minute!"

When Mama saw that her nagging didn't help she stopped. Revival started Monday of the following week and every day I expected her to try and get me to go. When Wednesday passed and she still didn't say anything about going, I was sure she had given up. Next day, Thursday, I walked around the house singing and beaming in the thought that I had beat her down. For the first time in days I sat at the same table with her.

"Ray, I want you to drive us out to revival tomorrow night," Mama said casually. "Reverend Bridge gonna preach out there."

"So *that's* why she cooked all this good food," I thought. "Who is Reverend Bridge?" I asked, thinking he must be someone like Sister Jones.

"You heard 'bout that minister who everybody go hear preach those sermons 'bout dry bones and the eagle stirred his nest. He's the best preacher they got around."

"Oh *that's* Reverend Bridge, hmm? I didn't know they were goin' to have him at Mount Pleasant." I sat there and thought for a while. I knew Mama was just trying to impress me that such famous ministers came to Mount Pleasant, so that I would be tempted to go to revival. I *was* tempted, too. I was really curious about the famous Reverend Bridge. "Besides," I thought, "it's the last night of revival and nobody can *make* me join."

The following evening Raymond drove me, Mama, and Adline out to Mount Pleasant. He left us as usual, saying he would pick us up after church. When we walked inside, I saw that the place was full, but I was surprised that it wasn't overflowing since Reverend Bridge was going to be there. We sat in the center pews. As the service began I asked Mama where was Reverend Bridge.

"I heard somebody say he ain't comin' to preach tonight," she said, trying to look disappointed.

"He ain't *comin'*?" I said, frowning. "Who told you he ain't comin'?"

"What's the difference who told me? Stop askin' so many questions all the time. Always gotta *know* everything. Shut up now! Church is startin'."

I was so mad with Mama, I sat through the prayers and testimonies without hearing one word that was said. When Reverend Tyson got up to speak, I thought, "Come all the way out here to hear this dull-assed sermon! Listen to this, listen to *this*," I mumbled to myself as he began in his usual soft sweet tones.

"Tonight, brothers and sisters, since it's the last night of revival and I know that there are still many of you sitting out there tonight who are undecided about serving Christ, we shall take as our text, Matthew 4. I want y'all out there who's been tempted by the Devil to stay out of the church, to take a *good* look at what Christ our Lord went through and remember his courage and strength in the face of great temptation."

He opened his Bible very slowly, cleared his throat slightly, and began to read:

"'Then was Jesus led up of the Spirit unto the wilderness to be tempted of the Devil and when he had fasted *forty days and forty nights*,' brothers and sisters, forty days and forty nights! 'he was afterwards mighty hungry. And when the Devil came to him, he said, if *thou* be the Son of *God*, command that these stones be made of bread. But he answered,' and listen, listen! 'and he said...'"

"Yes! Yes! What did he say?"

"'It is written, man shall not live by bread alone but by every word that proceedeth out of the mouth of God.' Do you hear that, sisters and brothers?" he shouted.

"Yes!"

"We don't need them fine cars! We don't need them fancy clothes."

"Yes, Jesus! Yes, Lord! Yes! Amen!" the crowd roared and hollered.

I sat there thinking, "Who in here got fine cars and fancy clothes?"

He let them holler and "amen" and shout for a while, then he said, "If you think *that* was courage, listen to *this*," he said, mopping his face with his handkerchief. "'Then the Devil taketh Jesus up unto the holy city and set him on the top of the highest temple and he said to him,' to Christ himself! 'if thou be the Son of God, cast thyself down, for it is said that his angels watch over thee, and in their hands they shall bear thee up, lest at any time thou dash thy foot against a stone. And Jesus said unto him,' listen what he said, children! 'it is written, that thou shalt not tempt the Lord thy God' and the Devil, not givin' up," Reverend Tyson said, closing his Bible, "took Jesus up to the *highest* mountain this time and showed him *all* the kingdoms of the world below, *all* them big houses, *all* them fine cars, *all* them beautiful clothes, and said, 'if thou will fall down and worship me, *all* these things will I give unto thee,'" he shouted, standing on the edge of the pulpit, spit flying in every direction.

"And this time Christ got a little angry," he said, coming down through the aisles. "And Jesus said, 'Get thee hence, Satan!'" he screamed, throwing out his arms and pointing his finger in my direction.

Women were shouting and jumping and hollering and screaming all over the place. Deacons were running around grabbing
fainting women and shouting "Amen" at the right times.

"Get thee *hence*, Satan!" he said again, "for it is written that
thou shalt worship the Lord thy God and him *only* shalt thou
serve." He paused for a while, breathing deeply, and it seemed like
everybody in the church was about to faint.

"Then the Devil left Jesus and the angels came and minis-
tered unto him," he said, almost whispering, as everyone in the
church leaned forward to catch his words. Suddenly he raised
his arms.

"He fought away the Devil!" he shouted, going down on his
knees. "He fought away temptation!" he said, getting up. "And
God's *angels* came to him!"

He walked past our row and as I turned to watch him my eyes
met Sister Jones's. I couldn't take my eyes from her sunken-eyed
wrinkled face.

"Aren't you ready to give up the Devil and come to Christ
tonight!" Reverend Tyson shouted. "Who's goin' to come? Who's
ready? Do we *have* anybody tonight? Do we *have* anybody tonight?
Will you come? Will you come?" he pleaded. As he did, Sister
Jones started singing and all the other sisters joined her. I turned
around and looked at Mama and she had tears running out of her
eyes. Even Adline looked like she was about to cry.

"Come to Je-e-sus,

"Come to Je-e-sus,

"Come to Je-e-sus right now," they all sang.

"He will *sa-a-ve* you," Reverend Tyson sang as he walked back
toward the pulpit.

"He will *sa-a-ve* you

"He will *sa-a-ve* you

"He will *sa-a-ve* you ri-i-ght now," the whole church sang.

Reverend Tyson reached the pulpit and turned to the audience.
"Will everybody stand?" he said, motioning with his arms.

Everybody stood, continuing to sing "Come to Jesus." Out of all the voices, Sister Jones's was the only one I heard.

"All the *Christians*, I want you to sit down!" Reverend Tyson shouted over the singing voices. "And all the *sinners*, I want you to remain standing! Now don't you *lie* to the Lord!"

People started sitting down.

"If you are a *sinner, repent* tonight! Stand up and let me *see* who you are!"

> Come to Je-e-sus,
> Come to Je-e-sus,
> Come to Je-e-sus right now.

It seemed like I was floating in the air and I had lost sight of where I was. Something was behind me, pushing me. All I could hear was Sister Jones's singing and Reverend Tyson saying, "Will you come, will you come tonight?" I could feel myself moving and I didn't know where I was going or what I was doing. I didn't see anybody.

When everything was quiet and the singing had stopped, I looked around and saw that I was standing right in the front row of the church, at the mourner's bench, with a few other candidates for baptism. I was standing face to face with Reverend Tyson.

"What's your name, young lady?" he asked gently.

"Essie Mae Moody," I stuttered.

"Speak up, young lady. Tell the Lord your name."

"Essie Mae Moody," I said, a little bit louder.

"You want to become a member of this church, Sister Moody?" he asked.

I didn't say yes. I just nodded my head.

"Brothers," he said solemnly, "do we accept Sister Moody as a candidate for baptism to become a member of this church?"

"Brother pastor," said Deacon Brown, standing near us, "we

accept Sister Moody as a candidate to be baptized into Mount Pleasant Church on the second Sunday of next month."

When Reverend Tyson finished with the last candidate, he motioned us to return to our seats. I hesitated. I didn't want to go back there to face Mama. When I realized that I was standing there by myself, I turned around and walked slowly back. As I came up to Mama, I didn't even look at her. I just stumbled into the row and sat down. Adline leaned over and said in a loud whisper, "You joined church!"

Then I looked at Mama. When she smiled at me, I felt like killing her and Sister Jones both.

During the next few weeks I hardly spoke to Mama at all. Since I had threatened to run away before baptism, I didn't have to avoid her, she was avoiding me. She was so pleased that I had joined Mount Pleasant that she was scared to say anything that would make me mad enough to really run off.

Baptism at Mount Pleasant was the biggest event of the year. Some people saved all year to buy a new outfit. Mama got busy planning what we both would wear. She went to the one store in Centreville that gave credit to Negroes and got a gray fall suit and a pair of shoes for herself. The candidates for baptism had to wear all white so Mama had a white dress made for me and bought me a blue one for after baptism. When she said that the white dress symbolized that I was entering the church pure and the blue one meant that I would always be true and faithful to the church, I felt more than ever like running away.

Saturday, the day before baptism it rained. I had hoped it would flood so that baptism would be called off, but it didn't rain that hard. On Sunday morning, baptism day, I got up and the rain had stopped. I was the last one up. Everybody else had eaten breakfast, dressed and everything. When I saw that Mama had laid my baptism clothes out at the foot of my bed, I sat there thinking of jumping out of the window and disappearing forever. Instead, I looked at that *white* dress, those *white* socks, that *white* slip, and those *white* drawers, and thought, "This shit means I've been washed clean of all my sins!"

"My sins!" I said, kicking everything off onto the floor like a wild woman.

Just then Mama came in.

"Gal! Looka here what you done! Gettin' this white dress all dirty! Get outta that bed!" she screamed angrily, picking up the dress like I had wounded it. "How you 'spect to be baptized layin' up in the bed pokin' your mouth out, kickin' these clothes on the floor. God'll *slap* the *breath* outta you, playin' with him like this! Get up! Take a bath and get these clothes on. It's nine-thirty and I gotta get you out there 'fore eleven o'clock," she continued, hollering all the way to the kitchen. "Can't do nothing with these hardhead chaps."

Getting out of bed, I looked at those white things again and thought, "Washed clean!" I threw off my pajamas and pulled on the drawers. "Washed clean!" I said, putting on the slip. "Washed clean!" I said louder, pulling on the socks. "Wa-a-a-shed cle-e-e-an!" I yelled, pulling the dress over my head.

"Get outta them clothes and take a bath!" Mama yelled and pushed me onto the bed, just as I was putting my arms through the sleeves of the dress, which was still over my head. As I hit the bed I heard a loud rip.

"Looka there! *Looka* there! Done *tore* that damned dress! Gal, I could *kill* your ass! Get on in there and *take* a bath while I sew this dress up! God*damn* you!" she yelled, pushing me out of the room.

Finally I put that white dress on and we were on our way out to Mount Pleasant. Everyone had left the church for the pond except the dozen or so candidates who were waiting for me. I was almost an hour late. A couple of deacons used their cars to drive us to the pond. As we drove past the pond where they usually had baptism and turned into the old gravel road I had walked so many times on my way to school, I asked Deacon Brown which pond we were going to.

"They just build a new pond out there right in front of Miss Rose them. That's a better setup 'cause it'll be easier for y'all to change clothes at Miss Rose's house."

Deacon Brown parked the car in front of Miss Rose's, saying "Oh, they're all out there, huh? Pretty big day today."

Getting out of the car, I looked down the hill and saw hundreds of people standing around near the levee of a big new pond. Opposite the levee, on the far side of the pond, stood a whole group of cows. They looked like they were part of the service.

We walked through the gate and headed toward the pond. I felt the dampness of the ground from yesterday's rain. It was a gloomy and chilly September morning and it looked as if it was going to rain again. As I got closer to the crowd, they looked to me like they were huddling together to keep each other warm. Looking at them made me even colder. The girls were shivering in their gaily colored nylon dresses. The young boys stood motionless in their thin suits, with their hands in their pockets. Even the old ladies were too cold to talk. I spotted Mama in the crowd in her new fall suit and thought, "At least she knew how to dress."

When we got to the edge of the pond where Reverend Tyson was standing with two deacons, we were told to line up. I looked over at the crowd and saw that they had spread out so everyone could see better. There were a lot more people than I had thought. Seeing all those brightly colored dresses and hats, the long earrings, beads, and fancy hairdos, the blood-red lipstick laid on so thick that on some lips it looked purple made me even more aware that we were all dressed in white, even the boys. I felt like a stuffed white rabbit in an Easter parade.

Now that we were all lined up, we were asked to slip our shoes off. Then Reverend Tyson was led out into the water by two deacons. Just as they stepped into the water, I heard Sister Jones's voice sing out, loud and clear, "Take me to the wa-a-ters . . ."

She was immediately joined by everyone else standing around the pond.

> *Take me to the wa-a-ters . . .*
> *Take me to the wa-a-ters . . .*
> *To be-ee bap-tized. . . .*

As the people caught their breaths for the next verse, several moos could be heard. The mooing got so loud that the singing stopped for a moment. Reverend Tyson, in water up to his knees, turned toward the cows and raised his hand as if to quiet them. When they stopped mooing, everybody laughed. Then the singing began again.

When Reverend Tyson and the two deacons were standing in water up to their chests, the first candidate was led out. Everyone continued to sing "Take Me to the Waters" but much lower. Most of the candidates looked scared, especially the girl in front of me. I couldn't tell whether she was shaking because she was scared or cold, or both. I heard Jack, one of the wildest, crap-shootingest boys around, whisper from behind me, "Lookit all that *cow* shit in that water!" I looked down at the water and saw big piles of cow manure floating around. The thought of being ducked under that water made me want to vomit. The water was so muddy, the whole pond looked like a giant mud pie. Then I looked at the girl standing between Reverend Tyson and one of the deacons.

"I baptize you in the name of the Father, in the name of the Son, and in the name of the Holy Ghost, *Amen*," Reverend Tyson said, drawing out the last syllable as he ducked her quickly under the water. She came up coughing and sputtering, her white dress was now dark brown. Her hair was dripping with mud. All the other candidates stared at her as the deacons helped her back to the edge of the pond. She was shaking and she looked like she wanted to cry so bad. All the candidates were aware of the saying that if you coughed when you were being baptized, it meant the Devil was coming out of you. I knew she was embarrassed because she had coughed.

"All dressed in white! Washed clean! Look at that!" I thought, looking at her.

As the girl ahead of me was being led out, Jack leaned close and whispered, "'Member, Moody, betta not cough out there. Sister Jones gonna say you were a *sinner*. Hee-hee-hee."

"You got a lot more to cough about than me," I said. I saw two deacons coming for me. As I waded into the water, I could feel the mud sticking to my legs. I was mad as hell, and I heard Sister Jones's voice singing "Nothing but the righteous . . ." along with the rest, I thought, "Nothing but the *righteous*. Some shit!"

I was so mad I barely heard Reverend Tyson shouting, "I baptize you in the name of the Father, in the name of the Son, and in the name of the Holy Ghost, A-*men!*" Suddenly a wet hand was slapped over my face and I felt the mud folding over me, sucking me down. Just as I began to feel the heaviness of the mud, I was lifted out of the water. I tried to open my eyes but mud was stuck to my lashes, so I just left them closed. I felt shitty all over. As they were leading me out of the water, I could hear the cows mooing, Jack laughing, and everyone singing, "Take Me to the Waters." Everything sounded far away. It took me a minute to realize that my ears were stuffed full of mud.

After the last candidate was baptized, we were all rushed up to Miss Rose's where we washed off and changed. Even then, I still smelled like wet mud, and the smell lingered for weeks.

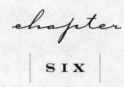

chapter

| SIX |

All that second winter in the new house, Raymond sat around talking about becoming a big-time farmer, raising lots of kids, making plenty of money, and being his own man. So in early March he went out scouting for a mule and a piece of land. Within a week he had found both, as cheap as he could get them. He bought a used-up old mule from a friend for twenty-five dollars, hoping that it could last at least one season. He rented a strip of cheap virgin land in the old army camp area. It was on a hill slanting down to the edge of some woods. Since there was only one little tree and not much grass, Raymond thought that plowing would be easy and that he had gotten a real bargain. For the first few days of plowing he went around grinning and boasting and even saying how nice Mr. Pickett was for letting him have the land so cheap. He enjoyed the plowing and he stayed in the field from sunup to sundown. He'd come in all sweaty and tired, dragging the poor old mule behind him.

One evening he came in a little early, all disgusted, cursing up a storm. He slammed into the kitchen with his lunch basket held in front of him.

"Looka this! Looka *this!* That goddamn mothafucka! I shoulda *known* he wasn't givin' me that land for nothin'. That whole damn bottom is just like plowin' into steel. Looka this shit!" he said, dumping the contents of his lunch bucket onto the table.

We all stood around the table looking. Mama picked up a big round rock, covered with dirt.

"What in the shit *is* this?" Mama asked, scraping the dirt from the rock.

"Don't you drop that thing! It may be *live!*" Raymond shouted.

"Live?" Mama screamed, throwing up both hands, dropping the object to the floor. It hit with a loud thud and rolled under the stove. Raymond tiptoed after it, with his arms out, like he was reaching for a baby. He got down on his knees, reached under the stove, and carefully picked the thing up.

"What you doin' bringin' stuff like that in this house! What you mean it's *live?*" Mama said, staring at the object in Raymond's trembling hands.

"Live? Shit! This is a goddamned *hand grenade!* That whole bottom is full of them! Some of 'em look like they ain't *never* been touched."

"*Hand grenade!* You mean a *bomb?*" Mama said.

"Sure, the bottom of that hill musta been a practice ground or something. Looka here," he said, picking up a big bullet. "If that steel plow hit this thing the right way, it'd kill the shit outta me."

"If them things been out there since the war they ain't hardly no good now," Mama said, looking at the pile of grenades and bullets on the table. "Take your hands off that stuff, boy!" she screamed at Junior, who was just about to pick up one of the grenades. "Ray, get that shit outta here."

From then on Raymond plowed very carefully. Every time he went out to the fields after that, he would act as if it might be his last day on earth. Even though Mama insisted that the old bullets and things weren't "live," she stopped fixing lunch for Raymond and had him come home at twelve. And every evening she'd pace around the kitchen worrying until he got home. After a few days of plowing with no explosions, Raymond and Mama began to relax a little.

"Next year I won't have to plow through all that shit," Raymond said to Mama.

"Shit, next year, Mr. Pickett will plant his own damn cotton out there," Mama said.

School wasn't out yet and I was still working for Mrs. Claiborne. She was teaching me so much and she was so good to me that I didn't want to stop working for her. But I knew as soon as school was over, I'd have to work in the field all day. I was scared to death. I never could take much sun without getting a headache, and I had heard that a lot of people had died in the field from sunstroke and different things.

One evening I came in from work and saw Mama, Raymond, and all of them standing around out under the pecan tree. I walked up to them. The mule was stretched out on the ground with foam bubbling out of his mouth, and Raymond was cursing.

"Why didn't that mothafucka die *next* week! Bring some water, Junior! Get that hose pipe and hook it up! Put some water in that tub! Goddamn, hurry up! This son of a bitch! Just got one more week of good plowing and this fucka gonna die now! Shit!"

"You're workin' him too hard, Ray. Why don't you take it easy? You ain't got but a little more plowing to do. You gotta give that mule some rest. You don't plow no old mule that much! Besides, Jim them prob'ly worked the hell outta this mule before you got him!" Mama said as Junior filled the tub up full of water.

"That damned cotton gotta be planted, though. That ground's gotta be broke. Soon everybody else's cotton gonna be comin' up!"

Raymond shouted, as he helped Junior drag the tub of water up to the mule. Then he grabbed the mule by the head and tried to make it drink from the tub, but its head was limp and its eyes were walling back. It looked like it didn't know where it was. When Raymond couldn't get it to drink any water, he slammed its head down on the ground some hard. I stood there feeling sorry for the poor old mule, but in the back of my mind I was saying, "I hope it die, I hope it die, I hope it die!" I went to bed that night praying that the mule would die, because I didn't want to quit working for Mrs. Claiborne to go out and get a sunstroke. But when I got up the next morning, that damned mule was up kicking and ready to go back to the field again.

Raymond finally finished his plowing and eventually got the cotton planted. It needed lots of rain to take root, so every day Mama and Raymond went around praying for rain. They prayed and prayed but the rain just didn't come. Raymond walked around grumbling and cursing and acting like he was mad with the whole world. Every day he would go out to look at the cotton. When he came in he'd start shouting, "That ground so hard out there, the sun is crackin' the ground up! Them damned cotton seed burnin' up in the ground! Fuck this shit! A man can't make a living, I don't care how hard he try! *Everythin*'s against him, even the god-damn sun!"

And every time I'd hear Raymond cursing, I'd think, "*Please* burn up in the ground! Oh, *please* burn up in the ground!"

Mama would sit on the porch rocking all day, watching the sky. Every time a little cloud would get in the sky, she'd start hollering, "It's comin', it's comin'! Look like we're gonna get some rain tonight!"

So then I started praying that it wouldn't rain. Often I went to bed and had dreams that there were big floods and water was just gushing everywhere, washing away mountains and trees and all the cotton.

But eventually it did rain and the cotton started to come up.

Every other day or so, Raymond would take us out to see the cotton. He wouldn't take us into the field when the cotton was just coming out of the ground because he was superstitious. He thought that we might interfere with "the works of Nature." So instead he parked the car alongside the road and we all sat looking out at the cotton field.

"Boy, looka there, Toosweet. It sure is growing," Raymond said, grinning like a wild man.

I thought he had lost his mind. I couldn't see *any* cotton. All I saw was a big empty field.

School ended and I sadly said good-bye to Mrs. Claiborne. Raymond had said that on Monday morning, my first week out of school, we would start chopping cotton. I was angry because I didn't expect to quit Mrs. Claiborne until it was time to *pick* the cotton. I didn't even know anything about chopping. All I thought you had to do to cotton once it was up was pick it.

That weekend Mama and Raymond both prepared for the chopping. Mama went into town and bought a whole lot of food and a straw hat for each of us, and Raymond stocked up on hoes. All day Sunday he sat out under the pecan tree sharpening the hoes. He called me and Adline out and had us make believe we were hoeing so he could cut handles the right length for us. As I watched Adline pretend to hoe, I thought, "Lord have mercy! Little Adline hoeing!"

That night as I went to bed, I thought of how hot it had been all day. I was sure the temperature was over a hundred degrees. I knew that it would be just as hot the next day and I could see myself standing out there sweating over a hoe. I fell asleep worrying about hoeing in that boiling hot sun, and I had a terrible dream.

In my dream a whole group of us were out in the cotton field, up on the hill where there was only that one tree that Raymond had left for shade. We were hoeing slowly down the hill when the sun came up so big that it seemed to fill up the whole sky. It came so close to us, it looked like a big mouth about to swallow us. The whole sky and everything around us was red. I was getting terribly hot and great big drops of sweat were dripping all over me. I looked at that little tree that was up on the hill and it was drying, bending, wizzling up to nothing. I looked around in the far distance and the trees were on fire, the whole forest was burning, the trees were just flapping down. I looked around for everybody else in the cotton field, for Raymond and all of them, and they were all dead, lying between the rows. I was leaning on my hoe and I was rocking and the sun came down even closer. I was the last one standing and I knew it was coming for me. I quickly glanced at all the dead bodies evaporating around me. And I felt myself crumbling under the heat of the sun. And then I woke up.

When I got out of bed that morning I was sweating and shaking like someone with palsy. I couldn't touch my breakfast. Mama kept asking me what was wrong, but I was too scared to tell her about the dream, so I just mumbled that I wasn't feeling well. I hoped that she would tell me to stay home but instead she handed me a couple of aspirins and sent me off to the cotton field with the rest.

Raymond took along Adline, Alberta, and me for the chopping and Junior and James as waterboys. When Raymond stopped the car in front of Miss Pearl's and Cherie and Darlene came running out in blue jeans, long-sleeved shirts, and straw hats, dressed just like we were, I was surprised. I didn't think Raymond could talk Miss Pearl into letting precious little Darlene and Cherie hoe cotton. I guessed he must have told her that if he made it big from the cotton he'd do something nice for her.

When Cherie and Darlene got into the car, I forgot my dream for a while. But as Raymond drove up the hill to the cotton field it all came back. I looked around at everybody in the car and thought to myself, "We're all gonna die this morning." It was about six-thirty and the sun was not up yet, but I could tell from the pink clouds and brightening sky that it was on its way. Raymond drove up to the gate and stopped the car. When Junior jumped out to open the gate, I felt like jumping out too and running away. I had a feeling that if I went through that gate, I'd be trapped in the cotton field forever. But I couldn't move. It was just like the time Mama had killed a hog and we had eaten a whole lot of fresh hog meat. I had gone to sleep and awakened just before daylight. Then, too, I couldn't move. I'd felt the need to call for help but I couldn't even open my mouth. I was calling and calling but no words came out. I tried to wiggle my toe or move my arm but I couldn't move anything. I couldn't even bat an eye. After a while, it passed away. When I told Mama about it, she said that I had eaten too much hog meat and that "the witch was riding" me. "The witch" was the evil in the hog meat that had stopped my blood from running.

As Raymond drove through the gate, I sat there screaming for help. But I knew no sound came because nobody looked at me. When he parked the car under the little tree, right by the cotton field and everybody got out, I was still sitting there screaming. I could hear Raymond calling me but I couldn't even answer. At last I saw him walking back to get me.

"Gal, what's wrong with you? You act like you're losin' your mind this morning!" Raymond shouted.

I jumped out of the car and ran right past him toward Alberta them walking to the cotton field. For a moment as Raymond shouted at me, I forgot my dream. Then suddenly it struck me that we were about to start hoeing on *that* hill and the whole dream came back. I stopped short and waited for Raymond. As he came up, I said, "Why don't we start hoeing in the bottom?"

"You ain't got a bit of sense, huh, gal? Don't you know it's harder to come up a hill than to go down it? Now why should we start hoeing at the bottom of the hill and hoe uphill?"

"It's cooler down there," I said meekly, looking up at the sky.

He shook his head as if I was crazy and walked away. I followed reluctantly.

Raymond and Alberta were the only ones who knew how to chop cotton, so they walked up and down the rows and showed us how to do it. The cotton was heavily planted. We had to thin it out so it would have enough earth and air to grow freely. Darlene and I caught on fast and we were soon hoeing by ourselves. Raymond and Alberta lagged behind, helping Adline and Cherie. I got all wrapped up in trying to outhoe Darlene. I finished three or four rows quickly, way ahead of her. Every now and then I looked back to see how far she was behind me. When she was one whole row behind, I stopped to shake my arms out. I could feel the sweat running down under them.

I was scared to look up at the sky because I knew the sun had come up. My heart began to beat like a loud drum. I shook all over. I could almost feel the sun rising in the sky. I stood there for a while, giving Darlene a chance to catch up with me. Then I hoed along slowly for a couple of hours pretending that the sun didn't even exist. Every now and then James or Junior brought someone water. I didn't want to look at them because I knew it was getting hotter and each trip they made reminded me of the sun.

Along about ten-thirty or eleven I could feel my shirt clinging to my body, like a big, wet crab. I was soaked to my waist. I didn't look up, but I knew that sun was up there just like it had been in my dream. Water was running down my face from under my hat. And big drops of sweat were dripping off my arms. It was getting harder and harder for me to hoe. Every time I reached out to chop some cotton, the row seemed to move away from me, like a big wiggling snake. I looked around at everybody else in the field and they were wiggling like the row in front of me. They looked like they were falling, just like in my dream. I didn't want to look at them. I looked up at the sun and for a moment I was completely blinded. Then I knew the others were dead. I could see the sun again. My eyes got fixed on it. I felt myself reeling and rocking on my hoe.

"Hey, Junior! Come over here, boy! Bring that water! This gal out here 'bout to *faint* or somethin'!" Raymond yelled.

Next thing I knew I was sitting on the ground and Raymond was trying to force me to drink some water. Everybody else had stopped hoeing and now they were all standing around me.

Raymond told me to rest awhile under the little tree. Thinking about how that tree shriveled up in the sun, I was afraid to go near it. I thought if I did, I would really die. When Raymond told me that we would be going home for lunch in about half an hour, I rested for a few minutes, picked up my hoe, and went back to hoeing with the rest of them. After eating lunch I felt much better, and when we went back to the field, the sun didn't seem very hot.

After a couple of days and didn't anybody die, my dream began to fade. Soon I even began to like the work. I'd pull off my shoes and let the hot earth fall over my feet as I was hoeing. It sent a warm feeling over my whole body. Even the burning of the hot sun no longer frightened me, but seemed to give me energy. Then when I went home there were those good hot meals Mama made. During the first few days of chopping cotton, we ate better than we had in our whole life. Mama was doing everything she could to keep us going. That first day she made a feast. She cooked at least five chickens, two big pones of bread, lots of rice and string beans, and even a couple of big coconut cakes. When we came in from the field, we found the picnic table out under the pecan tree loaded down with food.

I had never seen Raymond so happy as when he was sitting up at that table running over with food, surrounded by all his "workers," laughing and eating and listening to Mama's nasty jokes. While we sat at the table we didn't even think about the field. And when we went back, we felt like we were just beginning the day. It went on like that for days, until all the money was gone from the little loan Raymond had made from the bank. After that we went back to our usual beans and bread.

Finally we finished chopping the cotton for Raymond. Then Alberta, Darlene, and I took our hoes and went to chop cotton at two dollars a day for big-time farmers in the area, including some who were Raymond's relatives. They were among the few Negroes who had worked over the years to build up successful farms. When it came time to scrape the cotton a couple of weeks later, we returned to our field. We had to remove the weeds that had grown up among the cotton stalks. Then the cotton could grow freely until picking time.

In addition to the cotton for market, Raymond planted corn and potatoes for our own use. Within a couple of months I could really handle a hoe. When I wasn't chopping or scraping cotton, I was chopping corn or helping Mama in the garden. I had learned a lot about farming, but the more I learned, the surer I was that I would never become a farmer. I couldn't see myself becoming totally dependent upon the rain, sun, and earth like most farmers. I used to look at Raymond and Mama running around the house praying all the time and think that they were crazy. Farming was a fever they couldn't get rid of. When they first planted the cotton they prayed for rain. Once the cotton came up they didn't need rain any more, so they prayed for sun, so the cotton bolls would open. Then after the bolls opened, they worried about the boll weevils, and spent a lot of money on poison to kill them. When the poison didn't work, they started praying again. It was always something.

Mama and Raymond had been hooked to the soil since they were children, and I got the feeling, especially from Mama, that they were now trying to hook me. Sometimes I'd help Mama hoe in the garden and she'd be telling me how she used to pick so much cotton and how she used to do this and used to do that. Then she'd be pitty pattin' around in the soil, barefooted, bragging about her collard greens and how "old Mother Nature" took care of things. "Looka these mustard greens here! Gol-lee, wasn't nothin' but a seed a few weeks ago. Now they ready to eat." She would kick her foot into the soil and say, "Boy, you c'n put *any* kinda seed in this garden—'fore you know it you got somethin' to eat." I saw how happy she was in her garden and most of what she said was true. She did have the most beautiful garden I'd ever seen. The whole thing fascinated me—planting seeds, growing your own food, using the rain and the sun and the earth, and even the idea of making a living from it. But it was the hardest way I knew of making a living.

So whenever Mama started one of her long lectures on the pleasures of farming, I would drown her out with my thoughts of Mrs. Claiborne and all the traveling she had done and the people she had met. Mrs. Claiborne had told me how smart I was and how much I could do if I just had a chance. I knew if I got involved in farming, I'd be just like Mama and the rest of them, and that I would never have that chance.

After the cotton season was over I was surer than ever that I would never be a farmer. Out of all that work we had put into the cotton, we didn't even make enough money to buy school clothes. We had one good picking and that was it. The land was just no good. If Raymond hadn't planted corn and sweet potatoes, and Mama's garden hadn't been so good, we would have starved to death that winter.

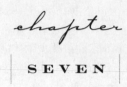

chapter

SEVEN

We started to school in our same old school clothes and broken-down shoes. I ran around looking for a job for a week or so but I couldn't find anything. I went back to Mrs. Claiborne but she had someone else working for her. She said she'd ask her friends if any of them needed help. I checked every day, and none of them did. Then one day we came in from school and Mama had a stack of croker sacks out on the porch.

As I walked into the house she said, "Essie Mae, y'all hurry up and eat. Shit, Mr. Wheeler came by here today. He want us to pick up pecans. He say that ground is just loaded with 'em. We could make enough money to buy all y'all school clothes."

As soon as we finished eating we grabbed the croker sacks and ran all the way to Mr. Wheeler's house. He lived right on the other side of the project from us, in a big white house. He was a rancher and he owned lots of land in the area. Right down the hill from his house he had a big pecan orchard. As we walked up the gravel driveway, we could see him out in his backyard playing with his children.

"I sure hope he ain't let nobody else pick 'em up," Mama said. "I told him we'd be up there as soon as y'all got outta school. He look like he don't even know we're comin'."

"Elmira, where you carryin' that baby to? She'll get fulla ticks out there in that grass," Mr. Wheeler said as we approached.

I was so excited about going to pick up pecans, I hadn't even noticed that Mama was carrying Jennie Ann.

"My little boy here gonna keep her while we pick up pecans. I didn't want to leave her in the house by herself," Mama answered.

"Oh, I see you brought your own sacks too. Good! C'mon, I'll drive y'all down in the bottom. I want y'all to pick them up next to the road first 'cause them little boys keep runnin' in there pickin' them up." Mr. Wheeler put his two little boys in front of the pickup truck and we all piled into the back—Mama, me, Adline, Junior, James, and the baby. As Mr. Wheeler drove past his cattle, Mama said, "Boy, looka that milk in them cows' titties. Shit, if I had all them cows, I would never get through eatin' steaks and drinkin' milk." As he drove through the pecan orchard, we could see pecans piled on the ground about two inches thick. "Look at 'im how he's drivin' the truck through them pecans! He coulda let us walk down here," Mama said, looking like she wanted to jump right out and get started. She was the first one off the truck when we got to the bottom.

It had rained heavily the day before and just about all the pecans on the trees had fallen. We all had gallon buckets and we could almost fill them just by raking them around on the ground. Even little Jennie Ann, who wasn't a year old, was stumbling around on the ground picking up pecans. "C'mon, Jennie Ann! Looka here! Help your mama make some money," Mama laughed every time Jennie Ann dropped some pecans in her bucket.

It was almost dark when Mama sent Junior up to the house to say we were ready to knock off. When Mr. Wheeler came down, we were all standing out there with muddy hands and knees.

Jennie Ann was muddy all over. We looked like a bunch of clowns standing there behind four full croker sacks.

"Boy, y'all look like y'all had fun down here today. My land, I ain't never had anybody work that fast! Look at all them pecans!" Mr. Wheeler said. The croker sacks were so heavy that all of us had to help him put them in the truck.

We had picked the pecans up on half. Since we had four sacks, I had expected Mr. Wheeler to give us two of them. But instead he measured them out, gallon for gallon, to make sure we didn't have an ounce more than he did. He kept us there for two hours measuring the pecans. We got home about eight that night. Next evening after school we went back and finished them up. That Saturday morning Mama and Raymond drove the pecans to Woodville, where they could get eighteen cents a pound instead of the fifteen cents they got paid in Centreville. In all we had picked up a hundred and twenty dollars' worth. Mama used the money to buy school clothes for us—shoes, dresses, and pants.

We picked up pecans the following week for Miss Minnie, an old lady who was living across the road from Mr. Wheeler. After we'd finished, Miss Minnie asked me to sweep her porch, then she asked if I would help her some evenings, so I began working for her. I had to burn her trash and then sweep her porches and halls. She paid me three dollars a week and also let me pick up the few pecans that were left after the first big picking. I sold them and made as much as six dollars a week during the season. Then when the pecans were all gone I started baby-sitting for Mr. and Mrs. Jenkins, a young couple who rented rooms next door from Miss Minnie. They had one child, a little girl named Donna who had just started walking, and another child on the way.

Since Mrs. Jenkins had had trouble giving birth to Donna, she was extremely nervous about her second pregnancy. She was expecting in two months and she had gotten so big that everybody thought she'd have twins. They couldn't really afford help, but little Donna was getting to be too much for Mrs. Jenkins, so they hired me to keep the child out of her way. I took her for walks, read her stories, and made up games for her to play. We would spend hours under Miss Minnie's pecan tree, playing and picking up pecans.

I used to feel funny calling Mrs. Jenkins "Mrs. Jenkins" because she didn't look too much older than me. When she saw that it bothered me, she told me that her first name was Linda Jean and that when I called her Mrs. Jenkins it reminded her too much of her mother, who demanded that everyone, especially Negroes, call her "Mrs." I began to really like Linda Jean after that. She treated me just like I was one of her friends and I never thought about our color difference when I was with her, except when she paid me. Only then was I reminded that I was her maid. When I told Linda Jean I was the oldest of five and that my mother was also expecting, she said, "Boy, you should know more about children than me." Sometimes, when she would get one of her sick spells, she would even ask me what to do, like I was an authority on having babies.

She was so nice to me that when I saw her struggling with the housework, I started helping her even though I was only paid to take care of Donna. A few weeks before she was about to get down they began paying me to do *all* the housework and take care of Donna too. Altogether they paid me twelve dollars a week, the most I had ever earned. I felt a little guilty about taking that much money from them because I knew they couldn't afford it, but things were so bad at home that I had to.

One day I was in the kitchen washing dishes for Linda Jean while she was up front talking to the lady who lived in the big white frame house next door. She was a good-looking, tall slim woman with mingled gray and black hair. I had just finished washing the cake mixer and I didn't know where to put it.

"Linda Jean," I called, "where do the cake mixer go?"

"Far left-hand corner of the cupboard," she yelled back.

A moment later the lady from next door appeared in the kitchen door.

"Is *that* what you call Mrs. Jenkins—Linda Jean?" she asked angrily.

I looked at her, puzzled, thinking to myself, "Now what in the shit does *she* mean?"

Suddenly Linda Jean was there, shouting.

"Mama! Essie works for *me!* I told you about trying to run my life!"

She was standing in the door behind the lady who I now realized was her mother. Linda Jean was so angry that she was shaking. Her mother glared at her for a moment, then walked out.

Linda Jean was so upset that she went to lie down for a while. As I finished the dishes I wondered why Linda Jean's mother, whom I had seen raking leaves in her backyard while Donna and I were playing under the pecan tree, had never said anything to me. I didn't even figure she *knew* Linda Jean.

When I finished the dishes I knocked softly at Linda Jean's door. She was awake and asked me in.

"I finished the kitchen. Would you like for me to do anything else while Donna is asleep?" I asked.

"Look, Essie, don't get upset by Mama. She's got to learn once and for all that I am not like her," she said, not even answering my question. She kept on talking and I just stood there listening.

"At the last minute she comes over and wants to know if she can help! She didn't approve of me marrying Bill and she didn't help me at all when I had my trouble with Donna. She even wanted me to kill the baby when I was pregnant. After Bill and I ran off and got married she didn't even speak to me for months. *Now* she wants to help! Bill doesn't want her in this house!"

On Saturday of that following week Linda Jean's mother, Mrs. Burke, was over again. She came in just as Linda Jean was paying me. She didn't say anything, but before I left for home I stopped on the back porch to pick up some towels that had fallen off the line and overheard her saying to Linda Jean, "I don't understand it! If you don't have any money why do y'all pay her twelve dollars? The richest people in town don't pay their help that much. Six dollars is the most *anyone* pays!"

"But, Mama, she does *everything*. It's not fair. I don't do *anything* around here," I heard Linda Jean say.

I was surprised to hear that I was making more than any maid in Centreville and it made me feel closer to Linda Jean. At the same time I felt even guiltier about taking it. I headed home, feeling sure that Linda Jean wouldn't let Mrs. Burke talk her into paying me less. But the next Saturday she gave me only six dollars. I was so shocked I couldn't say anything. I just took it and went home. I thought about it a lot and almost didn't go back. But since we needed even that six dollars so badly, I went back on Monday evening.

I noticed that Linda Jean and Mrs. Burke seemed to be getting along a little better, because Mrs. Burke was over a lot more. I figured Mrs. Burke was now helping them out. I knew that Linda Jean wasn't like her and that she still couldn't stand her, but that she was just going along with her for the money.

A few days later, Linda Jean went into the hospital. That Saturday I went up and gave the house a thorough cleaning. Mrs. Burke was watching Donna. I finished my work early, but since I had to wait for Mr. Jenkins to pay me, I went over to Miss Minnie's to see if she needed anything done. While I was rinsing out some clothes for her she happened to mention that Mr. Jenkins was the son of the sheriff of Woodville. I had heard a lot of bad things about the sheriff. He was known as a "nigger hater" and was one of the meanest sheriffs in the whole area. The thought that I was working for the son of such a terrible man frightened me.

When I finished Miss Minnie's wash, I found something else to do because I was too scared to go back next door. Finally I heard

Mr. Jenkins drive up in his big gasoline truck. Now I remembered how some evenings he came home all greasy and black and smelling of gas and oil, looking like he hated driving that truck for a living. The dirtier he was, the angrier he looked. Linda Jean would be quiet around him when he was in that mood. He had hardly ever said anything to me, so I couldn't tell what he thought about Negroes but now that I knew he was the sheriff's son, I could almost see him being mean and cruel too.

I knew that the first thing he did when he got home every evening was scrub all of that gummy oil and grease off his hands, so I stayed over to Miss Minnie's until I thought he had finished washing up. I didn't want to have to wait around for my pay. When I finally went over, there he was in the kitchen, just as dirty as anything, going through a box of tools. He had a big wrench in one hand and was digging into the box with the other. I could tell he was angry by the way he dug into the box. Beads of sweat were popping out on his balding head. I stood looking at him for a while wondering if I should go home without my pay. Just as I was about to leave, he looked up and said, "Oh, Essie, I thought you were gone. Go over next door and get Donna and dress her for me, please. I wanta take her to see Linda Jean."

On my way to Mrs. Burke's I decided that even though Mr. Jenkins was the sheriff's son, he didn't talk mean to me. As the weeks went by, I gradually forgot who his father was.

Shortly after Linda Jean had her baby, Mama had hers. And she almost had it in the courthouse. A few days before she gave birth, she made up her mind that she and Raymond would finally get married with or without Miss Pearl's consent. She had been pouting at Raymond for over a week. Then one day they got all dressed up. Raymond put on his old blue suit that had hung in the closet for so long it had turned purple. It was one of those old-fashioned, 1920's-looking, double-breasted suits with wide sleeves and legs.

Mama put on her best maternity dress. As they dressed, they barely said a word to each other. Raymond looked very sad and scared. I thought it was about time Mama made up her mind that she had had enough babies for Raymond without being married to him. She had told me that she didn't want Miss Pearl them to know that she and Raymond were getting married. But I felt like running over there and throwing it up in Miss Pearl's face.

I sat on the porch and watched them walk to the car, Mama all hump-shouldered and with her mouth still stuck out, Raymond walking a little behind her looking like he was about to cry. They looked just like they were going to a funeral.

It seemed as though it took them an hour to get to the car, when it was only a few feet away from the house. Mama got in without even looking at Raymond. She sat there staring straight ahead of her, not looking anywhere in particular. Raymond very slowly backed the car out of the driveway. He didn't have a rear-view mirror so usually he would turn to the right and look out of the back window to make his turn. But today, instead of looking in Mama's direction, he backed the car straight out of the driveway without looking back at all. As he turned, he cut too short and drove the car right into the ditch. Mama didn't even move. She just sat there putting a little more puff into her pout. Raymond slammed out of the car, gave a curse, got back in, gunned the accelerator and the car shot out of the ditch. In the mood they were in, I wondered if they would make it to the courthouse.

I was still sitting on the porch when they got back. My first thought was that they didn't go all the way to Woodville, they were back so quick, but I could tell that they had gotten married. When Raymond parked the car, I could hear the radio blaring rock-and-roll. Mama was grinning down. For the first time in a couple of weeks they were talking to each other. Raymond got out of the car, leaving the radio on, and went on down toward the hog pen, looking as if it was slowly dawning on him that he had just gotten married. Mama remained in the car listening to the song on the radio.

All of a sudden she got out of the car and started twisting to the fast beat. Her big pregnant belly swayed from side to side.

"Essie Mae," she called, "look at me!" as if I wasn't already looking.

"You better stop that 'fore you fall down and break a hip or somethin'!" Raymond yelled, looking back. Just then the song ended. As Mama hit that last note I thought she would sling that baby up on the porch.

The baby must have got the message that it was safe to come out, because a few days later he was there. Mama was loving Raymond so at the time that she named him Raymond, Jr. and called him Jerry. Now it seemed like I could never get away from crying babies. When I went to work, Linda Jean's baby, Johnny, was bawling, and when I got home little Jerry was at it. And it was like that for a long while.

chapter

| EIGHT |

I worked for Linda Jean throughout my seventh grade year. But that spring and summer Raymond tried farming again, and I was only able to help her on weekends. When I entered eighth grade the following fall we were poorer than ever. Raymond had worse luck with the farm than the year before, so we weren't able to buy any new school clothes. I had added so much meat to my bones that I could squeeze into only two of my old school dresses. They were so tight I was embarrassed to put them on. I had gotten new jeans for the field that summer, so I started wearing them to school two and three days a week. But I continued to fill out so fast that even my jeans got too tight. I got so many wolf whistles from the boys in the class that the faster girls started wearing jeans that were even tighter than mine. When the high school boys started talking about how fine those eighth grade girls were, the high school girls started wearing tight jeans too. I had started a blue jeans fad.

One Friday in early October before school let out, Mrs. Willis announced that first thing Monday morning the class would choose its queen for the Homecoming competition. I couldn't think of any girl in the class I liked enough to nominate. I figured that the boys would get together and pick one of the fast girls, so I didn't worry myself about it.

Homecoming Day was in November. Each grade from fifth to twelfth was represented by a queen in the parade before the football game; the queen whose class raised the most money became Miss Willis High and was crowned Homecoming Queen during half time. Every girl in my class knew that our queen would certainly be the winner because Mrs. Willis' class always raised the most money. Mrs. Willis knew more about raising money than any other teacher on campus.

On Monday morning, after roll call, Mrs. Willis passed out little slips of paper and asked us to write the names of our nominees. Just for the hell of it I nominated myself. I knew that the outcome of the election depended on how the boys voted because all the girls except Darlene and me, who stood alone, were split into two groups, the fast and the quiet. Even so it would be close since there were nearly twice as many girls as there were boys. All that day I could see the three groups in their separate huddles, speculating. When we finally got back to Mrs. Willis' class in the last period, everybody got quiet.

"Class, durin' my break I counted the votes," Mrs. Willis said, "and I'm mighty glad I did because we've elected ourselves *three* queens!"

Everybody gasped and oohed and ahed. All the girls were looking at each other wondering who was the third queen, the one the *boys* had undoubtedly picked.

"Will the queens come forward as I call your names, please," Mrs. Willis said. "Queen Amanda!"

Amanda, the prettiest girl in the quiet group, went shyly up to the front of the room and stood by the side of Mrs. Willis' desk, looking down at the floor.

"Queen Dorothy!" Mrs. Willis called.

Some of the girls in the fast group clapped their hands as Dorothy switched up front in a real tight pair of jeans and with an overconfident look on her face. As she stood next to Amanda, she put her hands on her hips and stuck out her ass. A couple of the boys gave a low "boo" and all of a sudden she didn't seem so confident. I was surprised at the boos because I also thought Dorothy was the boys' favorite since she was the fastest girl in the eighth grade.

Mrs. Willis cleared her throat. I could tell she was enjoying the surprises.

"Queen Essie," she said. The girls in both groups nearly fainted and the boys started whistling and cheering. I began to look around for Queen Essie. Suddenly it struck me that *I* was Queen Essie. "The boys picked *me?*" I thought, with my mouth wide open.

"Queen Essie, we're waitin'," Mrs. Willis said, smiling.

"You mean me?" I said, poking myself in the chest.

"You're Essie, ain't you?" Mrs. Willis said.

As I started to get up and the boys began to whistle even louder, I realized I had on those tight jeans. So I sat right back down in my seat. One of the fast girls who didn't like me whispered from behind me, "'Shamed to show that ass now, Moody?" I felt like spitting in her face, but instead I got up and purposely swayed my ass all the way up to Mrs. Willis' desk. The boys were going crazy, whistling all over the place. Mrs. Willis was laughing like she got a big kick out of the whole thing.

Now that the three of us were standing by Mrs. Willis' desk, she asked for a "standing vote," but it went on so long without a clear majority that Mrs. Willis decided to have a money-raising contest among the three nominees and their backers. We were given three weeks. So for the next three weeks we went around on campus selling popcorn, hot dogs, candied apples, and all kinds of stuff. Dorothy and her gang put on a big act like they were raising millions of dollars. The act was so good that Amanda and her group fizzled out, but I knew it was only a bluff because if Dorothy's gang were really raising lots of money they wouldn't have talked about it so much. Besides, I knew we had an advantage because most of the boys worked after school, and so did I, and we put every penny we made into buying and selling. When the three weeks were up, we had raised fifty dollars more than the other two groups put together, and I became the eighth grade's Homecoming Queen. Mrs. Willis and the whole class now worked to make me queen of the whole school.

I had always thought that because Mrs. Willis was the principal's wife, she had used the school money from the snack bar and other places to make sure her class queen won. But now that she was working the hell out of us every day, I saw that she won because she was better organized than the other teachers. She divided the class into five groups and each day of the week one of the groups was selling something. In addition to that she gave evening socials to raise still more money. At the rate we were going, I knew we couldn't lose.

A week before Homecoming, a special chapel meeting was called, and each class presented the money it had raised. The to tal amount raised by all the classes was about seventeen hundred dollars and our class had raised about eight hundred of that. This was far more than the nearest competition. The school secretary asked the eighth grade queen to come up on stage and present the money to Principal Willis. When she handed me the money I almost felt like I had earned it all, I was so tired. I really didn't want to hand it to Willis, who was standing there with that big fat grin on his face I couldn't stand.

Walking to work that evening, I got panicky as I remembered that Homecoming was less than a week away. I had worked so hard to raise money to become queen that I had completely forgotten that a queen had to get all dressed up in an evening gown and all that stuff. All I had to my name was one pair of blue jeans and two shrunken dresses.

When I got to Linda Jean's I was so depressed that I didn't feel like working.

"Why're you so blue, Essie?" she asked. "Did you lose the race?"

"I wish I *had* lost," I mumbled.

"What, do you mean you *won?* Then why are you so sad?" she asked.

When I explained to her that I had forgotten about the gown, that I didn't have any money left, that Homecoming was next week and I didn't know what I would do, she rushed to her closet. She returned with an old pink faded gown that looked like something Mrs. Burke had worn when she was a teen-ager. The gown depressed me even more. When she saw the expression on my face I didn't have to tell her what I thought about it. She just quickly put it back in the closet.

When I got home I went straight to my room and bopped down on the bed. Mama came right after me. I was looking so sad she also thought I had lost. When I told her I had won, she shouted around a bit like *she* had just been made queen or something.

"What you got your mouth all stuck out about then? I can see you sittin' up there on that float now," she said, looking in the mirror at herself.

"Yeah, sittin' up there with blue jeans on?" I sneered.

"Well that *is* a little problem," she said, prancing before the mirror, "but we may clear that up pretty soon."

"What you mean we're gonna clear that up pretty soon? Where we gonna get money from to buy a gown that look like anything?"

"Well, I tol' your daddy's cousin Clara about two weeks ago that you were gonna be queen and she tol' me that Diddly was workin' in New Orleans makin' a lotta money, and I gave her your dress size and tol' her to write him and tell him to *buy* you a gown."

"But Homecoming is Thursday and that's been two weeks ago," I protested.

"Don't you worry, he *better* buy it!" she said, leaving me on the bed.

I wondered why all of a sudden she was betterin' *Daddy* to do something when she wouldn't even let him help us when we were young and starving. I guessed she wanted me to look good and, since we were so broke, she was willing to swallow her pride. I was still a little worried because Homecoming was so close, but she had said "he better buy it" so threateningly that I figured Daddy would probably come through.

When Tuesday passed and I still hadn't heard from Daddy, I got so upset that I was ready to tell Mrs. Willis the next day that I couldn't be queen. But on Wednesday when I got to school and everybody was treating me so queenly, I changed my mind and figured that I would be queen even if I had to wear Linda Jean's old faded-out pink gown. I came home that evening after work with Linda Jean's gown under my arm. Mama was waiting for me on the porch.

"What's that in that box?" she asked.

I didn't say anything. I went into the house and, throwing open the box, I grabbed the gown and held it against me.

"How do you like Frankenstein's bride?" I said, putting on a monster face.

"Where in the shit you got that thing from?" Mama said. "Look like somethin' from the forty-ist century!"

"Ye-es? Well, *tomorrow* is the forty-ist century for me!" I said, throwing the gown on my bed and making a vomiting noise.

"Clara say come up there, she got a letter for you from Diddly," Mama suddenly whispered.

"A letter!" I screamed. "And the parade is tomorrow? What in the shit am I gonna do with a *letter!* I . . ."

"Shh! Shh!" Mama said, pointing wildly toward the kitchen. I knew Raymond was in the kitchen and that he probably didn't know anything about Mama contacting Daddy, so I didn't say anything else and just left for Clara's.

A few minutes later I was knocking on Miss Clara's door.

"Who is it?" I heard my cousin call.

"It's me, Essie Mae."

"Just a minute, honey!" I could hear a lot of bustling around inside. Then the door opened.

"I been waitin' for you. I thought you weren't comin'," Clara said, beckoning me to come into the living room.

"Mama said you had a letter for me from Daddy," I said, sitting down on her sofa.

"Wait a minute, I have to go in here and get it." She disappeared into the bedroom. A few moments later she appeared in the doorway with a big smile on her face.

"Here it is, signed, sealed, and delivered," she said, reaching her arm behind her, pulling someone into the room.

My mouth went wide open when I saw that it was Daddy. I hadn't seen him since the day he was squatting in the yard when Granddaddy died. He was standing there grinning, with a big box in his hand. He looked taller than I remembered and his mustache was much thicker. He was dressed like a real city slicker in matching sweater and suit. He looked good. I just stood there gaping at him.

"Well, you came for the letter and here it is," Miss Clara finally said, breaking the awkward silence. Then Daddy moved toward me as if he wanted to throw the box down and take me in his arms like I was his little girl. But instead he clumsily placed the box on the sofa and quietly said, "Go on, open it."

I quickly turned away from him to the box, glad to get away from the longing look in his eyes. It was a big white long box with blue ribbon tied around it. I opened it slowly.

"Oh!" I gasped. There in the box was a beautiful blue lace-bodiced gown. I sat there looking at it for a long time. I wanted to hug Daddy and kiss him and thank him for it, but I just couldn't draw myself to do it.

"Take it out, take it out and look at it," Daddy said.

I carefully removed it from the box and held it against me as I stood up.

"Boy, you gonna look *good* tomorrow!" Clara said, pulling me to a long mirror on the door to the bedroom. "Diddly, you sho' know yo' clothes!"

As I looked at myself in the mirror I could see him behind me looking and smiling.

"Ain't she just pretty?" he said to Miss Clara. I felt I had to say something.

"Oh, it's *so* pretty. Thank you *so* much," I said, wishing that I had the nerve to call him "Daddy," if only to please him. I could see a little flicker of hurt across his face but he covered it quickly by asking about Adline and Junior. We talked very briefly and then I ran out of the house, hugging the box to my breast. I glanced back as I ran and saw Daddy on the porch with Miss Clara, watching me.

I knew everyone was sitting in the kitchen so I went through the back door.

"Mama, y'all, look at this!" I yelled, running through the kitchen to my room. I took the gown out and was holding it in front of me when Mama, Adline, and all the children came in.

"Ooh, where did you get that?" Adline asked.

Just as I was about to answer I saw Raymond looking into the room.

"Where *did* you get that gown from?" Raymond asked, looking like he already knew the answer.

"My *daddy* bought it!" I said.

He didn't say anything. He just turned around and went back to the kitchen and Mama followed him. I didn't care what he thought. I spent the next couple of hours prancing around, but I wasn't really happy. Adline and Junior were jealous that Daddy didn't buy them anything. Raymond was angry because he thought Mama had been seeing Daddy again and Mama was upset because Raymond was upset. But I made up my mind that I wouldn't let them spoil it for me, so I lost myself in dreams of how I would look tomorrow in that gown.

I got up early Thursday morning, my big day. Because I was queen I felt I didn't have to rush. The morning at school would be spent decorating the floats. Since I had to go to the hair dresser, I told Adline to tell Mrs. Willis I'd be in about twelve. For the first time during the whole Homecoming excitement, I was relaxed, knowing I had that beautiful gown to put on. Going to the hairdresser made the day seem even more special, since I had only gone there once before in my life.

I walked up on campus around one o'clock. The whole place looked and sounded like a carnival. There were cars, tractors, trucks, and all kinds of vehicles everywhere, and kids were scrambling all over them taping on crepe paper. Clutching my gown box, I walked among them looking for my class. Now I was even more aware of the noise and excitement. Girls were walking around with their hair teased and curled, most of the boys had fresh haircuts and their best suits on, and everybody looked beautiful to me.

Turning a corner, I saw Mrs. Willis standing over the crowd on some sort of platform. As I got closer I saw that she was on a big trailer truck, pointing and yelling at my classmates. "Ben, Joe, c'mon, y'all boys, let's get busy and fix those chairs on these markings," Mrs. Willis shouted to some of the boys nearby. "Look, here comes the queen! *Everything* is late today! The truck is late, the queen is late, and the decorations aren't even here yet!" she said, shouting at no one in particular.

As I walked up to one of my "attendants," she warned me that Mrs. Willis was in a bad mood, that at the last minute we almost didn't get the truck. And the girls who had gone over three hours ago to pick up the decorations ordered by Mrs. Willis still hadn't returned. I stood around for a while not saying anything. Soon the girls came with the decorations and Mrs. Willis got everybody but me and my court busy working on the float.

Once she had gotten the others started, she led me and my six attendants to her house where we were to dress. We all crowded into her guest room and the girls immediately began opening their boxes and showing their gowns. It had been planned that all six of them would wear white, and I, the queen, would wear blue. As they pranced around showing their gowns off, I could see that each one thought that hers was the prettiest. And suddenly I couldn't keep myself from laughing. Dorothy, the girl I beat for queen, noticed that I was laughing and, thinking that I was making fun of her, said in a loud nasty voice, "What are *you* laughing at, Moody? You think jus' 'cause you're queen you should have a room all to yourself to dress in?"

A couple of Dorothy's pals laughed. I stood there with the unopened box in my hands, still smiling. All the girls looked at me, curious. One of Dorothy's friends said, "Why don't you show us *your* gown, Moody?"

Without saying a word, I walked slowly over to one of the two beds in the room, placed the box on it and carefully opened it, folding back the tissue paper. They all crowded around, as if I was unveiling a newborn baby. As I lifted the gown from the box and held it against me, they all went "ooh" and "where did you get *that?*" and I could see that not one of them thought her gown was pretty any more.

"Oh, so *that's* what you were standing there laughing for, making fun of *our* gowns!" Dorothy hissed. "Where did you get it from anyway? Borrow it from the *white* folks you work for?"

Just then Mrs. Willis appeared in the door.

"All right, girls, leave Moody alone! After all, she *is* queen and she *deserves* to have the prettiest gown! Now y'all stop this bickering and get washed up. I'm gonna go get some of the high school girls to help make you up. Okay, Dorothy, I don't want no stuff while I'm gone!"

By the time Mrs. Willis was back with the girls we were sitting there in our gowns ready to be made up. Because it was nearing four o'clock, parade time, the girls rushed right in, throwing towels around our necks and wildly brushing our hair into big bouffants. I sat there feeling like a pampered princess as they brushed on the powder, applied the mascara and blended two shades of lipstick together. I was sitting on a stool with my back to the mirror, and since I had never worn mascara before, I was scared that they were messing my eyes up, so I kept trying to turn my head and peep in the mirror. But every time I tried, the mascara brush would slip, drawing a heavy black line right into my ear, and the hairdressers would grab my head and scream, "Moody, we'll *never* get your hair fixed! Stop turnin' around! You can look in the mirror in a minute. Look at your face!" One girl seemed to be doing nothing but wiping mascara off my face with tissue. She looked like she wanted to poke my eyes out. They teased my hair up high in front, with long curls left hanging in the back.

Just as they were finishing, Mrs. Willis ran in with a crown in her hands. "Oh my! Is that *my* queen? How beautiful! Here, put this on her! If the rest of you are finished, go on out on the float," she said to the other girls, who were sitting around looking at me being made up. They got up reluctantly and went out. The only ones left in the room were Mrs. Willis, the two girls doing my hair, and me.

When they had carefully pinned the crown to my hair, Mrs. Willis said, smiling, "Turn around, Queen, look at yourself."

I pulled the stool out a bit. I was scared to look in the mirror now that they were all finished. But from the way Mrs. Willis was looking at me, I could tell that I must look pretty.

When I turned I had to touch my face to see if it was me. I sat there in front of the mirror for a good five minutes; I kept staring at myself, at my piled-up hair, my full breasts and wide hips—I realized that I was no longer a little girl. Then Mrs. Willis was tapping me on the shoulder, motioning that it was time to go. As I got up, I took one more glance at myself. Full figure, I seemed even less real. Seeing how perfectly the gown fitted, I thought of Daddy and wished that he could see me in it, riding down the main street of Centreville, Queen of Willis High.

As I stepped outside behind Mrs. Willis, the cold November breeze hit my bare shoulders, sending a chill through me. But as I looked around and saw all of my classmates staring at me, I grew warmer. The boys stood gaping and oohing and the girls looked on enviously. Mrs. Willis was now walking beside me, smiling proudly. As we walked up to the crowd, she gestured with her hands, and they made a space for me to walk through. I felt like I was walking on a velvet carpet. Suddenly I saw the float, all covered with blue and white crepe paper. My whole court was there, waiting for me, the girls sitting in their white gowns and the boys standing behind them in their dark blue suits. As I walked up to them, Joe Lee, my escort, came forward to the edge of the float. I looked up and saw that he had tails on. I figured he must have gotten them from New Orleans too.

There was a chair that was being used by everyone to step up on the float. Just as I was about to do so, one of the big guys in my class who liked me rushed up to me and, sweeping me into his arms, whispered, "The queen deserves to be carried." Then another guy, getting into the act, jumped up on the chair and I was passed into his arms and he carefully placed me on the float. Once I was seated with my court behind me and Joe Lee standing by my side in his tux, I felt more than ever like a queen.

As soon as I was seated, the floats started lining up behind the band. A few minutes later we were slowly moving toward town. As we turned the corner into Main Street, it looked like just about every Negro and white in Centreville had turned out for the parade. The stores were deserted and I saw salesmen I knew standing on the street. Everybody was waving and cheering. Then I saw Mama standing where she said she would be, in front of the service station. I waved at her and I could tell she wasn't sure that it was me. Turning slightly, I found myself looking into a group of white faces. There was Linda Jean, staring like she didn't know me either. She started to wave, but hesitated. Then I waved at her and she waved back, giving me a look that said, "My how beautiful you are," as if she was surprised that a Negro could look that beautiful. I wanted to answer her and say, "Yes, Linda Jean, it's me. Negroes can be beautiful too." I got an urge to yell it to her but instead I just smiled and waved some more.

When the band reached the center of Main Street, they stopped marching and began playing. As they hit the first notes of "Dixie," I thought I would die, especially when I saw some of the familiar white faces bellowing out the lyrics. There was one big fat man in the crowd that cracked up Joe Lee and the others on my float. He was so fat that every word sent his big pregnant-looking belly jolting up and down. I sat there for a while trying to keep my cool and not laugh and carry on like the girls behind me. But when he raised his arms and his pants fell under that big fat belly, I forgot I was queen. I just couldn't hold in the laughter. He was so overcome with sentimentality for "Dixie" that he just let his big naked red belly shake, and every time it shook, we laughed harder and harder. "Dixie" seemed to have made everyone happy, Negroes and whites. After the band finished that tune they played a very fast one and the majorettes did their little steps. Then they tuned up and swung into "Swanee River." It seemed like the whole town was singing now. As they sang I sat up there on that float and had the strangest feeling. Somehow I had chills all over my body and I was overcome by a sudden fear. The faces of the whites had written on them some strange yearning. The Negroes looked sad. I sat there wondering, trying to get some meaning from the song as I listened closely to the words:

> *Way down upon the Swanee River, far far away.*
> *There's where my heart is turning ever,*
> *There's where the old folks stay.*
> *All the world is sad and dreary*

Ev'rywhere I roam.
Oh! darkies, how my heart grows weary
Far from the old folks at home.

There was something about "Swanee River" that touched most of those old whites singing along with the band. There was also something that made the old Negroes even sadder. I got a feeling that there existed some kind of sympathetic relationship between the older Negroes and whites that the younger people didn't quite get or understand.

The feeling that the song conveyed stayed with me all evening, and I was cold. I shivered throughout the rest of the parade. That night, when I was crowned Homecoming Queen during half time of the football game, I felt even colder. As soon as the ceremony was over, I left for home. I felt like I was coming down with something.

chapter

| NINE |

Shortly after I was crowned queen, my name was changed. Graduation was approaching in May and Mrs. Willis had asked us to bring our birth certificates to her for school records. I found I didn't have one. It had been lost with Junior's and Adline's when Junior set the house on fire. So Mama sent off to Jackson to get new copies for each of us. They came about a month later. But instead of one for Essie Mae Moody, they sent one for Annie Mae. Mama returned it even though all the information on it was correct but the name. Two weeks later she got it right back again—this time with a long letter saying there must have been some mistake during the original printing. She was told she could get the name changed for a small fee, but by this time it was only two weeks before graduation and Mrs. Willis had received all the certificates but mine. After much persuasion on my part, Mama decided to let me keep the name Annie. I was so glad, I had always thought of Essie as a name suitable for a cow or hog.

I shall never forget when I handed the certificate to Mrs. Willis, and made my announcement: "Mrs. Willis, here is my birth certificate. Mama said it's too late to have it changed and to go on and use Annie."

Mrs. Willis held the certificate up so everyone could see it. "Class! Class!" she called out. "Queen Essie is now officially Queen Annie." When she said that I felt just like a real queen.

The changing of my name didn't really make a difference at school or at home. The first day I carried the certificate to school, a lot of my classmates had teased me about it but they kept on calling me Moody as they had before. And at home I was still called Essie Mae. Mama insisted that it was "bad luck" to change your name. So she wouldn't even let Adline them call me Annie.

A few days after I gave Mrs. Willis my certificate, we spent an entire day computing class averages to determine the scholastic rank of each student. Mrs. Willis told us it was now time to see who would be Valedictorian and Salutatorian. I hadn't even heard those words before. But within minutes I had learned what they meant from the student sitting next to me. Automatically I looked over at Darlene. She sat there looking so confident. I began to wonder what had caused the change in her.

Mrs. Willis drew a small square on the board in the left-hand corner. Within it she listed the numerical equivalent for each letter grade. After she had done this, she went and sat in the back of the classroom. She then began calling us to the board five at a time.

Didn't any of us know our final grades. But everyone in the class expected me and Darlene to be the Val and Sal because we had always maintained the highest averages. Most of the other students weren't as interested in their own grades as they were in ours. So they just sat tense in their seats and waited for our averages to be determined. And the way Darlene sat there smirking, I was sure she knew she had finally beaten me. Had it been any other time I wouldn't have cared so much but for graduation... She would never let me live it down.

As the students returned to their seats from the board, they discussed their grades with their friends. And the room was getting very noisy. But when Mrs. Willis called Darlene's name then mine, silence fell over the entire room. Now only Mrs. Willis' voice could be heard calling out grades. And Darlene and I stood at the board sweating. She had been cool and seemed so sure of herself when she was in her seat. Now she was shaking. She was second in line at the board. She had all A's and B's when her grades were called. After hearing her grades, chills went all over my body. "If I get just one C or three B's I have lost," I thought. I was the last in line. When Mrs. Willis called my first grade, it was a B. My hand was trembling as I wrote it on the board. I didn't even breathe until my last grade had been called. Discovering I had all A's and B's, I sighed with relief and heard the whole class sighing too. When I finished figuring out my average, I stood looking out of the window, afraid to even look in Darlene's direction. Suddenly there was a lot of noise in the room and I heard someone whisper, "Darlene won." I almost fainted. "What's your average, Darlene?" called Mrs. Willis. Darlene almost shouted her 97. When Mrs. Willis got to me my 96 could barely be heard.

I went to my seat sick inside. "How did I let that happen?" I asked myself over and over again. I jotted down Darlene's grades on a piece of paper and began adding them. But while I was doing this, someone shouted out, "Betty Posey got 98." All the eyes in the room stared at the board. Betty stood there—gasping over her average. I looked at Darlene and saw her jot down Betty's grades to add them as I had done with hers.

I didn't even pick up a pencil for Betty's grades. I just looked to Darlene for the answer. Then I saw some of the delight fade from her face. Betty had always been a pretty good student but Darlene and I had not considered her a threat at all. We were in for a lot of surprises that day. Betty had won. She was the Val, Darlene the Sal, and I was to give the Welcome Address on Class Night. So it was and school ended.

That summer Mama succeeded in getting Raymond off to California to look for a job. I hadn't believed she could ever get him out of that bottom, but somehow she did. For years his relatives in Los Angeles had been urging him to go out there, telling him he could easily find a job, but Raymond had wanted to try and make it as a farmer in Mississippi. Finally, after two years of bad luck with the farm, he gave it up. Now there was nothing else he could do.

In Centreville there weren't any factories or sawmills that employed unskilled Negro men. The nearest mills were fifteen to fifty miles away in Woodville, Crosby, and Natchez. White businesses in town employed Negroes as janitors only, and there was never more than one janitor in any single business. The Negro man had a hard road to travel when looking for employment. A Negro woman, however, could always go out and earn a dollar a day because whites always needed a cook, a baby-sitter, or someone to do housecleaning.

Raymond stayed in Los Angeles for about a month. Within that time he wrote home twice. The first letter came about two weeks after he left:

Los Angeles is a big city. But jobs are as hard to get out here as they are in Mississippi. And Negroes don't live as well out here as people at home think. I am coming back home.

The second letter came about two weeks later. It said:

I am headed home I am just wasting time out here.

Three days later he was back.
We were all disillusioned. Poor Mama was hurt some bad. All

of her hopes for ever getting out of that bottom were gone. She had sat around the house talking about California the whole time Raymond was gone. "Y'all can go to school with white children and be real smart"; or "We are gonna git a real nice house out in California 'cause Raymond kin make more money," or "Essie Mae, you kin make ten dollars a day doing housework."

The future looked very dim for us. It seemed as though we were doomed to poverty and more unhappiness than we had faced before. Raymond was out of work again. And again our diet consisted of dried beans and bread. In addition to the lack of food and money, Mama was about to have another baby. She would soon be the mother of seven. She always chose the wrong time to have babies. It seemed as though every time we were encountering a streak of bad luck she shot up. One day you would look at her and she was flat and the very next day seemingly she was in labor and Aunt Caroline was being summoned to the house.

As usual when she was pregnant and times were hard she cried a lot. She cried so now she almost drove us all crazy. Every evening I came home from work, she was beating on the children making them cry too. Raymond couldn't say a word without her biting his head off.

I was still working for Linda Jean during this family depression and contributed five of my six dollars to the cause. But that didn't help very much. There were just too many mouths to feed, and soon even my six dollars wouldn't be coming in. Mr. Jenkins had been building a house in the country for over a year and it was nearly finished. As soon as they moved I would be out of work. I looked forward to that time with intense fear. I began wondering what white woman I would end up working for next. The five I had worked for so far had been good to me. But I knew that all white women in Centreville weren't good to their maids.

By the time Linda Jean was ready to move, Raymond had gotten together a few men and started dealing (cutting and hauling) pulpwood. He had picked up a ragged old truck somewhere and most of his money was spent on repairing it every day or so. But a little money was coming in—enough to buy food with, anyway. Now I would be able to take a week or two and look for a good job.

But the day before Linda Jean moved, all my plans were upset. Mama had the baby, another boy—she named him Ralph. In addition to that, the pulpwood truck fell completely apart. I went to bed that night and prayed for something to happen so Linda Jean them would have to stay another week.

As soon as I got to work the next morning, I knew my prayer hadn't been answered. Linda Jean and Mr. Jenkins were wrapping all the china in newspaper. I just stood in the kitchen looking at them.

"Good morning, Essie," Linda Jean said when she noticed me there. "I left Donna and Johnny over to Mama's. She is gonna keep them until we finish packing. The man is coming to move us at two o'clock, so we've got a lot to do before then. Honey," she said to Mr. Jenkins, "let Essie help me with these dishes."

After we finished packing them, she asked me to take three glasses over to her mother and see if Donna and Johnny were all right. "Oh! Tell Mama to make some sandwiches for us for lunch, I don't have time," she said.

I took the glasses and headed for Mrs. Burke's. Walking to her house was like walking on quicksand. I had no desire to get involved with Linda Jean's mother. We shared a mutual dislike for each other. From the way she tried to treat me I knew how she felt about Negroes. She was one of those whites who would let her dog occupy a seat at her dining table before she would a Negro.

Now that I was facing that big white house, my knees were trembling. "Why am I shaking so?" I thought as I walked up the wooden steps into the front porch. I missed one and almost fell.

Trying to compose myself, I stood facing the screen door. "What am I scared of?" I thought. "Linda Jean will be gone tomorrow and I won't ever see this woman again." I knocked.

"Yes!" I heard her say as she came down the hallway. "Did you come for Donna and Johnny?" she called from behind the door.

"No. Linda Jean sent these glasses and told me to tell you to make some sandwiches for lunch for us, that she is too busy," I answered.

Mrs. Burke opened the door now and took the glasses from me. "Does *Mrs. Jenkins* want me to bring the children over, or will you come back for them?" She sounded very indignant.

"She didn't say, but I can come back for them," I said innocently.

"Tell *Mrs. Jenkins* to send some diapers for Johnny," she said as I was walking down the porch steps.

When I carried the diapers over a few minutes later, she met me at the door with a smile. I stood there looking at her baffled by the change in her attitude.

"Come on in, Essie, and change Johnny's diapers for me. I'm on the phone," she said in a pleasant tone of voice.

I followed her down a long hallway that was as big as our whole house. The only piece of furniture in it was an office desk with a telephone on it.

"The children are in the dining room, Essie," Mrs. Burke said, picking up the phone.

I stood there wondering where in hell the dining room was. "How does she figure I know where it is?" I thought as I walked into a bedroom. "It's over here, Essie," Mrs. Burke said, pointing to a room on the opposite side of the hall. I walked in there feeling a little stupid.

Donna and Johnny were sitting in a corner of the dining room as quiet as two mice. They looked as though they were scared to death. I realized then how mean Mrs. Burke was. Donna and

Johnny were as noisy as ten children when they were home, and they never stayed in one place.

Mrs. Burke came in just as I finished putting on Johnny's diaper. She stood smiling at me for a while.

"Essie, are you planning to take on another job now that Linda Jean is moving?" she asked. I just looked at her with my mouth wide open. She had purposely said "Linda Jean."

"I can use some help if you want work," she finally said, still smiling.

I was too stunned to answer.

"Well, you think about it and let me know before you leave Linda Jean's today."

I did think about her a lot the next few hours. She was a strange woman and she puzzled me. I just couldn't make up my mind to work for her. However, when I got home and was again faced with a sick mother, crying babies, an unemployed stepfather, and a plate of dried beans, my mind was made up for me. I knew that I had to take that job, I had to help secure that plate of dry beans if nothing else. I went to work for Mrs. Burke the following morning.

I was so uneasy that first day at Mrs. Burke's. However, I felt better after becoming familiar with the rest of the household, and making the discovery that Mrs. Burke was the only nasty person in there. Her mother, Mrs. Crosby, was a very nice old lady with long braids wrapped around her head. She thought I was a beautiful girl and took a keen interest in me from the start. Wayne, Mrs. Burke's son, was my same age and grade. He was very much like Linda Jean in the sense that he also treated me as his equal. It was hard for me to accept the fact that he and Linda Jean were Mrs. Burke's children. I didn't meet her eldest son, Dennis, who was her favorite. I didn't meet him, but I knew that if he was her favorite, he too must be evil with a negative attitude toward Negroes. Mr. Burke, her husband, was difficult to figure. He was very seldom home, and when he was he hardly ever said anything.

Mrs. Burke, an ex-schoolteacher, was a typical matriarch. She ruled her whole family and even tried to rule me. She had a certain way of doing everything in her house from sweeping to setting a table. I guess all the maids she had had before catered to these little wishes of hers. But I had no intention of doing so, and I had my own little ways of resisting her rule. When I first ironed some shirts for her she brought all fifteen of them back for me to redo. "Take out these cat faces, Essie. Wayne can't wear these shirts looking like this. I watched you do these and I see you have no set way of ironing shirts. Let me show you how it's done." I stood back and watched her do one shirt. Then I went over all of the remaining fourteen. But the very next week I did the ironing, I did all the shirts my way, and Mrs. Burke watched me do them too. But this time she didn't have me redo them. In fact, she didn't say anything.

I had always used the front door when entering and leaving her house. The morning after that second ironing I walked up on the front porch and discovered that the screen door was locked.

"Who is it?" Mrs. Burke called as she heard me knocking.

"It's me, Essie!" I answered.

"Use the back door, Essie, it's open!" she yelled to me.

The tone of her voice told me that she was again trying to subdue me. I went to the back door that morning. But the next morning I walked up on the front porch again and knocked at the front door. I knocked for what seemed like ten minutes and she still didn't answer. I didn't stop knocking though. Finally Mrs. Crosby came to the door and let me in. When I walked in, I noticed that as usual Mrs. Burke was occupying her favorite chair in the living room, which was the first room to the left as you entered the hall. I knew she had heard me knocking. "That's all right," I thought. "I will knock at the front door tomorrow morning again and the day after that too."

When I knocked the next morning, Mrs. Crosby was standing in the hallway as if she was waiting for me. She let me in that morning and every morning at seven-thirty after that.

Soon Mrs. Burke decided to let me do things my way. I would have quit had she not. And I think she knew it. She really had no complaints about my work so she let me be. In a way, working for her was a challenge for me. She was the first one of her type I had run into.

part two

HIGH SCHOOL

chapter

| TEN |

Not only did I enter high school with a new name, but also with a completely new insight into the life of Negroes in Mississippi. I was now working for one of the meanest white women in town, and a week before school started Emmett Till was killed.

Up until his death, I had heard of Negroes found floating in a river or dead somewhere with their bodies riddled with bullets. But I didn't know the mystery behind these killings then. I remember once when I was only seven I heard Mama and one of my aunts talking about some Negro who had been beaten to death. "Just like them low-down skunks killed him they will do the same to us," Mama had said. When I asked her who killed the man and why, she said, "An Evil Spirit killed him. You gotta be a good girl or it will kill you too." So since I was seven, I had lived in fear of that "Evil Spirit." It took me eight years to learn what that spirit was.

I was coming from school the evening I heard about Emmett Till's death. There was a whole group of us, girls and boys, walking down the road headed home. A group of about six high school boys were walking a few paces ahead of me and several other girls.

We were laughing and talking about something that had happened in school that day. However, the six boys in front of us weren't talking very loud. Usually they kept up so much noise. But today they were just walking and talking among themselves. All of a sudden they began to shout at each other.

"Man, what in the hell do you mean?"

"What I mean is these goddamned white folks is gonna start some shit here you just watch!"

"That boy wasn't but fourteen years old and they killed him. Now what kin a fourteen-year-old boy do with a white woman? What if he did whistle at her, he might have thought the whore was pretty."

"Look at all these white men here that's fucking over our women. Everybody knows it too and what's done about that? Look how many white babies we got walking around in our neighborhoods. Their mama's ain't white either. That boy was from Chicago, shit, everybody fuck everybody up there. He probably didn't even think of the bitch as white."

What they were saying shocked me. I knew all of those boys and I had never heard them talk like that. We walked on behind them for a while listening. Questions about who was killed, where, and why started running through my mind. I walked up to one of the boys.

"Eddie, what boy was killed?"

"Moody, where've you been?" he asked me. "Everybody talking about that fourteen-year-old boy who was killed in Greenwood by some white men. You don't know nothing that's going on besides what's in them books of yours, huh?"

Standing there before the rest of the girls, I felt so stupid. It was then that I realized I really didn't know what was going on all around me. It wasn't that I was dumb. It was just that ever since I was nine, I'd had to work after school and do my lessons on lunch hour. I never had time to learn anything, to hang around with people my own age. And you never were told anything by adults.

That evening when I stopped off at the house on my way to Mrs. Burke's, Mama was singing. Any other day she would have been yelling at Adline and Junior them to take off their school clothes. I wondered if she knew about Emmett Till. The way she was singing she had something on her mind and it wasn't pleasant either.

> *I got a shoe, you got a shoe,*
> *All of God's chillun got shoes;*
> *When I get to hebben, I'm gonna put on my shoes,*
> *And gonna tromp all over God's hebben.*
> *When I get to hebben I'm gonna put on my shoes,*
> *And gonna walk all over God's hebben.*

Mama was dishing up beans like she didn't know anyone was home. Adline, Junior, and James had just thrown their books down and sat themselves at the table. I didn't usually eat before I went to work. But I wanted to ask Mama about Emmett Till. So I ate and thought of some way of asking her.

"These beans are some good, Mama," I said, trying to sense her mood.

"Why is you eating anyway? You gonna be late for work. You know how Miss Burke is," she said to me.

"I don't have much to do this evening. I kin get it done before I leave work," I said.

The conversation stopped after that. Then Mama started humming that song again.

> *When I get to hebben, I'm gonna put on my shoes,*
> *And gonna tromp all over God's hebben.*

She put a plate on the floor for Jennie Ann and Jerry.

"Jennie Ann! you and Jerry sit down here and eat and don't put beans all over this floor."

Ralph, the baby, started crying, and she went in the bedroom to give him his bottle. I got up and followed her.

"Mama, did you hear about that fourteen-year-old Negro boy who was killed a little over a week ago by some white men?" I asked her.

"Where did you hear that?" she said angrily.

"Boy, everybody really thinks I am dumb or deaf or something. I heard Eddie them talking about it this evening coming from school."

"Eddie them better watch how they go around here talking. These white folks git a hold of it they gonna be in trouble," she said.

"What are they gonna be in trouble about, Mama? People got a right to talk, ain't they?"

"You go on to work before you is late. And don't you let on like you know nothing about that boy being killed before Miss Burke them. Just do your work like you don't know nothing," she said. "That boy's a lot better off in heaven than he is here," she continued and then started singing again.

On my way to Mrs. Burke's that evening, Mama's words kept running through my mind. "Just do your work like you don't know nothing." "Why is Mama acting so scared?" I thought. "And what if Mrs. Burke knew we knew? Why must I pretend I don't know? Why are these people killing Negroes? What did Emmett Till do besides whistle at that woman?"

By the time I got to work, I had worked my nerves up some. I was shaking as I walked up on the porch. "Do your work like you don't know nothing." But once I got inside, I couldn't have acted normal if Mrs. Burke were paying me to be myself.

I was so nervous, I spent most of the evening avoiding them going about the house dusting and sweeping. Everything went along fairly well until dinner was served.

"Don, Wayne, and Mama, y'all come on to dinner. Essie, you

can wash up the pots and dishes in the sink now. Then after dinner you won't have as many," Mrs. Burke called to me.

If I had the power to mysteriously disappear at that moment, I would have. They used the breakfast table in the kitchen for most of their meals. The dining room was only used for Sunday dinner or when they had company. I wished they had company tonight so they could eat in the dining room while I was at the kitchen sink.

"I forgot the bread," Mrs. Burke said when they were all seated. "Essie, will you cut it and put it on the table for me?"

I took the cornbread, cut it in squares, and put it on a small round dish. Just as I was about to set it on the table, Wayne yelled at the cat. I dropped the plate and the bread went all over the floor.

"Never mind, Essie," Mrs. Burke said angrily as she got up and got some white bread from the breadbox.

I didn't say anything. I picked up the cornbread from around the table and went back to the dishes. As soon as I got to the sink, I dropped a saucer on the floor and broke it. Didn't anyone say a word until I had picked up the pieces.

"Essie, I bought some new cleanser today. It's setting on the bathroom shelf. See if it will remove the stains in the tub," Mrs. Burke said.

I went to the bathroom to clean the tub. By the time I got through with it, it was snow white. I spent a whole hour scrubbing it. I had removed the stains in no time but I kept scrubbing until they finished dinner.

When they had finished and gone into the living room as usual to watch TV, Mrs. Burke called me to eat. I took a clean plate out of the cabinet and sat down. Just as I was putting the first forkful of food in my mouth, Mrs. Burke entered the kitchen.

"Essie, did you hear about that fourteen-year-old boy who was killed in Greenwood?" she asked me, sitting down in one of the chairs opposite me.

"No, I didn't hear that," I answered, almost choking on the food.

"Do you know why he was killed?" she asked and I didn't answer.

"He was killed because he got out of his place with a white woman. A boy from Mississippi would have known better than that. This boy was from Chicago. Negroes up North have no respect for people. They think they can get away with anything. He just came to Mississippi and put a whole lot of notions in the boys' heads here and stirred up a lot of trouble," she said passionately.

"How old are you, Essie?" she asked me after a pause.

"Fourteen. I will soon be fifteen though," I said.

"See, that boy was just fourteen too. It's a shame he had to die so soon." She was so red in the face, she looked as if she was on fire.

When she left the kitchen I sat there with my mouth open and my food untouched. I couldn't have eaten now if I were starving. "Just do your work like you don't know nothing" ran through my mind again and I began washing the dishes.

I went home shaking like a leaf on a tree. For the first time out of all her trying, Mrs. Burke had made me feel like rotten garbage. Many times she had tried to instill fear within me and subdue me and had given up. But when she talked about Emmett Till there was something in her voice that sent chills and fear all over me.

Before Emmett Till's murder, I had known the fear of hunger, hell, and the Devil. But now there was a new fear known to me— the fear of being killed just because I was black. This was the worst of my fears. I knew once I got food, the fear of starving to death would leave. I also was told that if I were a good girl, I wouldn't have to fear the Devil or hell. But I didn't know what one had to do or not do as a Negro not to be killed. Probably just being a Negro period was enough, I thought.

A few days later, I went to work and Mrs. Burke had about eight women over for tea. They were all sitting around in the living room when I got there. She told me she was having a "guild meeting," and asked me to help her serve the cookies and tea.

After helping her, I started cleaning the house. I always swept the hallway and porch first. As I was sweeping the hall, I could hear them talking. When I heard the word "nigger," I stopped sweeping and listened. Mrs. Burke must have sensed this, because she suddenly came to the door.

"Essie, finish the hall and clean the bathroom," she said hesitantly. "Then you can go for today. I am not making dinner tonight." Then she went back in the living room with the rest of the ladies.

Before she interrupted my listening, I had picked up the words "NAACP" and "that organization." Because they were talking about niggers, I knew NAACP had something to do with Negroes. All that night I kept wondering what could that NAACP mean?

Later when I was sitting in the kitchen at home doing my lessons, I decided to ask Mama. It was about twelve-thirty. Everyone was in bed but me. When Mama came in to put some milk in Ralph's bottle, I said, "Mama, what do NAACP mean?"

"Where did you git that from?" she asked me, spilling milk all over the floor.

"Mrs. Burke had a meeting tonight—"

"What kind of meeting?" she asked, cutting me off.

"I don't know. She had some women over—she said it was a guild meeting," I said.

"A guild meeting," she repeated.

"Yes, they were talking about Negroes and I heard some woman say 'that NAACP' and another 'that organization,' meaning the same thing."

"What else did they say?" she asked me.

"That's all I heard. Mrs. Burke must have thought I was listening, so she told me to clean the bathroom and leave."

"Don't you ever mention that word around Mrs. Burke or no other white person, you heah! Finish your lesson and cut that light out and go to bed," Mama said angrily and left the kitchen.

"With a Mama like that you'll never learn anything," I thought as I got into bed. All night long I thought about Emmett Till and the NAACP. I even got up to look up NAACP in my little concise dictionary. But I didn't find it.

The next day at school, I decided to ask my homeroom teacher Mrs. Rice the meaning of NAACP. When the bell sounded for lunch, I remained in my seat as the other students left the room.

"Are you going to spend your lunch hour studying again today, Moody?" Mrs. Rice asked me.

"Can I ask you a question, Mrs. Rice?" I asked her.

"You *may* ask me a question, yes, but I don't know if you *can* or not," she said.

"What does the word NAACP mean?" I asked.

"Why do you want to know?"

"The lady I worked for had a meeting and I overheard the word mentioned."

"What else did you hear?"

"Nothing. I didn't know what NAACP meant, that's all." I felt like I was on the witness stand or something.

"Well, next time your boss has another meeting you listen more carefully. NAACP is a Negro organization that was established a long time ago to help Negroes gain a few basic rights," she said.

"What's it gotta do with the Emmett Till murder?" I asked.

"They are trying to get a conviction in Emmett Till's case. You see the NAACP is trying to do a lot for the Negroes and get the right to vote for Negroes in the South. I shouldn't be telling you all this. And don't you dare breathe a word of what I said. It could cost me my job if word got out I was teaching my students such. I gotta go to lunch and you should go outside too because it's nice and sunny out today," she said leaving the room. "We'll talk more when I have time."

About a week later, Mrs. Rice had me over for Sunday dinner, and I spent about five hours with her. Within that time, I digested a good meal and accumulated a whole new pool of knowledge about Negroes being butchered and slaughtered by whites in the South. After Mrs. Rice had told me all this, I felt like the lowest animal on earth. At least when other animals (hogs, cows, etc.) were killed by man, they were used as food. But when man was butchered or killed by man, in the case of Negroes by whites, they were left lying on a road or found floating in a river or something.

Mrs. Rice got to be something like a mother to me. She told me anything I wanted to know. And made me promise that I would keep all this information she was passing on to me to myself. She said she couldn't, rather didn't, want to talk about these things to the other teachers, that they would tell Mr. Willis and she would be fired. At the end of that year she was fired. I never found out why. I haven't seen her since then.

I was fifteen years old when I began to hate people. I hated the white men who murdered Emmett Till and I hated all the other whites who were responsible for the countless murders Mrs. Rice had told me about and those I vaguely remembered from childhood. But I also hated Negroes. I hated them for not standing up and doing something about the murders. In fact, I think I had a stronger resentment toward Negroes for letting the whites kill them than toward the whites. Anyway, it was at this stage in my life that I began to look upon Negro men as cowards. I could not respect them for smiling in a white man's face, addressing him as Mr. So-and-So, saying yessuh and nossuh when after they were home behind closed doors that same white man was a son of a bitch, a bastard, or any other name more suitable than mister.

Emmett Till's murder provoked a lot of anger and excitement among whites in Centreville. Now just about every evening when I got to work, Mrs. Burke had to attend a guild meeting. She had more women coming over now than ever. She and her friends had organized canvassing teams and a telephone campaign, to solicit for new members. Within a couple of months most of the whites in Centreville were taking part in the Guild. The meetings were initially held in the various houses. There were lawn parties and church gatherings. Then when it began to get cold, they were held in the high school auditorium.

After the Guild had organized about two-thirds of the whites in Centreville, all kinds of happenings were unveiled. The talk was on. White housewives began firing their maids and scolding their husbands and the Negro communities were full of whispered gossip.

The most talked-about subject was a love affair Mr. Fox, the deputy sheriff, and one of my classmates were carrying on. Bess was one of the oldest girls in my class. She was a shapely, high brown girl of about seventeen. She did general housekeeping and nursing for Fox and his wife.

It was general policy that most young white couples in Centreville hired only older Negro women as helpers. However, when there were two or more children in the family, it was more advantageous to hire a young Negro girl. That way, they always had someone to baby-sit when there was a need for a baby-sitter. My job with Linda Jean had been this kind. I kept Donna and Johnny on Sundays and baby-sat at night when they needed me.

Even though the teen-age Negro girls were more desirable for such jobs, very few if any were trusted in the homes of the young couples. The young white housewife didn't dare leave one alone in the house with her loyal and obedient husband. She was afraid that the Negro girl would seduce him, never the contrary.

There had been whispering in the Negro communities about Bess and Fox for some time. Just about every young white man in Centreville had a Negro lover. Therefore Fox, even though he was the deputy sheriff, wasn't doing anything worse than the rest of the men. At least that's the way the Negroes looked at the situation. Fox wasn't anyone special to them. But the whites didn't see it that way. The sheriff and all of his deputies were, in the eyes of their white compatriots, honorable men. And these honorable men were not put into office because they loved Negroes. So when the white community caught on about Fox and Bess, naturally they were out to expose the affair. Such exposure would discourage other officers from similar misbehavior.

Mrs. Fox was completely devoted to her husband. She too thought he was an honest man and she was willing to do anything that would prove him innocent. Soon a scheme was under way. Mrs. Fox was to leave home every so often. It had been reported that every time she was out and Bess was left there alone, Fox found his way home for one reason or another. Mrs. Fox left home purposely a couple of times while the neighbors kept watch. They confirmed the report that Fox would always return home. So one day Mrs. Fox decided to take the children and visit her mother—but she only went as far as the house next door. Bess was to come and give the house a thorough cleaning on the same day.

Mrs. Fox waited almost an hour at her neighbors' and nothing happened. It was said she was ready to go home and apologize to Bess and call her husband and do likewise. But just as she was about to do so, Fox drove up and went inside. She waited about thirty minutes more, then went home.

When she walked into her bedroom there they were, her husband and Bess, lying in her bed all curled up together. Poor Bess was so frightened that she ran out of the house clothed only in her slip with her panties in her hands. She never set foot in Mrs. Fox's house again. Neither did she return to school afterward. She took a job in the quarters where we lived, in a Negro café. It was said that she didn't need the job, though. Because after her embarrassing episode with Fox, her reputation was beyond repair, and he felt obligated to take care of her. Last I heard of Bess, she was still in Centreville, wearing fine clothes and carrying on as usual. Fox is no longer deputy, I understand, but he and his wife are still together.

It appeared after a while that the much talked about maids

raids were only a means of diverting attention from what was really taking place in those guild meetings. In the midst of all the talk about what white man was screwing which Negro woman, new gossip emerged—about what Negro man was screwing which white woman. This gossip created so much tension, every Negro man in Centreville became afraid to walk the streets. They knew too well that they would not get off as easily as the white man who was caught screwing a Negro woman. They had only to look at a white woman and be hanged for it. Emmett Till's murder had proved it was a crime, punishable by death, for a Negro man to even whistle at a white woman in Mississippi.

I had never heard of a single affair in Centreville between a Negro man and a white woman. It was almost impossible for such an affair to take place. Negro men did not have access to white women. Whereas almost every white man in town had a Negro woman in his kitchen or nursing his babies.

The tension lasted for about a month before anything happened. Then one day, a rumor was spread throughout town that a Negro had been making telephone calls to a white operator and threatening to molest her. It was also said that the calls had been traced to a certain phone that was now under watch.

Next thing we heard in the Negro community was that they had caught and nearly beaten to death a boy who, they said, had made the calls to the white operator. All the Negroes went around saying, "Y'all know that boy didn't do that." "That boy" was my classmate Jerry. A few months later I got a chance to talk to him and he told me what happened.

He said he had used the telephone at Billups and Fillups service station and was on his way home when Sheriff Ed Cassidy came along in his pickup truck.

"Hey, buddy," Cassidy called, "you on your way home?"

"Yes," Jerry answered.

"Jump in, I'm goin' your way, I'll give you a lift."

Then Jerry told me that when they got out there by the scales where the big trucks weigh at the old camp intersection, Cassidy let him out, telling him that he had forgotten something in town and had to go back and pick it up. At that point, Jerry told me, he didn't suspect anything. He just got out of the truck and told Cassidy thanks. But as soon as the sheriff pulled away, a car came along and stopped. There were four men in it. A deep voice ordered Jerry to get into the car. When he saw that two of the men were Jim Dixon and Nat Withers, whom he had often seen hanging around town with Cassidy, he started to run. But the two in the back jumped out and grabbed him. They forced him into the car and drove out into the camp area. When they got about five miles out, they turned down a little dark dirt road, heavily shaded with trees. They pushed Jerry out of the car onto the ground. He got up and dashed into the woods but they caught up with him and dragged him farther into the woods. Then they tied him to a tree and beat him with a big thick leather strap and a piece of hose pipe.

I asked him if they told him why they were beating him.

"No, not at first," Jerry said, "but when I started screamin' and cryin' and askin' them why they were beatin' me Dixon told me I was tryin' to be smart and they just kept on beatin' me. Then one of the men I didn't know asked me, 'Did you make that phone call, boy?' I said no. I think he kinda believed me 'cause he stopped beatin' me but the others didn't. The rest of them beat me until I passed out. When I came out of it I was lying on the ground, untied, naked and bleeding. I tried to get up but I was hurtin' all over and it was hard to move. Finally I got my clothes on that them sonofabitches had tore offa me and I made it out to the main highway, but I fainted again. When I woke up I was home in bed.

"Daddy them was scared to take me to the hospital in Centreville. I didn't even see a doctor 'cause they were scared to take me to them white doctors. Wasn't any bones or anything broken. I was swollen all over, though. And you can see I still have bruises and cuts from the strap, but otherwise I guess I'm O.K."

When I asked him whether they were going to do anything about it, he said that his daddy had gotten a white lawyer from Baton Rouge. But after the lawyer pried around in Centreville for a few days, he suddenly disappeared.

Jerry's beating shook up all the Negroes in town. But the most shocking and unjust crime of all occurred a few months later, about two weeks before school ended.

One night, about one o'clock, I was awakened by what I thought was a terrible nightmare. It was an empty dream that consisted only of hollering and screaming voices. It seemed as though I was in an empty valley screaming. And the sounds of my voice were reflected in a million echoes that were so loud I was being lifted in mid-air by the sound waves. I found myself standing trembling in the middle of the floor reaching for the light string. Then I saw Mama running to the kitchen, in her nightgown.

"Mama! Mama! What's all them voices? Where're all those people? What's happening?"

"I don't know," she said, coming to my bedroom door.

"Listen! Listen!" I said, almost screaming.

"Stop all that loud talking fo' you wake up the rest of them chaps. It must be a house on fire or somethin' 'cause of all the screamin'. Somebody must be hurt in it or somethin' too. Ray is getting the car, we gonna go see what it is," she said and headed for the back door.

"You going in your gown?" I asked her.

"We ain't gonna git out of the car. Come on, you can go," she said. "But don't slam the door and wake them chaps up."

I followed her out of the back door in my pajamas. Raymond was just backing the car out of the driveway.

When we turned the corner leaving the quarters, Raymond drove slowly alongside hundreds of people running down the road. They were all headed in the direction of the blaze that reddened the sky.

The crowd of people began to swell until driving was utterly impossible. Finally the long line of cars stopped. We were about two blocks away from the burning house now. The air was so hot that water was running down the faces of the people who ran past the car. The burning house was on the rock road, leading to the school, adjacent to the street we stopped on. So we couldn't tell which house it was. From where we sat, it seemed as though it could have been two or three of them burning. I knew every Negro living in the houses that lined that rock road. I passed them every day on my way to and from school.

I sat there in my pajamas, wishing I had thrown on a dress or something so I could get out of the car.

"Ray, ask somebody who house it is," Mama said to Raymond.

"Hi! Excuse me." Raymond leaned out of the car and spoke to a Negro man. "Do you know who house is on fire?"

"I heard it was the Taplin family. They say the whole family is still in the house. Look like they are done for, so they say."

Didn't any one of us say anything after that. We just sat in the car silently. I couldn't believe what the man had just said. "A whole family burned to death—impossible!" I thought.

"What you think happened, Ray?" Mama finally said to Raymond.

"I don't know. You never kin tell," Raymond said. "It seems mighty strange, though."

Soon people started walking back down the road. The screams and hollering had stopped. People were almost whispering now. They were all Negroes, although I was almost sure I had seen some whites pass before. "I guess not," I thought, sitting there sick inside. Some of the ladies passing the car had tears running down their faces, as they whispered to each other.

"Didn't you smell that gasoline?" I heard a lady who lived in the quarters say.

"That house didn't just catch on fire. And just think them bastards burned up a whole family," another lady said. Then they were quiet again.

Soon their husbands neared the car.

"Heh, Jones," Raymond said to one of the men. "How many was killed?"

"About eight or nine of them, Ray. They say the old lady and one of the children got out. I didn't see her no-where, though."

"You think the house was set on fire?" Raymond asked.

"It sho' looks like it, Ray. It burned down like nothing. When I got there that house was burning on every side. If it had started on the inside of the house at some one place then it wouldn't burn down like it did. All the walls fell in together. Too many strange things are happening round here these days."

Now most of the people and cars were gone, Raymond drove up to the little rock road and parked. I almost vomited when I caught a whiff of the odor of burned bodies mixed with the gasoline. The wooden frame house had been burned to ashes. All that was left were some iron bedposts and springs, a blackened refrigerator, a stove, and some kitchen equipment.

We sat in the car for about an hour, silently looking at this debris and the ashes that covered the nine charcoal-burned bodies. A hundred or more also stood around—Negroes from the neighborhood in their pajamas, night-gowns, and housecoats and even a few whites, with their eyes fixed on that dreadful scene. I shall never forget the expressions on the faces of the Negroes. There was almost unanimous hopelessness in them. The still, sad faces watched the smoke rising from the remains until the smoke died down to practically nothing. There was something strange about that smoke. It was the thickest and blackest smoke I had ever seen.

Raymond finally drove away, but it was impossible for him to take me away from that nightmare. Those screams, those faces, that smoke, would never leave me.

The next day I took the long, roundabout way to school. I didn't want to go by the scene that was so fixed in my mind. I tried to convince myself that nothing had happened in the night. And I wanted so much to believe that, to believe anything but the dream itself. However, at school, everybody was talking about it. All during each class there was whispering from student to student. Hadn't many of my classmates witnessed the burning last night. I wished they had. If so, they wouldn't be talking so much, I thought. Because I had seen it, and I couldn't talk about it. I just couldn't.

I was so glad when the bell sounded for the lunch hour. I picked up my books and headed home. I couldn't endure another minute of that torture. I was in such a hurry to get away from the talk at school I forgot to take the round-about way home. Before I realized it, I was standing there where the Taplins' house had been. It looked quite different by day than it had at night. The ashes and junk had been scattered as if someone had looked for the remains of the bodies. The heavy black smoke had disappeared completely. But I stood there looking at the spot where I had seen it rising and I saw it again, slowly drifting away, disappearing before my eyes. I tore myself away and ran almost all the way home.

When I walked in the house Mama didn't even ask me why I came home. She just looked at me. And for the first time I realized she understood what was going on within me, or was trying to anyway. I took two aspirins and went to bed. I stayed there all afternoon. When it was time for me to go to work after school, Mama didn't come in. She must have known I wasn't in the mood for Mrs. Burke that evening. I wasn't in the mood for anything. I was just there inside of myself, inflicting pain with every thought that ran through my mind.

That night Centreville was like a ghost town. It was so quiet and still. The quietness almost drove me crazy. It was too quiet for sleeping that night, yet it was too restless for dreams and too dry for weeping.

A few days later, it was reported that the fire had started from the kerosene lamp used by Mrs. Taplin as a light for the new baby. Nobody bought that story. At least none of those who witnessed that fire and smelled all that gasoline. They were sure that more than a lampful of kerosene caused that house to burn that fast.

There was so much doubt and dissension about the Taplin burning that finally FBI agents arrived on the scene and quietly conducted an investigation. But as usual in this sort of case, the investigation was dropped as soon as public interest died down.

Months later the story behind the burning was whispered throughout the Negro community. Some of the Taplins' neighbors who had been questioned put their scraps of information together and came up with an answer that made sense:

Living next door to the Taplin family was a Mr. Banks, a high yellow mulatto man of much wealth. He was a bachelor with land and cattle galore. He had for some time discreetly taken care of a white woman, the mother of three whose husband had deserted her, leaving her to care for the children the best way she knew how. She lived in a bottom where a few other poor whites lived. The Guild during one of its investigations discovered the children at home alone one night—and many other nights after that. Naturally, they wondered where the mother was spending her nights. A few days' observation of the bottom proved she was leaving home, after putting the children to bed, and being picked up by Mr. Banks in inconspicuous places.

When the Taplin family was burned, Mr. Banks escaped his punishment. Very soon afterward he locked his house and disappeared. And so did the white lady from the bottom.

I could barely wait until school was out. I was so sick of Centreville. I made up my mind to tell Mama I had to get away, if only for the summer. I had thought of going to Baton Rouge to live with my Uncle Ed who was now married and living there with his family.

A few days before school ended I sat in the midst of about six of my classmates who insisted on discussing the Taplin family. By the time I got home, my nerves were in shreds from thinking of some of the things they had said. I put my books down, took two aspirins, and got into bed. I didn't think I could go to work that evening because I was too nervous to be around Mrs. Burke. I had not been myself at work since the Emmett Till murder, especially after the way Mrs. Burke had talked to me about the Taplin family. But she had become more observant of my reactions.

"What's wrong with you? Is you sick?" Mama asked me.

I didn't answer her.

"Take your shoes off that spread. You better git up and go to work. Mrs. Burke gonna fire you."

"I got a headache and I don't feel like going," I said.

"What's wrong with you, getting so many headaches around here?"

I decided not to wait any longer to tell Mama my plan.

"Mama, I am gonna write Ed and see can I stay with him this summer and get a job in Baton Rouge. I am just tired of working for Mrs. Burke for a dollar a day. I can make five dollars a day in Baton Rouge and I make only six dollars a week here."

"Ed them ain't got enough room for you to live with them. Take your shoes off," Mama said, and left me lying in bed.

As soon as she left, I got up and wrote my letter. About five days later I received an answer from Ed. He said I was welcome, so I started packing to leave the next day. Mama looked at me as if she didn't want me to go. But she knew better than to ask me.

I was fifteen years old and leaving home for the first time. I wasn't even sure I could get a job at that age. But I had to go anyway, if only to breathe a slightly different atmosphere. I was choking to death in Centreville. I couldn't go on working for Mrs.

Burke pretending I was dumb and innocent, pretending I didn't know what was going on in all her guild meetings, or about Jerry's beating, or about the Taplin burning, and everything else that was going on. I was sick of pretending, sick of selling my feelings for a dollar a day.

chapter

TWELVE

When I got off Greyhound in Baton Rouge, Ed was waiting for me. I hadn't seen him in a long time. He looked different, but he hadn't changed. He was still my favorite uncle and best-liked relative. Bertha, his wife, wasn't an easy person to deal with, though. She didn't have an extra bedroom, so I had to sleep in the living room. Her sofa was new, and she didn't really want me to sleep on it. I thought of going back home the very next day, but I told myself, "If I put up with Mrs. Burke for over a year, I sure can put up with Bertha for three months. I just won't eat much of their food, and I'll stay out of her way as much as possible."

Within three days I had found a job, or rather a job found me. Mrs. Jetson, a lady Bertha had once worked for, stopped in to see if Bertha would keep her children on the weekend. But Bertha had another job now. She worked six days a week in a restaurant. She suggested that Mrs. Jetson hire me instead.

"The sooner I get some money coming in, the better," I thought. So I took the job. However, that Sunday night when Mrs. Jetson paid me six dollars for two days' work, I was some disappointed.

When she asked me if I would consider working for her throughout the summer, I told her I would have to think about it.

Coming from work that evening, I walked the three blocks back to Ed's in what seemed like one minute flat. As soon as I stepped into the living room, where Ed and Bertha were watching TV, I said, "Bertha! Why didn't you tell me she just paid three dollars a day? I thought you got paid five dollars a day here."

"Look, Essie Mae, that woman is poor. Only the rich whites here pay five dollars a day for housework. You don't have to keep the job. You can just work there until you find something better to do."

"I was talking to my boss today," Ed said. "His wife is gonna try and find something for you. But you keep that job until you git something else."

I called up Mrs. Jetson the next day and told her I would take the job for the summer. I would be making eighteen dollars a week. I went to bed that night thinking that within two weeks I would have another job.

Mrs. Jetson worked in one of the big shoe stores on Third Avenue. Her husband was a construction worker. I didn't realize how poor they were until that Saturday, the end of my first week's work. I had finished everything and was watching TV with her two sons when she came home that evening.

"I'm going when this story is over, Mrs. Jetson," I said, indicating I was waiting for my money.

"Essie, I am gonna have to give you a check Saturday of next week. I won't be able to make any deposits until then."

I stood there looking and feeling like a stupid fool. I didn't say anything, though. I just left. "I will not go back there Monday for nothing," I thought as I went to bed. But by Monday I'd changed my mind. I knew if I didn't go back I would never get my money.

The next Saturday I walked up on the porch and found the house locked. I was shocked. After noticing the curtains had been removed from the front window, I looked inside and saw that the house was empty. I didn't believe it. I stood there looking in that window for about thirty minutes. Then I knocked on the door of the lady who lived in the next house.

"Excuse me, please, I just noticed that Mrs. Jetson moved last night. Did she leave any money with you for me?" I asked her.

"Money? They don't have any money. They were gonna be thrown out of the house today. That's why they left last night. She didn't pay you?" the lady asked.

"No. And she owes me for two weeks' work."

"Why don't you call her at the store on Monday?" she suggested. "That's pretty thoughtless of her to do such a thing."

On Monday I did call the shoe store, and was told Mrs. Jetson had quit on Friday. I had never before felt so gypped in all my life. Out of all the women I had worked for this woman was the worst. Even worse than Mrs. Burke.

The following week I went to see a girl I had once gone to school with who was also living with her uncle in Baton Rouge. Susie was working in a restaurant. She had promised me that she would let me know when there was an opening there, but that evening she told me bluntly, "Essie Mae, they ain't hired nobody at the restaurant in a long time and look like they ain't gonna be hiring nobody soon. Jobs are so hard to find, people just don't quit so fast now."

I went back to Ed's and packed up my suitcase. I would have gone back to Centreville that night, but Ed wouldn't let me leave until next morning.

I overslept and missed the nine o'clock bus. The only other bus going to Centreville was at four-thirty that afternoon, so I bought my ticket, with the five dollars Ed had given me, and put my suitcase in the locker, and went back to Ed's to wait. As soon as I walked in, Bertha told me that Susie had called because she'd found a job for me.

I called Susie that night. She told me that they needed someone right away, and she asked me to go with her the next morning for the interview. I made up my mind that I could get that job. "I'll pass the interview," I told myself, "I know I can." But I left my suitcase at the bus station in the locker, just in case.

When I met Susie I was wearing bangs and a ponytail and looked more like twelve than fifteen. She balled my hair up on my head and made me put on more powder and lipstick. "Now you tell them you are eighteen or nineteen 'cause they won't hire you if they know you are fifteen. And tell them you finished school too," she said to me as we got off the bus together.

The only thing Susie didn't warn me about was to lie about my social security card. I didn't even know what social security was at the time. Mississippi Negroes never made enough money to have any taken out for hard times. Times were always hard. And I guess white folks didn't think they would live long enough to enjoy it. Anyway I told the manager of Ourso's Department Store that I'd left my social security card at home in another purse. They needed someone so badly that they took me on, and I started work that very same day.

As soon as my lunch break came I ran next door to the restaurant to ask Susie about a social security card. She said we could pick one up on our way home that evening. We spent an hour together walking around the neighborhood. Susie pointed out several other businesses the Oursos owned. Among them were Ourso Hardware, Restaurant, Gas Station, Grocery, and Tastee Freeze. And one of the Oursos was president of the American Bank. They owned that whole section of Plank Road. They were the richest people I had ever heard of. One of them lived in a mansion almost two blocks long. All the white folks in Centreville put together didn't have as much as the Ourso family. I kept thinking of how unfair it was for any one set of people to have so much.

My job consisted of cleaning the showcase glass, pressing wrinkles out of new dresses, helping with display windows, and sometimes sweeping. There were two of us employed in the same capacity. The other lady was a middle-aged Negro woman who worked part time. She told me that she had worked for the Oursos for about ten years, and how nice and rich they were. We were both paid twenty-four dollars a week. I didn't consider that salary just at all. I felt that as rich as they were, they could have afforded more—much more.

In no time at all I was well liked by most of the Ourso family. They considered me a pretty little sweet colored girl. I was very shapely, with nice long legs. The young women in the Ourso family were always telling me how they envied my shape, and asking how I kept so nice and slim. "If you were fifteen, you would look slimmer too," I thought.

The lady working with me had been considered the Oursos' favorite Negro before me. Within two weeks she was almost completely out of the picture. I was now getting all of their attention. One day when she and I were out in the ironing room pressing dresses, she became extremely confidential with me. She told me all about her family, her ex-husband, etc. She and I even spent our lunch hour together. We had a beautiful time. I was so overcome by how nice she was to me that I told her all about myself—that I was only fifteen, and hadn't finished high school, that I was from Mississippi, and that I only had one month to work there.

When I came to work the next morning, I was told the manager was waiting in his office for me. He was sitting at his desk when I walked into his office. The only thing he said was, "Here is your check, Anne. We can't use you any more. Thanks. We liked you."

I stood there wondering what had I done. I wanted so badly to ask him. But the look on his face told me that it was best that I just leave. So I did. Walking out of the door I saw my confidential friend who had shared the work with me. I was about to walk up to her and say good-bye when she turned her head. Then I knew what I had done wrong.

I got off Greyhound in Centreville with sixty-five dollars in my pocket and new school clothes. Walking home swinging my suitcase, I began to think that the experience hadn't been so bad after all. I got so wrapped up in thinking about Baton Rouge that I forgot I was back in Centreville until I ran into Doris, one of my classmates.

"Moody, where you been? You certainly disappeared some fast after school. Someone said you were in New Orleans."

"I went to Baton Rouge and lived with Ed and got a job. What's been going on here?" I asked her.

"Nothing, really. They ran Benty and Mrs. Rosetta them out of town," she said.

"For what?" I asked.

"They claim Benty was screwing that little poor white girl who live down in that bottom," she said.

"The girl living in that bottom where that white woman with them three children lived?" I asked her.

"What white woman with three children?" she asked.

"The one Mr. Banks was suppose to be taking care of. The one who left town after the Taplin burning."

"Yes, that's the girl. The one living next to where that woman lived," Doris said.

"You know Benty wouldn't have nothing to do with that trash," I said.

"They say he did, anyway Benty them have moved now."

"Where?" I asked.

"To Woodville, so they say. Benty was kin to you, wasn't he?"

"Yes, he's my cousin, not close, though." Suddenly I was trembling. "I better get on home," I managed to say. "Mama them don't even know I'm coming."

I felt as bad as if I had never gone to Baton Rouge for the

summer. "Before I get home," I thought, "I'll have a nervous break-down in the street. I'll surely get sick if anything like the Taplin burning happens this year. I'll just crack up if I have to push any-thing else into the back of my mind."

I was still shaking as I walked up on the porch. Jennie Ann was playing there. "Essie Mae done come home!" she cried. She went running into the kitchen where Mama, Raymond, and the rest of them were sitting, while I went to my room to drop my suitcase and try to pull myself together.

"Look at you!" Mama said when I walked in the kitchen. "As skinny as a stick. Didn't Bertha and Ed feed you?"

"Sho'. I had plenty to eat," I said.

"Then how come you lost all that weight?" she asked.

"I don't know. I just lost weight, that's all. I met Doris on my way home and she told me they ran Mrs. Rosetta and Benty them out of town."

Raymond got up and walked out of the kitchen at that point. When I looked at Mama, she dropped her head. Then I looked at Adline, James, Junior, Jennie Ann, and Jerry. They seemed a little strange to me too. And I stood there trying to figure out just what was strange about them. Why had Raymond walked out? Why wouldn't Mama look at me?

I didn't say anything more to anyone. I walked out of the kitchen, went to my bedroom, and flung myself on the bed.

After a while Mama came in. "Take your shoes off that spread," she said angrily.

"What's wrong with everybody? What's wrong with Raymond?" I asked her as I kicked off my shoes.

"Ain't nothin' wrong with Ray! What's wrong with you? 'Fore you get in the house you start worryin' me 'bout who got run out of town. Why is you so interested in things like that?"

"Why can't I ask about Benty them? They *are* kin to us, ain't they? What's wrong with people talking? What's wrong with people? Negroes are being killed, beaten up, run out of town by these white folks and everything. But Negroes can't even talk about it. I shoulda stayed in Baton Rouge."

Mama didn't say a word after that. She just went away, looking hurt. After she left, I began to think of what Mrs. Rice told me once when I was talking to her about the NAACP: "You gotta find something to do, Essie, that will take your mind off some of this. It's not good for you to concern yourself too much about these killings and beatings and burnings. The Negroes here ain't gonna do nothing about them. You should be having fun and enjoying yourself like others your age. Why don't you take piano lessons or something."

"Yes, that's it," I thought, still lying there. "This year I'll take piano lessons, I'll join the band and play basketball again. I will keep busy from sunup to sundown. Then I won't have to think about the Taplins, Jerry, Emmett Till or Benty. No, I won't even have to talk to Mama them, or get up tight when Raymond stares at me all the time, because from now on, I'll spend as little time in this house as possible. Next summer I will go back to Baton Rouge and get a job. And as soon as I finish high school I am gonna leave Centreville for good."

chapter

| **THIRTEEN** |

That night, I lay in bed making plans for the whole year. Somehow I thought of everything except Mrs. Burke and the job after school. And I didn't even think of her the next day until she happened by the house. Mama, Adline, and the rest of the children were sitting on the porch when she drove up. I was in my room going through my old school clothes.

"Essie Mae! Miss Burke here to see you," Mama called to me.

"Is Essie here?" I heard Mrs. Burke say. "I just stopped by to see when she was coming back."

"Is Essie here?" I thought, going to the porch. Why did she just happen by here today?

"My, but you lost weight! How did you like Baton Rouge?" Mrs. Burke asked me as I went to the car.

"It was O.K.," I said.

"What did you do while you were there?" she asked.

"I got a job," I said.

"Oh, you didn't tell me you were going to work. I thought you were going for a vacation."

I stood looking at her, thinking to myself, "Why are you so interested in what I did while I was in Baton Rouge?"

"I would like for you to come back and work for me; if you are not doing anything Friday and Saturday I would like for you to help me give the house a good cleaning."

"I gotta get my school clothes together before school start," I said. "I could help you next weekend."

"And when does school start?" she asked.

"A week from Monday."

"But I was kinda hoping you could help me *this* weekend. We are having company Sunday." She waited for me to answer.

I didn't say anything.

"O.K.," Mrs. Burke finally said. "I'll see you next Friday." Then she drove off.

"That's how you talk to white folks?" Mama said to me as I walked back on the porch.

"Now what did I say to Mrs. Burke? How *am* I suppose to talk to her?" I asked.

"You didn't have nothing to do Friday and Saturday that you couldn't help her."

"I do have something to do. You heard what I told her. I gotta get my school clothes together."

"You got all next week to do them clothes," Mama said.

I still didn't understand the change that had taken place in Mama while I was in Baton Rouge. Again, I knew that Raymond had something to do with it. He wasn't just looking at me longing like he used to. Since I had come back from Baton Rouge, he had barely spoken to me. Whenever he was around, I got this strange feeling that for some reason or other he hated me.

About two weeks after school opened, all my plans were in operation. I was busy for a total of eighteen hours a day. Each day I spent the last two periods of school on the band or on basketball.

Then I would go straight to work. I was never home until eight or nine at night and as soon as I entered the house, I'd begin helping Adline them with their lessons so I wouldn't even have to talk to Mama or Raymond. On Wednesday and Friday nights I took piano lessons. On Sundays I taught Sunday school and B.T.U.

I was so busy now that I could work for Mrs. Burke and not think of her or her guild meetings. I would fall asleep at night without dreaming old, embedded, recurring dreams. I had to keep a lot of things in the back of my mind until I finished high school.

When our mid-semester grades were released, I discovered I had made A's in all my subjects. Everything seemed so easy now. Sometimes I got scared because things were moving along too smoothly. Things had always seemed hard before. But now I was doing three times as much and I felt as if I could take on the whole world and not be tired by it. I was even better in basketball than I had ever been. In fact, I was the number one girl on the team.

Mr. Hicks, our new coach, was a nut for physical fitness—especially for girls. He hated women who were dumb about sports and he used to practice us until we were panting like overplowed mules. Sometimes he'd even take us out to play touch football with the boys so that we could learn that game. All the girls who didn't go along with his physical fitness program or who were fat and lazy he dismissed immediately. He was determined to have a winning team and was interested only in tall, slim girls who were light and fast on their feet. I think I worked harder than almost anyone else.

Shortly after mid-semester, Mr. Hicks organized a gymnastic and tumbling team. All the basketball players were required to participate. Running and heaving a ball on that open basketball court wasn't so bad, but falling on it when we did somersaults, handsprings, and rolls was like falling on steel.

Mr. Hicks was the most merciless person I had ever met. The first few weeks some of the girls could hardly walk, but he made them practice anyhow. "The only way to overcome that soreness and stiffness is to work it out," he would say. We all learned to like Mr. Hicks, in spite of his cruelty, because in the end he was always right. After three weeks our stiffness was completely gone and we all felt good. Now I took in all the activities without even getting short-winded. And I finished the semester with straight A's.

One Wednesday, I was ironing in Mrs. Burke's dining room as usual when she came to me looking very serious.

"Essie, I am so tired and disgusted with Wayne," she said, sitting down in one of the dining room chairs. "He almost flunked out of school last semester. At this rate he won't finish high school. I don't know what to do. He's in algebra now and he just can't manage it. I've tried to find someone to tutor him in math, but I haven't been able to. How is *your* math teacher?" she asked me.

"Oh, he is very good, but he hardly ever teaches our class. Most of the time he lets me take over," I said.

"Are you that good in algebra?" she asked.

"Yes, I make all A's in algebra, and he thinks I am one of his best students."

She looked at me for a moment as if she didn't believe me. Then she left the dining room.

"Look, Essie," she said, coming back with a book. "These are the problems Wayne is having trouble with. Can you work them?"

"Yes, we've passed these in my book. I can do them all," I said.

"See if you can work these two," Mrs. Burke said to me. "I'll press a couple of these shirts for you meanwhile."

I sat down at the dining room table and began working the two problems. I finished them before she finished the first shirt.

When I gave her the paper, she looked at me again like she didn't believe me. But after she had studied it and checked my answers against the ones given in the back of the book, she asked me if I would tutor Wayne a few evenings a week. "I'll pay you extra," she said. "And I can also help you with your piano lessons sometimes."

Within a week I was helping Wayne and a group of his white friends with their algebra every Monday, Tuesday, and Thursday night. While Mrs. Burke watched television in the living room, we would all sit around the dining room table—Wayne, Billy, Ray, Sue, Judy and me. They were all my age and also in the tenth grade. I don't think Mrs. Burke was so pleased with the even proportion of boys to girls in the group. Neither did she like the open friendship that was developing between Wayne and me. She especially didn't like that Wayne was looking up to me now as his "teacher." However, she accepted it for a while. Often Wayne would drive me home after we had finished the problems for the night.

Then, one Tuesday, she came through the dining room just as Wayne was asking me a question. "Look Essie," he said, "how do we do this one?" He asked this as he leaned over me with his arms resting on the back of my chair, his cheek next to mine.

"*Wayne!*" Mrs. Burke called to him almost shouting. Wayne and I didn't move, but the others turned and stared at her. "Listen to what Essie is saying," she said, trying to get back her normal tone of voice.

"Mother, we *were* listening," Wayne said very indignantly, still cheek to cheek with me.

The room was extremely quiet now. I felt as if I should have said something. But I couldn't think of anything to say. I knew Wayne was purposely trying to annoy his mother so I just sat there, trying to keep from brushing my cheek against his, feeling his warm breath on my face. He stared at her until she looked away and went hurriedly into the kitchen.

Wayne straightened up for a moment and looked at each of his friends as they looked to him for an explanation. His face was completely expressionless. Then he leaned over me again and asked the same question he had asked before. At that point, Mrs. Burke came back through the dining room.

"Wayne, you can take Billy them home, now," she said.

"We haven't done this problem, Mother. If you would stop interrupting maybe we could finish."

"Finish the problem then and take Billy them home, but drop Essie off first," Mrs. Burke said and left the room.

I explained the problem. But I was just talking to the paper. Everyone had lost interest now.

When we left the house Mrs. Burke watched us get into the car and drive off. Didn't anyone say a word until Wayne stopped in front of my house. Then Billy said, "See you Thursday, Essie," as cheerfully as he could. "O.K.," I said, and Wayne drove away.

The following evening when I went to work, Mrs. Burke wasn't home and neither was Wayne. Mrs. Burke had left word with Mrs. Crosby that I was to do the ironing and she had put out so many clothes for me to do that by the time I finished I was late for my piano lesson. I ran out of the house and down the front walk with my music books in my hand just as Mrs. Burke and Wayne were pulling into the driveway.

"Did you finish the ironing already, Essie?" Mrs. Burke asked me, as she got out of the car.

"I just finished," I said.

"Where are you going in such a hurry?" Wayne asked.

"I'm late for my piano lesson."

"Let me drive you then," he said.

"I'm going to use the car shortly, Wayne," Mrs. Burke snapped.

"It's not far from here. I can walk," I said, rushing down the sidewalk.

The next evening Sue and Judy didn't show up. Only the boys came. Mrs. Burke kept passing through the dining room every few minutes or so. The moment we finished doing the problems, she came in and said, "Essie, I gotta stop in and see Mrs. Fisher tonight. I'll drop you off."

I had begun to get tired of her nagging and hinting, but I didn't know what to do about it. In a way I enjoyed helping Wayne and his friends. I was learning a lot from them, just as they were from me. And I appreciated the extra money. Mrs. Burke paid me two dollars a week for helping Wayne and Wayne's friends paid me a dollar each. I was now making twelve dollars a week, and depositing eight dollars in my savings account. I decided not to do anything about Mrs. Burke. "She will soon see that I won't mess with Wayne," I thought.

That Saturday afternoon I was out in the backyard hanging clothes on the line while Wayne was practicing golf.

"Essie, you want to play me a round of golf?" he asked as I finished and headed for the back door.

"I don't know how to play," I said.

"It's easy. I'll teach you," he said. "Come, let me show you something."

He gave me the golf club and tried to show me how to stand, putting his arms around me and fixing my hands on the club.

"Essie, the washing machine stopped long ago!" Mrs. Burke suddenly yelled out of the house.

"I'll show you when you finish the wash," Wayne said as I walked away. I didn't even look back at him. Walking into the house, I felt like crying. I could feel what was happening inside Wayne. I knew that he was extremely fond of me and he wanted to do something for me because I was helping him and his friends with their algebra. But the way he wanted to do it put me up tight. By trying to keep him from doing it, Mrs. Burke only made him want to do it more. I knew Wayne respected me and wouldn't have gotten out of his place if I'd remained distant and cool. Now I wanted to tell him that he didn't have to do anything for me— but I didn't know how.

Wayne, Billy, and Ray received B's on the mid-semester exams. They were so happy about their marks they brought their test papers over for me to see. I shall never forget that night. The four of us sat around the table after we had corrected the mistakes on their papers.

"Gee, Essie, we love you," Billy said. "And just think, Wayne, we could have gotten A's, and if we make an A on the final exam we will get a B for a final grade." Wayne didn't say anything for a while. He just looked at Billy, then at me. When he looked at me he didn't have to speak.

"Boy, let's call Sue and Judy and see what they got," he finally said. He ran to the phone in the hall, followed by Billy and Ray.

When they left me sitting there, I began to wonder how it was that Wayne and his friends were so nice and their parents so nasty and distasteful.

Sue and Judy came back to me for help because they almost flunked the exam. Mrs. Burke seemed more relaxed once the girls were back. However, they were not relaxed at all. They felt guilty for leaving in the first place. For a week or so they brought me little gifts and it made me nervous. But after that we were again one little happy family.

The dining room in Mrs. Burke's house had come to mean many things to me. It symbolized hatred, love, and fear in many variations. The hatred and the love caused me much anxiety and fear. But courage was growing in me too. Little by little it was getting harder and harder for me not to speak out. Then one Wednesday night it happened.

Mrs. Burke seemed to discuss her most intimate concerns with me whenever I was ironing. This time she came in, sat down, and asked me, "Essie, what do you think of all this talk about integrating the schools in the South?"

At first I looked at her stunned with my mouth wide open. Then Mama's words ran through my head: "Just do your work like you don't know nothin'." I changed my expression to one of stupidity.

"Haven't you heard about the Supreme Court decision, and all this talk about integrating the schools?" she asked.

I shook my head no. But I lied.

"Well, we have a lot of talk about it here and people seemingly just don't know what to do. But I am not in favor of integrating schools. We'll move to Liberty first. I am sure that they won't stand for it there. You see, Essie, I wouldn't mind Wayne going to school with *you*. But all Negroes aren't like you and your family. You wouldn't like to go to school with Wayne, would you?" She said all this with so much honesty and concern, I felt compelled to be truthful.

"I don't know, Mrs. Burke. I think we could learn a lot from each other. I like Wayne and his friends. I don't see the difference in me helping Wayne and his friends at home and setting in a classroom with them. I've learned a lot from Judy them. Just like all Negroes ain't like me, all white children I know ain't like Wayne and Judy them. I was going to the post office the other day and a group of white girls tried to force me off the sidewalk. And I have seen Judy with one of them. But I know Judy ain't like that. She wouldn't push me or any other Negro off the street."

"What I asked you, Essie, is if you wanted to go to school with Wayne," Mrs. Burke said stiffly. "I am not interested in what Judy's friends did to you. So you are telling me you want to go to school with Wayne!" She stormed out of the dining room, her face burning with anger.

After she left I stood at the ironing board waiting—waiting for her to return with my money and tell me she didn't need me any more. But she didn't. She didn't confront me at all before I left that evening. And I went home shaking with fear.

The next evening when I came to work I found a note from Mrs. Burke stating she was at a guild meeting and telling me what to do. That made things even worse. As I read the note my hand shook. My eyes lingered on "the Guild." Then when Wayne and his friends didn't show up for their little session with me, I knew something was wrong. I didn't know what to do. I waited for an hour for Wayne and Judy them to come. When they didn't, I went to Mrs. Crosby's room and knocked.

When Mrs. Crosby didn't answer my heart stopped completely. I knew she was in there. She had been very ill and hadn't been out in a month. In fact, I hadn't even seen her because Mrs. Burke had asked me not to go to her room. At last I put my hand on the knob of her door and slowly turned it. "She can't be dead, she can't be dead," I thought. I opened the door slowly.

"Mrs. Crosby," I called. She was sitting up in bed as white as a ghost. I saw that she must have been sleeping. Her long, long hair was not braided as usual. It was all over the pillow everywhere.

"How do you feel, Mrs. Crosby?" I asked, standing at the foot of her bed. She beckoned for me to come closer. Then she motioned for me to sit on the side of her bed. As I sat on the bed, she took my hands and held them affectionately.

"How do you feel?" I repeated.

"Weak but better," she said in a very faint voice.

"I was suppose to help Wayne them with their algebra this evening, but they didn't come," I said.

"I know," she said. "I heard Wayne and his mother fighting last night. Wayne is a nice boy, Essie. He and his friends like you very much. However, his mother is a very impatient woman. You study hard in school, Essie. When you finish I am going to help you to go to college. You will be a great math teacher one day. Now you go on home. Wayne and his friends aren't coming tonight." She squeezed my hands.

The way she talked scared me stiff. When it was time to go home and I walked out on the porch, it was dark. I stood there afraid to move. "I can't go through the project now," I thought. "Mrs. Burke them might have someone out there to kill me or beat me up like they beat up Jerry. Why did I have to talk to Mrs. Burke like that yesterday?" I took the long way home that went along the lighted streets. But I trembled with fear every time a car drove past. I just knew that out of any car five or six men could jump and grab me.

The following day, I didn't go to work. I didn't even go to school. I told Mama I had a terrible headache and I stayed in bed all day.

"Essie Mae, it's four o'clock. You better git up from there and go to work," Mama called.

"My head's still hurting. I ain't going to work with my head hurting this bad," I whined.

"Why is you havin' so many headaches? You been lazin' in bed all day. Miss Burke gonna fire you. Junior, go up there and tell Miss Burke Essie Mae is sick."

I lay in bed thinking I had to find some other ache because Mama was getting wise to my headaches. If I could only tell her about Mrs. Burke, I wouldn't have to lie to her all the time. I really missed Mrs. Rice. Mrs. Rice would have told me what to do. I couldn't talk to any of the other teachers. "What can I do?" I thought. "I can't just quit, because she'll fix it so I can't get another job."

When Junior came back, I called him into my room.

"What did Mrs. Burke say?" I asked him.

"She ain't said nothing but for you to come to work tomorrow, 'cause the house need a good cleanin'. She want me to come with you to mow the yard."

I felt a little better after Junior told me that. But I couldn't understand Mrs. Burke's actions. It worried me that she was still going to keep me on. What if she was doing that just to try and frame me with something? "I'll see how she acts tomorrow," I finally decided.

At seven o'clock on Saturday morning Junior and I headed through the project for Mrs. Burke's house. Usually I took advantage of my walk through the project to think about things and compose myself before I got to work, but today I didn't have a single thought in my head. I guess I had thought too much the day before. When I walked up on her porch and saw her standing in the hall smiling it didn't even register. I was just there. I realized at that point I was plain tired of Mrs. Burke.

I went about the housecleaning like a robot until I got to the dining room. Then I started thinking. I stood there for some time thinking about Mrs. Burke, Wayne, and his friends. It was there I realized that when I thought of Wayne my thoughts were colored by emotions. I liked him more than a friend. I stood softly looking down at the table and the chair where Wayne sat when I helped him with his lessons.

When I looked up Mrs. Burke was standing in the doorway staring at me. I saw the hatred in her eyes.

"Essie," she said, "did you see my change purse when you cleaned my room?"

"No," I answered, "I didn't see it."

"Maybe I dropped it outside in the yard when I was showing Junior what to do," she said.

"So, that's how she's trying to hurt me," I thought, following her to the back door. "She better not dare." I stood in the back door and watched her walk across the big backyard toward Junior. First she stood talking to him for a minute, then they walked over to a corner of the yard and poked around in the grass as though she was looking for her purse. After they had finished doing that, she was still talking to Junior and he stood there trembling with fear, a horrified look on his face. She shook him down and turned his pockets inside out. I opened the door and ran down the steps. I didn't realize what I was about to do until I was only a few paces away from them.

"Did you find it out here, Mrs. Burke?" I asked her very coldly, indicating that I had seen her shake Junior down.

"No, I haven't found it," she answered. She looked at Junior as if she still believed he had it.

"Did you see Mrs. Burke's purse, Junior?" I asked him.

"No, I ain't saw it." He shook his head and never took his eyes off Mrs. Burke.

"Junior hasn't seen it, Mrs. Burke. Maybe we overlooked it in the house."

"You cleaned my bedroom, Essie, and you said you didn't see it," Mrs. Burke said, but she started back to the house, and I followed her.

When we got inside, she went in the bedroom to look for her purse and I went back to housecleaning. About thirty minutes later she interrupted me again.

"I found it, Essie," she said, showing me the change purse in her hand.

"Where was it?" I asked.

"I had forgotten. Wayne and I watched TV in his room last night." She gave me a guilty smile.

"I am glad you found it." I picked up the broom and continued sweeping.

"I'll just find me another job," I thought to myself. "This is my last day working for this bitch. School will be out soon and I'll go back to Baton Rouge and get a job. Ain't no sense in me staying on here. Sooner or later something might really happen. Then I'll wish I had quit."

"Essie, I don't have enough money to pay you today," Mrs. Burke said, sitting at the big desk in the hallway. She was looking through her wallet. "I'll pay you on Monday. I'll cash a check then."

"You can give me a check, now, Mrs. Burke. I won't be back on Monday."

"Do you go to piano lessons on Monday now?" she asked.

"I am not coming back, Mrs. Burke," I said it slowly and deliberately, so she didn't misunderstand this time.

She looked at me for a while, and then said "Why?"

"I saw what you did to Junior. Junior don't steal. And I have worked for white people since I was nine. I have worked for you almost two years, and I have never stole anything from you or any-body else. We work, Mrs. Burke, so we won't have to steal."

"O.K., Essie, I'll give you a check," Mrs. Burke said angrily. She hurriedly wrote one out and gave it to me.

"Is Junior still here?" I asked.

"No. I paid him and he's gone already. Why?" she asked.

I didn't answer. I just slowly walked to the front door. When I got there, I turned around and looked down the long hallway for the last time. Mrs. Burke stood at the desk staring at me curiously as I came back toward her again.

"Did you forget something?" she asked as I passed her.

"I forgot to tell Mrs. Crosby I am leaving," I said, still walking.

"Mama doesn't pay you. I do! I do!" she called to me, as I knocked gently and opened Mrs. Crosby's door.

Mrs. Crosby was propped up on pillows in bed as usual. But she looked much better than she had the last time I was in her room.

"How are you feeling. Mrs. Crosby?" I asked, standing by the side of her bed.

"Much better, Essie," she answered. She motioned for me to sit down.

"I just came to tell you this is my last day working for Mrs. Burke, Mrs. Crosby."

"What happened? Did she fire you, Essie?" she asked.

"She didn't fire me. I just decided to leave."

"I understand, Essie," she said. "And you take care of yourself. And remember when you are ready for college let me know, and I'll help you." She squeezed my hand.

"I gotta go, Mrs. Crosby," I said. "I hope you'll be up soon."

"Thanks, Essie, and please take care of yourself," she said.

"I will, Mrs. Crosby. 'Bye."

"'Bye, Essie," she said. She squeezed my hand again and then I left her room.

When I walked out of Mrs. Crosby's room, Mrs. Burke was still standing in the hallway by the desk.

"Maybe you would like to come back tonight and say good-bye to Wayne, too," she said sarcastically.

I didn't say anything to her. I walked past her and out of that house for good. And I hoped that as time passed I could put not only Mrs. Burke but all her kind out of my life for good.

I was in town about three days later when my next job found me. I had just mailed a couple of letters and was going through the post office doors as Mrs. Marcia Hunt, one of the owners of Hunt and Taylor Ladies Shop, was entering.

"Excuse me, ain't you Essie, the girl who worked for Mrs. Burke?" she asked.

"Yes," I answered, wondering what she wanted. She was a friend of Mrs. Burke's and lived across the street from her and no doubt was a member of the Guild.

For a moment she seemed baffled because I had answered her so bluntly. "I need a girl to help me in the store a couple of days a week," she said. "I can pay you two dollars a day if you will help."

I thought for a minute. The four dollars a week would keep me going until school was out.

"What evenings would you like for me to work?" I asked her.

"Tuesday and Thursday, if you can fit it in," she said.

"You want me to start next Tuesday?" I asked.

"Yes, that will be fine. I'll see you then," she said.

I thought I might really enjoy the new job. I liked the idea of working in a store again. But when I got there after school on Tuesday and discovered I was to be the janitress, I was disheartened. The first thing Mrs. Hunt asked me to do was clean the display windows.

As I walked out of the store hugging a stepladder under one arm and hauling a pail of water with the other, I stepped right into a group of my classmates. I was so embarrassed, I felt like running and hiding somewhere. But I didn't. I walked outside, placed the pail on the pavement, and opened up the stepladder. The Negro students who came through town were still passing by as I climbed up. I expected them to shout insults at me or something, but they didn't. Some called out, "Hey, Moody," as they passed and some simply passed without saying anything. Those who called out or spoke to me didn't sound as if they were poking fun at me. Once I dropped the sponge and one of the boys picked it up. "Hold it. I'll get it," he said.

Just as he handed it to me, I saw Wayne turning the corner with some of his friends. I lost my balance and almost fell flat on my back. "Essie, watch it or you'll hurt yourself," Wayne cried, running to me and grabbing hold of the ladder. He stopped it from rocking and said, "Mama told me you were working for Mrs. Hunt. But I thought you were working at her house. You shouldn't be doing this. What happened to the man Mrs. Hunt had helping her?" His friends looked on curiously as he talked to me.

"I don't know. How's the algebra coming along?" I asked. I climbed down to the first step of the ladder.

"O.K., but we miss you. We all go over to Judy's on Thursday night now. Maybe you can come over and help us before the finals," he said.

Just then I saw Mrs. Hunt standing inside the door, observing Wayne and me closely. I was sure Mrs. Burke had told her about me. I got the feeling she had hired me more out of curiosity than out of need. Following the direction of my eyes, Wayne noticed Mrs. Hunt for the first time. "Well, we gotta be going, Essie. I'll come by and see you before the finals and see if you can help us out, O.K.?"

"All right," I answered, and he and his friends left.

I climbed back up the ladder and started on the window again. Then the expression on Wayne's face when he saw Mrs. Hunt registered on my mind. He had looked scared—not for himself but for me. And now I got scared too. "I won't be here too long," I thought. "School will soon be out and I'll go back to Baton Rouge for the summer."

Within a few weeks Mrs. Hunt had formed her own opinions about me. At first she acted as though she thought I was some kind of smarty who needed to be taught a lesson. She was always telling me what to do—making sure I did it just the way she wanted it done. Then gradually she let me do things my own way. When I told her I was saving money for college, she began to show a lot of respect for me, and said she would pay me five dollars if I would clean her house each Saturday. She also arranged for me to baby-sit for her daughter on Sunday nights for another five dollars. In addition, her sister, Mrs. Taylor, paid me three dollars to clean her house on Fridays. I was soon making fifteen to twenty dollars a week all told and my savings were growing nicely.

By the time school ended, I realized that despite Mrs. Burke, it had been a good year. I had finished tenth grade with straight A's and was outshooting all the other girls on the basketball team. At Centreville Baptist, I sang in the choir, was the regular substitute pianist for Sunday school, and did all the things I had dreamed of doing since the first time I had attended there.

I still wanted to leave home for the summer, but I was not up tight with anxiety the way I had been the year before. This time Mama could see the happiness in me and she didn't mind letting me go. She knew I would be back in the fall.

I wrote to Ed and Bertha but it turned out they had no room for me this summer. Ed suggested I write to my Aunt Celia (Mama's sister) who was in New Orleans. I did and received a letter a few days later saying I was welcome to come, if I didn't mind sharing a bed with her sister, Sis. I wrote Celia that I would sleep on the floor if she didn't have a bed for me. I took the bus that evening and arrived two days before my letter.

chapter

| FOURTEEN |

I went to New Orleans with the intention of getting a job as a waitress in a big-time restaurant. I had been told that a waitress could make as much as fifty dollars a week, and I hoped to save three hundred dollars that summer and add it to the two hundred that was already in my bank account. What I didn't know at the time was that most of the big-time restaurants used only waiters who were very skilled and who had chosen the job as a career. I spent two weeks looking for a big-time waitress job, but when I couldn't find one, I tried for bus girl. Bus girls and busboys made from twenty-five to thirty-five dollars a week plus tips.

Before I realized it, I had wasted a whole month looking for a restaurant job. Sis was working as a domestic, doing work for five dollars a day. She earned twenty-five to thirty dollars a week and had saved about seventy-five dollars during the month of June. It was now July and I had yet to earn my first penny. Sis tried very hard to get me to take on a job as a domestic, but I wouldn't. I hadn't come to New Orleans to do housework. I'd go back home and work for Mrs. Hunt first.

My Grandmother Winnie, who had recently come to New Orleans, also lived with Celia, and worked as a dishwasher in Maple Hill, a little restaurant on Maple Street. They used only waiters, too. But occasionally they hired bus girls and needed an additional dishwasher. She had spoken to the owner about me, and I spent the first week in July sitting around praying and waiting for someone to quit at Maple Hill. But didn't anyone quit and that weekend I packed my things to go back home.

Sunday, the day before I was to leave, Sis and I were sitting out on the back steps, both of us feeling sad. All that past month we had had fun together. Sis had treated me to a movie almost every weekend on the promise that I would treat her as soon as I was working. Now I felt very guilty. I found myself wanting to stay if only to take her to a movie and repay her for being so nice to me.

We had been sitting in gloom and silence for about an hour when a car drove up and stopped in front of the back gate. Two boys got out. One of them waved to us and I recognized him as Little Eddie, one of Sis's classmates who had quit Willis High two years ago.

"Well, if it ain't Eddie!" Sis cried, as Eddie and his friend walked through the gate.

"Jones's mama told me you here with Celia and Johnny," Eddie said. "What in the world you doin' in New Orleans?"

"Just here for the summer. Where is you working anyway?" Sis asked.

"That's what I come by here for," Eddie said, "to see if you had a job. I'm over at the chicken factory. I been working out there for about a year. They need a lot of workers now."

"What happen out there? Did everybody quit?" Sis asked him.

"Yes, last week a whole lot of people walked off the job. They was crazy to quit a job like that. Women out there make forty or fifty dollars a week. And we make from sixty-five to eighty dollars. At home I used to work from sunup to sundown to make fifteen dollars a week mowin' them white folks' yard. Now I'm makin' sometime seventy-five and eighty dollars a week. They're crazy if they think um gonna quit my job," he said.

"Forty or fifty dollars a week!" I said, almost shouting.

"You workin', Essie Mae?" he asked innocently.

"No, and I was going back home tomorrow, too. Do you think they'll hire me out there?" I pleaded.

"Sho'. They need people some bad and y'all could start work tomorrow if you wanted to."

"I got a job making twenty-five dollars a week doing housework now, but I'd sho' quit if I thought I could get fifty dollars," Sis said.

"Y' all want to go tomorrow then?" Eddie asked.

"I know what I'll do. I'll call the lady I work for and tell her I'm sick and me and Essie Mae kin go to the chicken factory tomorrow. You want to go, Essie Mae?" she asked me.

"Sho' if you go," I answered.

"We'll pick y'all up in the morning," Eddie said. "What time will you be by here, Buck?" he asked his friend.

"'Bout six o'clock. You see, we have to git out there early 'fore the people start walkin'. We gotta be already inside the factory workin'," Buck said. "Can you all be ready for six?"

"Sho'," said Sis. "All right, Essie Mae?" She looked at me and I nodded my head Yes.

As they headed back to their car, I sat there with my eyes closed and my head back. I was thanking God because I knew this was the answer to the prayer I had prayed for a week. I thought of what Mama always used to say, "He may not come when you want him, but he is always right on time."

The next morning Sis and I got up, dressed and sat on the front steps. We waited out there for Buck from about 5:45 until 6:30, then we went back inside the house. We didn't say a word to each other. Sis sat on the side of the bed and looked miserable as I picked up my suitcase and started to pack again. I was half finished when we heard a horn blowing outside. Sis ran to the window, but I didn't stop packing. People were always blowing their horns in front of the house.

"It's him!" Sis shouted.

I left my open suitcase on the bed, picked up my purse, and followed Sis outside. Buck was sitting behind the wheel of what looked like a delivery truck, smiling at us as we walked toward him. Sis opened the door and we started to climb in beside him.

"Wait," he said. "Y'all gotta git in the back." He got out and took us around to the back of the truck. He knocked on the door twice and someone opened it.

When we peered inside, it was like looking from day into night. It was almost pitch black and hot as hell in there because the truck didn't have any windows. We saw about a dozen people packed in already.

Sis suddenly recognized another old classmate. "Rosemary! What you all doing in here?"

"Shit!" cried Rosemary. "Where you and Essie Mae goin'?"

"Y'all get in," said Buck. "I'm late already and I gotta pick up some more people." As soon as we jumped up, he closed the door and locked it.

"Shit," said Rosemary, as we scrambled for seats. "It looks like all the niggers in Mississippi is workin' out there at that chicken factory."

"I know one thing," one girl said, "I'm so scared. Them people walkin' out in front looked mighty mad with us last time. They been breakin' car glasses and beatin' up people."

After that, everyone got very quiet. Sis and I just looked at each other. I began to get a funny scary feeling. Somehow I felt that we were doing something wrong. I thought of myself as a criminal and I didn't even know why.

Buck made two more stops before we got to the factory, and then at last he opened the door and said. "We here." We all scrambled out and found that we were right inside the factory itself, in some sort of loading area. I thought that was kind of funny. I had wanted to see the outside of the building because I had never seen a big factory before. Now I felt even more like a criminal.

Sis and I joined the others on a long line. I was surprised that all the people on the line were Negroes. I had always pictured a big factory as a place where Negroes and whites worked side by side—at least that was what the pictures of factories in magazines showed. Until I got to the head of the line, I didn't see any whites at all. But then there were two white men sitting inside a door at a makeshift desk. They asked us our names and addresses, and wrote them down. When we got past that desk, we were inside the factory. It was very noisy. I looked up and there were hundreds of naked dead chickens hanging from the ceiling. They were moving very slowly along an assembly line of about fifty workers. The workers looked so tired, I began to feel sorry for them. Some of them looked as dead as the chickens hanging before them.

While we were standing there, a big husky white man, whom I later discovered was the foreman, came up to us. "Y'all git over there at them troughs and find a spot," he said. Then several young Negro guys were called over to help us. They stood at our sides telling us what to do until we had caught on. Then they moved on to other new workers as they came in and were given positions.

Earlier I had felt sorry for the people who were working when we came in. Now after about two hours of work, they not only felt sorry for us but were openly laughing at us. The chickens had been moving very slow in the beginning. Now the rate of speed was doubled. I stood there with sweat running down my face and legs. It was so hot, I felt as though I would faint. The chickens were now moving as fast as I could blink my eyes. I was on the end of the trough which pulled the insides out. There were five of us at this spot. I stood there reaching up and snatching out those boiling hot guts with my bare hands as fast as I could. But I just wasn't fast enough. The faster the chickens moved, the sicker I got. My face, arms, and clothes were splattered with blood and chicken shit. I got so disgusted at one point that I stood there and let about a dozen chickens half full of shit pass me by. So many chickens left the trough half clean that the foreman moved the five of us and put some of the older hands there. Before the ten o'clock break, I had been moved about five times.

As soon as the assembly line stopped for the fifteen-minute break, I headed outside. I was with a group of new workers. We all ran out suffocating as though we were running from death.

"Hey! Where y'all going? Y'all can't go outside!" some big black guy said. He stood just outside the entrance we had used to enter the factory.

We stopped dead in our tracks. A few feet outside the factory a long line of men and women walking up and down the sidewalk with signs on their backs began to yell at us.

"Scabs! Strikebreakers! Hicks! Country niggers! Go back to Mississippi!"

I had never seen such an angry bunch of Negroes in all my life. We stood there with our eyes popping out of our heads as we slowly backed into the factory. As I turned around, I noticed that the older hands hadn't even attempted to go outside. They were now sitting around on the floor, on crates and on stools. I just backed against the wall and sat down. Sis came over and joined me. We didn't exchange a single word. We just sat there looking out at the people walking up and down the sidewalk. Some of the signs read: NO MORE SLAVE LABOR. WE WANT MORE PAY. And some simply said SCABS.

During the lunch hour, we still weren't allowed outside of the factory. About five of the big Negro helpers were sent out to get sandwiches for us. By the time we had all gotten something to eat, the lunch hour was over. We worked until eight o'clock that night. We cleaned about three to four thousand chickens. And still two trailers full were left undone.

When Buck stopped in front of Celia's to let Sis and me out, we both stumbled out of the truck half blinded with fatigue. I felt like crawling up the porch steps on my fours.

"My goodness, look at how dirty and stinky y'all is," Celia said. "Don't sit down in that chair, Sis, pull off them filthy clothes."

I was too tired to speak. I walked straight through the house to the bathroom. I was in a tub of warm water up to my neck when Sis walked in.

"Celia say Johnny is some mad with us," she said.

"'Bout what?" I asked.

"Breaking the strike at the chicken factory," she answered.

"I won't be breaking it tomorrow," I said.

"What you mean?" she asked.

"'Cause I ain't going back out there. That work is too hard. Every bone in my body is aching," I said.

"Buck said it won't be that hard after we get caught up on the chickens and get used to it," Sis said, standing there looking at me somewhat puzzled. "Do you know we made $9.60 today?"

"That ain't worth it," I said.

When Sis left the room, I leaned back in the tub and closed my eyes. I was about to fall asleep when I heard Johnny yelling at her.

"Yeah, but why did you and Essie Mae have to go out there? Them people didn't quit their jobs 'cause they just got tired of them. They quit them 'cause they is out there makin' chicken feed. Those are slavey jobs," he said. "Don't you and Essie Mae go back out there tomorrow, you hear. I just finished with a strike out there on the river front and Celia them was starvin' until I started back to work. Now heah my own sister is taking bread outta some starvin' baby's mouth. Where is Essie Mae?" he asked Sis.

"She's taking a bath," Sis answered.

Johnny came and knocked on the bathroom door. "Essie Mae, look, don't you and Sis go back out there to that chicken factory tomorrow. You hear me!" he shouted.

"I heard you," I yelled back to him.

Later that night after I had slept for about two hours I sat up in bed and thought about the $9.60 we had made. I told myself over and over again that it wasn't worth it. And besides, Johnny had made me feel guilty. Tomorrow I would take the bus to Centreville, I decided. But at five-thirty the next morning Sis was tapping me on the shoulder. She didn't say a word. I guess I had known all along that I would be going to that damn factory. You just didn't make $9.60 anywhere.

Sis and I were in the bathroom getting dressed when Celia knocked on the door. "Essie Mae, what you'n Sis doin'? Y'all ain't goin' out to that chicken factory. You'n Sis know what Johnny said last night."

After five minutes of talk with her about how bad we needed that money, we were outside waiting for Buck.

I worked at the chicken factory for about a month. Within that time I saw the entire place. I shall never forget the slaughterhouse—the men pulling feathers from the bloody chickens, sloshing in blood up to their knees, the globs of blood dripping off their rubber aprons right into the boots they wore. The taut faces of the two men who stood at the door haunt me still. They stood there grasping chickens by the neck and knifing them one after the other, their eyes sparkling with what looked to me like pleasure. During the breaks I often overheard these same two men cracking jokes: "I musta killed three thousand of them mother fuckers already," one would brag. "Shit, I hear them fuckers squawking all day and all night. They're driving me crazy," the other would say. I felt sick every time I looked into the slaughterhouse or saw the men who worked there.

But there was something even more sickening to me—those rotten chickens that came in with sores all over them. I would see women take them, cut the knots and rotten sores off and box the remaining parts. These women would often have terrible rashes break out on their hands from the hot blood and diseased flesh.

I couldn't think of eating chicken for years after working in that factory and I still don't eat boxed chicken today.

chapter

FIFTEEN

When I entered school that fall, I realized that the chicken factory had not only turned me off chickens but on to life. Now that I was back with the same old classmates and teachers, I was bored. The little games we often played in class seemed so stupid now. And all the girls seemed silly and the boys childish. Even my teachers seemed dumb. I used to sit in class when some lesson was being explained and say to myself, "Everybody knows that," or "Can't you talk about something new?" I was making straight A's without studying half as much as before. I think Darlene bored me more than the rest of my classmates. She had been my only rival for years. Now she appeared just as dumb as the others. Often when I got bored in class, I would look at her and hate her because she wasn't giving me any competition any more. I missed the excitement of looking for ways of beating her. Now I felt as though I was in a class all by myself, and I didn't want it that way. I was lonesome.

After I gave up on the class, my only outlets were basketball, gymnastics and tumbling, and the church. I intensified these ac-

tivities and never missed a day's practice. Then I bought a piano
for fifty dollars from a classmate. Now that I had the piano, I practiced all the time. Within a few months, I became the regular
pianist at Centreville Baptist. I played for Sunday school and
B.T.U., and the church paid me four dollars each Sunday. I was
still working for Mrs. Hunt, so I was now earning a lot.

At the end of the year, for the first time in the history of the
school, Mr. Hicks sponsored a Gymnastics and Tumbling Night. I
was the only girl tumbler on the program. When it was over,
several people from the audience came backstage and crowded
around me and said, "We just wanted to see if you had any bones
in your body." This made me feel so silly and embarrassed, I almost didn't feel human.

But Mr. Hicks, my coach, was beaming. Mama came backstage
that night beaming too. In her own little way she was trying to be
extra nice to me.

"Put your clothes on before you git a cold. Look how wet you
is!" she said, helping me get dressed.

"Mama, how do you like your daughter? She is something special, huh!" Mr. Hicks said to Mama.

"Sho' is," Mama said, blushing.

All the way home that night Mama was talking about Mr.
Hicks. "They sho' need some mo' teachers like Mr. Hicks. That
was the best program they ever had here yet." She said a million
little nice things about Mr. Hicks and not a word about me. But I
knew she must have felt good about me being star of the program.

Stunt Night was held a few days before my class program. And
I had what I thought were my two best aces coming off on the
class program. I had written a one-act comedy called "Mama's
Apron String." The play was about three teen-age girls whose
father was in the service and who were under their mother's watch
twenty-four hours a day. Every night one of the girls could be seen
pulling a trick on her mother as the others covered for her. They
each managed a date a week without their mother ever knowing

about it. The play ended as one of the girls was slipping out one night and discovered that on the nights they were supposed to be playing tricks on their mother, she was actually tricking them and having three dates to their one per week. The play was a hit that night—especially among the teen-age girls who were looking for ideas.

My second ace took the audience by storm. When seven girls, including me, walked out on the stage dressed in extra short black crepe-paper skirts over black bikini panties that started below our belly buttons, and black paper bras, the whole auditorium rocked as we swayed into what I called "An Exotic African Café Style Dance." Principal Willis almost had a heart attack before he could get up front to stop us. He came running up the center aisle waving his arms with saliva dripping from his mouth. He was opening and closing his mouth as he approached the stage. I don't think anyone heard him, because the air was filled with the boys' wolf whistles and the old ladies' cries of disapproval. The principal scrambled straight up on the platform and headed for us as though he was going to push us backstage. Looking at the audience, I said, "That's all, folks," and wiggled off as everyone roared.

I looked back as I headed down the steps backstage. The audience was leaving and I saw Mama coming after me through the side entrance with fire leaping out of her eyes.

"Put your clothes on, gal. Let's go home," she yelled at me. She seldom called me "gal," so I knew she was real mad with me. "You got some nerves comin' out on that stage naked like that," she said.

"I told you about the dance. I told you it was an African dance," I said.

"What you know about some African dance? You don't know nothin' about Africa. Ain't never seen a African in your life," she shouted.

The rest of the girls were scared stiff. They were mad as hell with me. So were Principal Willis and my teacher. Everybody stayed out of Mama's reach backstage. I guess they thought she would have hit them or something worse the way she was slinging my clothes and pushing me around. All this time my teacher was hiding behind the curtains. She wasn't only hiding from Mama but from the principal too.

All the way home that night Mama kept saying, "You just gittin' besides yourself ever since that stunt night and people talkin' 'bout how good you is. People ain't doin' nothin' but making you git besides yourself."

Two days later school was out and I was on good old Greyhound, sitting in the back of the bus as usual headed for New Orleans and Aunt Celia's. I hunted around three weeks for a job. Before I realized it, I was walking into the chicken factory again out of pure desperation. When I was told they weren't hiring anyone, I was glad. I was just about to give up on New Orleans and write to my cousin Ivory Lee in Kansas City when one night Winnie came to me.

"One of the boys that wash dishes with me is sick," she said. "He gonna be outta work for two weeks. I told Mr. Steve that you may wanta work in his place. It don't pay but twenty-six dollars a week. You kin work the two weeks anyway and if Ivory Lee say you kin come you would have made your busfare."

I knew I wouldn't like that job but I decided to take it. "I will do good if I can stand it two weeks," I thought.

The first time I walked in the side door of Maple Hill that read EMPLOYEES ONLY, I wanted to walk right out again. It was so cramped and hot in the little narrow kitchen. I saw Winnie standing there stacking dirty dishes into a dishwasher. Her clothes were wet to her waist and big drops of sweat were dripping off her face. Two cooks kept colliding with each other in the little space between the stoves and steam table. One was a big tall red man who weighed about three hundred pounds or more. The other was about four feet high. Waiters were running in and out of the doors leading from the kitchen to other parts of the restaurant. They picked up plates of food as fast as those two cursing cooks put them down. A tall boy entered and set a big aluminum tray of more dirty dishes on an iron stand at Winnie's side. They were all too busy to notice me standing there in the door.

"Shit, Howard, that mothafuckin' steak is raw," the little short cook said to the big one.

"Who's running this goddamn kitchen, Mike? Keep your mothafuckin' mouth closed 'fore I ram your head in that hot grease," the fat one said.

"That's *my* order, Waite," a tall skinny waiter yelled as he ran after an old waiter who had just picked up a plate from the kitchen.

"Like shit this your order, Percy. Go ask Howard!"

I stood there thinking, "What kind of place is this? It's worse than the chicken factory. Shit, I'm goin' home."

"Essie Mae! You jus' gitting here?" Winnie called. "Come on help me wit' these dishes. Lunch hour done started and these dishes is pilin' up like crazy! Mike, you'n Howard look. This is my oldest grandchild." Winnie said, pointing to me. "Ain't she pretty? Jus' like I was when I was her age."

"Mama, I shoulda known you in your younger days," Howard said, giving me a fresh grin. "You sure you looked this good, Mama?"

Mike and Howard looked me over carefully, and within a couple of hours all the other workers in the restaurant got around to taking a look at me too. I started washing dishes without speaking to anyone. The dishes were coming in so fast that I really didn't have time. Every two minutes the busboy brought in another tray. It got so hot in that little kitchen with everybody running around, and all the stoves and ovens burning full blast, I thought that if I could only last through the rush hour, I would be doing well. As I raked the food off the plates into the garbage cans, I thought about all the hungry people I knew, and how those white folks could just throw away so much food.

Around two o'clock the rush hour was over and we finally had a chance to breathe. Winnie and I caught up on the dirty dishes and took a lunch break. We had our choice of any of the day's specials. Suddenly I began to like the job.

During the lunch break Winnie and I sat at a little table in the pantry, where all the employees usually ate. As we sat there, I was again carefully observed by the workers. The place was flooded with men. Dorothy, the pantry girl, Winnie, and I were the only women working there. Four waiters and a busboy worked the dining room, two waiters and a cook worked the counter, and two cooks were in the kitchen. Every one of them was Negro except Mike, the owner's son-in-law. From the way all the men stared at me, I got the feeling that they'd never seen a pretty girl before. Some insisted on being overly nice to me, in spite of the "hands off" expression on my face. Percy and Jack, the two tall young waiters from the counter, and P.J., a big husky waiter from the dining room, kept running in and asking me questions about school, and whether I was planning to stay long, and if I wanted them to steal me some ice cream, cake or pie from the counter. I got tired of them declothing me with their eyes. Just as I was about to explode with anger, Winnie spoke up.

"Percy! Y'all leave Essie Mae alone! She ain't come here to mess with you, she jus' come here to work. You oughta be shame of yourself with a wife an' house full of chillun at home."

"Mama, why you gotta single *me* out all the time? Why you gotta broadcast to the whole world that um *married* anyhow?" Percy asked, annoyed. The rest of the men laughed. "What *you* gigglin' at, Lily White?" Percy said to a Chinese-looking Negro who worked in the dining room.

"Trying to make 'em all as usual, huh, Percy?" Lily White said in a high-pitched effeminate voice. "That's right, Mama, you protect your granddaughter from these *lechers* around here," he giggled and walked to the other side of the room, shaking his ass at Percy.

"Yeah, Mama don't have to worry 'bout *you*, hah, 'cause you think you got the same thing *she's* got," Percy said, pointing to me, as everybody laughed again.

I sat there unable to take my eyes off "Lily White." He sounded so much like a woman I didn't believe it. And he seemed to be flirting with Percy too.

"Don't you let that bum ruffle you, honey," Lily White said to me as though he were speaking woman to woman.

"C'mon, Essie Mae, 'fore them dishes start stackin' up again," Winnie said to me, picking up her plate from the table.

Winnie was supposed to leave at five but the dishes were coming in so fast that she decided to stay and help me until her replacement came. She kept looking up at the clock and saying, "Lola better hurry up an' come. I been here since eight o'clock." A little past six, a tall slim figure appeared outside the screen door.

"Mama! Open the door!" a frail girlish voice called to Winnie.

"It's about time you got here, Lola," Winnie said, going to let her in. Lola had long wavy auburn hair hanging down to her shoulders and wore what might have been a man's or woman's sport shirt with skin-tight pants. I was startled when she dashed into the men's room.

"Winnie, is that a woman or a man?" I asked uncertainly.

"That's a man. This place is full of 'em," she answered.

I opened my mouth to ask her "full of what?" but I didn't say anything because I was too stunned. Winnie finished stacking the dishes she had taken out of the machine. Then she went to the ladies' room to change, leaving me at the dishwasher alone.

Shortly, Lola came out of the men's room, pinning his hair up on his head with a few bobbies, then adding a comb to make a pompadour in the front. He caught me looking at him. "You Mama's granddaughter?" he asked coldly.

"Yes," I muttered, as Lily White appeared in the door.

"Where you been, comin' in here two hours late?" he asked, swishing in the pantry doorway.

"What *business* is it of yours, long as I ain't sleeping with *you*," Lola snarled, throwing his head back, the comb falling out as he did so. He gracefully picked it up and replaced it.

"What are you so *nervous* about? Are you scared Jimmy's gonna find out you're comin' to work two hours late every day?" Lily White asked.

"Just don't make it your business to tell him," Lola hissed back.

"Will you two girls cut that out and respect Mama's grand-daughter," Big Howard said, smirking, as he saw how attentive I was to their conversation.

I had forgotten Winnie until she showed her face in the door-way. She had changed clothes and was now ready to leave.

"Mama, you go home and rest now," Lily White said, patting Winnie on the shoulder. "You look pretty tired."

"Shucks, it's after seven! I think I'll set down and rest a bit. You'll be off soon, Essie Mae, and then we kin catch the bus to-gether," Winnie said to me.

"Aw, Mama, Lola ain't gonna hurt your granddaughter," Lily White said, throwing his hands up to his mouth as he swished away laughing.

I could tell Winnie was angry. She didn't say anything. She turned and went into the pantry leaving me and Lola at the dish-washer alone.

Lola now acted as if he was angry with me. He forced me out of the way and started raking the dirty dishes and stacking them. I didn't say a word. I just stepped to the other side of the machine and took the clean dishes out, stacking them on the shelf. We hardly spoke until I left.

I couldn't wait until I got outside to ask Winnie about Lola and Lily White and the others. But I didn't have to ask. Winnie started talking, telling me everything I wanted to know and more.

"Essie Mae, don't you let them things in that restaurant upset you. You jus' do your work and pay no mind to them and they won't bother you. That place ain't fit for young people like you to be workin' in. I is old and done seen or heard jus' about everything. And they don't bother me 'cause um old. But can't no young single woman work there. If they don't end up bein' whores for them no-good married men and Steve fire them, Lola them scare them off. I sho' hope Ivory Lee send fo' you 'cause you can't find no jobs fit to work at in New Orleans. You might find somethin' to do in Kansas City," she said, sighing as if she was tired.

We walked to the bus stop in silence. As we stood waiting for the bus, Winnie took out her handkerchief and blew her nose. I thought she was crying, but it was so dark I couldn't tell for sure. When we got on the bus, I saw tears running down her face.

I sat beside her remembering the day I went to her house and saw her two white sons, Sam and Walter. I knew that out of her thirteen children they were the only two she kept. My Mama was the only one who married out of Winnie's house, because she was the oldest. As the others got older, Winnie gave them away one by one to the Negro families who didn't have many children and were farmers on Mr. Carter's plantation. Winnie never had a husband of her own so she didn't farm. She spent twenty-some years working as Mr. Carter's cook and she got Sam and Walter by one of the white hired hands.

She loved Sam and Walter more than any of the others. Everything she had she put on them. She looked to them as her salvation. She wanted them to finish school and be big successes. But they had both quit high school the year before and come to New Orleans to get jobs and Winnie had come right behind them.

Looking at her out of the corner of my eye, I could see her whole life of hardship on her face. The ends of her frizzled graying hair showed from under her scarf. Her skin sagged off her high Indian cheekbones which had become more prominent with the years. Her deep sad eyes were filled with tears.

I got the feeling we were thinking about the same things—her twenty-some years on Mr. Carter's plantation, thirteen children and no husband, and always the hope for something better. But now she'd ended up in Maple Hill Restaurant washing dishes, sharing the kitchen with two cursing cooks and a bunch of strange men who thought they were women.

One day during my second week at Maple Hill, Steve, the owner, came into the kitchen with a uniform and an apron in his hands. He told me he wanted me to work in the dining room for the day. I changed into the uniform, thinking, "At last, I'm a waitress," and went out to report to Waite, the headwaiter.

"Mmm, but you look nice in that uniform," he said, smiling. "You ever bus dishes before?"

"Bus dishes? Is that what I'm gonna do?" I asked, disappointed.

"Oh, ain't nothin' to it. C'mon, I'll show you." He walked to a table where a couple had just finished eating. "Watch me," he said as he began to remove the dirty dishes. The couple looked up and Waite said to them, "Oh, just breakin' in a new bus girl." The couple smiled but their eyes said, "You must be pretty stupid if you don't know how to bus dishes." All of a sudden I felt that I wasn't cut out to be a bus girl because if all the white folks who ate in the restaurant gave me looks like that I would probably break all the dishes.

There were three waiters working the dining room, Waite, P.J., and Lily White, and they each had a customer as I started bussing the tables. I removed the dirty dishes from each table, placed them on a tray, and took the tray into the kitchen. A new couple came in and Waite said I was to serve them water. He went to the pantry and showed me where the ice and glasses were. When I returned with the two glasses of water, I was shocked to see that just about every table in the dining room was full. I began to panic. I stood there in front of the swinging doors with the water in my hands as Waite them ran past me ordering salads from the pantry.

I was still standing there holding the water when they came back out.

"C'mon, Annie, serve that water and get water for the other tables," Waite said as he went by.

I put the two glasses down in front of the first two people I saw. Then I ran back to the pantry, took a small tray, and quickly filled ten more glasses with water. Just as I started through the swinging doors, sideways, with the water tray held in front of me, P.J. came through the other door and raked off all ten glasses. They hit the floor with a tremendous crash, sending ice, broken glass and water in all directions. As I stood in the door, still holding the empty tray, all the customers turned to see what was going on.

"Don't you come through that door sideways durin' a rush hour! Kick that door with your foot if your hands are full!" Waite snapped as he passed me. "Some mess you made here!" he said. I rushed in behind him and began to pick up the broken glass with my hands.

"Leave that stuff there and let Willie clean it up! Don't you know better to pick up glass with your hands? Get some water to the customers out there."

I quickly refilled the tray and entered the dining room again, this time making sure that no one was coming through from the other side. It seemed as though everyone in the dining room was looking at me when I came through the door. I stood there for a moment, composing myself. Then I started distributing the water like nothing had happened. I managed to serve them all water without any more trouble. While they were eating I stood up front with the waiters and had a chance to look over the customers. I saw that they were mostly students. Schoolbooks were piled on the floor next to many of the tables. A few of the students were even doing their work while they ate.

"They must be puttin' it on 'em pretty heavy over there at Tulane, eh?" P.J. said to me as he noticed me watching a guy do his homework. This was the first time he had said anything to me without being fresh. I figured he felt bad about knocking those glasses out of my hands. "I can see you studyin' like that when you get to college," he said, trying to draw me into conversation. "Yeah, I wish I was one of them students sittin' out there. Most of 'em that come in here is from up North. Got them rich-assed parents up there in New Yo'k and dif'rent places, sendin' 'em a whole lotta money and all they do is lay around on their ass and mess with these fast girls...."

"Shut up, P.J.," Waite whispered loudly. "Go back there to your own station and talk that shit if you want to. Don't you be messin' up my tips."

A long line of students waited near the entrance, so as soon as a table was empty I quickly bussed it. I noticed that most of the students had left tips of more than twenty-five cents each. "Boy, if I was a waitress, I could make some money," I thought.

"Hey, sonny, wait, you forgot your change," P.J. called after a white boy who had just left a table. The white boy acted as if he didn't even hear P.J. and went on to pay his check.

"See that fuckin' cracker? He from Mississippi," P.J. grumbled as he picked up ten pennies from the table. "Annie, I swear, you can have yo' Mississippi rednecks. We got a bunch of telephone men that come in here, all from Mississippi. They'll eat a big steak 'cause the telephone company have to pay for the food. Then them cheap-assed fuckers'll get up and leave a nickel tip. Shit!" he spat, as he helped me clean the dishes from the table.

That night I went home with my back killing me from toting those heavy trays full of dishes. I looked forward with pleasure to going back to the kitchen the next day. Even more satisfying was the thought that I would be leaving the restaurant the following week. However, when I got to the restaurant the next morning I learned that the busboy had quit. I was asked to bus dishes until they found someone for the job. A week passed and they still hadn't found a replacement. By this time I had gotten used to bussing dishes and I was beginning to like the job—especially the fifteen-dollar difference in salary. Whenever I was in the dining room, I felt like I was somebody, that I was human, because I had to react to living people. But when I was in the kitchen using the dishwasher I felt just like a machine. Besides that, I liked being around the students. Watching them made me look forward to college, living away from home and having the freedom they had.

After my second week of work in the dining room, P.J. quit. At first Waite and Lily White worked the dining room alone. Then one day the dining room got packed. Steve threw a checkbook at me and told me to take orders. He was so pleased with how I handled myself that from that day on I was a waitress, earning more money than I had ever made.

Before the summer was over, I had worked all over the restaurant. I learned to do everything from cooking to making salads. Even more important, I learned a lot about the people I was working with, especially Lily White and Lola.

I got to know Lily White first. He told me his real name was James and soon he let me call him James outside of the dining room. We had many conversations during our breaks. He talked mostly about his nightlife and about his career as an "exotic" dancer. Lily White was his stage name. He'd tell me how pretty and smooth his body was and how when he went on stage he used a light powder so that when he stripped under the spotlights he looked snow white. He bragged so much about how good a dancer he was and how the men all raved that I agreed to go to one of his performances.

The new busboy, Robert, a freshman at Dillard, was also from Mississippi and didn't know very much about James and Lola types. He told me he knew where James danced and would take me if I wanted to go. I got the feeling that he was more curious about James than I was, but he was afraid to go alone because he knew James might think he liked him.

Finally one Saturday night we decided to see Lily White's midnight show.

We were ten minutes late and, as we entered, James was just being introduced by a tall handsome well-dressed Negro. A small combo came out and started playing some strip-tease music. As Robert and I made our way through the customers, I noticed that most of them were homos. There were hardly any women, and the ones who were there looked to me like they might have been men in women's clothes.

"Ladies and gentlemen, again tonight we present the fabulous Miss Lily White," the tall program announcer said just as Robert and I found an empty table.

I looked to the stage and I was shocked. James didn't look like James. His pot belly had completely disappeared. If I hadn't known him I would have sworn he was a woman with that wig and costume he wore. When he came on, all the people in the place began to whistle and call "Lily White," and make all kinds of cracks. "C'mon, Lily, show us what you got," someone shouted.

"Old Lily got plenty," someone else answered, and everybody laughed.

James wiggled on the stage as if he was out to please them all. He really seemed to enjoy the shouting crowd down below. I was still standing, gaping at him, as he went into his stripping act. I was dying to see if his body was as white as he said it was.

"C'mon, Mama, set yo' pretty ass down! It ain't transparent, y'know," a girlish voice cried indignantly behind me. I turned to see who she was talking to and noticed I was the only one standing, so I bopped down real quick in a chair next to Robert. I realized from the way she said it, she probably thought I was one of them.

"Shit, everybody in here must be queer," Robert whispered as I sat next to him.

The combo drummer began a roll on his drum and all the lights gradually faded out except the big spotlight on James. My eyes were sitting on the end of my nose as I watched James remove his costume piece by piece. Each piece he removed caused a wave of loud sighs, whistles, and cries from the audience. I looked at James's rigged-up tits and couldn't tell them from real ones. He removed everything but his G-string and turned around. I thought my eyes were playing tricks on me as his snow-white ass glittered in the spotlight. The whole place reeled and rocked as he went into his "snake-dance wiggle." Robert and I were speechless at the end of the performance.

The next day at work the whole place knew that we had gone to see James. I had expected them to tease us and carry on all day, but they did nothing more than comment. I got the feeling that most of them wanted to go see James themselves but hadn't had the nerve to do so. Anyway a lot of them got around to seeing him after we went. James seemed really pleased that we had seen him. I waited for him to crack on me when I told him that he was good, but he just smiled. He and I became friends after that, and he told me a lot about Lola.

Lola had a record and was known to be dangerous, so didn't anyone in the restaurant bother him much. When he came to work at Maple Hill, he was just out of "Tulane and Broad" (Louisiana State Prison), where he had spent three years in jail for armed robbery and assault. He smuggled a razor into prison, lodged in the roof of his mouth. While he was serving his time, a big fight broke out between the homos and the straight men in the prison. Lola cut up three or four men in the cell and earned the name Killer.

Lola looked so lonesome around Maple Hill. He never talked to anyone but James. Unlike James, he thought of himself as a real woman. James never acted queer around the restaurant until he was a little drunk. Lola was the helpless, little, fragile female type. It was hard for me to believe all that James had said about how tough and violent Lola was when I saw him at work in the restaurant. But everyone else in the place knew about his prison fight and I had seen him poke his razor out of his mouth at James. He had a way of holding his mouth like it was full of food. James told me that he had the razor resting on his tongue then and that if you said something to him, you could actually see him fit the razor into the top of his mouth before he spoke.

One day I was sitting in the pantry alone, at the little table where the workers usually ate, when Lola came in and stood over me. He stood there for a while without saying anything. I began to tense up because I couldn't sense what was on his mind.

"Why do you wear your hair like that?" he asked like he was trying to be nice.

"Huh!" I replied in a trembling voice.

"Are you scared of me?" he asked and paused for me to answer. "I'm not a monster even though you think I am. So you don't have to be scared of me."

"I don't think of you like that!" I said defensively.

"Why do you treat yourself like you do? You could look much better even though everybody around here thinks you're hot shit."

"What do you mean?" I asked, sincerely interested.

"Look at you with your hair pinned up in that little ducktail in the back. If you want short hair why don't you cut that little piece off in the back? What's it back there for anyway? It's not long enough to do anything with. Then look at your plain eyes. Some women would give anything for your long eyelashes. A little mascara wouldn't hurt you. I don't understand women like you. You are pretty and seem to know it. Yet you treat yourself like a plain Jane. You remind me too much of my sister," he said, then hurried back to the kitchen as Waite came into the pantry.

I didn't know what to think of Lola after that. It frightened me that he was interested in how I looked. I thought he was attracted to me at first, but a few minutes later, I saw him swishing up in some man's face. I thought it over and came to the conclusion that he was just trying to be nice and wanted to be my friend.

The following morning, I went to work with my hair pinned in the back in what Lola had called a ducktail. I had tried for half an hour to change the style and couldn't do anything with it so I finally just pinned it up. Lola gave me a good sermon on why I insisted on being ugly. He talked about me from head to toe. He commented on my hair, the sagging clothes I wore to hide my body, and even the shoes I wore. He finally convinced me that I could look much better, so that evening I stopped at a beauty shop and had my hair cut and bought some mascara. Before long Lola also had me wearing straight dresses and uplift bras.

chapter

| SIXTEEN |

When school started that fall, I began to really appreciate what Lola had done for my appearance. Most of my classmates and teachers commented on how I had changed and how good I looked. I had made good money from tips after I became a waitress, so I bought a lot of cheap clothes. I bought them all in the style Lola had said was best for me and just about every day for the first month or so I wore a different outfit to school. The clothes emphasized my body just like Lola had said they would. I really looked good especially with the mascara and the new hairdos he suggested.

I looked so good that it became somewhat of a problem. Whenever I was in town white men would stare me into the ground. I was shopping with Mama one Saturday when a group of white men followed us. One of them walked up to me and asked me where I lived. "What y'all wanta know where she live for? That ain't none of yo' business! What y'all doin' followin' us anyhow? If I catch y'all doin' it again um gonna tell Ed Cassidy," Mama spoke up quickly before I said anything. She spoke so forcefully, the white men went away.

When they left, Mama said to me, "They think every Negro woman in Centreville who look like anything should lick their ass and whore around with them." She warned me that I must never be caught in town after dark alone and if I was ever approached by white men again, I should walk right past them like I was deaf and blind.

It was easy for me to ignore the white men in town. But it wasn't so easy for me to ignore Mr. Hicks, my basketball coach, and the only single male teacher at school. I knew before that Mr. Hicks liked me a lot, but I thought he liked me because I was his best tumbler and basketball player. I never suspected he had any long-range plans for me or desired me physically. Now the only looks he ever gave me were looks of affection and whenever he spoke to me it was in the tone of a lover. Every other Sunday or so he would just happen by the house to see if I were home, or to say something about what would happen next week, or to show me some new pointers in basketball or just because he was driving through the community. He dropped by so frequently Mama started hinting around that he liked me. I got the feeling that she didn't mind that he did. In fact, she seemed pleased. Once we were sitting on the porch when Hicks drove by and waved and Mama commented, "I sho' wish I had married a schoolteacher." Then I knew she was hoping I would marry Hicks.

It became obvious at school that Hicks liked me, and a lot of the girls on the basketball team began to get jealous. We had shown great teamwork before. Now when we practiced, the girls would freeze me out of the game. Then when Hicks scolded them for not passing the ball to me and messing up most of our plays, they would throw me the ball as hard as they could or over my head. Things got so bad that Mr. Hicks threatened to cut out the girls' team altogether. One evening while we were practicing one of the girls knocked me down, then ran flat-footed over me like I was part of the ground. I was so mad I jumped up and ran after her ready to tear her to bits. Just as I reached out to grab her, Mr. Hicks stepped between us. He stopped the game and lectured to us right there on the court. He told us to think seriously about why we were playing ball. He asked why we were fighting each other if we really wanted to play and continue to have a winning team. Then he dismissed us and gave us a week to think about the questions he had asked.

Within that week, the girl who knocked me down came to me and apologized, and the captain went to each of the girls for her decision about abolishing the team. When Hicks called us together again, the captain got up and said that the girls had unanimously voted to continue playing. After that Hicks didn't treat me any better than the other girls. He didn't call me sweet names or look for excuses to touch me every time he was near me; now I began to respect him again. I think I appreciated his change of attitude toward me more than any of the other girls did.

Right after Hicks had cooled off on me, I began having problems with Raymond. I would come in from work in the evening and he would be hanging around the house. Sometimes he would be sitting in the yard, under the pecan tree and when I walked out there, he would stare at me long and hard. One evening I was sitting in my room in front of the mirror, combing my hair. I was wearing a real low-cut blouse. He had walked out of the kitchen past my bedroom window and suddenly I saw him in the mirror standing outside staring at me. I pretended I didn't see him. He stood out there for a long time giving me wanting eyes. After that I became a little frightened of him. I stopped wearing low-cut blouses and even stopped wearing shorts or tight pants around him. But he still continued to look at me wantingly. I got the feeling he thought that I had begun screwing around when I was in New Orleans because I had matured so. Then too he knew Hicks liked me because he had come by the house so much. I knew that he was jealous of Hicks and didn't want Hicks or anyone else to touch me.

Once when Mama, Raymond, and all the children were sitting around watching TV, I came into the room and sat down. Raymond glanced at me angrily, got up grumbling to himself, and stormed out of the room. Mama looked at him as he left and a hurt expression came across her face. I could tell she knew exactly what was going on with Raymond. She got up and followed him out of the room and I heard them exchange angry words in the kitchen. As I sat there, I remembered the day I had mentioned to Lola that I had a stepfather and Lola had said:

"Stepfathers ain't no damn good. Once my cousin remarried some no-good man and put him over her teen-age daughter. One day she came home and caught that fucker in bed with her child."

"All stepfathers ain't like that," I had said defensively.

"Like hell they ain't! He never touched you or brushed up against you or looked at you funny?"

"Raymond ain't like that. Besides, if he did like me he would never mess with me 'cause he know I can't stand him."

"But why you can't stand him then?" Lola had asked.

Then I told him about Miss Pearl them and how bad they treated Mama. I told him that I hated Raymond because he let them treat Mama like dirt.

Now I knew that Lola was right, and I knew if things got any worse, I would have to leave Centreville.

Two weeks later, Samuel O'Quinn was murdered. One night as he was walking the few blocks from town to his house he was shot in the back from close range with a double-barreled shotgun. The blast left a hole through his chest large enough to stick a fist through.

His death brought back memories of all the other killings, beatings, and abuses inflicted upon Negroes by whites. I lay in bed for two days after his death recalling the Taplin burning, Jerry's beating, Emmett Till's murder, and working for Mrs. Burke. I hated myself and every Negro in Centreville for not putting a stop to the killings or at least putting up a fight in an attempt to stop them. I thought of waging a war in protest against the killings all by myself, if no one else would help. I wanted to take my savings, buy a machine gun, and walk down the main street in Centreville cutting down every white person I saw. Then, realizing that I didn't have it in me to kill, I slowly began to escape within myself again.

The following Sunday on my way to Centreville Baptist, I walked the same sidewalk I always walked, the one where Samuel O'Quinn had died. As I stood looking at the bloodstained spot where he had fallen, pangs of anger hit me like lightning, paralyzing me emotionally. Sitting up in church later, I couldn't make myself feel anything when the preacher casually mentioned "the passing of Mr. O'Quinn."

Samuel O'Quinn had just returned from a long stay up North. A few weeks after he was murdered, it was whispered among the Negroes that he was killed because he was an NAACP member. He was said to have joined during his stay. His plans were to come back to Centreville and try to organize the Negroes. He supposedly knew all the facts underlying the Taplin burning and other mysterious killings in and around Centreville and Woodville. However, when he returned to Centreville and began seeking out Negroes whom he thought he could trust, he found only a few. And out of that few, someone squealed. Before he was able to organize his first meeting, he was killed. The other men involved hushed up or left town in fear of their lives.

Later talk among the Negroes about his death brought out that Principal Willis was one of the biggest Uncle Toms in the South. It was said that he was the one who squealed on Samuel O'Quinn and also helped plot his death. Even later, a Negro on his deathbed confessed that he and another Negro, who is walking around alive and healthy today, were paid five hundred dollars to murder Samuel O'Quinn and the money was delivered by Willis. It never came out which whites were behind the killing, but everyone figured it was the same bunch that had pulled all the others. Every time I saw Willis at school after that, I hated his guts. At night I used to have dreams about killing him.

After Samuel O'Quinn's murder, I became a real loner. I spent most of my time in school, at work or in church. Whenever I was home, I stayed in my room to avoid Raymond. I even moved the piano in there. I didn't have any contact with my classmates or teachers outside the classroom. When I was at work I hardly spoke to Mrs. Hunt. Because she was a part of Centreville's white community and didn't condemn what they were doing, I considered her as guilty as the ones who did the killing.

It became almost impossible for me to go to school or work. I had hoped that I could finish high school and then leave Centreville for good. Now I made plans to leave at the end of that semester. I would go to New Orleans to work at the restaurant, then finish high school at night. I planned to take Adline with me because I didn't want to leave her there around Raymond.

One Sunday morning, in early November, Adline and I went to Sunday school and church as usual. It was about two o'clock that afternoon when church let out and I headed home to spend the rest of the day in my room at the piano. When we got home, Mama and Raymond were sitting on the porch. Mama was sitting there picking bumps in her face with a needle looking in a small piece of broken mirror as she did every Sunday. When I walked up on the porch, I pulled Mama's hair playfully and ran past her into the house as she hit at me. I went straight to my bedroom, sat down at the piano, and started playing "Does Jesus Care."

"Essie Mae, ah'll sing while you play. All right?" Mama yelled from the porch.

"O.K. Wait till I change clothes and then come in here," I answered.

After I had changed into something comfortable I began play-ing again and waited for Mama to come in. I played a couple of songs and she still hadn't come so I went onto the porch to tell her I was ready. Raymond was sitting there alone. I walked out in the yard to see if she was under the pecan tree. She wasn't, so I sat on the corner of the bottom step and looked under the house to see if she was in the backyard. I looked up at Raymond. Just as I was about to ask him where Mama was, he jumped up out of the rock-ing chair and stormed into the house cursing.

"Goddamn! Can't see no fuckin' peace 'round here," he said, slamming the screen door.

Something inside me popped.

"You mothafucka! I'm *tired* of you! What's wrong with you, you can't see no peace? What have I done to you? *You're* the one. Can't nobody see no peace for you going around here cussin' and fussin' all the time." I ran up on the porch and picked up the piece of bro-ken mirror Mama had left there. "I'll kill you! You son of a bitch! You *need* to be dead!" I screamed, rushing to the screen door.

I was so mad I was stone out of my mind. When I ran for the door, Raymond immediately latched it from inside. He stood be-hind it looking at me like he wanted to strike me. But he knew if he opened the door I would cut him with the mirror. I was crying like crazy. I could hardly see for the water in my eyes. As I was jerking on the door, Mama came up behind him.

"What's wrong with you, Essie Mae? Put that mirror down! You losin' your mind or somethin'?" she yelled at me.

"I didn't do nothin'! I came out on the porch for you and this fucker come talkin' 'bout um driving him crazy, he can't see no peace for me! What in the shit have I done? Um getting tired of this shit around here! Um gonna leave right now! Open this door! Let me get my clothes!" I cried, jerking on the door again with all my might.

They wouldn't open it and I ran around to the back door and found it latched too. All the other children came running to the house from down the hill, where they had been playing, as I ran to the front of the house. When I came up on the porch, Mama was opening the door, but Raymond forced her back into the house when he saw me and latched it again.

"Open this door!" I screamed, pulling and kicking at the wooden frame.

"Shut up your mouth!" Mama yelled. "What's wrong with you? Shut up! People all up in the quarters can hear you."

"I don't give a goddamn about people hearing me! Nobody in this fuckin' town ain't no good no way. Um *tired* of this shit! What have I done to Raymond? What have I done to him!! I know what his problem is! I know what's wrong with him . . ."

"Shut up, gal! Shut up! Everybody is listenin' to you!"

"I *told* you once, Mama! I *told* you he wasn't no good. He ain't *no* good! I hear him fussin' at you *every* mornin' and you don't say *nothin'* to him! What do you say? You just sit there and take it and let him walk all over you! Um *tired* of him walkin' all over you and treatin' us like we're dirt or somethin'. If you don't want me to get my clothes," I screamed, "I'm just gonna leave without them. I don't need them no way. Um just gonna go away, Mama. Um just gonna go away and kill myself!" I walked down off the porch. I was so mad, I was talking to myself.

"That's all right, Mama, um goin'. Um leavin' this town. Ain't *nobody* no good here, black or white."

"Where you goin', gal?" Mama yelled from the house with a tone of sorrow in her voice.

"I don't know, Mama. I don't know," I muttered to myself.

As I walked toward Miss Pearl's house, they were all standing out in the yard staring at me. I wanted to kill all of them. "They ain't worth it," I thought, walking by them. As I passed, they stared at me like I had lost my mind. I turned the little curve in front of Miss Pearl's, and walked up toward the highway. My cousin, Miss Clara, and all of them were standing out in the road.

"Essie Mae! What's wrong wit' you? What's goin' on down

there?" Miss Clara asked, walking toward me. "Come on in and tell me what's wrong," she said, leading me to her house. She took me inside and wiped my face with a towel. I lay on her sofa and cried for a while as she patted me on the back.

"Essie Mae, what happen? What were you screamin' and carryin' on 'bout?" her husband, Mr. Leon, asked.

"I had a fight with Raymond and I'm not gonna stay there any more."

"Did he beat you?" he asked angrily.

I just shook my head no.

"You want me and Clara to take you to Diddly?"

"I wanta get my clothes," I said. "But Mama them won't let me in the house."

"You want me to go and get your clothes?" Leon asked.

"No! Raymond and Mama won't give them to you. They will just get mad with you."

"Then why don't you just leave them and let Diddly git them," he said.

"My daddy won't go down there. And I don't want him to go because Raymond would be mad with Mama if Daddy went there." I sat there thinking for a while. "I know what. Take me to the sheriff. He would come back with me and I'll get my clothes 'cause Mama ain't gonna give them to nobody else."

As Mr. Leon and Miss Clara drove me to Ed Cassidy's house, they acted like they were scared, but I wasn't. I figured the sheriff could get my clothes if nobody else could. I was old enough to leave home. I had bought all the clothes myself out of what I had earned.

Mr. Leon and Miss Clara waited in the car for me as I walked up on the sheriff's porch. I was still crying as I knocked. Mrs. Cassidy came to the door.

"Yes?" she asked. "What can I do for you?" She stood on the other side of the screen door staring at me suspiciously.

"Is Mr. Cassidy home?" I asked, tears still running down my face.

"Yes, but he's eatin' dinner. Is it serious?" she asked.

"Yes, it *is* serious and I would like to see him now," I said.

"Well, I'm sorry, he's eatin' dinner right now. He'll be out in a little while. You can sit in the swing and wait for him," she said, going back into the house.

"How long is it gonna take?" I asked.

"Fifteen twenty minutes," she answered without turning around.

When she went back and told him, he came right out. I guess she must have told him I was crying.

"What happened?" he asked, looking at me as though he was trying to remember my name.

"I just had a fight with Raymond and I left home. They won't let me get my clothes and I bought them. They're my clothes and I want them and I'm gonna take them. Now if you don't come and go back with me to get them, I'm goin' back by myself and if Raymond touch me, I'm gonna kill him, and it's gonna be *your* fault 'cause I told you. I want my clothes so you better come go back with me."

"Are you sure you know what you're doin'?"

"I'm old enough to know what I'm doin'. I was old enough to go to New Orleans and Baton Rouge and work and buy them. I'm old enough to send myself to school too. I don't owe Raymond nothin' and I want my clothes from there."

"What your mama think about this?"

"Mama ain't got nothin' to do with it."

"Wait a minute till I finish eatin', then I'll drive you down there and talk to Ray. Are you sure you wanna leave home?"

"I know what I'm doing!" I said sharply.

He gave me a funny look and went back into the house. I told Mr. Leon and Miss Clara, who were still sitting in the car, that they could leave me. They drove off and I went back and sat on Cassidy's steps and waited for him to finish his dinner. As I sat there crying, I thought of how much I hated Raymond and wanted to kill him and how much I hated Centreville. Sitting on Ed Cassidy's steps, remembering how he took Jerry out in the camp area to be beaten up by Withers them, I hated him more than all the whites in Centreville. I hated the thought of him taking me any-where. But I knew Mama and Raymond wouldn't let me get my clothes if I went back alone.

In a little while, Cassidy came out, backed his little pickup truck out into the street, and opened the door for me to get in. I jumped up beside him without even looking at him. As he drove through the quarters, all the Negroes were sitting out in their yards or on their porches. They all stared at me sitting up in Ed Cassidy's truck.

"I know Ray," Cassidy said. "This ain't like Ray. We never had no trouble outta Ray. I can't understand this. What's goin' on there? Ain't Ray your daddy?"

"No, he ain't my daddy!" I answered coldly, knowing he knew Raymond wasn't my daddy.

"Where is your daddy?" he asked.

"My daddy live in Woodville...."

"Are you gonna go live with your daddy?"

"I don't know!" I snapped, hinting that I wasn't interested in talking to him. We drove along for a while in silence.

"Well, look like everybody is out this evening," he said, looking around at the Negroes staring at us as we went by. I didn't answer or look at the Negroes. I kept my eyes straight ahead of me, fixed on the road.

When he got to our house, he stopped right at the front gate. Raymond was sitting out under the pecan tree and most of the children were out in the yard. I jumped out of the truck.

"Wait, I'm gonna get my clothes. I'll just put them in the back of the truck," I said to Cassidy as he got out of the truck too.

"Hey, Ray! Come over here a minute. I wanna talk to you," Cassidy called to Raymond.

I stood by the gate for a while and looked at Raymond as he shuffled toward the sheriff, half grinning like he was scared of him. Instead of coming through the gate past me, he went through the driveway. I ran up the walk into the house. Mama was standing right inside the living room as I entered.

"What you have to go git Cassidy fer? All them people up in the quarter was sittin' out there lookin', I bet. Everybody's gonna be talkin'. What you call yourself doin'?"

"What I'm doin' is I'm leavin' here because I am *tired* of this shit. Mama, I'm sorry. I just can't take it. I just can't take this stuff."

"What stuff? What Ray did to you now?" she asked me with her eyes full of water.

"What has he *done*? You know what he's done. Besides he can't *stand* me. I hear him fussing at you every morning. Adline hear it too," I said. Adline was standing there looking sad. When I mentioned her name, she began to cry.

"Don't you take these clothes outta here!" Mama yelled.

"These are *my* clothes! I bought every one of them. Raymond or you didn't pay a penny for them! I'm gonna take them outta here, every one of them," I said as I snatched clothes off the wall, took them out of the cedar chest, and looked for my shoes. "Where my shoes? I want everything I got in this house! I'm sorry, Mama, but I'm never comin' back in this house again. I wish you have a long happy life with Raymond. And if I ever see you again it won't be here."

Adline cried even more when I said I was never coming back and Mama began grabbing the clothes away from me. I could tell she wanted to hit me, but she was scared because Cassidy was outside. I jerked the clothes out of her hands.

"Looka there!" Mama wept. "Just a *wild* woman! Just crazy! People are gonna be talkin' for *years* about this."

"I just don't care how people talk, Mama. I just don't care. They can talk all they want. I'm just *tired* of this! These people just ain't no damn good! Everybody in this fuckin' town ain't no good. I'm gonna *leave* this goddamn town right now!"

After I had piled all my clothes on the bed, I took them out by

armfuls and threw them into the back of Cassidy's truck. I ran in
and out of the house with a load every few minutes or so. Mama
and Adline them stood at the foot of the bed without moving.
Their eyes followed every move I made. Once I came out and
threw clothes clear over the other side of the truck where Raymond and Cassidy were standing. I ran around to pick them up.

"Don't look at me!" I screamed at Raymond as he looked down
at me picking up the clothes. "I'll kill you! Don't you look at me!
These are my clothes! I wish you had been in that house, I'da
killed you!"

"All right, you're leavin' now, whatta you gonna still kill him
about?" Cassidy asked me.

I didn't even answer him. I just turned around and walked back
toward the house.

"I ain't tellin' her to leave here. She is leavin' on her own. Now
if she leaves here, she betta not come back. Makin' a big scene
'bout nothin'," Raymond said, loud enough for me to hear.

"About nothin'!" I shouted. "You know what it's about!"

"Calm down, girl! Calm down! I've had enough of this," Cassidy
said as I stood there puffing at Raymond. I looked around as I was
going into the house for another load. Miss Pearl and everyone living down the road was standing out in their yards looking. *Everybody* was looking. When I had taken everything I thought I had in
the house I got in the truck.

"I'm finished now, let's go," I said to Cassidy.

"Let's go! Let's go where? To Woodville?" Cassidy asked as he
got into the truck.

It struck me then that I didn't really know where I wanted
to go.

"Take me up to Miss Clara and Mr. Leon," I finally said, and we
drove off, leaving Raymond standing in the road.

Miss Clara and Mr. Leon were standing out in the yard when
Cassidy drove up. They helped me take my things out of the
truck. Cassidy just sat there as we unloaded it and didn't say a

word. When we finished, I told him thanks and he left. I sat at
Miss Clara's a long time trying to decide what to do. I wanted very
much to finish the semester in Centreville so I tried to think of
someone I could live with for the remaining six weeks of that semester. I couldn't think of anyone. Miss Clara and Mr. Leon offered to let me stay with them, but I refused because they lived
too close to Raymond and Mama and Miss Pearl. I didn't want any
part of that bottom again. I was about to panic when Miss Clara
suggested that they drive me over to see my daddy and ask him to
help me decide what to do.

As Mr. Leon drove to Woodville, I thought of all my daddy's old
habits—drinking, gambling, and women. I still remembered him
rolling his dice on the floor and how he left Mama for Florence. I
wondered what type of woman he was living with now—if she was
yellow like Florence or brown like Mama. I knew Daddy wasn't
married to her and I wondered if he would be leaving her soon for
someone else.

When Mr. Leon drove up in Daddy's yard, I definitely decided
not to live with him whatever happened. The little rotten-wood
L-shaped house he had rented on my Cousin Hattie's place reminded me of all the little shacks we had lived in before.

"Look like ain't nobody here," Mr. Leon said as he honked his
car horn.

"It's after ten o'clock. They're probably in bed. Emma and
Diddly both go to work pretty early, you know," Miss Clara said,
looking at her watch.

"Who is it?" a heavyset yellow woman asked, peeping out of the
door.

At the first sight of her, I got angry. "So this is Emma, Daddy's
new wife," I thought. "She is just like Florence—yellow, straight
black hair and all."

"Hey, Clara! Y'all get out and come on in," she said. "Diddly and
I were just gettin' ready for bed. Who is that y'all got wit' you?" she
asked as we got out of the car.

"We thought you and Diddly needed some company over here so we brought you some," Mr. Leon said, going into the house.

"Well, we do get kinda lonesome. But who is the company?" Emma asked, looking at me curiously.

"That's Diddly's oldest child. Can't you tell? That's Essie Mae," Miss Clara said.

"Aw! Y'all stop kidding me. It's impossible for Diddly to make a child that pretty," she said, looking at me like she didn't really believe I was Essie Mae. "Y'all come on back in the kitchen. Diddly is back here soaking his corns," she said, leading us to the kitchen.

Because the outside of the house was so broken down and the porch gave under our weight as we stepped on it, I expected to find old broken-down furniture inside. But as Emma led us through the house to the kitchen, I was surprised to see how comfortably the place was furnished. The little living room had a big reclining chair, a plush sofa, a nice set of lamps, and other new-looking things. As we walked through the bedroom, I noticed a big four-poster covered with a beautiful white spread.

Daddy was sitting by the gas range in the kitchen with his feet submerged in a tub of steaming hot water. I hadn't seen him since I was in the eighth grade and hadn't anything changed about him but his mustache which was thicker. He was still as slim as the day he left Mama and didn't look a bit older.

"Diddly, guess who's here?" Emma said to Daddy. "Clara, y'all sit down," she said, motioning to the little dinette set in the corner of the kitchen.

"Essie Mae! What is the matter wit' you?" Daddy demanded after studying me carefully.

Because he had demanded that I tell him what was wrong with me, I didn't answer. I stood there looking at him as though he was a complete stranger who was nosing into my business. In thought, I had considered him my daddy even after he left us. But now he didn't seem like my daddy at all. Standing there, I hated myself for running to him.

"What's wrong wit' you?" he asked again angrily.

I still didn't answer him. Then Mr. Leon spoke up and told him that I had had a fight with Raymond and left home. As I listened to him tell Daddy what had happened, it didn't sound like he was talking about me. Daddy looked astonished when Mr. Leon said that I had gotten Sheriff Cassidy to get my clothes. Suddenly it struck me that I had gone to Cassidy to get help—Cassidy the quiet "nigger hater"!

"Did Raymond put his hands on you?" Daddy asked, cutting off Mr. Leon's story.

"No," I answered.

"Well, what did he do to you then?" he asked.

"Nothing! He just can't stand me. Be running around the house cursing all the time," I said.

Daddy didn't say anything for a while and everybody in the kitchen was silent. I could tell he was angry when he suddenly looked at me and said, "I sho' hate Toosweet get mixed up with them Davises. Ain't none of them no good. How is Raymond treating Adline and Junior?" he asked.

"He don't hate them like he hate me," I answered.

During the course of my conversation with Daddy, I slowly began to feel warm toward him. He didn't seem restless any more and his old urge to gamble and play around with women seemed to have disappeared. He appeared to be having a good honest relationship with Emma. Noticing how much concern Emma showed toward me, I began to like her too. She didn't seem snobbish about being yellow and having straight black hair like Florence did. In fact, she was the first high yellow Negro I had seen who didn't think or act like she was any better than darker Negroes.

Emma and Daddy both seemed eager to have me live with them. They had an empty bedroom and said they were able to furnish it for me. But I had only six weeks left to finish the semester at Willis High so we agreed I would go back and live with my Aunt Alberta. Even though there was a chance I would run into Raymond again, it was better for me to finish the semester in Centreville before transferring.

It was well after midnight when Mr. Leon, Miss Clara, and I left Daddy's. All the way to Alberta's I was scared she wouldn't let me stay with her. She and Mama got along well and I didn't think she would get involved with me leaving home, especially if Mama didn't want me to leave. Alberta and her husband were still up when we got to her house. When Mr. Leon honked, she ran out like she was expecting me. She had visited Mama that evening and knew all about my leaving home. She took me in without a single question and was careful not to mention Raymond. She just said Mama thought I would come and live with her and that she was hoping I would. I was furious that Mama had figured me out so well, but I decided to stay anyway.

The following morning I got up and went to school as usual. I went early because I had expected to be whispered about and pointed at around campus that day. Walking among the students before classes began I didn't notice any whispering or pointing. Once I was in class, I could tell all of my classmates knew I had left home but didn't any of them mention it to me. The whole morning passed without incident. But during the lunch hour I ran into Principal Willis. He was quick to ask me if what he heard was true. When I told him that it was, he immediately offered me the use of his guest room. Looking at him as he stood there pretending he was so interested in me, I thought of Samuel O'Quinn and I hated his guts.

The next person I ran into was Adline and I felt worse after seeing her. She looked so sad and her eyes were all red as if she had cried a lot. I knew she had been crying about me. She hardly had anything to say. I told her that I was living with Alberta and asked her to come see me on Sundays. She smiled a little then.

When I got back to Alberta's that evening, I discovered a note from Mama. The note read:

Essie Mae if you don't come home I'm gonna kill myself. Ray ain't mad with you. He told me he won't bother you if you come back home. Please come back home! I miss you.

Mama

I didn't know what to say. I just knew that it would be best in the long run if I didn't go back there to live. So I didn't answer the note.

A couple of days later, it rained and I found I had left my raincoat and umbrella at home. I sent Alberta's little girl with a note and asked Mama to send them. She sent the raincoat and umbrella back with everything else I had forgotten and she also sent another note, saying that if she found anything else she would send it too because she didn't want me to keep sending down there for stuff. I realized then that Mama wouldn't let me see any peace as long as I was living with Alberta. She would always be sending me notes or something, trying to make me feel sorry for her and guilty about leaving home.

That evening after making arrangements with my teachers to take midterm exams, I moved my things to my daddy's.

Daddy was glad that I had come back. He didn't know how to act around me. He went out of his way to be nice and treated me as though I was a child. I could tell it gave him pleasure just having me around. Sometimes I caught him looking at me with a grin on his face like he didn't believe I was there. I knew he wanted me to call him Daddy. But I couldn't. However, every time I called him Diddly he looked sad and I felt awful. I managed to choke out "Daddy" for a while. Finally I stopped calling him either Daddy or

Diddly. I just said "hey, look" or "you" whenever I wanted his attention.

Emma made the matter worse by bluntly asking me to call her Mama. She kept telling me about "my baby Lillian," who was her only child and was now twenty-five years old, married, and living in Baton Rouge. "Lillian is crazy about Diddly," Emma would say. "She hugs and kisses him and calls him Daddy and have no qualms about it. I don't know why I should expect you to call me Mama when you don't even call your own daddy Daddy." But I didn't stop calling her Emma and she got used to it.

Emma and Daddy both worked. Emma worked at a potato factory in a nearby town in Louisiana and Daddy as partner in a four-man independent timber business. The most enjoyable thing about living with them was the fact that I didn't have to get a job. They passionately disliked most of the whites in Woodville and were against me working for them.

"I don't want you working for these no-good ass white men around here," Daddy said bitterly. "They don't do nothing but mess over those Negro girls working in their houses."

Knowing what I did about Negro maids and white men in Centreville, I had no argument for him. I just took his word and accepted their offer of ten dollars' allowance a week to do the general housework and mow the lawn at home.

It was Thursday when I left Alberta's to live with Daddy. That following Saturday before he went to work, he told me he had given Emma money for us to go into town and buy furniture for my room. He said he had given her enough for me to get whatever I wanted. I was all excited about buying furniture. It was the first time in my life that I would have a room to myself and I was seventeen years old. All that morning I was thinking about how I would fix my room up. I wanted to make it look just like the students' rooms I had seen in magazines, with a single bed, a bookshelf filled with books, and a desk with a good lamp. I had planned to go to a secondhand store and get most of what I wanted, since I wanted to save most of the money for books. But when we got into town, I discovered Emma had other ideas. She went straight to the most expensive furniture store in Woodville. I said, "Are we gonna buy stuff here? Don't they have any second-hand stores in town?"

"Secondhand stores! I wouldn't have no shit in my house other people done slept on. We can afford furniture here!" Emma snapped as she looked around for a salesman.

"Well, Mr. Brooks, I'm back again," she said to a tall, slim red-haired salesman who came running over to us as soon as he recognized Emma. "Have y'all got them Hollywood bedroom sets in yet?" she asked, grinning.

"Hollywood bedroom set! In that little raggly-ass house," I thought to myself.

"Sho'," said the salesman, leading us to the bedroom section. "So you finally talked Diddly into buying that set, huh? I thought you would, so I kept you in mind when we placed the order."

Since I had come there to live I had gotten the feeling that Emma didn't really want me around even though she had acted very friendly when I first met her. I had thought the way Daddy treated me made her a little jealous or something. Now, I thought she was just using me to get furniture money out of Daddy.

I asked the salesman if he had any single beds. He pretended he didn't even hear me. He was too busy pointing out a cream-white bedroom set that looked like it should belong to some movie star. The dresser looked longer than the room Emma was going to put it in. There was a big bed with a beautiful pink bedspread, a dresser, and another piece too. The whole thing nauseated me. When Emma said, "I'll take it," I felt like running back to Daddy's and packing my suitcase again.

The morning after we went shopping for furniture, Emma woke me up early, knocking on the living room door and yelling, "Essie Mae! Essie Mae! Get up. We're gonna spend the day with Mama them."

I got mad with her because she didn't ask me if I would *like* to spend the day with her parents. She just told me that I would, as if I didn't have any choice. "Just like I didn't have any say-so in buying the furniture for my room yesterday," I thought.

I got up but took my time getting dressed and eating breakfast. I didn't want to go out there to see her parents and relatives because I thought they were all high yellow and would treat me like Miss Pearl them.

All of Emma's close relatives, except her sister Janie who lived next door to us with her husband Wilbert and their five children, lived off Highway 61 between Woodville and Natchez. Our first stop was at Emma's sister Ola's house. Ola had ten children. Before Daddy stopped the car they were swarming around it like bees. When Daddy got out, they swung around his neck almost pulling him down to the ground. "Uncle Moody, we thought y'all wasn't comin'. We was just about to go play," a tall teak-colored teen-ager with light brown wavy hair hanging to her waist yelled as she clung to Daddy's neck. Another teen-ager who looked just like her stood clinging to Emma's arms. They were two of the most beautiful girls I had ever seen. They didn't look Negroid, Caucasian or anything, they just looked pretty. They were so outstandingly beautiful they overshadowed the other children to the point where one hardly noticed them.

After all the excitement died down, Emma introduced me, saying, "Mildred, I want y'all to meet Diddly's oldest child, Essie Mae."

Mildred looked at me startled for a moment, then said, "Uncle Diddly, I don't believe it. Auntie, are you kidding?"

"Sho' didn't take after Diddly, huh?" Emma added.

"Uncle Diddly, how did you get a child that pretty?" one of the teak-colored twins asked. Looking at her I felt so ugly. In comparison to her, Daddy and I both looked like monkeys.

We were at their house for about an hour when Emma suggested that I go with her to meet her mother and father who lived next door. When we walked in, her mother was sitting at the fireplace with a blanket wrapped around her feet. I was startled to see that she was even darker than I was. "Poppa," as Emma called her father, was out in the woods in the back of the house. Because Emma looked like the product of a mixed marriage and her mother turned out to be so dark, I wondered about Poppa. I knew of cases in Centreville where white men lived openly in common-law marriage with Negro women. Even though they were not allowed to marry because of the state law against mixed marriages, the children bore the name of the father. In another case I'd heard of, a Negro preacher had performed the marriage ceremony and the white man was listed as Negro on the marriage license.

As Emma and I were leaving, Poppa came walking around the house with an armful of logs. I wasn't surprised when I saw that he was as white as any white man I had ever seen. I stood in the yard a few feet from him and Emma as they talked, trying to decide whether he was actually white. He even talked like a white man. I wanted to ask Emma if he was white but I was too embarrassed. So I just assumed that he was.

When we left her parents, Emma carried me to meet her younger brother Clift and his wife Ruby who lived in the next house. Clift had five children. When they saw Emma coming up the little hill to their house, the two older ones ran and swung around her neck. They looked like they were so glad to see her. It was then that I began to really like Emma. She seemed to be the big influence in that family. The children and adults alike all admired her. She had a way of making people turn on to each other.

Walking back to Miss Ola's house, I saw people going in and out of the big, empty-looking building that sat just across the road.

As we got closer, I could hear lots of noise like a party was going on. It was the family café.

When we walked inside, I felt the closeness of Emma's family. The children were dancing to a tune on the juke box. Daddy and all of the adults sat around in one corner talking and telling dirty jokes. I felt a little out of place in the beginning so I stood alone watching the teen-agers. Emma had gone over where Daddy and the rest of them were. She told one of those dirty jokes of hers which sent Daddy them into a roar of laughter. Now she started dancing with the teen-agers, her big belly shaking more than any other part of her. All the teen-agers stopped and gave her the floor. She did some reels and rocks that I had never seen before, while all the children chanted, encouraging her to put on nastier cuts. When the record stopped, she called to Mildred, "Hey, Mildred, bring me that deck of cards behind that bar." Right away Mildred rushed them to her. "Come on, Essie Mae, I'll beat you twenty straight!" Emma shouted to me.

We walked over to one of the little broken-down tables and pulled up a couple of crates and started a game of Coon King as all the teen-agers stood around looking. I beat her three games in a row and she gave up. Then all the teen-agers in the café wanted to play me. All that evening I sat playing Coon King and thinking, "If only Raymond had been as strong as Emma, Mama wouldn't have all that trouble with his people."

chapter

S E V E N T E E N

The following Sunday, as usual, Emma, Daddy, and I went out to Ola's café and spent the entire day there. It was about ten o'clock when we returned home. We had had a bite to eat and were getting ready for bed when we heard screaming. It was Emma's sister Janie, next door.

"Lord Jesus somebody help me! Help me! This man done gone crazy."

Emma jumped up and ran onto the porch. Daddy and I ran after her. By the time we got to our front door, Emma had crossed the yard and was entering Janie's kitchen. Suddenly Daddy stopped short.

"Wilbert! What's wrong wit' you?" he shouted. He made an attempt to move but stopped abruptly again. Looking over his shoulder as he spoke, I saw Wilbert, Janie's husband, standing outside their house pointing a shotgun in their kitchen window. "Man, don't shoot in that window, you'll kill all them children."

"That bitch better open this door! Um gonna kill her goddamm ass tonight," Wilbert exclaimed, running around to the porch. He leaped up on it like a wild man and almost jerked the screen door off its hinges.

"Y'all help me wit' this door!" Janie screamed to her children as Wilbert kicked the wooden door with enough force to shake the entire house.

"Emma! Don't just stand there, help wit' this door. I tell you this man done lost his mind!"

Wilbert had broken the latch and upper hinge and the door was now tilted open at the top. The weight of bodies propped against it inside kept the bottom hinge from crumbling. Wilbert pushed until almost the entire door tilted. Then all of a sudden he stopped pushing, stood back, pointed the gun at the bottom of the door, and fired a shot. The door now hung loosely as if the weight on the opposite side had disappeared, and Wilbert stood there calmly looking at it. Gradually the calmness left his face and he started trembling like a frightened child. For a while everyone inside the house was quiet. Then we heard Emma moaning incoherently.

Daddy leaped off the porch and ran into Janie's kitchen. I started to follow him but stopped. I was sure I would find Emma near death on the floor.

Just as I finally made my mind up to go in and see what had happened, Daddy appeared in the door with Emma in his arms. He held her nearly two hundred pounds as if she were weightless. As he came into the light, I could see that Emma was covered with blood from her waist to the tip of her toes. I looked into her drawn face and walled-in eyes. I was sure she was dead. Daddy's face was hard and cold. He looked as if he was dead himself. He walked past Wilbert on the porch and didn't even look at him as Wilbert said:

"Oh, Emma, what have I done to you? Oh God, what have I done? Diddly, I didn't mean it, I didn't mean it. . . ."

Daddy walked carefully down the steps. As he walked toward the truck that belonged to Cousin Hattie's husband, Albert, I got a feeling that it wasn't his strength that supported Emma but some supernatural force that carried them both. I couldn't move as I watched Daddy carefully place Emma in the back of Albert's pickup truck. He got up in the truck with her, placed her head in his lap, and then sat there as though he expected the truck to know what to do. I had just thought of going to get Albert to drive the truck for them when Albert and Cousin Hattie came running out of their house. Albert didn't even look at Daddy sitting in the back of the truck. Without a word he and Hattie got up in the front and drove away. Then Janie came running out of the house with her blouse half on looking like a ghost. She didn't even look at Wilbert as she ran to their car. Wilbert ran after her and jumped into the driver's seat.

I stood on the porch for a while looking out into the darkness. I felt as if I had just witnessed the end to some weird movie and my life was all wrapped up in it. I looked over at the broken door to Janie's kitchen. I knew that Janie's five kids were inside and that they were awake. It frightened me that I didn't hear any stirring around. Somehow I got up enough nerve to go and see what they were doing.

I walked up on Janie's porch as if I was treading on an earthquake. The door hanging on its bottom hinge made the house look like it was collapsing and I got the feeling I was collapsing with it. Inside the kitchen, all five of Janie's children stood with their eyes fixed on the pool of coagulating blood. I had never seen so much blood before; I noticed fragments of flesh and shattered bone mixed with it. Leon, the oldest boy, was crying. The younger ones appeared to be in a trance. "Let's put them to bed, Leon," I said. After I helped him do that, we cleaned up the blood together.

"Her whole foot, Essie Mae—her whole foot is gone, shot to pieces," Leon said, still crying. When he told me that, I was glad—glad that it was only her foot. From the way she looked when Daddy brought her out, I had thought it was her stomach. "Auntie ain't never did nothin' to us. She even gives Mama money to buy us food when we run out. Now look what Wilbert done done to her. I could kill him, I could just shoot that man's brains out."

As dawn approached that morning, Leon and I were still up, nodding over a cup of black coffee. I sat up all night while he talked to me about Wilbert and Janie and voiced his concern about what would happen to the children if they separated. As I had listened, I relived all the fears I had had when Mama and Daddy separated. Leon knew that he would have to stop school and work to help Janie take care of the children if Wilbert left them, because he knew Janie was pregnant. I shed a few tears with him as he said, "What kin I do, Essie Mae? These white people here don't pay nothin' to grown men. You know they ain't gonna pay a twelve-year-old boy nothin'. I use to work for that old white lady who live up the road and she paid me four dollars a week to work like a slave." I thought of the old white woman I had worked for who paid me seventy-five cents and two gallons of clabber milk a week and all the others I had worked for for practically nothing.

At seven that morning, I left Leon sitting before a cup of black coffee. I still remember his trembling hands as he motioned to thank me, his red swollen eyes, the tight lines across his forehead, and his nervously shaking feet. He looked like an old worried man with a twelve-year-old frame.

I was just beginning to enter a restless sleep when Daddy came home. He told me that Emma's brother Clift was going to pick me up at ten o'clock before he went to work and drive me to Centreville to spend the day with Emma in the hospital. Then Daddy was off to work himself like nothing at all had happened. I didn't even have time to ask him about her.

At the thought that I would have to go to Centreville, I got sick enough to be in the hospital myself. I hadn't planned to go back at all. As Clift drove down the main street later, I rested my head on the back of the seat and pretended I was asleep. I didn't want to see the town or recognize anyone I knew. Once I was in the hospital, I didn't leave Emma's room except for occasional use of the rest room.

I spent a week with Emma in the hospital. During that time, I learned to admire her strength even more. She was livelier than anyone who visited her and refused to let anyone feel sorry for her. Each day when the doctor came in, she cracked jokes with him and carefully observed what he was doing. When I saw her foot for the first time, I turned away unable to look at it. It was all swollen and bloody and one side of her ankle and heel had been blown off.

What I admired most about her was the fact that she didn't blame Wilbert for shooting her. She placed the blame where it rightfully belonged, that is, upon the whites in Woodville and how they had set things up making it almost impossible for the Negro men to earn a living. "It ain't Wilbert's fault," she told a group of her relatives. "Him and Janie wouldn't be fightin' if Wilbert could get a good job and make enough money to take care of them children. If these damn white folks ain't shootin' niggers' brains out they are starvin' them to death. A nigger can't make it no way he try in this fuckin' place. Don't y'all go blamin' Wilbert for this. It wouldn't bring my foot back or make it well. Neither would it help him feed his children." "If there were more Emmas in this world, Negroes would be a whole lot better off," I thought every time I looked at her in the hospital.

After a little over two weeks in the hospital, she was discharged. Once she was home, we all got back on regular schedules. Her only visitors now were members of the family who came and spent a few hours with her on Sundays. After about a week of sitting up in the house all day alone, she began to feel sorry for herself. The old spirited Emma I admired gradually disappeared. Every evening when I got home from school, she would have thought up a million little things for me to do. Then she would complain about everything. I couldn't sweep the floor clean enough to please her. I began counting the weeks until graduation when I could leave there for good.

Meantime, I was going to Johnson High School every day. But the students were so boring there, that I longed for my old classmates at Willis High. The Johnson boys and girls didn't seem to care about anything but each other. They sat up in class all day passing notes back and forth. And most of the teachers didn't give a damn whether they learned anything or not.

The one thing I didn't miss was my old basketball team. The team at Johnson High was much better and more exciting. While I was at Willis, I had heard a lot of talk about the big tall Johnson players. I went out and watched them practice a few times to discover everything I had heard about them was true. They shot jump shots and passed the ball like boys. I tried to talk myself into a practice game but every time I went out and watched them I got scared and chickened out.

One afternoon I was sitting up in class bored stiff when one of the players came in and told me Coach Dunbar wanted to see me. When I got outside, Dunbar was sitting on the ground in the middle of the court surrounded by the players. The girls stared curiously at me as I walked toward them. Some whispered and hunched each other.

"Miss Moody, we have been waiting long enough for you to make up your mind to play with us," Dunbar said without even looking at me. I didn't know what to say so I just stood there. "Hicks called me up a few weeks ago and accused me of stealing his best player," he continued. "I thought the man was out of his mind. And today I discovered the fine new chick who I've had my eyes on for weeks turns out to be Hicks's best player." All the girls laughed when he said that and one asked:

"What Mrs. Dunbar gotta say about that?"

"Shhh! Shhh," Dunbar said holding a finger up to his mouth. "Pull up a chair and sit down," he said to me.

I sat down on the ground among the girls. Dunbar then told me that his best player was sick. He said they had some tough games coming up and that he wanted me to replace her. I told him that I wasn't interested in basketball any more and hadn't planned to play with their team. But somehow he talked me into getting into the practice game that evening.

During that game, he put three big guards on me who looked like female football players, then stood back and watched them slaughter me. He stood watching every move I made without saying a word. I knew he was sizing me up as a player and I tried to impress him, but those big girls were smothering me and I couldn't even move. When the game was over, I walked away hurting all over and vowing that I would never touch a basketball again.

But one evening, when I passed the basketball court and the girls were out practicing, Dunbar spotted me and called me over. He told me that they had their toughest game coming up the following day and asked me to play. I was going to refuse, but then I remembered how basketball had helped me forget my troubles and pass the time at Willis High, and I changed my mind.

The next morning around nine o'clock we boarded one of the school buses. Our destination was Liberty, Mississippi, where we were to meet one of the toughest teams in the state. On the way, I was extremely nervous. I began to wonder if I were as good as Dunbar and Hicks thought.

When we got to Liberty, we were greeted by a woman who was the exact picture of Emma. She reminded me of the fight we had had the night before. The strategy I had thought up on the bus vanished and throughout the entire game I thought of Emma and played as if I was playing against her. When the game was over, all my teammates ran to me and began swinging around my neck. We had won by two points. The score was 43 to 41. I had shot 27 points and had broken a tie of 41–41 the last ten seconds of the game.

During that spring I hardly saw Emma or Daddy at all. Johnson High had become one of the most challenged teams in the state and I was one of its most valuable players. In addition, I organized Johnson High's first gymnastic and tumbling team, ran track, did substitute teaching, and spent all day Sunday in church. Before I realized it, I was practicing for graduation.

Wilkinson County was a recipient of one of the new "Separate but Equal" schools built throughout the South as a result of the 1954 Supreme Court Decision. It had been under construction on a fifty-two-acre plot in Woodville for almost a year, when I graduated in 1959. The following September all the Negro high schools in Wilkinson County would consolidate into the new school, giving it nearly three thousand students and eighty to ninety teachers. It was supposed to be the largest new school in the state and it caused much bickering among the Uncle Tom principals and teachers in the county. Many of the teachers sought positions as heads of various classes or departments and the principals challenged each other for the position of head principal. Since Willis was the biggest Tom among the principals of the merging schools, he was the one chosen by the state board for this job.

My class was scheduled to be the first to graduate in the new school building. Most of my classmates were all excited about this but not me. As most of them, students, teachers, and principals alike, were bragging about how good the white folks were to give us such a big beautiful school, I was thinking of how dumb we were to accept it. I knew that the only reason the white folks were being so nice was that they were protecting their own schools. Our shiny new school would never be equal to any school of theirs. All we had was a shiny new empty building where they always had the best teachers, more state money, and better equipment. The only exciting thought I had about graduation was the fact that I was finishing high school and that would enable me to leave Woodville.

During the graduation ceremony each merging school was to be represented by the student with the highest average. I had a straight A average—the highest of all the seniors. But because I was a product of two schools, I had been ruled ineligible to represent either. My homeroom teacher thought it was very unfair for me not to be the main speaker. She wanted to make an issue out of it but I wouldn't let her. She didn't understand and thought it was stupid of me not to want the speech after earning it. I told her I felt that the only thing I had truly earned was my diploma and if she could arrange for me to get it without marching and becoming a part of all that confusion, I would be grateful. Then she called me crazy and forgot the whole thing.

The night before graduation, I packed all of my clothes and prepared to leave for New Orleans the following morning. I said good-bye to Daddy before going to bed because I wouldn't see him again before I left. I had expected him to object to my leaving so soon after graduation but he didn't. He just told me that I should try and get into college in New Orleans and that he would help me as much as he could. That night I felt closer to him than ever. I realized that he had known all along that I was not happy there, that Emma mistreated me when he wasn't home, and that he also understood Emma too and loved her enough to be patient with her until she was up and out of the house again. As Emma listened, I could tell she was touched by the feeling Daddy had shown toward me. The next morning, she got up and was nicer to me than she had been in a long time. She acted as though she was sorry that I was leaving. She even told me she would come to my graduation if she could wear shoes. I responded politely to her newly shown interest in me but by this time I didn't care whether she came to my graduation or not, and I knew Daddy wouldn't come because he had never been to a public event in his life. So the next morning I walked out of the house alone, my cap and gown swinging on my arm.

When I got to the auditorium, the seniors from Willis High and the other schools had arrived. There were about three hundred seniors standing around in caps and gowns. The whole scene was a barrel of confusion. I stood back looking at everything as if I were not a part of it. Once all the students were there, the teachers went through a big ordeal about which class should lead the march. It was finally decided that the Willis High seniors would lead. Then the seniors at Johnson High objected and the whole thing started all over again.

We were about two hours late. About five hundred restless people were sitting in the auditorium and Mr. Willis was pacing the stage nervously. The teachers who were lined up to march ahead of us shouted to our teachers in an attempt to rush them into a decision as to how we would march. At about ten o'clock the pianist started playing. I don't remember which class marched in first or who led the lines. But somehow we all got seated. I was so tired that I fell asleep as soon as I sat down.

When everything was over with, one of the students tapped me on the shoulder and told me we were about to march out. Marching down the aisle half asleep, I spotted a woman who looked just like Mama sitting next to the aisle in back of the auditorium. At first I had thought she was Mama but as I got closer she looked much too old. I couldn't make up my mind if it was Mama or not. As I passed, staring at her, she whispered, "Essie Mae, wait on me outside." I stopped, holding up the entire line as I took a good look at her. I saw that it was Mama and I was too hurt to say anything. I just walked away as tears began forming in my eyes. Instead of continuing the march outside with the rest of the students, I cut out of line and ran to the ladies' rest room. I stayed in there a long time crying and blaming myself for the way Mama looked. When I left home, I hadn't written her once even though I knew she worried about me. I was so concerned about getting my feelings hurt that I forgot that she even had feelings. At that moment, I hated myself for the way I had treated her.

I must have been in the rest room a long time, because when I got outside, everyone was leaving. A long line of cars and buses moved slowly off the school grounds, and a steady flow of people walked alongside them. There were only a few people left standing in front of the auditorium. I looked for Mama among them. When I didn't see her, I almost panicked. I thought she had left. If she had, I knew she was terribly hurt because I didn't wait on her. I ran down the walk toward the road.

"Essie Mae! Essie Mae!" I heard her calling me.

I looked around but I still didn't see her. "Essie Mae! Essie Mae!" I heard her voice again and started running up the road.

"Girl, where you runnin' to?" a voice called out of a pickup truck moving slowly along beside me. I turned my head slightly and kept running. "Essie Mae!" This time Mama's voice sounded as if it came from the truck. I turned and there was Mama leaning over Junior waving at me.

"Where you runnin' to? Kin we give you a lift?" she said jokingly. Junior stopped the truck and I ran around and jumped in beside Mama. She was grinning as if she was so glad to see me. She looked at me as if she wanted to hug me but she didn't.

"How you gonna git out to Emma them?" she asked me.

"I was gonna catch a ride back with Cousin Hattie."

"Hattie them done gone. I thought you was going back wit' them. But they said they hadn't seen you." Mama paused for a while, then asked, "Why don't you come go spend the night wit' me?" I didn't answer, I just looked at her. She dropped her head and said, "You don't have to stay wit' us, you kin spend the night with Alberta and come see me tomorrow...." I looked at Mama again and she seemed even older, she had lost weight and an air of sadness surrounded her. I sat there feeling so guilty.

"O.K., Mama," I said at last, "I'll go but I can't stay but a couple of days because I want to go to New Orleans and get my job at the restaurant."

Mama smiled and for a second she looked young again.

part three

COLLEGE

chapter

EIGHTEEN

Two days after graduation, I arrived in New Orleans hoping to earn enough money at Maple Hill so I could go to one of the inexpensive colleges there. I had spent all my little savings while living with my daddy. After Emma was shot, Daddy was the only one bringing in any money and he had cut off my ten dollars a week allowance. I was afraid to work for the whites in Woodville, so I just lived off my savings.

But now I found myself in a real mess. Business in the restaurant that summer turned out to be worse than usual. For some reason, many of the regular summer school students hadn't returned. Every evening, I got sick as I counted my tips. I was averaging only two or three dollars a day. At this rate, it would take me a whole year at the restaurant to save enough money for college, and I was scared to take the chance of being out of school that long.

In a panic I wrote Coach Dunbar. He had said that I had a good chance of getting a basketball scholarship to one of the junior colleges in Mississippi that had a girls' team. I hadn't even considered going to college in Mississippi and I was tired of playing basketball. But now I had no other choice. I received a reply from Coach Dunbar about a week later, saying that the Natchez College coach, Mr. Lee, was considering me for a scholarship and would write me soon. While I waited to hear from him, I didn't even count my tips. I just threw them in a big cigar box and prayed that Mr. Lee would say that I was accepted.

It was well past midsummer before I got a letter and all Mr. Lee could say was that he was "considering" me. I began thinking that maybe I was stuck in the restaurant and that I would probably never get to college. But finally late in August, a second letter came, telling me that I had gotten a scholarship, and that I was to report to school in two weeks. I ran to my cigar box and was surprised to find that I had saved nearly four hundred dollars. I still didn't know whether I'd gotten a full scholarship, so I was scared to spend any money. I bought only a few cheap clothes, and since I had always wanted a suitcase of my own, I splurged on a three-piece eighteen-dollar luggage set.

All the way from New Orleans to Natchez, I was excited and anxious. I sat on the bus dreaming about Natchez College. I had seen all of the colleges in New Orleans with their beautiful spacious campuses, large modern dormitories, and many new buildings. The only thing I knew about Natchez was that it was a Baptist school. That didn't impress me one bit. I just hoped it was a *rich* Baptist school and that it would be modern like the schools in New Orleans.

When the bus arrived in Natchez, there were lots of cabs lined up waiting. I grabbed the first one I saw. As the cabby headed for the college, I checked myself over. I thought I was looking real good with my little blue luggage set and the matching blue dress I wore. I leaned back in the seat and ran my hand admiringly over the largest piece in the set, which lay on the seat beside me. I stroked it gently, feeling proud that it was mine. Suddenly my eyes jumped. My hand had come to a big hole in the side of the suitcase. My pajama top was sticking out of it. I felt like I had been wounded and that what was showing through that hole was my own insides. "Look at this," I thought. "Eighteen dollars for three pieces of cardboard." I didn't feel so pretty any more as I tried to glue the cardboard back together with spit. I got so wrapped up in trying to fix the suitcase before getting to the college that I didn't realize we were there until the cabdriver said, "O.K., miss, this is it."

"Is *this* Natchez College?" I asked as I sat there looking out of the cab at an old two-story red brick building, on which was engraved "Women's Auxiliary."

"You never been here before?" the driver asked as he opened the door for me.

"No, it's my first year. Is this all there is to the school?" As I stepped out of the cab, I could see only three little old brick buildings.

"Sho' is!" he said, pointing to the red brick building. "This is where the women live."

When he said that, I felt like jumping right back in the cab and going back to New Orleans. I didn't want to get involved with this place. I didn't even want to see anyone connected with it. I was so upset I walked off without paying the man. I was halfway up the walk with my eyes fixed on that "Women's Auxiliary," thinking how it sounded so religious and looked so dead and dull, when he called after me, "Hey, miss! The fare is thirty-five cents."

I walked back and handed him a dollar, telling him to keep the change. I never would have given him such a big tip, if I hadn't been so depressed.

"So this is what I left New Orleans for," I thought, walking toward Women's Auxiliary again.

When I got inside the building an old lady came up to me and said, "I'm Mrs. Evans, the matron, and you is ... ?"

"Miss Moody," I said.

"Just bring in your luggage and follow me," she said. Her speech was too proper. I could tell that she was one of those uneducated women who get this kind of a job and try to pretend that they're educated. "They always give themselves away with those broken verbs," I thought as I listened to her. "I bet the teachers here don't even have college degrees."

Mrs. Evans showed me to a room, told me where the showers were, and said I could rest until dinner. She asked me so many questions and seemed so concerned about me, that I got a nice motherly feeling from her.

I didn't see any other girls around, and I began to wonder if I were the only student there. I put some of my things away and went to take a shower. When I looked out of the window in the shower room, and saw a big beautiful school building down the hill from the dorm, my mood changed. "Oh, that's where we have our classes," I thought happily.

When I went down to dinner that evening, I discovered that more students had arrived. I asked one of them about the new building I had seen. My gay mood disappeared when the student said, "Oh, that's a high school. I wish it *was* a part of this place."

As soon as I took a look at the food I got an urge to take over the kitchen. I met the cook and told her about my restaurant experience. She asked me if I wanted to work in the kitchen and I told her I would love to. Later I found out that all students on full scholarships had to work part-time. I was glad that I had found something to do that I really liked. However, after working in the kitchen for a while, I found I couldn't stand it or Miss Harris, the cook. I had thought I could really help improve the food, but I came to realize there wasn't much you could do with baloney and potatoes, our two main dishes.

What was even worse than that was the fact that Miss Harris was the biggest Uncle Tom on campus. I soon discovered the main reason she liked me. She wanted me to be her stool pigeon and tell her everything that was happening in the girls' dorm. Every morning she would ask me something personal about one of the girls. I wouldn't tell her anything so she started being nasty.

She would crack little jokes about my looks to the other girls in the kitchen and always found some criticism of me. One morning I got up feeling a little sick. When I got to the kitchen a few minutes late Miss Harris was cursing and slinging spoons everywhere. She threw a spoon at me and told me to stir the grits. I threw it right back at her and walked out. I went straight to the Dean's Office and asked for another work assignment. That morning I started work as an assistant librarian.

In high school, I had thought that Johnson High had the biggest girls on any basketball team. But the Natchez College team had the biggest girls I had ever seen on or off the basketball court. One girl was six feet four. She was so big she could hardly move. There was only one girl on the team shorter than me. All the rest were five feet nine and over. At first I was a little frightened of playing on the team but Dunbar had spread the news through Mr. Lee, the boys' coach, that I was good. I found out after a few days' practice that all the girls were scared of me.

The coach of the girls' team, Miss Adams, was a well-built young woman in her late twenties. Mr. Lee had worked with us for a few days then turned the team over to her. Most of the girls didn't like her because she was real tough and was the Dean's secretary and suspected secret lover. She set up a lot of stupid rules for the basketball girls and was always crying to the Dean if the girls got out of hand and wouldn't obey the rules. She was jealous of every girl the Dean looked at and the Dean looked at plenty. She was especially suspicious of me because the Dean was always giving me "bad eyes." Oddly enough she was not suspicious of the two girls who were actually known to be screwing the Dean. In fact, the three of them were almost buddies. They all probably had the same attitude where the Dean was concerned. "He doesn't want any more from her than from me," was the way one of the girls had put it.

The Dean was a tall, slim, well-preserved mulatto in his late forties. He liked tall shapely girls and seemed to like me a lot. He had told one of the boys that I had one of the most beautiful bodies he had ever seen in a pair of shorts. He even went so far as to tell him he knew that I was scared of men. He often came over to the gym when we were practicing. He would sit and look at us like a sex maniac who hadn't had a woman in years. Every time I passed him he would stare at me and I would look away, then he would laugh like a lunatic.

Some of Miss Adams' rules were just too much. I constantly felt like I was in prison. We couldn't even go out of our rooms at night. We were only allowed to room with basketball girls. And I turned out to be the odd player without a basketball roommate. We always practiced a couple of hours before dinner. Then we had a compulsory study period from seven to nine, during which time Miss Adams checked to see if we were studying; at ten she would check again to see if we were in bed.

One day I was feverish and stayed in bed all day. The next day, I met Miss Adams on my way to class.

"Did you check the bulletin board to see what your assignment is, Moody?" she asked.

"No. What is my assignment?" I asked, thinking to myself, "What in the hell have I done?"

"Check the board and see," she said, switching away.

I went back to the dorm to check the bulletin board. There she had posted her punishment list, and my name headed it. "Moody—wash windows in the library," it said. I got furious. I ran all the way from the dorm to her office. She was sitting behind her typewriter when I opened the door.

"Don't you know to knock before you enter an office if the door is closed?" she scolded.

"What did I do, Miss Adams? Why have I gotta wash all those library windows?"

"Don't come asking me what you did! You know well enough!"

"If you don't tell me what I did, I ain't gonna wash no windows," I snapped.

"Look, Moody, don't you come screaming at me! You know damn well you had company during study hour last night."

"And where was I?" I asked.

"You were in bed with your back turned to me!" she shouted.

"I was in bed because I was sick! I didn't even go out of my room all day. And I am not gonna wash no windows!" I said, really getting worked up. "I noticed one thing on the board, Miss Adams. You assigned me to do the windows and all the other girls gotta do is sweep a floor or dust a chair or something. Yet I gotta wash a whole library full of windows when I didn't even do anything. I wouldn't get up on a ladder and be embarrassed before all the other students even if I *had* done something!"

"Stop shouting at me, Moody! Who do you think you are? Are you going to obey the rules or not?" she shouted.

"I am not gonna do it."

Without saying another word, she got up from her desk and rushed past me into the Dean's office. She seemed glad she finally had an excuse to see him about me.

I went back to my room and got in bed. I was so mad I didn't even feel like going to class. A few minutes later, Mrs. Evans knocked on my door and said the Dean wanted to see me downstairs in the lounge. When I got downstairs, he was standing in the door. He glanced at me freshly then quickly changed to his official look.

"Miss Adams tells me that you just cursed her out and said you were not going to obey her basketball rules. What's your story?" he asked suspiciously.

"My story is this," I said and went on to tell him what had happened. I made it clear to him that I thought Miss Adams' rules for the basketball girls were very unfair.

When I had finished talking, he said, "Well, your story is inter-esting, but are you gonna wash the windows? I think you ought to since Miss Adams said you should."

"Even if I didn't do anything, but just because *she* said I gotta wash some windows, I gotta do them?" I asked angrily.

"Well, in a dispute between the teachers and the students, the teacher is always right," he said stuffily.

"Well, I don't see things that way and I am not going to wash those windows."

"We'll see! Let's see what the President has to say about this!" he said. I was sure he was bluffing.

"You do what you gotta do!" I said angrily and walked away. I went on back upstairs and got in bed again. About an hour later, Mrs. Evans knocked on my door and said the President wanted to see me. I went downstairs and there he was, standing out on the walk waiting. He was rared back with his hands on his hips and his pot belly in the air. I walked up to him and looked down at his greasy slicked-down hair. I was more than a foot and a half taller than he was.

He looked up at me and asked, "What's going on with you and Miss Adams them? The Dean tells me you just sacked out him and Miss Adams. What's going on with you?" he said, puffing and blowing like a little dragon.

"Nothing is going on with me. I have been in my room sick for two days. Miss Adams came to my room last night and found another girl in there. I was asleep and didn't even know she had been there or the other girl. I am not gonna wash those win-dows...."

"What's this about washing windows?" he asked.

"She got all these stupid rules made up about what basketball girls gotta do. I think they are absurd. First of all, Miss Adams don't like me. Now you look, come on go in the dorm and look at what she assigned the other girls...."

"Now don't get excited," he said. "Where is this here list?" he asked, following me up the steps.

"It's right here on the bulletin board," I said, going into the lounge. He stood on his tiptoes to read it. "When I leave here," I said, "I'm going back to bed. Now if you insist that I wash those windows, I'm going home." He didn't say anything, he just left.

A few days later, I found out that the President had scratched out all Miss Adams' rules. Dean and Miss Adams were furious with me after that. Miss Adams immediately dropped me from first string to second to side girl. Then basketball became the biggest drag I had ever known.

After about two months of Natchez College, I was completely fed up with it. I had never in my entire life felt so much like a prisoner, not even when I worked for white Klan members at home. When I was home Mama had trusted me to take care of myself. She never told me I couldn't go here or do this or that. During the summer when I went to New Orleans and Baton Rouge in search of work she never questioned my reason for going. Now at Natchez College, I couldn't even go to the store a block away alone or without permission from the matron. She would always send two of us together and then time us. If we were gone longer than she expected, she would come after us.

Every Friday evening she would post two lists on the bulletin board in the dorm—one for movies and one for shoppers. Then she called the movie house on Saturday morning to find out when the picture started and ended. When we were all ready to go into town, on Saturday afternoon, our regular shopping time, she would line us up like cows and march us up Union Street. On Franklin, the main shopping street in Natchez, we all split up. We were usually given two or three hours to shop or see a movie. Then we were supposed to meet her at five on the corner of Franklin and Union so she could march us back to the dorm. She didn't really have to come into town with us. It was just a front so the good sisters of the Baptist churches in Natchez, who supported the college, would see that she was protecting us from evil influences.

In spite of that big front Mrs. Evans put on, the faster girls put on an even bigger front. As soon as we split up in town, I would see them bopping around corners, hopping in cars and going here and there when they were thought to be in the movie. At the end of the shopping period as Mrs. Evans and the rest of us stood on the corner waiting for them, they'd come running up smiling and blushing and out of breath. All the girls would look at them and know they had done something. But Mrs. Evans would give them her motherly smile and asked innocently, "Did you see a nice mooo-vv-eee? What was playing?"

"Mrs. Evans, it was such a *nice* picture. But they had a little trouble with the film, that's why we're a little late," Bernice, one of the little fast sex pots, would answer sweetly. As soon as Mrs. Evans turned away, Bernice would give us a big wink and we would all crack up inside.

Sometimes Mrs. Evans would ask what the picture was about. One of the girls always knew the title of the picture and could make up a story about it. We would stand there hurting with laughter as we watched gullible Mrs. Evans nod her head and take it in.

As we marched back down Union Street to the dorm, we would pass the house of one of the little old Baptist sisters who always sat on the porch every Saturday. Mrs. Evans would nod and smile and the little old sister would smile back, giving Mrs. Evans her approval. A lot of the girls would smile and nod at her too. But Bernice always took the cake. Instead of smiling and just nodding like the rest of the girls, she would say something like, "How you feeling, Sister? It's really a nice day, isn't it?" The old lady would smile back at Bernice and look as if she wanted to say, "They sho' got some nice girls over there at the college." When she gave Bernice that little smile, Bernice, in her little short Saturday dress with the deep open pleat in the back showing half of her thigh, would switch away laughing.

Everything the girls did on campus was also supervised by Mrs. Evans. Every evening after dinner, we were allowed to walk around on the campus in front of the dorm. Mrs. Evans always found some excuse to be in front of the dorm too. If she wasn't out there picking flowers in the spring, she was raking leaves in the fall and feeding birds in the winter. Just before dark, she would go into the dorm and blink the lights. This was a signal for all the girls to come inside. She would blink the lights three or four times, then come out and stand on the steps to watch the boys walk the girls back to the dorm. "Come on in, girls, the social period is over," she would call, just like a mother talking to a seven- or eight-year-old playing in the yard after dark.

The only times we went out of the dorm at night were on Wednesdays and Thursdays. Wednesday we spent an hour in prayer meeting and Thursday the library was open from seven to nine. Mrs. Evans would walk out with her Bible on Wednesday, and Thursday night she sat in the library knitting.

Once every two weeks on Friday or Saturday night, a social was given in the dining room. This was the only time boys and girls got together after six o'clock at night. The social usually started at seven and was over by nine-thirty or ten. We weren't allowed to dance and the only games we could play were Bingo, Pin the Donkey's Tail, Scrabble, and other word games. We couldn't play any game that resembled a card game, not even Old Maids. But we were allowed to make up games and play them. One night one of the girls made up a game similar to Simon Said which went like this:

Stand up, turn around, comb your hair and sit down.
Stand up, turn around, stomp twice, sit down.

Everyone in the room would participate. They all tried to outdo each other and come up with something more original than the last person had come up with. One of the boys in calling his turn said, "Stand up, turn around, do the twist, sit down." He let us twist about fifteen minutes before he called the other move. Some of the students did some nasty cuts. Mrs. Evans, taking part in the games too, was so upset that she threatened to have the boy expelled. After that, the boys stopped attending the socials and the girls were very unhappy. Soon the socials were cut out altogether because didn't enough girls go to them. Now the only time girls with boyfriends on campus got together was on Sunday from four to six. Then they sat up in the lounge with the door open and Mrs. Evans sat right across in the next lounge knitting.

The boys weren't too upset over the campus rules because they could go anywhere without permission, spend the night off campus, and do just about anything else except openly tamper with the girls on campus. And most of the boys had no desire to mess with the campus girls because they had three or four girls in the city.

The majority of the girls living in the dorm came from homes with real strict Baptist parents. And a lot of them had been sent on church scholarships. They were some of the most backward girls I had ever seen. They had lived a sheltered life of Baptist fantasy. They were the girls who had courted the nice boys at church, who sneaked kisses in parked cars on the church lawn, who had never spent a night away from home except with relatives who were just as strict as their parents. For them, it was a big thing to be away from home even in a place as prison-like as Natchez College. Once away from their parents and relatives, they were also the girls most likely to end up pregnant—because at home sex was a big mystery, tabooed in conversation and bitterly condemned in church.

With the exception of Bernice and her three or four friends, the basketball girls were the healthiest girls on campus. Most of them had boyfriends, loved sports, had a good sense of humor, and didn't care too much about anything. I didn't particularly consider myself in their class. But if it was necessary for me to be in a class at all, I would have chosen theirs. Instead, I was a loner just as I had been in high school. The only thing I had in common with them was basketball.

When the basketball team started traveling, I really saw how hypocritical everyone at the college was, especially Mrs. Evans. Even though we had a lady coach, Mrs. Evans came along to chaperone us. She was as glad to get away from Natchez as we were. As we boarded the bus on campus to leave, she came on the bus in her long dark "mourning" dress, all plain-faced and motherly. But as soon as we got to the college we were playing, she pulled off that long black dress, put on a short stylish one, and made herself up with powder, rouge, and lipstick. She shocked all of us. She didn't follow us everywhere like she did at Natchez. Neither did she speak in her little proper speech. She was an entirely different lady and the girls liked her because she let them dance and do anything they wanted to—just about. But as soon as we got back to Natchez College, she put on her old self again.

By the time the school term ended, I was so sick of Natchez that I was sure I wouldn't return the following year. But the schools in New Orleans cost just too much money, so a few weeks before the new term I decided to go back.

chapter

NINETEEN

That second year at Natchez, I discovered that I had changed. The year before almost every boy on campus had tried to make it with me, especially the basketball boys, and I had turned them down one after the other. Now I found myself wondering whether I should have been so rude to them. When I saw girls and boys sneaking kisses out under the trees, I got curious. Sometimes I wished I had a boyfriend. I was twenty years old and I had never been kissed, not even a smack on the lips. I wanted to know how it felt.

There was a new basketball player on campus named Keemp, whom all the girls and boys were talking about. He was tall—six feet five—and slim. Besides being tall, he had a "cool" about him that most girls liked. So they all went around talking about how handsome he was. It was early October and we hadn't started practicing yet, so I didn't know whether he was a good player or not, but I certainly didn't think his looks were anything special. He looked just like my daddy without a mustache and I never thought Daddy was handsome. I used to see Keemp walking

around on campus and wondered what was it that all the girls saw
in him. Then too he made me wonder what all the women had
seen in my daddy when he was young.

One Sunday after church, I was leaving chapel when Keemp
walked up to me and said, "So you are Anne Moody, huh?"

"Yes. Why?" I asked, and kept walking.

"I heard a lot of talk about you," he said, walking beside me.
"Where are you going now?"

"To the dorm," I answered.

"If you'll slow down, I'll walk you over there," he said coolly.

For the first time in my life I slowed down for a boy. I was a little surprised at myself.

As we walked together, Keemp didn't try to force the conversation. He hardly said anything and whenever he did it was like a
brother to a sister. When we got to the dorm he asked if he could
walk me to dinner. I again surprised myself by answering yes.

Because Natchez College was so small, most of the relationships between girls and boys were a public thing. Everybody knew
everybody else's business. The students were all shocked when I
started going with Keemp, especially the sophomore boys who
had tried to make it with me the year before. A couple of the guys
who had tried hardest came up and bluntly asked me what did I
see in Keemp or what did Keemp have to offer me that they didn't.
I was a little surprised at the girls' reaction. Most of them seemed
glad that I had finally decided to join the club. So much so that
they started giving me all kinds of advice about how to handle
men.

When Keemp started playing basketball, I really began to like
him. He had the longest limbs I had ever seen. As he moved down
the basketball court, he was so light he looked like he was flying.
He could just walk up to the goal and dunk the ball with ease.
Through basketball, he became the most popular boy on campus.

Keemp tried to kiss me many times but I wouldn't let him. I
always told him that I had a headache or something. When we

traveled to play other teams, all the other boys and their girls on the team kissed around on the bus. Keemp, the best player on the team, sat beside me begging me to kiss him. Everyone else on the bus knew that Keemp wasn't getting anywhere with me, and most of the boys began to tease him.

There were a couple of girls on the team who were having spasms over Keemp. One of them sat in the seat behind us and late at night she would start clawing on the seat like a big cat. When Keemp started answering her clawing, I went to one of my friends, seeking advice on how to kiss. She told me that I didn't have to do anything but part my lips to Keemp and he would do the rest. For the next two months I thought of how I would part my lips. Then one night I dreamt that Keemp and I were kissing around nude on the back seat of the bus and just as we were about to have intercourse, I woke up screaming. I was so frightened by the dream, I began to think that if I kissed Keemp it might lead to something else. The mere thought of getting sexually involved caused me all kinds of anxieties. But I had a tremendous guilt about treating Keemp the way I did when another girl would have treated him better, so I made up my mind to quit him and let that clawing girl have him.

One night in November, when we were playing Philander Smith College in Little Rock, Arkansas, I decided that this would be the night I would quit Keemp. Since the game was one of our biggest, I decided to wait and tell him after it was over. I knew we would lose if he wasn't at his best.

Keemp shot forty-some points during that game. He played better than I had ever seen him play. Just about every time he raised his arms, it was two points for us. When the game was over, the rest of the boys hugged him down to the floor, then picked him up and declared him "King of Basketball." As I watched him play and then saw how everyone loved him, it suddenly dawned upon me that he was a terrific person and that I was a fool to be thinking about quitting him.

When the boys let him go, he walked up to me smiling. Without saying a word, he put his arms around my shoulders and walked me to the bus. As he touched me, a warm current ran through my body.

As I sat on the bus beside Keemp that night, a feeling I had never known before came over me. He held my hands, and it seemed like every hormone in my body reacted. Neither one of us said a word. As the bus was coming to a stop, Keemp leaned over and gently placed his lips on mine. They were like a magnet slowly pulling my lips apart. Once my mouth was open his tongue explored areas that had never been touched by anything but a toothbrush. I completely forgot where I was until one of the boys sitting near us started banging on the basketball and yelling.

"Jesus! Y'aaaall! It finally happened! Keemp done did it!"

The bus had stopped. The lights were on and everybody was looking at us. Keemp wouldn't stop. He pretended that he didn't even hear the yelling, that we weren't on a bus surrounded by spectators. I tried to pull away but I was so weak I couldn't control myself, so I just gave in to his kisses.

Didn't anyone on the bus say one word or stir, not even Mrs. Evans. No one made a move to get off the bus until Keemp and I did. When Keemp finished kissing me, I saw that he had lipstick all over his mouth. My first reaction was to wipe it off real quick before anyone could see it. Keemp just smiled as I wiped it off. When I finished, he took me by the hand, pulled me up out of the seat, buried my head in his shoulder and we walked off the bus.

I was very embarrassed about the fact that my first kiss had been such a public thing. But I didn't regret the kiss at all. Once we were back on campus, Keemp and I greeted each other with a kiss every time we met.

We never did hide behind trees or posts to sneak kisses like the other students. When Mrs. Evans blinked the lights for the girls to come in, I'd give Keemp a smack on the lips right in front of her. Soon most of the other girls started smacking kisses on their boyfriends in front of Mrs. Evans too. Finally, one day Mrs. Evans called me in for a "conference" and accused me of leading the kissing game on campus.

During the first six months of our relationship I was happier than I had ever been. Keemp turned me on so much that I made the first straight-A average that had been made at Natchez in many years. Studying was a cinch and everything else seemed so easy. But that spring when the basketball season was all over and the excitement of traveling was gone and boys and girls began swarming all over each other like bees, I slowly began to drift away from the whole scene. I had gotten tired of being part of "the club." There was something about the way couples were relaxing into relationships and making them everything that bothered me. I didn't want to get all wrapped up in Keemp the way some of the other girls did with their boyfriends. My relation with him had gradually become a brother-sister thing. He could tell I was moving away from him, so he got himself a girl in the city. I wasn't even jealous and I didn't say anything. I just didn't care. I knew I would be leaving him behind next year and figured he'd have somebody else. I pretended that I didn't know he had another girl and went on being friends with him. He was the best friend I had had since Lola, and I told him everything.

I had spent all of my money buying foxy clothes when I was high on Keemp. Now I was down to ninety dollars, and I was beginning to worry about where I would go to college next year. It was about two months before school ended and I tried to hold on to that money. I figured I could make at least two hundred dollars at the restaurant the coming summer even if business was bad. But I knew that still wouldn't be enough to get me into a good senior college. The closer it came to school ending, the more depressed I got.

One Saturday morning I got up feeling disgusted. I was sick of having to worry about where my next penny was coming from and how I would get to school next year. I looked at that ninety dollars in my drawer and thought to myself, "This time I'm gonna go out and have me a big steak and buy me a fifty-dollar dress!" I went down to breakfast a little late, and when I got there I saw a whole commotion going on. I stood on the steps looking for a while wondering what in the hell was happening. A large group of students were standing around a table, talking and gesturing. Others were picking in their plates like they were looking for something. The noise was tremendous. As I headed down the steps, Inez, one of my classmates, who was sitting at the table where all the students were gathered spotted me and called out:

"Hey! Moody, come here! Will you look at *this!*"

Then someone else called, "Go and get yours, Moody, and see if you can find any."

I walked over to Inez. She pointed with her fork to the half-eaten plate of grits in front of her. At first I didn't see anything.

"What's going on?" I asked.

"Can't you see? Looka there!" she said, poking something in the grits with her fork.

"What's that?" I asked, seeing a little white lump at the end of her fork.

"What's that? A goddamn *maggot*, that's what it is," one of the boys said loudly.

"A *maggot!* In the *grits?* Where did it come from?"

"Don't y'all get mad, that's just a little present from Miss Harris, tryin' to show us how much she love us," somebody cracked, and we all laughed. I looked to the kitchen, and saw her standing in the door. I remembered the mornings she used to sling those spoons at me because I wouldn't Uncle Tom to her. I hated her guts.

"Oh-oh," somebody said, as Miss Harris started to come over to us, "here come Mother Maggot now."

"What's goin' on out here?" she asked.

When she said that everyone pointed to Inez's grits. Miss Harris looked. "What's wrong with the grits, they's a little too done?" she asked.

"Look a little closer, Mama. We're just admiring your latest ingredients," some wise guy said.

She leaned over, almost sticking her big nose into the grits.

"Watch out, it'll bite you!" someone screamed in mock fright. This really cracked everyone up.

When she finally saw the maggot she turned angrily on the crowd and demanded, "Who's playin' jokes out here?" She glared at one of the boys who was still laughing. Everybody suddenly shut up. Miss Harris stood there with her hands on her hips, blowin' and a puffin' like she was about to blow us all away. I could feel everyone tense up and grow angry. Suddenly I noticed one of the girls who helped in the kitchen motioning frantically and pointing toward the pantry. I walked very deliberately past Miss Harris toward the kitchen.

"Where you goin', Moody!" Miss Harris yelled as I neared the kitchen. "You stay outta that kitchen! You don't work down here any more!"

"Yes, but I am a student here and I do have to eat this *shit!*" I shouted back. By that time the others had seen the girl beckoning too and a lot of them began following me to the kitchen.

"What's goin' on here! What's goin' on here! Calm down! Stop it!" Miss Harris screamed, running after us. "Come outta that kitchen, Moody! Somebody go get President Buck! Moody, I'm goin' to have you sent away from here yet!"

I knew exactly where the grits were kept from the time I had worked in the kitchen. I went straight to the pantry and saw that there was a big leak from the showers upstairs. The water was seeping right down onto the shelves.

"How long has this been leakin' down here?" I called to the girl who had been motioning to us. But now that Miss Harris was standing there she was too scared to answer.

"That's okay. I'll find out," I said. "You want President Buck? *I'll* get him," I yelled at Miss Harris, who was standing there fuming. I went angrily by her once again, followed by several students. We were about to go over to President Buck's house, which was right next to the dorm, when somebody remembered that he was in Vicksburg for a big meeting.

"O.K.," I said. "We don't eat until he gets rid of Miss Harris and that leak is fixed!"

We were just outside the dining room door and a couple of the guys stormed back inside, hollering, "Boycott! Boycott!" One of them started yelling, "Maggots in the grits, maggots in the grits! We ain't gonna eat this cooked-up shit!" Then students began to walk out, leaving their plates on the tables right where they were. (Usually we were required to empty our own trays.) Then we all gathered in front of the dorm. Some of the students were arguing. I could tell that a lot of them weren't too hot on boycotting. One of the guys came up to me.

"Okay, Moody," he said so everyone could hear, "you runnin' this shit! How we gonna eat? I don't have one penny in my pocket!" Several of the others joined in with him. "Yeah, Moody, what's your bright idea now? How we gonna come up with some money?"

"Just 'cause you ain't got no money, you gonna go down there and eat that shit? I would *starve* first!" I shouted. There was a mixed reaction of yells and boos. The same guy who had come up continued the debate.

"O.K., so we don't go to the kitchen! You tell us how we're goin' to eat!"

"I got some money," I said quickly, thinking of my ninety dollars. "Who else got some?" There was dead silence.

"I got twenty bucks," Inez yelled out.

"Ain't nobody else got some money?" I asked.

"Fuck money, man!" one of the guys shouted. "Let's telegram Buck and tell him to come back here and take *care* of this shit."

The crowd cheered.

"O.K.," I said. "But meantime, stay outta that dining room!"

We tried to telegram Buck but we couldn't get him. Since it was Saturday and Mrs. Evans was going to march us into town shortly I took fifty of my ninety dollars and gave twenty-five of it to the boys. I told them to buy enough food to last a couple of days. Then a group of girls and I went to town as if we were going to do our regular Saturday shopping. Instead, we borrowed a couple of hot plates from students who lived in the city and bought enough food to last us for a while.

On Sunday, the next day, we all sat around on the campus eating fried chicken that we cooked ourselves. It was like a big all-day picnic. Miss Harris had a girl from the kitchen telling the students there was lots of chicken, ice cream, and homemade cake in the dining room, but the students just called her an Uncle Tom and told her to get lost.

Monday morning, just as my alarm clock went off at six-thirty, Mrs. Evans knocked on my door and said that President Buck was in the lobby to see me. When I got down to the lobby, he was standing with his back to me looking outside. He didn't look like a little fiery dragon this time.

"Mrs. Evans said you wanted to see me," I said to his back.

He turned quickly as if I had frightened him out of his thoughts. "Look here, Moody, I came in last night at two o'clock and found Miss Harris and Mrs. Evans sitting on my doorstep waiting on me. I'm getting pretty tired of you upsetting everybody around here...."

I stood there listening until he had his say. Evidently, Mrs. Evans and Miss Harris hadn't told him anything about the maggots in the grits or the leaking shower. They just told him that I had started a boycott and hadn't any of the students eaten since Saturday and barrels of food had gone to waste.

When he finished I told him what had happened. Then I denied that I was responsible for keeping the other students out of

the dining room. I told him that I could only account for myself
and that I would never go back down there and eat Miss Harris'
cooking. When he said that he would get the showers fixed immediately and have Miss Harris throw out the grits, I told him that it
wasn't only that but that Miss Harris herself was nasty—she knew
the grits weren't any good and she cooked them anyway.

By Wednesday the showers were fixed and the spoiled grits had
been thrown out but Miss Harris was still there so none of the
students went back. I split my last forty dollars with the boys and
we bought food to last till the weekend, hoping that Miss Harris
would be gone by then. But she wasn't. On Sunday, President
Buck called a special chapel meeting. He got up and made a lot of
excuses for Miss Harris. He said that she had reported the leak
over two weeks ago to him but that he was so busy running around
trying to get money for the school to *buy* food for us that he had
forgotten about it. The students didn't really believe his sob story,
but since all our money and food were gone, the students slowly
began to drift back, one by one. I didn't go back at all, but one of
my friends told me that now Miss Harris was wearing a snow-
white uniform and a hair net every day.

I managed to get by for a while on what friends brought me
from the city. But I started losing so much weight and got so hungry all the time that I wrote Mama and told her what had happened. She and Junior came up and brought me a couple of
cartons of canned food to last the remainder of the semester.

At mid-semester when our averages were tallied, I had the
highest average in the class. Soon after the averages were posted,
I was called to President Buck's office. He asked me if I had any
plans for going on to college next year. I didn't know what he had
up his sleeve so I came on very cool with him in the beginning.
But before our meeting was over I could tell that he really liked
me in spite of all the disturbances I had caused on campus. So I
broke down and admitted my worries about going on to college.
Then he told me that I could probably get a full scholarship with

my high grades. He said that a test would be given in a week or so for scholarships to a couple of the colleges in Mississippi and that he wanted me to try for them.

The following week, the registrar from Tougaloo College, the best senior college in the state for Negroes, came down. I took the test, and a week before school ended, I received notice that I had received a full-tuition scholarship.

I could barely wait until September, when I was to enroll in Tougaloo College as a junior. Meanwhile, I tried to find out as much as I could about the school. A girlfriend of mine at Natchez, after learning of my scholarship, told me that Tougaloo was not for people my color. When I asked her what she meant, she merely said, "Baby, you're too black. You gotta be high yellow with a rich-ass daddy." At first, I thought she was jealous because she didn't get a scholarship. But then I thought of the high-yellow registrar who had given me the scholarship exam. So I went back to my girlfriend for more information. She tried so hard to convince me not to go, I ended up by accusing her of being jealous and we had a big fight. A few days later she came to my room.

"Look out that window, Moody, I want to show you something," she said, pointing at a white student out on the lawn talking to some of the guys. "She's a student at Tougaloo and she ain't white either," she said and left my room. I didn't believe her—that girl was as white as any woman I had ever seen. I went right downstairs and asked her if she was a student at Tougaloo. When she said, "Yes, I go there," without even looking at me, I just walked away thinking that Tougaloo wasn't the place for me, after all.

That summer, while working at the restaurant, I seriously started looking for a school to attend in New Orleans. Since L.S.U. was only thirty-five dollars a semester for off-campus students I thought of going there. But when I learned that it had just been integrated and that all the teachers were white, I talked myself out of going. I was afraid that those white students would murder me in class. I was an A student but those A's were from Natchez. I didn't have much competition there, I thought. Besides Natchez wasn't anywhere near as good as L.S.U. I didn't want the white students to act like they were smarter than me just because they had gotten off to a better start.

I kept thinking and talking to myself until September rolled around. By then it was too late to register in any of the schools in New Orleans, and I knew it. So I sent Tougaloo ten dollars to reserve a room for me and five dollars for my registration fee.

One morning in mid-September, my grandmother woke me before she went to work. I got up and made sure all my things were packed. Four hours later I was headed for Tougaloo on "good old Greyhound."

By the time I arrived in Jackson, Mississippi, that evening, I was tired as hell. After wandering around the small segregated station for a while, I asked a little dark-skinned man with glasses how to get to Tougaloo. He smiled and asked, "Are you a freshman?"

"No. I'm a junior," I said.

We introduced ourselves. He told me his name was Steve and that he was a senior.

"I'm waiting for a cab," he said. "We could split the fare if you would like."

All during the seven and a half miles to the college I was dying to ask if he was the only black student there. But instead we talked about our majors. I didn't like him because he tried too hard to impress me so I just sat back in the seat without saying much. At last, we came to a sign that said TOUGALOO SOUTHERN CHRISTIAN COLLEGE 1/4 MILE. Soon we were riding on campus, but by now it was too dark for me to see what it looked like.

The driver dropped Steve off first because he had about five suitcases and two trunks stacked in front of my luggage. When we stopped in front of the boys' dormitory, some of the boys ran out to help with his suitcases. One of them looked inside the car and said, "I'm Jimmy. What's your name, pretty?" I was so mad, because he was yellow, that I didn't answer. I wondered how many of the other students were yellow, and probably with rich-ass daddies. Anyway, it pleased me to know that mulattos liked dark brown-skinned girls. Maybe some of the others would too, I thought.

A few minutes later, as I was carrying my own luggage into Galloway Hall, the girls' dormitory, I noticed several girls passing in and out of the lounge and going upstairs. Not all of them were yellow, either. As a matter of fact, some of them were even black. This really pleased me. I was disappointed when I went to the room that had been assigned me and found one of those white-looking girls sitting on a bed, smoking a cigarette. "Hi. I'm your new roommate," I said.

"I have a roommate," she answered. "You mean you are *one* of my roommates." I looked at her and wondered if the other one was as white as this one. If so, I couldn't take this diplomatic shit.

"Trotter sleeps there," she said, pointing to the lower half of the bunkbed against the opposite wall. "Therefore, you gotta sleep up there."

"Fine with me," I said, but I was thinking I would ask to be assigned to another room no later than tomorrow morning. Without saying anything more to her, I began to roll my hair in big rollers. While I was looking in the mirror, I could see her smiling and sizing me up.

"My name is Gloria," she said.

"Mine's Anne," I answered.

"Where are you from? I take it that you're a junior since they put you on this hall."

"Yes, I'm a junior. I'm from Natchez College."

"My home is Natchez," she said. "I lived down the street from the college."

I was getting tired of her probing, so I simply said, "Oh." I took my pajamas from a suitcase and got into bed—the top bunk.

"Trotter's not coming until next week. You can sleep in her bed if you like."

"Thanks," I said, and went to sleep thinking how much I would hate the school.

The next morning I got up around six because I wanted to get a glimpse of the campus. After I had taken a shower and dressed, I went outside. I could not believe it—this place was beautiful. It was large and spacious. There was evenly cut grass everywhere and huge old oak trees with lots of hanging moss. Birds were singing, and the air was fresh and clean. I must have walked all over the campus in a trance before I realized I was hungry and went to find some breakfast.

I spent the first two days going through the regular college routine—registration, meeting faculty. On Thursday it was announced that there was going to be a "freshmen and new students Talent Show" to be held on Saturday. All that night I tried to think of something I could do that would get me off to a good start. I had the feeling that I had to make that first good impression. I thought of singing a song. That was out—I didn't know the type of song that would impress intellectuals. I could sing real well, but nothing but good old Baptist hymns. Since some of my teachers were white, I knew they would not have the right impression after that. Eliminating singing, I thought of dancing. I could not do anything except exotic, café-style dances. I remembered the exotic dance we'd had in high school. The one that the principal stopped before it got started. I couldn't do that, because I didn't want my white friends to think I was vulgar. Finally, I gave up the idea of participating in the talent show and went to sleep.

The next morning, walking through the lounge, I noticed some girls doing exercises. That's it, I thought. If I could get them to help me, I could do some tumbling. One of the girls was very agile and graceful.

I walked over to her and said, "Hi. My name is Anne. You're very good."

"I'm Freddie," she said. "Are you a freshman?"

"No, I'm a junior."

"Lucky you, I'm just beginning."

"That's not so bad. It seems like only yesterday that I started. Once you get that start, the time really rolls."

"Yeah, but the thing is getting started," she said.

"I'm on my way to breakfast," I said. "We could talk on our way over, if you like." She looked at me as if she thought I was funny or something. I guess she thought I had a hangup on girls. Finally, sounding a little embarrassed, she said yes. By the time we got to that old white frame dining hall, she had said she was willing to do the tumbling in the talent show. We agreed to practice in the lounge that same afternoon.

We met around three. She was good, she was really good. We practiced the Fly and the Bear until we had them perfect. While we were doing the Fly for the last time, we were interrupted by a short, muscular dark-skinned boy.

"My, my, my. What acrobats," he said. "I'm Paul. Do you girls mind letting me in on what's going on?"

Freddie, who was standing on my knees, seemed a little embarrassed again. I was too. I had to set this cat straight.

"Look," I said, "we're practicing for the talent show tomorrow night."

"No! No! I didn't mean no harm," he said. "You see, my major is P.E. I was just interested. I was trying to think of something to do in the talent show, too. I think maybe the three of us could win first prize."

He looked sincere, so I said, "O.K. What can you do?"

"Just about anything."

"Can you tumble?" I asked.

"Yes," he nodded.

"What about the Logroll?"

"Sure."

"O.K. That's great," I said. "We have a team. Here is what we're going to do. The Bear, the Fly, the Logroll and some tumbling."

"I can walk on my hands," he said. "Let's do that."

"I can't do that," I said, "but it's O.K. if you do it."

The three of us agreed to meet the next day and practice for an hour or so. We needed other people, so I went around looking for other girls to squat for us. I found three just before dinner. They thought I was crazy, but I didn't mind. Freddie also had three or four friends she could depend on, so in about three hours we were to go on stage as unorganized as could be.

The show started around eight-thirty or a little after. I was kind of nervous about all those scared freshman girls that were supposed to squat for us. They were so damn scared we would fall on them or something that they might suddenly disappear before we went on. I kept an eye on them to make sure they didn't. There was not too much on the show except singing for quite some time. It was getting boring. Then just as I began to think of how we were going to show up all those singers, I was shocked. My eyes were glued to the stage as a tall, skinny guy was doing the limbo. He was well over six feet four. Each time he passed under the pole, it was lowered. It kept going down lower and lower, but no part of his body ever touched it and I mean it was low. Finally it was lowered about a foot from the floor. Boys in the audience began betting each other that he couldn't do it. Everyone was all worked up.

I knew he was going to win. He went under that pole twelve inches from the floor, feet still flat, and didn't touch that damn pole anywhere.

Next a guy came on playing a set of bongo drums. The audience seemed impressed. They were rocking heads and clapping hands rhythmically with the drums. I didn't think he was so good. I just thought they were still excited from the performance of that limbo cat, because I was.

Now it was our turn. I beckoned to my crowd, and we walked backstage looking like a bunch of beatniks or something. Boys began bellowing, to Romana, the M.C., "What's going on, Ramona? What are they going to do?" Ramona shrugged her shoulders, indicating she didn't know. When she introduced us, she said, "Next on the program we have Anne Moody and the Tumblers."

I put my best smile on and walked to the center of the stage. The reaction from the crowd was wild, especially the boys. They started shouting, whistling, and carrying on something terrible. I wore some skin-tight red short shorts over black leotards and looked even taller than five feet nine. I guess it was the contrast of the colors that started the boys. Maybe they thought they were going to see some sort of a burlesque. I stopped blushing and smiling long enough to say, "We'll do the Bear followed by the Fly, the Logroll and a little bit of tumbling." Someone in the audience said, "Sho-o-o-o-nuff!"

I beckoned for Freddie. She walked to the center of the stage and we stood facing each other. I again turned to the audience and said, "If this act reminds you of a bear, let us know by your generous applause." As I stood facing Freddie again, I opened my legs by placing my feet about two feet apart; then I braced myself. Freddie placed a hand on each of my shoulders. She then jumped around my waist, locking her legs behind my back with her hands clasped to my ankles. I leaned forward until the palms of my hands were flat on the floor. I began to walk on my hands and feet. The audience applauded long after we had stopped. The Fly and the Logroll also received lots of applause. Then Paul and I tumbled. We started by diving over one person squatted on hands and knees on the floor. Each dive was completed with a forward roll. Another person squatted next to the first one, we then dove over two, then three lined up side by side. After that, one person was placed on top of the one squatting on the center. We completed that dive successfully. This left the audience tense and worried that something would happen. By the time Paul and I had dived over nine bodies stacked like a pyramid, the entire audience was standing. The applause went on and on. We all came to the center of the stage and bowed. As we were about to walk off the stage, Paul started walking all around on his hands. The audience laughed, whistled and applauded even louder, and some shouted, "More! More! More!" I knew we were too much for them. After a couple of songs the show ended. We received first prize, the limbo cat second and one of the girls that sang got the third prize.

After the show was over and our prize had been awarded, the Dean of the College stopped me to say that we were good, and that if we would like to do something with our talent, the school was ready to help us. He asked me if I was a physical education major. I said no, that my intention was to major in biology. A few days later he sent the physical education instructor to talk to me and I told her the same thing.

Soon after classes began, I discovered I had only one Negro teacher for the semester. I began to get scared all over again. I had never had a white teacher before. Now I wished I had gone to L.S.U. I knew the whites in New Orleans weren't half as bad as the ones in Mississippi. I kept remembering the ones in my hometown, those that had Samuel O'Quinn murdered, those that burned the entire Taplin family, and those I worked for who treated me like a secondhand dirty dish towel. I got so damn mad just sitting there thinking about those white teachers, chills started running down my back. I knew that if they were at all like the whites I had previously known, I would leave the school immediately.

By this time I had become friendly with my second roommate, Trotter, who was even darker than me. I asked her whether or not she thought I could take it at Tougaloo. If I couldn't, I didn't want to waste my little bit of money.

Trotter laughed and said, "Girl, I had the same feeling when I was a freshman. I came here scared stiff. I didn't know what to expect. I had heard about the white teachers, the high yellow students and all."

"I'm an A student, Trotter, but I've never had any of those tough white teachers. I know I'm going to have some problems."

"No, no, Moody. I came from a little country high school too. Here I am an honor student. You can do the same. All teachers start off pretending they are hot shit. It's the same with Negro teachers. You know that."

"If their disposition is anything similar to the whites in my hometown, I couldn't take that shit either," I said.

"But these teachers here on campus are all from up North or Europe or someplace. We don't have one white teacher here from the South. Northern whites have a different attitude toward Negroes."

"I certainly hope so," I said, relieved of some of my fright.

By the time mid-semester exams rolled in, I had gotten off to a very good start. It looked as though I could make the honor roll if I continued at this pace. I began to relax. I started taking time with my clothes, watching my weight, and wanting to look good. Keemp had not written in about a month. I started to worry because I knew that most of my girlfriends at Natchez College wanted him. I thought I'd better find me someone at Tougaloo to pass the time with. I knew I'd have to do some looking since there were three girls on campus to every boy. Three or four guys showed lots of interest in me, but they were already dating girls I knew. Finally, in December, I started dating one of them—a guy named Dave Jones.

As it turned out, when the semester ended, I didn't make that damn honor roll. I came out with three points less than I needed. I rationalized by blaming my downfall on my adjustment to the white teachers. However, the real cause was that damn Dave. All he could think of after we had gone together for a month was going to bed. I didn't even like him that much—not enough to go to bed with him anyway. When we had a so-called "adult discussion" about sex, as he called it, I told him that I was a virgin and I was afraid to be screwing around on campus. He kept telling me that he would take care of me, that he wouldn't hurt me, and all that shit. To get him off my back, I told him that I would only when I felt that I was ready. After another month or so when I still wasn't ready, he got mad, and one night in the park, he tried to take me. We were walking back from the "Greasy Spoon," a little student hangout right outside the campus gate. He had drunk quite a bit of beer and now he suggested that we sit on a bench and talk for a while. I agreed only to discover that he wanted to start petting and going on.

"Dave, let's go. O.K.?" I said.

"Why are you in such a hurry? It's Saturday night. You could sleep late tomorrow."

"I just want to go," I said, trembling.

"O.K.," he said, "give me one sweet kiss and we can leave."

When I kissed him, I could taste the beer and cigarettes he'd had at the Greasy Spoon. I didn't like this at all, so I drew away. He got mad and jerked me to him, kissing me hard. He started caressing my breasts and breathing on my neck and everything.

"Let go of me, Dave!" I started crying. Then we saw another couple coming through the gate. Dave didn't want to act as if something was going on, so he let me go, but held on to my sweater. I jumped up to leave and tore every button off it. I ran back to the dormitory, vowing I would never see Dave again.

On Monday I got a letter from him begging me to forgive him. He promised to buy me a new sweater and everything. I didn't want to go through that shit again, so I just acted as if I hadn't got the letter. He had asked me to call him, but I wouldn't. I was through and that was that.

One night, shortly after Dave and I had broken up, I asked Trotter what kind of meetings she was always going to. She said, "I thought you knew. I'm secretary of the NAACP chapter here on campus."

"I didn't even know they had a chapter here," I said.

"Why don't you become a member? We're starting a voter registration drive in Hinds County and we need canvassers. Besides, it would give you something to do in your spare time, now that you don't see Dave any more."

I promised her that I would go to the next meeting. All that night I didn't sleep. Everything started coming back to me. I thought of Samuel O'Quinn. I thought of how he had been shot in the back with a shotgun because they suspected him of being a member. I thought of Reverend Dupree and his family who had been run out of Woodville when I was a senior in high school, and all he had done was to get up and mention NAACP in a sermon. The more I remembered the killings, beatings, and intimidations, the more I worried what might possibly happen to me or my family if I joined the NAACP. But I knew I was going to join, anyway. I had wanted to for a long time.

chapter

TWENTY-ONE

A few weeks after I got involved with the Tougaloo chapter of the NAACP, they organized a demonstration at the state fair in Jackson. Just before it was to come off, Medgar Evers came to campus and gave a big hearty speech about how "Jackson was gonna move." Tougaloo sent four picketers to the fair, and one of them was Dave Jones. Because he was chosen to be the spokesman for the group, he was the first to be interviewed on TV. That evening when the demonstration was televised on all the news programs, it seemed as though every girl in the dorm was down in the lounge in front of the set. They were all shooting off about how they would take part in the next demonstration. The girl Dave was now seeing was running all around talking about how good he looked.

Dave and the other demonstrators had been arrested and were to be bailed out around eight that night. By eight-thirty a lot of us were sitting outside on the dormitory steps awaiting their arrival, and they still hadn't shown up. One of the girls had just gone inside to call the NAACP headquarters in Jackson, when suddenly two police cars came speeding through the campus. Students came running from every building. Within minutes the police cars were completely surrounded, blocked in from every direction. There were two cops in the front seat of each car. They looked frightened to death of us. When the students got out of the cars, they were hugged, kissed, and congratulated for well over an hour. All during this time the cops remained in their seats behind locked doors. Finally someone started singing "We Shall Overcome," and everyone joined in. When we finished singing, someone suggested we go to the football field and have a big rally. In minutes every student was on the football field singing all kinds of freedom songs, giving testimonies as to what we were going to do, and praying and carrying on something terrible. The rally ended at twelve-thirty and by this time, all the students were ready to tear Jackson to pieces.

The following evening Medgar Evers again came to campus to, as he put it, "get some of Tougaloo's spirit and try and spread it around all over Jackson." He gave us a good pep talk and said we would be called upon from time to time to demonstrate.

That spring term I had really wanted to do well in all my subjects, but I had become so wrapped up in the Movement that by the time mid-semester grades came out, I had barely a one-point average. Other students who had gotten involved with the NAACP were actually flunking. I started concentrating more on my work—with little success. It seemed as though everything was going wrong.

In addition to my academic problems, I was running out of money. In May I was so broke, I could not pay my last month's bill and was forced to write Mama and ask her to send me thirty dollars. A couple of weeks went by without a letter from her. If Mama had the money, I knew she would have sent it. Apparently she didn't have it, but why didn't she write anyway? Finally I got a letter from Adline, who was working in New Orleans. Mama had written Adline and asked her to send me some money, because Raymond wouldn't let her send me any herself. Adline could only spare ten dollars, and she wrote me that she was sorry I had gone to Tougaloo when I knew I could not afford it.

The letter made me so mad that I was sick all the next week. I decided to write Emma and ask her for the thirty dollars. She sent me forty right away and said that she and my daddy would have helped me more and that they wanted to, but my daddy had been bothered with his back and had not been working.

Emma's money took care of the spring term, but now I was faced with the problem of the summer. I had to make up some credits in summer school, and I was counting on getting a student loan.

One day as I passed the main bulletin board on campus, I noticed a memorandum from the Dean, saying that applications for federal loans had to be turned in before the week was up. The next day I stopped in at the Dean's office to pick up a form. His secretary told me that I was too late. There were too many applicants already. I went to see the Dean, and had to give him my whole damn life history. I didn't like that at all, but I needed the money. I told him I wouldn't be able to graduate next year if I couldn't go to summer school. He wasn't very encouraging, but he gave me a form to fill out just in case one of the other students had a change in plans. My luck was so bad, I didn't believe this could possibly happen.

By now I was so low I needed someone's comfort. I started seeing Dave again, and the same old trouble started. But this time I didn't care so much. School would be out soon and I wouldn't see him again. Dave would graduate if anyone did. He had even received a Woodrow Wilson fellowship.

I took my final exams and was preparing to leave the campus, when I received a notice from the Dean's office. It said that I had been given the sum of one hundred fifty dollars to assist me in summer school. Even though I had asked for three hundred, I started feeling better—better than I had felt in a long time. I didn't know how I would manage on a hundred and fifty dollars, but I knew I would find some way to do it.

During the summer a white student moved into the room across the hall from me. Her name was Joan Trumpauer, and she told me she worked for SNCC as a secretary. In a short time we got to know each other very well, and soon I was going into Jackson with Joan and hanging out at her office. SNCC was starting a voter registration drive in the Delta (Greenwood and Greenville) and was recruiting students at Tougaloo. When they asked me if I wanted to canvass every other weekend, I agreed to go.

The first time I went to the Delta, I was with three other girls. A local family put us up and we slept two to a room. The second time I was there I stayed at the Freedom House—a huge white frame house that SNCC was renting from a widow for sixty dollars a month. This time I was with Bettye Poole, who had been canvassing for SNCC for a couple of months, and Carolyn Quinn, a new recruit like me. We arrived at the Freedom House on a Friday night about twelve-thirty and found fifteen boys all sleeping in one large room on triple-decker beds. They were all sleeping in their clothes. Some of the boys got up and we played cards for a while. A couple of them were from McComb, Mississippi, which was only twenty miles from Centreville. We cracked jokes about how bad the whites were in Wilkinson County. Around 2 A.M. I started to get sleepy and asked where the girls were going to stay. I was told we were going to stay right in the same room with all those boys. I was some shocked. Now I understood why Bettye Poole was wearing jeans; just then she was climbing into one of the empty bunks and settling down for the night. Here I was with only a transparent nylon pajama set to sleep in. Carolyn Quinn wasn't prepared either. The two of us just sat up in chairs until some extra pairs of pants were found for us. The boys explained that they slept in their clothes because they had had bomb threats, and had to be ready to run anytime. They all slept here in this one big room because it was sheltered by another house.

The next morning I woke up to the sounds of someone banging on a skillet and hollering, "Come and get it! Come and get it!" When we walked in the kitchen, the boy who'd made the racket said, "All right, girls, take over. Us boys have been cooking all week." Most of the guys were angry because he had gotten them up in that manner, but they didn't make a big fuss over it. Carolyn and I started cooking. When we announced that the food was ready, the boys ran over each other to get to the kitchen. It seemed they thought the food would disappear. It did. Within five minutes, everything on the table was gone. The food ran out and three boys were left standing in line.

I really got to like all of the SNCC workers. I had never known people so willing and determined to help others. I thought Bob Moses, the director of SNCC in Mississippi, was Jesus Christ in the flesh. A lot of other people thought of him as J.C., too.

The SNCC workers who were employed full-time were paid only ten dollars a week. They could do more with that ten dollars than most people I knew could do with fifty. Sometimes when we were in the Delta, the boys would take us out. We did not finish with our work some Saturdays until ten or eleven, and all the Negro places had a twelve o'clock curfew. But we would have more fun in an hour than most people could have in twenty-four. We would often go to one place where the boys had made friends with the waitresses, and they would sneak us fifths of liquor. Those SNCC boys had friends everywhere, among the Negroes, that is. Most whites were just waiting for the chance to kill them all off.

I guess mostly the SNCC workers were just lucky. Most of them had missed a bullet by an inch or so on many occasions. Threats didn't stop them. They just kept going all the time. One Saturday we got to Greenville and discovered that the office had been bombed Friday night. The office was located up two flights of outside steps in a little broken-down building. It seemed as though a real hard wind would have blown it away. The bomb knocked the steps off, but that didn't stop the rally on Saturday night. Some of the boys made steps. When the new steps began to collapse, we ended up using a ladder. I remember when the rally ended, we found that the ladder was gone. For a few minutes we were real scared. We just knew some whites had moved it. We were all standing up there in the doorway wondering what to do. There was only one exit, and it was too high up to jump from. We figured we were going to be blown up. It seemed as though the whites had finally trapped us. The high school students were about to panic, when suddenly one of the SNCC boys came walking up with the ladder and yelled up to ask if the excitement was over. A lot of the other guys were mad enough to hit him. Those that did only tapped him lightly and smiled as they did it. "The nerve of those guys!" I thought.

Things didn't seem to be coming along too well in the Delta. On Saturdays we would spend all day canvassing and often at night we would have mass rallies. But these were usually poorly attended. Many Negroes were afraid to come. In the beginning some were even afraid to talk to us. Most of these old plantation Negroes had been brain-washed so by the whites, they really thought that only whites were supposed to vote. There were even a few who had never heard of voting. The only thing most of them knew was how to handle a hoe. For years they had demonstrated how well they could do that. Some of them had calluses on their hands so thick they would hide them if they noticed you looking at them.

On Sundays we usually went to Negro churches to speak. We were split into groups according to our religious affiliation. We were supposed to know how to reach those with the same faith as ourselves. In church we hoped to be able to reach many more

Negroes. We knew that even those that slammed doors in our faces or said, "I don't want no part of voting" would be there. There would also be the schoolteachers and the middle-class professional Negroes who dared not participate. They knew that once they did, they would lose that $250 a month job. But the people started getting wise to us. Most of them stopped coming to church. They knew if they came, they would have to face us. Then the ministers started asking us not to come because we scared their congregations away. SNCC had to come up with a new strategy.

As the work continued that summer, people began to come around. I guess they saw that our intentions were good. But some began getting fired from their jobs, thrown off plantations and left homeless. They could often find somewhere else to stay, but food and clothing became a problem. SNCC started to send representatives to Northern college campuses. They went begging for food, clothing and money for the people in Mississippi, and the food, clothing and money started coming in. The Delta Negroes still didn't understand the voting, but they knew they had found friends, friends they could trust.

That summer I could feel myself beginning to change. For the first time I began to think something would be done about whites killing, beating, and misusing Negroes. I knew I was going to be a part of whatever happened.

A week before summer school ended, I was in town shopping with Rose, a girl from the dorm. We had planned to split cab fare back to campus, but discovered we did not have enough money. Cab fare out to Tougaloo was $2.50 and bus fare was thirty-five cents one way. We decided to take the Trailways back. When we got to the station, I suggested to Rose that we use the white side. "I'm game if you are," she said.

I walked in the white entrance. When I looked back, I saw that

Rose had not followed. I decided I would not go back to see what had happened, because she would try and talk me out of it. As I was buying my ticket, she walked up behind me.

"Shit, Moody, I thought you were kidding," she said.

I didn't answer. I was noticing the reaction of the man behind the counter. He stood looking at me as if he were paralyzed.

"Make that two tickets, please," I said to him.

"Where is the other one to?" he said.

"Both to Tougaloo," I said.

As he was getting the tickets for us, another man had gotten on the phone. He kept looking at us as he was talking. I think he was reporting to the police what was taking place. The man that sold us the tickets acted as if that was the last thing in the world he wanted to do. He slapped the tickets down on the counter, and threw the change at me. The change fell off the counter and rolled over the floor. That bastard had the nerve to laugh as we picked it up. Rose and I sat opposite each other, so we could see what was happening throughout the terminal. The bus was to leave at three-thirty, and we had gotten there about two-forty-five. We had some time to wait. Rose had a watch. I asked her to keep a check on the time.

People came in and stared. Some even laughed. Nothing happened until a bunch of white soldiers sat with us and started talking. The conversation had gone on for some time when a Negro woman got off one of the incoming buses. She saw us sitting in there and walked right in. She had about six small children with her. The little Negro children started running around the station picking up things from the counter and asking if they could buy them. At that point the excitement started. A drunken white man walked into the station behind the Negro lady with all the children. He started cursing, calling us all kinds of niggers.

"Get them little dirty swines outta heah," he said, pulling one of the little boys to the door.

"Take your filthy hands off my child," the Negro woman said. "What's going on here anyway?"

"They got a place for you folks, now why don't you take them chilluns of yours and go on right over there?" the drunkard said, pointing to the Negro side of the bus station.

The lady looked at us. I guess she wanted us to say something. Rose and I just sat there. Finally she realized a sit-in or something was going on. She took her children and hurried out of the door. Instead of going to the Negro side, she went back on the bus. She looked as though she was really angry with us.

After that the drunkard started yelling at us. I didn't get too scared, but Rose was now shaking. She had begun to smoke cigarettes one after the other. She looked at her watch. "Moody, we have missed the bus," she said.

"What time is it?" I asked.

"It's almost four-thirty."

"They didn't even announce that the bus was loading," I said.

I walked over to the man at the ticket counter. "Has the bus come in that's going to Tougaloo?" I asked him.

"One just left," he said.

"You didn't announce that the bus was in."

"Are you telling me how to do my job?" he said. "I hear you niggers at Tougaloo think you run Mississippi."

"When is the next bus?" I asked.

"Five-thirty," he said, very indignant.

I went back and told Rose that the next bus left at five-thirty. She wanted to leave, but I insisted that we stay. Just as I was trying to explain to her why we should not leave, the white drunk walked up behind her. He had what appeared to be a wine bottle in his hand.

"Talk to me, Rose," I said.

"What's going on?" Rose said, almost shouting.

"Nothing. Stop acting so damn scared and start talking," I said.

The drunk walked up behind her and held the bottle up as though he was going to hit her on the head. All the time, I was looking him straight in the face as if to say, "Would you, would you really hit her?" Rose knew someone was behind her. She wouldn't have been able to talk or act normal if someone in the station threatened to shoot her if she didn't. The drunkard saw that I was pleading with him. He cursed me, throwing the bottle on the floor and breaking it. At this point, more people got all rallied up. They had now started shouting catcalls from every direction. Some bus drivers walked into the station. "What's wrong? What's going on heah?" one of them shouted. One took a chair and sat right in front of us. "Do you girls want to see a show?" he said. "Did you come here for a little entertainment?"

We didn't say anything.

"I guess you didn't. I'll put it on anyhow," he said. "Now here's how white folks entertain," putting his thumbs in his ears and wiggling his fingers, kicking his feet and making all kind of facial expressions. The rest of the whites in the bus station laughed and laughed at him. Some asked him to imitate a monkey, Martin Luther King, Medgar Evers. His performance went on for what seemed to be a good thirty minutes. When he finished, or rather got tired of, clowning, he said, "Now some of you other people give them what they really came for."

All this time the man was still on the phone talking to someone. We were sure he was talking to the police. Some of the other people that were sitting around in the bus station starting shouting remarks. I guess they were taking the advice of the bus driver. Again Rose looked at her watch to report that we had missed the second bus. It was almost a quarter to seven.

We didn't know what to do. The place was getting more tense by the minute. People had now begun to crowd around us.

"Let's go, Moody," Rose began to plead with me. "If you don't I'll leave you here," she said.

I knew she meant it, and I didn't want to be left alone. The crowd was going to get violent any minute now.

"O.K., Rose, let's go," I said. "Don't turn your back to anyone, though."

We got up and walked backward to the door. The crowd followed us just three or four feet away. Some were threatening to kick us out—or throw us all the way to Tougaloo, and a lot of other possible and impossible things.

Rose and I hit the swinging doors with our backs at the same time. The doors closed immediately behind us. We were now outside the station not knowing what to do or where to run. We were afraid to leave. We were at the back of the station and thought the mob would be waiting for us if we ran around in front and tried to leave. Any moment now, those that had followed us would be on us again. We were standing there just going to pieces.

"Get in this here car," a Negro voice said.

I glanced to one side and saw that Rose was getting into the back seat. At that moment the mob was coming toward me through the doors. I just started moving backward until I fell into the car. The driver sped away.

After we had gotten blocks away from the station, I was still looking out of the back window to see who would follow. No one had. For the first time I looked to see who was driving the car and asked the driver who he was. He said he was a minister, that he worked at the bus station part-time. He asked us not to ever try and sit-in again without first planning it with an organization.

"You girls just can't go around doing things on your own," he said. He drove us all the way to campus, then made us feel bad by telling us he probably would get fired. He said he was on a thirty-minute break. That's a Negro preacher for you.

Summer school ended the following week. I headed for New Orleans to get that good three weeks of work in before the fall term of my senior year began.

part four

THE MOVEMENT

In mid-September I was back on campus. But didn't very much happen until February when the NAACP held its annual convention in Jackson. They were having a whole lot of interesting speakers: Jackie Robinson, Floyd Patterson, Curt Flood, Margaretta Belafonte, and many others. I wouldn't have missed it for anything. I was so excited that I sent one of the leaflets home to Mama and asked her to come.

Three days later I got a letter from Mama with dried-up tears on it, forbidding me to go to the convention. It went on for more than six pages. She said if I didn't stop that shit she would come to Tougaloo and kill me herself. She told me about the time I last visited her, on Thanksgiving, and she had picked me up at the bus station. She said she picked me up because she was scared some white in my hometown would try to do something to me. She said the sheriff had been by, telling her I was messing around with that NAACP group. She said he told her if I didn't stop it, I could not come back there any more. He said that they didn't need any of those NAACP people messing around in Centreville. She ended the letter by saying that she had burned the leaflet I sent her. "Please don't send any more of that stuff here. I don't want nothing to happen to us here," she said. "If you keep that up, you will never be able to come home again."

I was so damn mad after her letter, I felt like taking the NAACP convention to Centreville. I think I would have, if it had been in my power to do so. The remainder of the week I thought of nothing except going to the convention. I didn't know exactly what to do about it. I didn't want Mama or anyone at home to get hurt because of me.

I had felt something was wrong when I was home. During the four days I was there, Mama had tried to do everything she could to keep me in the house. When I said I was going to see some of my old classmates, she pretended she was sick and said I would have to cook. I knew she was acting strangely, but I hadn't known why. I thought Mama just wanted me to spend most of my time with her, since this was only the second time I had been home since I entered college as a freshman.

Things kept running through my mind after that letter from Mama. My mind was so active, I couldn't sleep at night. I remembered the one time I did leave the house to go to the post office. I had walked past a bunch of white men on the street on my way through town and one said, "Is that the gal goin' to Tougaloo?" He acted kind of mad or something, and I didn't know what was going on. I got a creepy feeling, so I hurried home. When I told Mama about it, she just said, "A lotta people don't like that school." I knew what she meant. Just before I went to Tougaloo, they had housed the Freedom Riders there. The school was being criticized by whites throughout the state.

The night before the convention started, I made up my mind to go, no matter what Mama said. I just wouldn't tell Mama or anyone from home. Then it occurred to me—how did the sheriff or anyone at home know I was working with the NAACP chapter on campus? Somehow they had found out. Now I knew I could never go to Centreville safely again. I kept telling myself that I didn't really care too much about going home, that it was more important to me to go to the convention.

I was there from the very beginning. Jackie Robinson was asked to serve as moderator. This was the first time I had seen him in person. I remembered how when Jackie became the first Negro to play Major League baseball, my uncles and most of the Negro boys in my hometown started organizing baseball leagues. It did something for them to see a Negro out there playing with all those white players. Jackie was a good moderator, I thought. He kept smiling and joking. People felt relaxed and proud. They appreciated knowing and meeting people of their own race who had done something worth talking about.

When Jackie introduced Floyd Patterson, heavyweight champion of the world, the people applauded for a long, long time. Floyd was kind of shy. He didn't say very much. He didn't have to, just his being there was enough to satisfy most of the Negroes who had only seen him on TV. Archie Moore was there too. He wasn't as smooth as Jackie, but he had his way with a crowd. He started telling how he was run out of Mississippi, and the people just cracked up.

I was enjoying the convention so much that I went back for the night session. Before the night was over, I had gotten autographs from every one of the Negro celebrities.

I had counted on graduating in the spring of 1963, but as it turned out, I couldn't because some of my credits still had to be cleared with Natchez College. A year before, this would have seemed like a terrible disaster, but now I hardly even felt disappointed. I had a good excuse to stay on campus for the summer and work with the Movement, and this was what I really wanted to do. I couldn't go home again anyway, and I couldn't go to New Orleans—I didn't have money enough for bus fare.

During my senior year at Tougaloo, my family hadn't sent me one penny. I had only the small amount of money I had earned at Maple Hill. I couldn't afford to eat at school or live in the dorms, so I had gotten permission to move off campus. I had to prove that I could finish school, even if I had to go hungry every day. I knew Raymond and Miss Pearl were just waiting to see me drop out. But something happened to me as I got more and more involved in the Movement. It no longer seemed important to prove anything. I had found something outside myself that gave meaning to my life.

I had become very friendly with my social science professor, John Salter, who was in charge of NAACP activities on campus. All during the year, while the NAACP conducted a boycott of the downtown stores in Jackson, I had been one of Salter's most faithful canvassers and church speakers. During the last week of school, he told me that sit-in demonstrations were about to start in Jackson and that he wanted me to be the spokesman for a team that would sit-in at Woolworth's lunch counter. The two other demonstrators would be classmates of mine, Memphis and Pearlena. Pearlena was a dedicated NAACP worker, but Memphis had not been very involved in the Movement on campus. It seemed that the organization had had a rough time finding students who were in a position to go to jail. I had nothing to lose one way or the other. Around ten o'clock the morning of the demonstrations, NAACP headquarters alerted the news services. As a result, the police department was also informed, but neither the policemen nor the newsmen knew exactly where or when the demonstrations would start. They stationed themselves along Capitol Street and waited.

To divert attention from the sit-in at Woolworth's, the picketing started at J. C. Penney's a good fifteen minutes before. The pickets were allowed to walk up and down in front of the store three or four times before they were arrested. At exactly 11 A.M., Pearlena, Memphis, and I entered Woolworth's from the rear entrance. We separated as soon as we stepped into the store, and made small purchases from various counters. Pearlena had given Memphis her watch. He was to let us know when it was 11:14. At 11:14 we were to join him near the lunch counter and at exactly 11:15 we were to take seats at it.

Seconds before 11:15 we were occupying three seats at the previously segregated Woolworth's lunch counter. In the beginning the waitresses seemed to ignore us, as if they really didn't know what was going on. Our waitress walked past us a couple of times before she noticed we had started to write our own orders down and realized we wanted service. She asked us what we wanted. We began to read to her from our order slips. She told us that we would be served at the back counter, which was for Negroes.

"We would like to be served here," I said.

The waitress started to repeat what she had said, then stopped in the middle of the sentence. She turned the lights out behind the counter, and she and the other waitresses almost ran to the back of the store, deserting all their white customers. I guess they thought that violence would start immediately after the whites at the counter realized what was going on. There were five or six other people at the counter. A couple of them just got up and walked away. A girl sitting next to me finished her banana split before leaving. A middle-aged white woman who had not yet been served rose from her seat and came over to us. "I'd like to stay here with you," she said, "but my husband is waiting."

The newsmen came in just as she was leaving. They must have discovered what was going on shortly after some of the people began to leave the store. One of the newsmen ran behind the woman who spoke to us and asked her to identify herself. She refused to give her name, but said she was a native of Vicksburg and a former resident of California. When asked why she had said what she had said to us, she replied, "I am in sympathy with the Negro movement." By this time a crowd of cameramen and reporters had gathered around us taking pictures and asking questions, such as Where were we from? Why did we sit-in? What organization sponsored it? Were we students? From what school? How were we classified?

I told them that we were all students at Tougaloo College, that we were represented by no particular organization, and that we planned to stay there even after the store closed. "All we want is service," was my reply to one of them. After they had finished probing for about twenty minutes, they were almost ready to leave.

At noon, students from a nearby white high school started pouring in to Woolworth's. When they first saw us they were sort of surprised. They didn't know how to react. A few started to heckle and the newsmen became interested again. Then the white students started chanting all kinds of anti-Negro slogans. We were called a little bit of everything. The rest of the seats except the three we were occupying had been roped off to prevent others from sitting down. A couple of the boys took one end of the rope and made it into a hangman's noose. Several attempts were made to put it around our necks. The crowds grew as more students and adults came in for lunch.

We kept our eyes straight forward and did not look at the crowd except for occasional glances to see what was going on. All of a sudden I saw a face I remembered—the drunkard from the bus station sit-in. My eyes lingered on him just long enough for us to recognize each other. Today he was drunk too, so I don't think he remembered where he had seen me before. He took out a knife, opened it, put it in his pocket, and then began to pace the floor. At this point, I told Memphis and Pearlena what was going on. Memphis suggested that we pray. We bowed our heads, and all hell broke loose. A man rushed forward, threw Memphis from his seat, and slapped my face. Then another man who worked in the store threw me against an adjoining counter.

Down on my knees on the floor, I saw Memphis lying near the

lunch counter with blood running out of the corners of his mouth. As he tried to protect his face, the man who'd thrown him down kept kicking him against the head. If he had worn hard-soled shoes instead of sneakers, the first kick probably would have killed Memphis. Finally a man dressed in plain clothes identified himself as a police officer and arrested Memphis and his attacker.

Pearlena had been thrown to the floor. She and I got back on our stools after Memphis was arrested. There were some white Tougaloo teachers in the crowd. They asked Pearlena and me if we wanted to leave. They said that things were getting too rough. We didn't know what to do. While we were trying to make up our minds, we were joined by Joan Trumpauer. Now there were three of us and we were integrated. The crowd began to chant, "Communists, Communists, Communists." Some old man in the crowd ordered the students to take us off the stools.

"Which one should I get first?" a big husky boy said.

"That white nigger," the old man said.

The boy lifted Joan from the counter by her waist and carried her out of the store. Simultaneously, I was snatched from my stool by two high school students. I was dragged about thirty feet toward the door by my hair when someone made them turn me loose. As I was getting up off the floor, I saw Joan coming back inside. We started back to the center of the counter to join Pearlena. Lois Chaffee, a white Tougaloo faculty member, was now sitting next to her. So Joan and I just climbed across the rope at the front end of the counter and sat down. There were now four of us, two whites and two Negroes, all women. The mob started smearing us with ketchup, mustard, sugar, pies, and everything on the counter. Soon Joan and I were joined by John Salter, but the moment he sat down he was hit on the jaw with what appeared to be brass knuckles. Blood gushed from his face and someone threw salt into the open wound. Ed King, Tougaloo's chaplain, rushed to him.

At the other end of the counter, Lois and Pearlena were joined by George Raymond, a CORE field worker and a student from

Jackson State College. Then a Negro high school boy sat down next to me. The mob took spray paint from the counter and sprayed it on the new demonstrators. The high school student had on a white shirt; the word "nigger" was written on his back with red spray paint.

We sat there for three hours taking a beating when the manager decided to close the store because the mob had begun to go wild with stuff from other counters. He begged and begged everyone to leave. But even after fifteen minutes of begging, no one budged. They would not leave until we did. Then Dr. Beittel, the president of Tougaloo College, came running in. He said he had just heard what was happening.

About ninety policemen were standing outside the store; they had been watching the whole thing through the windows, but had not come in to stop the mob or do anything. President Beittel went outside and asked Captain Ray to come and escort us out. The captain refused, stating the manager had to invite him in before he could enter the premises, so Dr. Beittel himself brought us out. He had told the police that they had better protect us after we were outside the store. When we got outside, the policemen formed a single line that blocked the mob from us. However, they were allowed to throw at us everything they had collected. Within ten minutes, we were picked up by Reverend King in his station wagon and taken to the NAACP headquarters on Lynch Street.

After the sit-in, all I could think of was how sick Mississippi whites were. They believed so much in the segregated Southern way of life, they would kill to preserve it. I sat there in the NAACP office and thought of how many times they had killed when this way of life was threatened. I knew that the killing had just begun. "Many more will die before it is over with," I thought. Before the sit-in, I had always hated the whites in Mississippi. Now I knew it was impossible for me to hate sickness. The whites had a disease, an incurable disease in its final stage. What were our chances against such a disease? I thought of the students, the young Negroes who had just begun to protest, as young interns. When these young interns got older, I thought, they would be the best doctors in the world for social problems.

Before we were taken back to campus, I wanted to get my hair washed. It was stiff with dried mustard, ketchup and sugar. I stopped in at a beauty shop across the street from the NAACP office. I didn't have on any shoes because I had lost them when I was dragged across the floor at Woolworth's. My stockings were sticking to my legs from the mustard that had dried on them. The hairdresser took one look at me and said, "My land, you were in the sit-in, huh?"

"Yes," I answered. "Do you have time to wash my hair and style it?"

"Right away," she said, and she meant right away. There were three other ladies already waiting, but they seemed glad to let me go ahead of them. The hairdresser was real nice. She even took my stockings off and washed my legs while my hair was drying.

There was a mass rally that night at the Pearl Street Church in Jackson, and the place was packed. People were standing two abreast in the aisles. Before the speakers began, all the sit-inners walked out on the stage and were introduced by Medgar Evers. People stood and applauded for what seemed like thirty minutes or more. Medgar told the audience that this was just the beginning of such demonstrations. He asked them to pledge themselves to unite in a massive offensive against segregation in Jackson, and throughout the state. The rally ended with "We Shall Overcome" and sent home hundreds of determined people. It seemed as though Mississippi Negroes were about to get together at last.

Before I demonstrated, I had written Mama. She wrote me back a letter, begging me not to take part in the sit-in. She even sent ten dollars for bus fare to New Orleans. I didn't have one penny, so I kept the money. Mama's letter made me mad. I had to live my life as I saw fit. I had made that decision when I left home.

But it hurt to have my family prove to me how scared they were. It hurt me more than anything else—I knew the whites had already started the threats and intimidations. I was the first Negro from my hometown who had openly demonstrated, worked with the NAACP, or anything. When Negroes threatened to do anything in Centreville, they were either shot like Samuel O'Quinn or run out of town, like Reverend Dupree.

I didn't answer Mama's letter. Even if I had written one, she wouldn't have received it before she saw the news on TV or heard it on the radio. I waited to hear from her again. And I waited to hear in the news that someone in Centreville had been murdered. If so, I knew it would be a member of my family.

On Wednesday, the day after the sit-in, demonstrations got off to a good start. Ten people picketed shortly after noon on Capitol Street, and were arrested. Another mass rally followed the demonstrations that night, where a six-man delegation of Negro ministers was chosen to meet Mayor Thompson the following Tuesday. They were to present to him a number of demands on behalf of Jackson Negroes. They were as follows:

1. Hiring of Negro policemen and school crossing guards
2. Removal of segregation signs from public facilities
3. Improvement of job opportunities for Negroes on city payrolls—Negro drivers of city garbage trucks, etc.
4. Encouraging public eating establishments to serve both whites and Negroes
5. Integration of public parks and libraries
6. The naming of a Negro to the City Parks and Recreation Committee
7. Integration of public schools
8. Forcing service stations to integrate rest rooms

After this meeting, Reverend Haughton, the minister of Pearl Street Church, said that the Mayor was going to act on all the suggestions. But the following day, Thompson denied that he had made any promises. He said the Negro delegation "got carried away" following their discussion with him.

"It seems as though Mayor Thompson wants to play games with us," Reverend Haughton said at the next rally. "He is calling us liars and trying to make us sound like fools. I guess we have to show him that we mean business."

When Reverend Charles A. Jones, dean and chaplain at Campbell College, asked at the close of the meeting, "Where do we go from here?" the audience shouted, "To the streets." They were going to prove to Mayor Thompson and the white people of Jackson that they meant business.

Around ten the next morning, an entire day of demonstrations started. A little bit of everything was tried. Some Negroes sat-in, some picketed, and some squatted in the streets and refused to move.

All of the five-and-ten stores (H. L. Green, Kress, and Woolworth's) had closed their lunch counters as a result of the Woolworth's sit-in. However, this did not stop the new sit-ins. Chain restaurants such as Primos Restaurant in downtown Jackson were now targets. Since police brutality was the last thing wanted in good, respectable Jackson, Mississippi, whenever arrested demonstrators refused to walk to a paddy wagon, garbage truck, or whatever was being used to take people to jail, Negro trusties from Jackson's city jail carted them away. Captain Ray and his men would just stand back with their hands folded, looking innocent as lambs for the benefit of the Northern reporters and photographers.

The Mayor still didn't seem to be impressed with the continuous small demonstrations and kept the streets hot. After eighty-eight demonstrators had been arrested, the Mayor held a news conference where he told a group of reporters, "We can handle 100,000 agitators." He also stated that the "good colored citizens are not rallying to the support of the outside agitators" (although there were only a few out-of-state people involved in the movement at the time) and offered to give Northern newsmen anything they wanted, including transportation, if they would "adequately" report the facts.

During the demonstrations, I helped conduct several workshops, where potential demonstrators, high school and college students mostly, were taught to protect themselves. If, for instance, you wanted to protect the neck to offset a karate blow, you clasped your hands behind the neck. To protect the genital organs you doubled up in a knot, drawing the knees up to the chest to protect your breasts if you were a girl.

The workshops were handled mostly by SNCC and CORE field secretaries and workers, almost all of whom were very young. The NAACP handled all the bail and legal services and public relations, but SNCC and CORE could draw teen-agers into the Movement as no other organization could. Whether they received credit for it or not, they helped make Jackson the center of attention throughout the nation.

During this period, civil rights workers who had become known to the Jackson police were often used to divert the cops' attention just before a demonstration. A few cops were always placed across the street from NAACP headquarters, since most of the demonstrations were organized there and would leave from that building. The "diverters" would get into cars and lead the cops off on a wild-goose chase. This would allow the real demonstrators to get downtown before they were noticed. One evening, a group of us took the cops for a tour of the park. After giving the demonstrators time enough to get to Capitol Street, we decided to go and watch the action. When we arrived there ourselves, we met Reverend King and a group of ministers. They told us they were going to stage a pray-in on the post office steps. "Come on, join us," Reverend

King said. "I don't think we'll be arrested, because it's federal property."

By the time we got to the post office, the newsmen had already been informed, and a group of them were standing in front of the building blocking the front entrance. By now the group of whites that usually constituted the mob had gotten smart. They no longer looked for us, or for the demonstration. They just followed the newsmen and photographers. They were much smarter than the cops, who hadn't caught on yet.

We entered the post office through the side entrance and found that part of the mob was waiting inside the building. We didn't let this bother us. As soon as a few more ministers joined us, we were ready to go outside. There were fourteen of us, seven whites and seven Negroes. We walked out front and stood and bowed our heads as the ministers began to pray. We were immediately interrupted by the appearance of Captain Ray. "We are asking you people to disperse. If you don't, you are under arrest," he said.

Most of us were not prepared to go to jail. Doris Erskine, a student from Jackson State, and I had to take over a workshop the following day. Some of the ministers were in charge of the mass rally that night. But if we had dispersed, we would have been torn to bits by the mob. The whites standing out there had murder in their eyes. They were ready to do us in and all fourteen of us knew that. We had no other choice but to be arrested.

We had no plan of action. Reverend King and some of the ministers who were kneeling refused to move; they just kept on praying. Some of the others also attempted to kneel. The rest of us just walked to the paddy wagon. Captain Ray was using the Negro trusties. I felt so sorry for them. They were too small to be carrying all these heavy-ass demonstrators. I could tell just by looking at them that they didn't want to, either. I knew they were forced to do this.

After we got to jail we were mugged and fingerprinted, then taken to a cell. Most of the ministers were scared stiff. This was the first time some of them had seen the inside of a jail. Before we were mugged, we were all placed in a room together and allowed to make one call. Reverend King made the call to the NAACP headquarters to see if some of the ministers could be bailed out right away. I was so glad when they told him they didn't have money available at the moment. I just got my kicks out of sitting there looking at the ministers. Some of them looked so pitiful, I thought they would cry any minute, and here they were, supposed to be our leaders.

When Doris and I got to the cell where we would spend the next four days, we found a lot of our friends there. There were twelve girls altogether. The jail was segregated. I felt sorry for Jeanette King, Lois Chaffee, and Joan Trumpauer. Just because they were white they were missing out on all the fun we planned to have. Here we were going to school together, sleeping in the same dorm, worshiping together, playing together, even demonstrating together. It all ended in jail. They were rushed off by themselves to some cell designated for whites.

Our cell didn't even have a curtain over the shower. Every time the cops heard the water running, they came running to peep. After the first time, we fixed them. We took chewing gum and toilet tissue and covered the opening in the door. They were afraid to take it down. I guess they thought it might have come out in the newspaper. Their wives wouldn't have liked that at all. Peep through a hole to see a bunch of nigger girls naked? No! No! They certainly wouldn't have liked that. All of the girls in my cell were college students. We had a lot to talk about, so we didn't get too bored. We made cards out of toilet tissue and played Gin Rummy almost all day. Some of us even learned new dance steps from each other.

There were a couple of girls in with us from Jackson State College. They were scared they would be expelled from school. Jackson State, like most of the state-supported Negro schools, was an

Uncle Tom school. The students could be expelled for almost anything. When I found this out, I really appreciated Tougaloo.

The day we were arrested one of the Negro trusties sneaked us
a newspaper. We discovered that over four hundred high school
students had also been arrested. We were so glad we sang freedom
songs for an hour or so. The jailer threatened to put us in solitary if
we didn't stop. At first we didn't think he meant it, so we kept
singing. He came back with two other cops and asked us to follow
them. They marched us down the hall and showed us one of the
solitary chambers. "If you don't stop that damn singing, I'm gonna
throw all of you in here together," said the jailer. After that we didn't
sing any more. We went back and finished reading the paper.

We got out of jail on Sunday to discover that everyone was talking
about the high school students. All four hundred who were arrested had been taken to the fairgrounds and placed in a large
open compound without beds or anything. It was said that they
were getting sick like flies. Mothers were begging to have their
children released, but the NAACP didn't have enough money to
bail them all out.

The same day we went to jail for the pray-in, the students at
Lanier High School had started singing freedom songs on their
lunch hour. They got so carried away they ignored the bell when
the break was over and just kept on singing. The principal of the
high school did not know what to do, so he called the police and
told them that the students were about to start a riot.

When the cops came, they brought the dogs. The students refused to go back to their classrooms when asked, so the cops
turned the dogs loose on them. The students fought them off for a
while. In fact, I was told that mothers who lived near the school
had joined the students in fighting off the dogs. They had begun
to throw bricks, rocks, and bottles. The next day the papers stated

that ten or more cops suffered cuts or minor wounds. The papers didn't say it, but a lot of students were hurt, too, from dog bites and lumps on the head from billy clubs. Finally, one hundred and fifty cops were rushed to the scene and several students and adults were arrested.

The next day four hundred of the high school students from Lanier, Jim Hill, and Brinkley High schools gathered in a church on Farish Street, ready to go to jail. Willie Ludden, the NAACP youth leader, and some of the SNCC and CORE workers met with them, gave a brief workshop on nonviolent protective measures and led them into the streets. After marching about two blocks they were met by helmeted police officers and ordered to disperse. When they refused, they were arrested, herded into paddy wagons, canvas-covered trucks, and garbage trucks. Those moving too slowly were jabbed with rifle butts. Police dogs were there, but were not used. From the way everyone was describing the scene it sounded like Nazi Germany instead of Jackson, USA.

On Monday, I joined a group of high school students and several other college students who were trying to get arrested. Our intention was to be put in the fairgrounds with the high school students already there. The cops picked us up, but they didn't want to put us so-called professional agitators in with the high school students. We were weeded out, and taken back to the city jail.

I got out of jail two days later and found I had gotten another letter from Mama. She had written it Wednesday the twenty-ninth, after the Woolworth's sit-in. The reason it had taken so long for me to get it was that it came by way of New Orleans. Mama sent it to Adline and had Adline mail it to me. In the letter she told me that the sheriff had stopped by and asked all kinds of questions about me the morning after the sit-in. She said she and Raymond told them that I had only been home once since I was in college, that I had practically cut off all my family connections when I ran away from home as a senior in high school. She said he said that he knew I had left home. "He should know," I thought, "because I had to get him to move my clothes for me when I left." She went on and on. She told me he said I must never come back there. If so he would not be responsible for what happened to me. "The whites are pretty upset about her doing these things," he told her. Mama told me not to write her again until she sent me word that it was O.K. She said that I would hear from her through Adline.

I also got a letter from Adline in the same envelope. She told me what Mama hadn't mentioned—that Junior had been cornered by a group of white boys and was about to be lynched, when one of his friends came along in a car and rescued him. Besides that, a group of white men had gone out and beaten up my old Uncle Buck. Adline said Mama told her they couldn't sleep, for fear of night riders. They were all scared to death. My sister ended the letter by cursing me out. She said I was trying to get every Negro in Centreville murdered.

I guess Mama didn't tell me these things because she was scared to. She probably thought I would have tried to do something crazy. Something like trying to get the organizations to move into Wilkinson County, or maybe coming home myself to see if they would kill me. She never did give me credit for having the least bit of sense. I knew there was nothing I could do. No organization was about to go to Wilkinson County. It was a little too tough for any of them. And I wasn't about to go there either. If they said they would kill me, I figured I'd better take their word for it.

Meantime, within four or five days Jackson became the hotbed of racial demonstrations in the South. It seemed as though most of the Negro college and high school students there were making preparations to participate. Those who did not go to jail were considered cowards by those who did. At this point, Mayor Allen Thompson finally made a decisive move. He announced that Jackson had made plans to house over 12,500 demonstrators at the local jails and at the state fairgrounds. And if this was not enough, he said, Parchman, the state penitentiary, 160 miles away, would be used. Governor Ross Barnett had held a news conference offering Parchman facilities to Jackson.

An injunction prohibiting demonstrations was issued by a local judge, naming NAACP, CORE, Tougaloo College, and various leaders. According to this injunction, the intent of the named organizations and individuals was to paralyze the economic nerve center of the city of Jackson. It used as proof the leaflets that had been distributed by the NAACP urging Negroes not to shop on Capitol Street. The next day the injunction was answered with another mass march.

The cops started arresting every Negro on the scene of a demonstration, whether or not he was participating. People were being carted off to jail every day of the week. On Saturday, Roy Wilkins, the National Director of NAACP, and Medgar Evers were arrested as they picketed in front of Woolworth's. Theldon Henderson, a Negro lawyer who worked for the Justice Department, and had been sent down from Washington to investigate a complaint by the NAACP about the fairgrounds facilities, was also arrested. It was said that when he showed his Justice Department credentials, the arresting officer started trembling. They let him go immediately.

Mass rallies had come to be an every night event, and at each one the NAACP had begun to build up Medgar Evers. Somehow I had the feeling that they wanted him to become for Mississippi what Martin Luther King had been in Alabama. They were well on the way to achieving that, too.

After the rally on Tuesday, June 11, I had to stay in Jackson. I had missed the ride back to campus. Dave Dennis, the CORE field secretary for Mississippi, and his wife put me up for the night. We were watching TV around twelve-thirty, when a special news bulletin interrupted the program. It said, "Jackson NAACP leader Medgar Evers has just been shot."

We didn't believe what we were hearing. We just sat there staring at the TV screen. It was unbelievable. Just an hour or so earlier we were all with him. The next bulletin announced that he had died in the hospital soon after the shooting. We didn't know what to say or do. All night we tried to figure out what had happened, who did it, who was next, and it still didn't seem real.

First thing the next morning we turned on the TV. It showed films taken shortly after Medgar was shot in his driveway. We saw the pool of blood where he had fallen. We saw his wife sobbing almost hysterically as she tried to tell what had happened. Without even having breakfast, we headed for the NAACP headquarters. When we got there, they were trying to organize a march to protest Medgar's death. Newsmen, investigators, and reporters flooded the office. College and high school students and a few adults sat in the auditorium waiting to march.

Dorie Ladner, a SNCC worker, and I decided to run up to Jackson State College and get some of the students there to participate in the march. I was sure we could convince some of them to protest Medgar's death. Since the march was to start shortly after lunch, we had a couple of hours to do some recruiting. When we got to Jackson State, class was in session. "That's a damn shame," I thought. "They should have dismissed school today, in honor of Medgar."

Dorie and I started going down each hall, taking opposite classrooms. We begged students to participate. They didn't respond in any way.

"It's a shame, it really is a shame. This morning Medgar Evers was murdered and here you sit in a damn classroom with books in front of your faces, pretending you don't even know he's been killed. Every Negro in Jackson should be in the streets raising hell and protesting his death," I said in one class. I felt sick, I got so mad with them. How could Negroes be so pitiful? How could they just sit by and take all this shit without any emotions at all? I just didn't understand.

"It's hopeless, Moody, let's go," Dorie said.

As we were leaving the building, we began soliciting aloud in the hall. We walked right past the president's office, shouting even louder. President Reddix came rushing out. "You girls leave this campus immediately," he said, "You can't come on this campus and announce anything without my consent."

Dorie had been a student at Jackson State. Mr. Reddix looked at her. "You know better than this, Dorie," he said.

"But President Reddix, Medgar was just murdered. Don't you have any feelings about his death at all?" Dorie said.

"I am doing a job. I can't do this job and have feelings about everything happening in Jackson," he said. He was waving his arms and pointing his finger in our faces. "Now you two get off this campus before I have you arrested."

By this time a group of students had gathered in the hall. Dorie had fallen to her knees in disgust as Reddix was pointing at her, and some of the students thought he had hit her. I didn't say anything to him. If I had I would have been calling him every kind of fucking Tom I could think of. I helped Dorie off the floor. I told her we'd better hurry, or we would miss the demonstration.

On our way back to the auditorium we picked up the Jackson *Daily News*. Headlines read JACKSON INTEGRATION LEADER EVERS SLAIN.

Negro NAACP leader Medgar Evers was shot to death
when he stepped from his automobile here early today as he
returned home from an integration strategy meeting.
    Police said Evers, 37, was cut down by a high-powered
bullet in the back of the driveway of his home.

I stopped reading. Medgar was usually followed home every night by two or three cops. Why didn't they follow him last night? Something was wrong. "They must have known," I thought. "Why didn't they follow him last night?" I kept asking myself. I had to get out of all this confusion. The only way I could do it was to go to jail. Jail was the only place I could think in.

When we got back to the auditorium, we were told that those who would take part in the first march had met at Pearl Street Church. Dorie and I walked over there. We noticed a couple of girls from Jackson State. They asked Dorie if President Reddix had hit her, and said it had gotten out on campus that he had. They told us a lot of students had planned to demonstrate because of what Reddix had done. "Good enough," Dorie said, "Reddix better watch himself, or we'll turn that school out."

I was called to the front of the church to help lead the marchers in a few freedom songs. We sang "Woke Up This Morning With My Mind on Freedom" and "Ain't Gonna Let Nobody Turn Me 'Round." After singing the last song we headed for the streets in a double line, carrying small American flags in our hands. The cops had heard that there were going to be Negroes in the streets all day protesting Medgar's death. They were ready for us.

On Rose Street we ran into a blockade of about two hundred policemen. We were called to a halt by Captain Ray, and asked to disperse. "Everybody ain't got a permit get out of this here parade," Captain Ray said into his bull horn. No one moved. He beckoned to the cops to advance on us.

The cops had rifles and wore steel helmets. They walked right up to us very fast and then sort of engulfed us. They started snatching the small American flags, throwing them to the ground, stepping on them, or stamping them. Students who refused to let go of the flags were jabbed with rifle butts. There was only one paddy wagon on the scene. The first twenty of us were thrown into it, although a paddy wagon is only large enough to seat about ten people. We were sitting and lying all over each other inside the wagon when garbage trucks arrived. We saw the cops stuff about fifty demonstrators in one truck as we looked out through the back glass. Then the driver of the paddy wagon sped away as fast as he could, often making sudden stops in the middle of the street so we would be thrown around.

We thought that they were going to take us to the city jail again because we were college students. We discovered we were headed for the fairgrounds. When we got there, the driver rolled up the windows, turned the heater on, got out, closed the door and left us. It was over a hundred degrees outside that day. There was no air coming in. Sweat began dripping off us. An hour went by. Our clothes were now soaked and sticking to us. Some of the girls looked as though they were about to faint. A policeman looked in to see how we were taking it. Some of the boys begged him to let us out. He only smiled and walked away.

Looking out of the back window again, we noticed they were now booking all the other demonstrators. We realized they had planned to do this to our group. A number of us in the paddy wagon were known to the cops. After the Woolworth's sit-in, I had been known to every white in Jackson. I can remember walking down the street and being pointed out by whites as they drove or walked past me.

Suddenly one of the girls screamed. Scrambling to the window, we saw John Salter with blood gushing out of a large hole in the back of his head. He was just standing there dazed and no one was helping him. And we were in no position to help either.

After they let everyone else out of the garbage trucks, they decided to let us out of the paddy wagon. We had now been in there well over two hours. As we were getting out, one of the girls almost fell. A guy started to help her.

"Get ya hands off that gal. Whatta ya think, ya goin' to a prom or somethin'?" one of the cops said.

Water was running down my legs. My skin was soft and spongy. I had hidden a small transistor radio in my bra and some of the other girls had cards and other things in theirs. We had learned to sneak them in after we discovered they didn't search the women but now everything was showing through our wet clothes.

When we got into the compound, there were still some high school students there, since the NAACP bail money had been exhausted. There were altogether well over a hundred and fifty in the girls' section. The boys had been put into a compound directly opposite and parallel to us. Some of the girls who had been arrested after us shared their clothes with us until ours dried. They told us what had happened after we were taken off in the paddy wagon. They said the cops had stuffed so many into the garbage trucks that some were just hanging on. As one of the trucks pulled off, thirteen-year-old John Young fell out. When the driver stopped, the truck rolled back over the boy. He was rushed off to a hospital and they didn't know how badly he had been hurt. They said the cops had gone wild with their billy sticks. They had even arrested Negroes looking on from their porches. John Salter had been forced off some Negro's porch and hit on the head.

The fairgrounds were everything I had heard they were. The compounds they put us in were two large buildings used to auction off cattle during the annual state fair. They were about a block long, with large openings about twenty feet wide on both ends where the cattle were driven in. The openings had been closed up with wire. It reminded me of a concentration camp. It was hot and sticky and girls were walking around half dressed all the time. We were guarded by four policemen. They had rifles and kept an eye on us through the wired sides of the building. As I looked through the wire at them, I imagined myself in Nazi Germany, the policemen Nazi soldiers. They couldn't have been any rougher than these cops. Yet this was America, "the land of the free and the home of the brave."

About five-thirty we were told that dinner was ready. We were lined up single file and marched out of the compound. They had the cook from the city jail there. He was standing over a large garbage can stirring something in it with a stick. The sight of it nauseated me. No one was eating, girls or boys. In the next few days, many were taken from the fairgrounds sick from hunger.

When I got out of jail on Saturday, the day before Medgar's funeral, I had lost about fifteen pounds. They had prepared a special meal on campus for the Tougaloo students, but attempts to eat made me sicker. The food kept coming up. The next morning I pulled myself together enough to make the funeral services at the Masonic Temple. I was glad I had gone in spite of my illness. This was the first time I had ever seen so many Negroes together. There were thousands and thousands of them there. Maybe Medgar's death had really brought them to the Movement, I thought. Maybe his death would strengthen the ties between Negroes and Negro organizations. If this resulted, then truly his death was not in vain.

Just before the funeral services were over, I went outside. There was a hill opposite the Masonic Temple. I went up there to watch the procession. I wanted to see every moment of it.

As the pallbearers brought the body out and placed it in a hearse, the tension in the city was as tight as a violin string. There were two or three thousand outside that could not get inside the temple, and as they watched, their expression was that of anger, bitterness, and dismay. They looked as though any moment they were going to start rioting. When Mrs. Evers and her two older children got into their black limousine, Negro women in the crowd began to cry and say things like "That's a shame," . . . "That's a young woman," . . . "Such well-looking children," . . . "It's a shame, it really is a shame."

Negroes formed a seemingly endless line as they began the march to the funeral home. They got angrier and angrier; however, they went on quietly until they reached the downtown section where the boycott was. They tried to break through the barricades on Capitol Street, but the cops forced them back into line. When they reached the funeral home, the body was taken inside, and most of the procession dispersed. But one hard core of angry

Negroes decided they didn't want to go home. With some encouragement from SNCC workers who were singing freedom songs outside the funeral home, these people began walking back toward Capitol Street.

Policemen had been placed along the route of the march, and they were still there. They allowed the crowd of Negroes to march seven blocks, but they formed a solid blockade just short of Capitol Street. This was where they made everyone stop. They had everything—shotguns, fire trucks, gas masks, dogs, fire hoses, and billy clubs. Along the sidewalks and on the fringes of the crowd, the cops knocked heads, set dogs on some marchers, and made about thirty arrests, but the main body of people in the middle of the street was just stopped.

They sang and shouted things like "Shoot, shoot" to the police, and then the police started to push them back slowly. After being pushed back about a block, they stopped. They wouldn't go any farther. So the cops brought the fire trucks up closer and got ready to use the fire hoses on the crowd. That really broke up the demonstration. People moved back faster and started to go home. But it also made them angrier. Bystanders began throwing stones and bottles at the cops and then the crowd started too; other Negroes were pitching stuff from second- and third-story windows. The crowd drew back another block, leaving the space between them and the fire trucks littered with rocks and broken glass. John Doar came out from behind the police barricade and walked toward the crowd of Negroes, with bottles flying all around him. He talked to some of the people at the front, telling them he was from the Justice Department and that this wasn't "the way." After he talked for a few minutes, things calmed down considerably, and Dave Dennis and a few others began taking bottles away from people and telling them they should go home. After that it was just a clean-up operation. One of the ministers borrowed Captain Ray's bull horn and ran up and down the street telling people to disperse, but by that time there were just a few stragglers.

After Medgar's death there was a period of confusion. Each Negro leader and organization in Jackson received threats. They were all told they were "next on the list." Things began to fall apart. The ministers, in particular, didn't want to be "next"; a number of them took that long-promised vacation to Africa or elsewhere. Meanwhile SNCC and CORE became more militant and began to press for more demonstrations. A lot of the young Negroes wanted to let the whites of Jackson know that even by killing off Medgar they hadn't touched the real core of the Movement. For the NAACP and the older, more conservative groups, however, voter registration had now become number one on the agenda. After the NAACP exerted its influence at a number of strategy meetings, the militants lost.

The Jackson *Daily News* seized the opportunity to cause more fragmentation. One day they ran a headline THERE IS A SPLIT IN THE ORGANIZATIONS, and sure enough, shortly afterward, certain organizations had completely severed their relations with each other. The whites had succeeded again. They had reached us through the papers by letting us know we were not together. "Too bad," I thought. "One day we'll learn. It's pretty tough, though, when you have everything against you, including the money, the newspapers, and the cops."

Within a week everything had changed. Even the rallies were not the same. The few ministers and leaders who did come were so scared—they thought assassins were going to follow them home. Soon there were rallies only twice a week instead of every night.

The Sunday following Medgar's funeral, Reverend Ed King organized an integrated church-visiting team of six of us from the college. Another team was organized by a group in Jackson. Five or six churches were hit that day, including Governor Ross Barnett's. At each one they had prepared for our visit with armed policemen, paddy wagons, and dogs—which would be used in case we refused to leave after "ushers" had read us the prepared resolutions. There were about eight of these ushers at each church, and they were never exactly the usherly type. They were more on the order of Al Capone. I think this must have been the first time any of these men had worn a flower in his lapel. When we were asked to leave, we did. We were never even allowed to get past the first step.

A group of us decided that we would go to church again the next Sunday. This time we were quite successful. These visits had not been publicized as the first ones were, and they were not really expecting us. We went first to a Church of Christ, where we were greeted by the regular ushers. After reading us the same resolution we had heard last week, they offered to give us cab fare to the Negro extension of the church. Just as we had refused and were walking away, an old lady stopped us. "We'll sit with you," she said.

We walked back to the ushers with her and her family. "Please let them in, Mr. Calloway. We'll sit with them," the old lady said.

"Mrs. Dixon, the church has decided what is to be done. A resolution has been passed, and we are to abide by it."

"Who are we to decide such a thing? This is a house of God, and God is to make all of the decisions. He is the judge of us all," the lady said.

The ushers got angrier then and threatened to call the police if we didn't leave. We decided to go.

"We appreciate very much what you've done," I said to the old lady.

As we walked away from the church, we noticed the family leaving by a side entrance. The old lady was waving to us.

Two blocks from the church, we were picked up by Ed King's wife, Jeanette. She drove us to an Episcopal church. She had previously left the other two girls from our team there. She circled the block a couple of times, but we didn't see them anywhere. I suggested that we try the church. "Maybe they got in," I said. Mrs. King waited in the car for us. We walked up to the front of the church. There were no ushers to be seen. Apparently, services had already started. When we walked inside, we were greeted by two ushers who stood at the rear.

"May we help you?" one said.

"Yes," I said. "We would like to worship with you today."

"Will you sign the guest list, please, and we will show you to your seats," said the other.

I stood there for a good five minutes before I was able to compose myself. I had never prayed with white people in a white church before. We signed the guest list and were then escorted to two seats behind the other two girls in our team. We had all gotten in. The church service was completed without one incident. It was as normal as any church service. However, it was by no means normal to me. I was sitting there thinking any moment God would strike the life out of me. I recognized some of the whites, sitting around me in that church. If they were praying to the same God I was, then even God, I thought, was against me.

When the services were over the minister invited us to visit again. He said it as if he meant it, and I began to have a little hope.

chapter

TWENTY-THREE

In July, CORE opened up an office in Canton, Mississippi, to start a voter registration campaign in Madison County. By this time, I was so fed up with the fighting and bickering among the organizations in Jackson, I was ready to go almost anywhere, even Madison County, where Negroes frequently turned up dead. Shortly before Christmas a man's headless corpse had been found on the road between Canton and Tougaloo with the genitals cut off and with K's cut into the flesh all over his body. Around the time the body was found, Tougaloo College had received a lot of threats, so an inventory was made of all the males on campus to see if any were missing.

When Reverend King discovered that I had agreed to work with CORE in the area, he was very much concerned. He discussed Canton with me, telling me he thought the place was too rough for girls. Some of my girlfriends also begged me not to go. But I just had to. I don't know why I felt that way, but I did.

Because I had come from Wilkinson County, I just didn't think Madison could be any worse. Things might even be a little better,

I thought, since in Madison there were three Negroes to every white. I remembered that in Jackson there had been one point when I could see the white folks actually tremble with fear. At times when we were having mass demonstrations we had them so confused they didn't know what to do. Whenever I could detect the least amount of fear in any white Mississippian, I felt good. I also felt there was a chance of winning the battle regardless of how costly it turned out to be.

Disregarding all acts of violence, Madison County was considered a place with a possible future for Negroes. In addition to the fact that our records showed that there was a population of twenty-nine thousand Negroes as against nine thousand whites, Negroes owned over 40 percent of the land in the county. However, there were only about one hundred and fifty to two hundred registered to vote, and these had registered as a result of a campaign conducted by a few local citizens a couple of years earlier. Of this number, less than half were actually voting.

I arrived in Canton with Dave Dennis one Friday evening, and was taken straight to the CORE office, a small room adjoining a Negro café. The café was owned by C. O. Chinn and his wife, a well-established Negro family. It was located on Franklin Street in the center of one of Canton's Negro sections. Dave and I were just in time to have supper there with George Raymond, the project director, and Bettye Poole, my old Tougaloo buddy.

Dave introduced me to Mrs. Chinn. She was a stout lady with a warm and friendly smile. I liked her right away. I spent the entire evening sitting around the office talking to her and George Raymond about Madison County.

The office had been open only a few weeks, and in that time, Mrs. Chinn had already had her liquor license taken away. The place had been broken into twice, and many Negroes had been physically threatened. George reported that so far mostly teen-agers were involved in the Movement. He said that about fifty dedicated teen-age canvassers showed up each day. They were

sent out daily, but had little success. Most of the Negroes just
didn't want to be bothered, Mrs. Chinn told me. "That's the way it
is all over," I thought. "Most Negroes have been thoroughly brain-
washed. If they aren't brainwashed, they are too insecure—either
they work for Miss Ann or they live on Mr. Charlie's place."

I just didn't see how the Negroes in Madison County could be
so badly off. They should have had everything going for them—
out-numbering the whites three to one and owning just about as
much land as they did. When I discussed this point with Mrs.
Chinn, I discovered that, although they did own the land, they
were allowed to farm only so much of it. Cotton is the main crop
in Mississippi, and, as Mrs. Chinn explained that night, the federal government controls cotton by giving each state a certain al-
lotment. Each state decides how much each county gets and each
county distributes the allotments to the farmers. "It always ends
up with the white people getting most of the allotments," Mrs.
Chinn said. "The Negroes aren't able to get more, regardless of
how much land they have." Most of the farmers in Madison
County were barely living off what they made from their land. Besides, they were never clear from debt. The independent farmers
were practically like sharecroppers, because they always had their
crop pledged in advance. The more I thought about it, the more it
seemed that the federal government was directly or indirectly responsible for most of the segregation, discrimination, and poverty
in the South.

Later, I was taken to the Freedom House, which had been provided by Mrs. Chinn's brother, Sonny. The house was newly built
and very nice. There were three bedrooms, a living room, dining
room, and kitchen. Sonny was a young man who had recently separated from his wife. Since his brother Robert lived with him now,
we kind of crowded them, forcing them to share a bed. But they
didn't seem to mind. The more I saw of the Chinns, the more I began to like and respect them. They were the one Negro family in
Canton who had put their necks on the chopping block. "If a

couple of other families made similar commitments," I thought, "we might just get this place moving."

There was a rally that night at the CORE office. Mrs. Chinn was the only adult there among about twenty teen-agers. We sang freedom songs for about two hours. After that, George gave a brief talk, and introduced me, saying, "I want you people to meet one of my co-workers. She is going to spend some time with us here in and around Madison County. She is a real soul sister. Why don't you stand, Anne?"

As I rose, one of the boys in the back gave a wolf whistle. "I don't mean that kind of soul sister, Esco," George said. "What I mean is, she is dedicated, man. She has been beaten and kicked all over Jackson. Remember that bloody sit-in, and the other demonstrations? She was in all of them. She has been in jail four or five times, and as a result, she can't even go home again. She is all right and don't you guys go getting any notions. Anne, why don't you say a few words?"

I felt I had to say something real serious after those remarks. "Anyway," I thought, "I better take advantage of such an introduction to put those teen-age boys in their place from the get-go. If not, I might have a little trouble on my hands later." Therefore, I decided to pull the religious bit. Now that I was facing the street, I saw that outside the cops were on the ball. There they were, two carloads of them. They were taking it all in. "The watchdogs of the Klan. They wouldn't miss a meeting for anything." I was beginning to hate them with a passion. "I just might try and give them something to think about, too," I thought.

"It seems as though a few of us have the spirit tonight," I started.

"Yes, we got it all right," one of the boys said, somewhat freshly.

"A few is not enough," I continued. "If a change is gonna take place in Canton, as we just said in one of the songs, then it's gonna take more than a few believers. Where are the rest of the adults besides Mrs. Chinn? Where are your parents, sisters and brothers and your other friends? We sit back and say that we want Freedom. We believe that all men are created equal. Some of us even believe we are free just because our constitution guarantees us certain 'inalienable' rights. There are the thirteenth, four-teenth, and fifteenth amendments that make us citizens and give us the right to vote. If you are depending on the writing on the wall to free you, you better forget it, it's been there a long time. We've gotta be the ones to give it meaning. Some of us believe that once we get enough nerve, all we gotta do is walk up to Mr. Char-lie and say, 'Man, I want my freedom.' Do you think that Mr. Charlie is going to dish it out to you on a silver platter?"

"No, he'll tell me that I am already free," one of the boys said.

"If he is that bold and thinks you are that crazy, then you should be bold and crazy enough to ask him a few more questions," I said.

"Questions like what?" he said.

"Like 'what am I free to do?'" I said. "Then name a few things you can't do if he continues. In fact, if you ever get enough nerve to do it, let me know what happens."

"I probably won't live to tell you about it," the boy said.

"So you see, it's not that simple, and all of you know that," I said. "Now that we know that we are not free and realize what's in-volved in freeing ourselves, we have to take certain positive ac-tions to work on the problem. First of all, we have got to get together. I was told that it's twenty-nine thousand Negroes in this county to nine thousand whites. What's wrong with you? Don't you realize what you have going for you?" When I said this, those overseers outside began to pace nervously. I had touched a nerve in them and I felt good, but I decided to stop before I overdid it. I ended by saying, "I am looking forward to the work ahead of me. I will certainly do my best to help you get the message across to Mr. Charlie." Then I took a seat.

George got up and said, "See, I told you she was all right. Now let's sing a few more songs. Then go home and see what we can come up with to start on Mr. Charlie. *All right*, soul brothers and sisters."

"All right," Mrs. Chinn said. "We are going to get that freedom yet, ain't we?"

A few shouts of Amen and Sho-nuff came from the teen-agers. We sang three songs, ending with "We Shall Overcome," and everyone went home. All that night I kept thinking about that pitiful meeting. We just had to get some more adults involved somehow.

The next day, Saturday, I went to the office to check over some of the reports by previous canvassing teams. I had been working for a few hours when George came in. "Come outside. I want to show you something," he said.

I ran into the street thinking someone was being beaten by the cops or there was some other kind of Saturday night happening out there.

"Take a good look at that," George said. "Just about every Negro in Madison County for miles around."

It wasn't hard for me to believe what I was seeing. I had seen it too many times before. In Centreville, my home-town, the same thing took place. Saturday night was known as Nigger Night. That's how the whites put it.

"Come on," George said, "let's walk out on Pear Street" (the main street in Canton). As we walked there, we had to push our way through crowds of Negroes. On Pear Street itself, everything was at a standstill. There were so many Negroes, and they were packed so closely together, they could barely move.

"Look over there," I said to George.

"Where?" he asked.

"At the two white cops standing on that corner," I said.

"They look pretty lonely and stupid, huh?"

"They sure do," I said. "Look just like they are in a completely black town at this moment."

"Most whites don't even bother to come in on Saturdays, I've noticed," George said.

I stood there looking and thinking. Yes, Saturday night is Nigger Night all over Mississippi. I remembered in Centreville, when it was too cold for anyone to walk the streets, Negroes would come to town and sit in each other's cars and talk. Those that didn't believe in sitting around or hanging out in bars, like my mother, just sat or moved from car to car for four or five hours. Teen-agers who were not allowed in cafés went to a movie and watched the picture three or four times while they smooched. There was a special "lovers" section in the movie house on Saturday nights. Often you saw more stirring and arousing scenes in the lovers' section than on the screen. Some Negroes would come to town on Saturday night just to pick a fight with another Negro. Once the fight was over, they were satisfied. They beat their frustrations and discontent out on each other. I had often thought that if some of that Saturday night energy was used constructively or even directed at the right objects, it would make a tremendous difference in the life of Negroes in Mississippi.

The next week or so, things went along fairly well. Within a few days, I had gotten to know most of the canvassers. They were more energetic than any bunch of teen-agers I had known or worked with before. There were about forty or fifty that reported daily. We kept running into problems. I found it necessary to keep dividing them into smaller teams. First I divided them into two teams, one for the mornings and one for the afternoons. Most of the eligible voters worked during the day, so a third team was organized for the evenings. Some of the teen-agers were so energetic that they often went out with all the teams. I usually canvassed with the last team for a couple of hours, then rushed to the Freedom House to cook.

It didn't take me long to find out that the Negroes in Madison County were the same as those in most of the other counties. They were just as apathetic or indifferent about voting. Nevertheless, we had begun to get a few more adults out to rallies at night. Pretty soon the whites saw fit to move in. They wanted to make sure that more adults would not get involved. Since our recruitment and canvassing was done mostly by the teen-agers, they decided to scare the teen-agers away. One night after a rally, George, Bettye and I had just walked back to the Freedom House when C. O. Chinn came rushing in after us. He kept repeating over and over again, "Five kids were just shot. Five kids were just shot." We stood there motionless, not wanting to believe what we had just heard, afraid to ask any questions. Were they seriously hurt? Was anyone dead?

Before any of us said a word, Mr. Chinn was saying, "They are at the hospital now, George, let's go over and see how they are." George got his cap and headed for the door, with Bettye and me right behind him.

As we were all getting into Mr. Chinn's car, Mr. Chinn said, "I'm going to leave you girls by my house with Minnie Lou. Anne, you and Bettye can't go to the hospital. How do you know they weren't trying to kill one of you? Maybe one of the girls was taken for you or Bettye."

As we approached his house, we saw Mrs. Chinn standing in the doorway as if she was about to leave.

"Where do you think you're going, Minnie Lou? You're goin' to stay right here with Anne and Bettye," Mr. Chinn said.

Mrs. Chinn didn't answer—the voice of authority had spoken. Mrs. Chinn, Bettye and I simply did as we were told. We sat around the house talking until about 4 A.M., and then we all tried to get some sleep. I didn't sleep at all. I kept thinking of what might possibly happen. This was probably just a warning. Something else was coming on. I could feel it. Finally, it was daylight and Mr. Chinn and George still hadn't returned. Maybe they didn't want to face us and say So-and-so died.

"Anne! Anne!" Mrs. Chinn was calling me. "Are you asleep?"

"No," I answered.

"Let's go down to the office. Maybe C.O. and George are there," she said. We all got up and headed for the office. We arrived just as Mr. Chinn and George were getting out of the car. "They're O.K.," Mr. Chinn told us. "They were released from the hospital about five-thirty this morning." He explained that they had been hit with buckshot.

That afternoon when the five teen-agers came to the office to fill out affidavits to be sent to the Justice Department, I heard the full story. They had been walking home down Pear Street after last night's rally when the incident occurred. As they passed the service station on the opposite side of the street, Price Lewis, the white owner, had been standing in the doorway. This did not seem unusual—they generally saw him there. Then just as they were crossing the railroad tracks to the left of the service station, they heard a loud noise. They looked back and noticed that Price Lewis was now holding a shotgun pointed in their direction. At this point, one of the girls said she looked down and discovered blood was running down her legs into her shoes. She realized she had been shot and saw that the others had been wounded by buckshot pellets too.

Price Lewis had been arrested at the service station and taken to jail during the morning. Immediately he posted a small bail and was released. Within an hour or so he was back to work at the service station, carrying on as though nothing had happened. His Negro service attendant was still there too. He acted as if he really hated being there and he must have known how other Negroes were looking at him, but I knew he couldn't afford to leave his job.

The shooting really messed up our relationship with the teen-agers. Within two or three days they had stopped coming to the office. I knew that their parents were responsible for most of them not coming back. From the beginning most of the parents had not approved of their participation in the voter registration drive. Several kids had told me that they came against their parents' wishes, but they always refused to let me go home with them to talk things over with the adults. They took too much pride in the work they were doing with us to let me do that. I think they knew as well as I that it was for themselves and themselves alone that they were working—because within a few years they would be the ones who would have to deal with the whites.

Now, however, I felt I had an obligation to go and see their parents. I did so with very little success. Some flatly refused to see me. Those that did gave made-up excuses as to why their children had to stay home. One sent her little boy to the door to tell me she was not home; "Mama say she ain't heah," he said.

I hardly knew what to do. I was not prepared to cope with this situation. I kept trying to think of some way to get the teen-agers involved again. For one thing, we would not be able to get our work done without them. Bettye and I tried canvassing alone for a day or so and ended up almost dead from exhaustion.

During this lapse in the project, I got one of those weeping letters from Mama again. As usual, she was begging me to leave Mississippi, and as usual she peeved the hell out of me, but I couldn't take lightly what she said about Wilkinson County. I knew too well what I was up against.

The next day, in an attempt to forget her letter, I decided to busy myself with cleaning the office. I got the one teen-ager that still hung around to help me, and sent him to the café for a pail of water. When he came back, he said, "Anne, there are two white men outside in a car asking to see the person in charge of the office."

"Are they from Canton or around here?" I asked.

"No," he said. "I've never seen them before."

My heart almost jumped right out of me. It was not until then that I really began to think of some of the things in Mama's letter. She had said that the white folks in Centreville had found out that I was in Canton, and that some Negro had told her he heard they planned to bump me off. She had been pleading with me this time as she had never done before. Why did I want to get myself killed? she kept asking. What was I trying to prove? Over and over again she said that after I was dead things would still be the same as they were now.

Now here I was standing in the middle of the office trembling with fear, not wanting to face the white men outside. Maybe they were here to tell me something terrible had happened. Maybe they came just to make sure I was here. George was out in the country talking to some farmers, and Bettye was cleaning the Freedom House. How I wished one of them were here now, so they could go outside instead of me. Finally I stopped shaking long enough to make myself walk out of the office. "You can't be getting scared without finding out who they are or what they want," I kept telling myself.

As I approached the car, and took a good look at the two men inside, I was almost positive I didn't recognize them from Centreville. Feeling almost limp from relief, I walked up to the driver and said, "I was told you would like to see the person in charge."

"Yes, we are from the FBI," he said, showing me his identification. "We are here to investigate the shooting. Where can we find the five kids who were involved?"

I stood there mad as hell. "The stupid bastards!" I thought. There I was getting all flustered and scared because of my mother's letter, not knowing who they were. "Why didn't you come inside and present yourselves as officials from the FBI?" I asked angrily. "We just don't happen to run out into the streets to see every white man that drives up in front of this office, you know. After all, it might just be someone ready to blow our heads off."

"Can you tell me where I could find those five kids that were shot?" he asked again, a little indignant.

"I'll see if I can find the addresses for you," I said sweetly. "Why don't you two come inside for a minute?"

I knew they weren't particularly interested in getting out of their car and coming into the office. However, I gave them a look that said, "You'll never get those addresses unless you do," so they followed me. They stood around impatiently, looking at our broken-down chairs and sofa, as if to say, "What a shame these niggers have to come into a place and open up a joint like this and cause all this trouble for us."

"I can find only three of the addresses for you," I said, "I would like that you wait and see George Raymond, our project director. He should be back soon and he'll be able to show you where they live. Why don't you two have a seat until he comes?"

"What time do you expect him?" one asked.

"Within fifteen or twenty minutes," I said. Realizing they had to wait that long, they decided to sit. They placed themselves carefully on the sofa, as if it was diseased or something. They must be from the South, I thought. "Where are you two from?" I asked.

"New Orleans," one said.

They waited restlessly until George returned. He spent a few hours driving around with them and they saw all the kids and questioned them. That was the extent of their "investigation." The same afternoon they left town and we never saw or heard from them after that.

By the beginning of August when the teen-age canvassers still had not returned, Dave Dennis decided to bring in three other workers—two girls, who were students from Jackson, and a boy called Flukie, a CORE task force worker. There were now six of us, but there was still more work than we could handle. George and Flukie went out in the country each day to talk with farmers and to scout for churches to conduct workshops in. The rest of us were left to canvass and look after the office.

So far we had only been able to send a handful of Negroes to the courthouse to attempt to register, and those few that went began to get fired from their jobs. This discouraged others who might have registered. Meanwhile, we were constantly being threatened by the whites. Almost every night someone came running by to tell us the whites planned to bump us off.

One evening just before dark, someone took a shot at a pregnant Negro woman who was walking home with her two small sons. This happened in a section where a few poor white families lived. The woman stood in the street with her children, screaming and yelling for help. A Negro truck driver picked them up and drove them to the Boyd Street housing project, which was right across the street from the Freedom House. She was still yelling and screaming when she got out of the truck, and people ran out of all the project houses. The woman stood there telling everyone what had happened. She was so big it looked as though she was ready to have the baby any minute. As I looked at the other women standing around her, I didn't like what I saw in their faces. I could tell what they were thinking—"Why don't you all get out of here before you get us all killed?"

After this incident, Negro participation dropped off to almost nothing, and things got so rough we were afraid to walk the streets. In addition, our money was cut off. We were being paid twenty dollars a week by the Voter Education Project, a Southern agency which supported voter registration for Negroes. They said that since we were not producing registered voters, they could not continue to put money into the area. It seemed things were getting rough from every angle. We sometimes went for days without a meal. I was getting sick and losing lots of weight. When the NAACP invited me to speak at a Thursday night women's rally in Jackson, at one of the big churches, I tried to prepare a speech that would get across to them how we were suffering in Canton.

Everything went wrong the night of the rally. Ten minutes before Dave arrived to pick me up, Jean, one of the new girls, had a terrible asthma attack, and we had to drop her off at the hospital in Jackson. I arrived at the church exhausted and an hour late, still wearing the skirt and blouse I had worked in all day; they looked like I had slept in them for weeks. The mistress of ceremonies was just explaining that I was unable to make it, when I walked straight up on the stage. She turned and looked at me as if I was crazy, and didn't say another word. She just took her seat, and I walked up to the mike. By this time I had completely forgotten my prepared speech, and I don't remember exactly what I said at first. I had been standing up there I don't know how long when the mistress of ceremonies said, "You are running overtime." I got mad at her and thought I would tell the audience exactly what I was thinking. When I finished telling them about the trouble we were having in Canton, I found myself crying. Tears were running down my cheeks and I was shaking and saying, "What are we going to do? Starve to death? Look at me. I've lost about fifteen pounds in a week." I stood there going to pieces, until Reverend Ed King walked up on the platform, put his arm around me and led me away.

Outside he said, "You touched them, Anne. I think you got your message across." He was still standing with his arm around me, and I was drying my eyes when Dave came up.

"What's wrong with her?" he asked.

"She just finished a speech which I think was tremendous," Reverend King said. "But I think she needs a rest, Dave."

Dave took me to his apartment in Jackson and said I could rest there a couple of days. I didn't really think about what had happened during my speech until I was in bed trying to sleep. Then I realized I was cracking up, and I began to cry again.

When I got back to Canton on Sunday, I discovered that a tub of food had been brought in from Jackson. We arrived just in time to find Flukie helping himself to some golden brown chicken. He gave me a note that had been left with the food:

> *Dear Anne,*
>
> *Brought some food for your people. Your speech was something Thursday night. However, you need a rest. Why don't you come spend a week with me? See you next week. Let me know if the food runs out before then. You take care of yourself.*
>
> *Mrs. Young*

I knew Mrs. Young through her sons, who had gone to jail with me during the demonstrations in Jackson. She had nine children, five of whom had been arrested. She was a beautiful lady and I appreciated the food she brought. But I felt bad about taking it, thinking about all those children she had and no husband.

Dave and Mattie Dennis, and Jerome Smith, another CORE field secretary, moved in to Canton with us the next week. Dave felt that the only way we were going to get any money put back into the area was if we got more people registered.

Suddenly we began to get quite a lot of support from the local Negroes. Mr. Chinn began working with us almost full time. They saw that we were trying hard and that we were doing our best under the circumstances. Every day now we managed to send a few Negroes to the courthouse. Soon we had a steady flow moving daily. But the registrar was flunking them going and coming. Sometimes out of twenty or twenty-five Negroes who went to register, only one or two would pass the test. Some of them were flunked because they used a title (Mr. or Mrs.) on the application blank; others because they didn't. And most failed to interpret a section of the Mississippi constitution to the satisfaction of Foote Campbell, the Madison County circuit clerk.

All of the Negroes who flunked but should have passed the test were asked to fill out affidavits to be sent to the Justice Department. Hundreds of these were sent and finally two men came down from Washington to look at the county registrar's books. They talked with the registrar and persuaded him to register four or five people who had been flunked because of using "Mr." or "Mrs." One of them was a blind man who had failed several times, and who should not have had to take the test anyway.

To keep up the pace, Dave brought in two more workers. Now there were nine of us working full time. When this news got to the white community, and they sensed the support we must be getting, they began to threaten us again.

One Friday evening, just as we were finishing dinner, Sonny's brother Robert came running into the kitchen. He was sweating and panting as if he had been running for a long time. At first, he didn't say anything. We all sat and stared, waiting. He just stared back. He looked like he was trying to decide how to tell us something. I thought that he had been chased by someone.

"Man, what's wrong with you?" George finally asked.

"Uh...uh..." Robert began. "Man, y'all better get outta Canton *tonight!* I got a funny feelin' when I was walkin' aroun' in town tonight so I went over to that Black Tom's café to see what people were talkin' 'bout. Sho' nuff, one o' them drunk bastards sittin' up there sayin' they gonna kill all them damn freedom workers tonight."

"What? *Who* said that?" Jerome Smith yelled. "You got more sense, Robert, than to go believe what you hear some drunkard sayin' in a café."

"Man, lissen, lissen, you don't believe me, go ask Joe Lee. He was sittin' there a *long* time. He said he was just about to come over and tell y'all. They really gonna do it, they really gonna do it tonight! Did Dave go to Jackson yet? Man, y'all better get outta Canton!"

"What do you mean, Robert?" I asked. "How did that guy find out? Them whites probably spread that shit just so it'll get back to us. If they were really gonna kill us, wouldn't any nigger in town know anything about it till it was all over with."

"Moody, that man work for Howard, who's behind *all* this shit here in Canton, and if he say he heard somethin', he *heard* it."

"That's what I just said, it was intended for him to hear," I said.

"George, y'all can sit here and listen to Annie Moody if you want to, but I swear to *God*, you betta get outta here! You think that fuckin' nigger woulda said anything if he *hadn'ta* been drunk?"

It was hard for us to believe what Robert was saying; however, none of us had ever seen him this nervous before. Finally George and Jerome decided that they would go into town to see if they could find out anything. By the time they got back it was pitch black outside. As soon as Jerome burst in the door we could all see that Robert had been right.

"Them white folks in town's *together*, man, and we better do something but quick," he said, almost out of breath.

I knew we were in bad shape. Dave had taken the car into Jackson for the weekend and the only people in town that would put us up were C.O. and Minnie Lou and they weren't home. So we just sat there until after eleven, trying to figure out a way to get out of Canton. We couldn't walk because there was only one way in and one way out, and we knew they could just as well mow us down on the highway.

"We are just wastin' time sittin' here bullshittin' like this. I ain't about to go down that dark-ass road. And I ain't about to stay in this damn house either," Flukie said.

"Y'all can sit here and talk *all night* if you want to," Bettye said, suddenly appearing in the door with a blanket in her arms. "But

I'm gonna take my ass out back in that tall grass and worry about gettin' outta here tomorrow."

Since Sonny's house was new, he hadn't cultivated a garden yet, so the space behind the house where the garden would have been had grown wild with tall weeds. Sonny them just mowed the back lawn right up to the weeds and let them grow like hedges.

It didn't take us long to agree that the weeds were our only way out. Even so, we knew that there was still a good chance that we would be discovered back there, but we had no other choice. So we pulled open the curtains and left the lamps on dim so that anyone could see that the house was empty. We also removed the sheets and blankets and left the spreads so the beds looked made. We waited until about twelve-thirty when all the lights in the neighborhood had been turned out. Then we sneaked out back with blankets and sheets clutched in our arms. The nine of us spaced ourselves so that from a distance no one patch of grass would look mashed down. The five guys made us girls stay behind them. We agreed not to do anything but look and listen without saying a word to each other.

I was wrapped in one of the spreads and after lying still for what seemed like hours, I began to get very cold and stiff. I couldn't hear a sound not even a cricket and I began to feel like I was all alone out there. I listened for Bettye's breathing, but I heard nothing. I wondered if the others were feeling as alone and scared as I was. I could feel the grass getting wet with dew and I began to get colder and colder. I kept thinking about what might happen to us if they found us out there. I tried hard not to think about it. But I couldn't help it. I could see them stomping us in the face and shooting us. I also kept thinking about the house and whether we had left some clue that we were out back. Suddenly I heard a noise and I could almost feel everyone jump with me.

"Don't get scared, it's that damn dog next door. Just be quiet and he'll shut up," one of the guys whispered.

Now I knew we were in for it. That damn dog kept on whimpering. I could see the neighbor coming out and discovering us just when the Klan drove up. But finally the dog was quiet again.

I must have begun to doze off when I heard a car door slam.

"Quiet! Quiet! They're here," Flukie whispered as someone moved in the grass.

I couldn't even breathe. My whole chest began to hurt as I heard the mumbling voices toward the front of the house. When the mumbling got louder I knew that they were in the back. But I still couldn't make out what they were saying. As I heard them moving around in the backyard, I had a horrible feeling that they could see us as plain as daylight and I just trembled all over. But in a few minutes I heard the car door slam again and they were gone.

We lay quietly in case they had pulled a trick. Finally Jerome whispered loudly, "They think we're at C.O.'s. They'll probably be back."

Soon the roosters were crowing and it began to get light. Sure enough they drove up again but this time they must have just taken a quick look, because they were gone almost immediately. We knew they wouldn't be back because it was too light. So we sneaked back in the house before the neighbors got up.

George, who had been in a position to see and hear them, told us what happened. He said that there was a pickup truck with about eight men who had obviously been drinking. They had all sorts of weapons. They discussed burning the house down, but decided that they would come back and get us another night.

After this incident, Robert and a group of men all in their middle or late twenties formed a group to protect us. Three or four of them had already lost their jobs because they tried to register. They couldn't find other jobs so they followed us around everywhere we went, walking with us as if they were bulletproof. They also spread rumors that the Freedom House was protected by armed men. We were all still a little up tight and afraid to sleep at night, but after a while, when the whites didn't come back, we figured the rumors worked. The threats didn't bother me as much now. I began to feel almost safe with those men around all the time. Their interest, courage, and concern gave all of us that extra lift we needed.

Now every Negro church in the county was opened for workshops. The nine of us split into groups of three. Almost every night we had workshops in different churches, sometimes sixteen to thirty miles out of town.

One or two of our protective guys had cars. They were usually sent along with the girls out in the country. It was dark and dangerous driving down those long country rock roads, but now that we always had two or three of the guys riding with us, it wasn't so bad. In fact, once we got to the churches, everything was fine. Listening to those old Negroes sing freedom songs was like listening to music from heaven. They sang them as though they were singing away the chains of slavery. Sometimes I just looked at the expressions on their faces as they sang and cold chills would run down my back. Whenever God was mentioned in a song, I could tell by the way they said the word that most of them had given up here on earth. They seemed to be waiting just for God to call them home and end all the suffering.

The nightly church workshops were beginning to be the big thing going for us at this point in the campaign. However, the white folks found out about this and tried to put a stop to it. One night out in the country three carloads of whites chased George and a group of the guys all the way to Canton. George said they were shooting at them like crazy. Since George thought the whites could have killed them if they had wanted to, we took it as a warning. We were extra careful after that.

The luckiest thing that happened to us was that we had succeeded in getting C. O. Chinn to work with us. He was a powerful man, known as "bad-ass C. O. Chinn" to the Negroes and whites alike. All of the Negroes respected him for standing up and being a man. Most of the whites feared him. He was the type of person that didn't take shit from anyone. If he was with you he was all for you. If he didn't like you that was it—in that case he just didn't have anything to do with you. Because he was respected by most of the local Negroes, he was our most effective speaker in the churches. He was in a position to speak his mind and what he said was taken without offense to anyone in particular.

Just as Mr. Chinn opened up full force, the whites cut in on him. Within a week he was forced to close his place and he began moving out most of his things. This still wasn't enough to satisfy the whites. One evening, when he was taking home the .45 he had kept around for protection, he was stopped and arrested by those damn cops that hung around the office all the time. He was immediately taken to jail and charged with carrying a concealed weapon—actually he had placed the gun on the seat beside him. His bail was set at five hundred dollars. He was in jail for a week before his family could find anyone to post a property bond. Most of the local Negroes had borrowed money on their property, which meant that it couldn't be used for bail purposes.

I think this was the beginning of C. O.'s realization of what had happened to him. Not only had he lost everything he had, he was sitting in jail with no one to go his bail. Instead of this putting the damper on his activities as the whites had expected, it increased them. He began hitting harder than ever. Often when he was speaking, he would say, "Take me, for example, they have completely put me out of business. I have lost practically everything I have. These young workers are here starving to death trying to help you people. And for what? A lot of you ain't worth it!" Not one of us working for CORE could have talked to the local people like that.

It was the middle of August now, and we had been working in the county for two months. Up until this time, not one of the ministers in Canton had committed himself to helping us. When they did give us a chance to speak in their churches, it was only for two or three minutes during the announcements. The biggest Negro church in Canton was pastored by Canton's biggest "Tom." Most of his congregation were middle-class bourgeois Negroes. We all knew that if we could somehow force him to move, every other large church in Canton would open its doors to us.

We set up a meeting and invited all the ministers, but since the number one minister didn't show up, all the others did was mumble to each other and tell us, "We can't do anything until Reverend Tucker says so." After that we decided to forget the ministers and go to work on their congregations. At this point the ministers started coming around. In fact, they called a meeting to talk things over with us. But the talk was fruitless. The ministers tried to play the same game the Southern white people played when things got too hot for them. That is, to find out what you are thinking and try and get you to hold off long enough for them to come up with some new strategy to use on you. Those Toms weren't as dumb as they appeared, I thought. They had learned to play Mr. Charlie's game pretty well.

We had a surprise for them, though. We had made headway with several of their most influential members, and they put us right where we wanted to go—behind the pulpits for more than five minutes. Now we could hit the Canton churches hard.

For a little while that good old Movement spirit was on the surge again. Everyone began to feel it. We still were not getting any money, but for the most part we didn't need any. The Canton Negroes began to take good care of us, and we were never hungry. A Negro service station owner even let us have gas on credit. What pleased me most was that many of our teen-agers had come back. I had really missed them.

chapter

TWENTY-FOUR

Toward the end of August, it suddenly seemed as if everyone in our group was leaving. The Jackson high school students went back to school, one girl left for New York to get married, and one guy went to California. Soon George and I were the only ones left. To make things worse, the high schools in the Canton area were opening in a week. Dave promised to bring in a couple of more people, but meanwhile it seemed as though George and I would have to do all the work ourselves. We also had to find a new place to stay, since Sonny and his wife went back together. This was a problem because people just didn't want to risk letting us live with them. Within a week, however, we found a place which was ideal—a two-apartment house. One apartment for the girls and one for the boys. "Great," I thought, "just when everyone's leaving."

I was so busy moving into the new place, that I completely forgot that the August 28 March on Washington was only a few days off. I had been planning to go ever since it was announced. Suddenly it was August 26 and I didn't even have a ride lined up.

There had been no room for me and other staff people on the bus, since there were so many local Negroes who wanted to make the trip.

Reverend King and his wife were driving up and offered to take me, though they warned me it would be quite risky driving through most of the Southern states in an integrated car. I told them I was willing to take the chance if they were.

On August 27 at 6 A.M., we headed for Washington. There were five of us, three whites (Reverend King, his wife, and Joan Trumpauer), and two Negroes (Bob, a student returning to Harvard, and myself). In the beginning, we were all a little uneasy, but somehow we made it through the Southern states without incident.

After driving all day and night, we arrived at the grounds of the Washington Monument just in time for the march, and joined the section of Southern delegates. Up on a podium near our section, various celebrities—Mahalia Jackson, Odetta, Peter, Paul and Mary—were singing. During a break in the entertainment the Mississippi delegates were asked to come to the podium and sing freedom songs. I got up and followed the others to the platform reluctantly. I think I was the only girl from Mississippi with a dress on. All the others were wearing denim skirts and jeans. We sang a couple of songs and shortly after, it was announced that the march to the Lincoln Memorial was about to start. Thousands of people just took off, leaving most of their leaders on the podium. It was kind of funny to watch the leaders run to overtake the march. The way some of them had been leading the people in the past, perhaps the people were better off leading themselves, I thought.

The march was now in full motion, and there were people everywhere. Some were on crutches, some in wheel chairs, and some were actually being carried down Pennsylvania and Constitution avenues. There were all kinds of signs and placards—one group of men acting as pallbearers carried a casket that said BURY JIM CROW.

By the time we got to Lincoln Memorial, there were already thousands of people there. I sat on the grass and listened to the speakers, to discover we had "dreamers" instead of leaders leading us. Just about every one of them stood up there dreaming. Martin Luther King went on and on talking about his dream. I sat there thinking that in Canton we never had time to sleep, much less dream.

I left Washington two days later with Joan Trumpauer and the Kings. As we drove out of town, no one had very much to say. I guess they were thinking about the historic event that had just taken place. I was thinking about it too, and I was also thinking that this was the first time in well over a year I had been away from my work with the Movement and away from Mississippi. I had really forgotten what it was like to be out of an atmosphere of fear and threats. I had even gone to a movie. The last movie I had seen had been in New Orleans the previous summer. "It's kind of strange," I thought. "I never really think of going to a movie when I'm in Mississippi." There was always so much work, so many problems, and so many threats that I hardly ever thought of anything except how to best get the job done and survive from day to day.

I noticed that Washington seemed like a deserted town compared to two days ago. How had 250,000 people disappeared so quickly? I seriously began to wonder whether those 250,000 people had made any impact on Congress.

As we began to drive through Virginia, I started to worry about the trip back. I was now the only Negro in the car. The white people of the South must really have some strong feelings about the march by now, I thought. I knew when we returned to Mississippi, we would be faced with twice as many threats and acts of violence. And maybe we'd never even get back to Mississippi. After all, we had to go back through the rest of those backward-assed states. We were going to go through Alabama and I knew damned well how bad that state was.

Reverend King must have thought of the dangers of the trip back, too. When we stopped at a Howard Johnson Restaurant right inside the Tennessee border, he suggested that we spend the night in Tennessee, then get up and drive through Alabama during the day.

When I discovered where we were going to sleep, I realized how much consideration he had given the matter. We were going to sleep in a Federal Park in the Tennessee mountains. I guess he thought that because the park was federal land most likely we would not run into any trouble there. The more I thought about it, the madder I got. Here I was forcing my white friends to sleep in a park because I was black and could not sleep in the same hotel with them. If it was not for me they could have slept in one of those luxurious hotels.

Reverend King and his wife were still asleep the next morning when Joan and I got up and wandered off through the park to find the rest room. We discovered showers there and decided to use them, since we seemed to have been the first to have gotten up that early. There were lots of parked cars around but we didn't see anyone stirring. We thought we could manage to get a good shower before all the other people in the park got up.

As we were finishing, two white women came in. They were from Georgia. We heard them talking as they used the toilets. Joan and I hadn't bothered to go back to the car and get towels. We were using the paper towels instead. When the women came from behind the little partition that gave privacy to the toilets, they saw us standing in the middle of the floor naked, drying each other's backs with paper. They didn't know how to react. It was a shock to them. Here we were, a black girl and a white girl, standing in a Southern public shower naked. I guess they thought we were having a "nude-in" or a "wash-in" or something. Anyway they didn't stay around to watch the demonstration. As they were leaving one sniffed, "Niggers everywhere."

Getting back to the car we found Reverend King and his wife awake. We told them that we had found some terrific showers without telling them the rest of the story, and they went off to shower too. Just before the Kings came back, several white women came snooping around the car. Joan and I were sitting in the back seat. We recognized two of them as the women from the showers. I guess they had found more women and gone back to the showers to beat us up. When they hadn't found us there, they had gone looking for us. For a while they were all staring at the Mississippi license plate. They didn't know what to do. I guess they thought I was a maid or some kind of governess working for the owner of the car. When the Kings returned, the women really looked bewildered. Reverend King was wearing his clerical collar. He didn't look exactly old or rich, but just like one of those "civil rights preachers." Before they could make up their minds what they were going to do about us, Reverend King and his wife got into the car and drove off, with Joan and me looking out the back window laughing. At this point I think it dawned upon those ladies that we were, in their language, professional agitators. "Too bad," I cracked to Joan, "now it's too late—that's a bunch of women for you."

Fortunately, the drive through Alabama went without incident. We arrived in Canton about 6 P.M. Reverend King dropped me at the Freedom House and drove straight on to Tougaloo. It was too dangerous for white civil rights workers to be caught in Canton after dark.

chapter

TWENTY-FIVE

Now that school was in session in Canton, I became more and more aware of the terrible poverty in the area. Many of the teen-agers who had worked with us had been unable to return to classes because their parents had been fired from their jobs and could not afford to buy their children school clothes. Some of these teen-agers had worked every summer to keep themselves in school, but this summer, because of the voter registration drive, had not been able to find jobs. To see those kids out of school standing around hungry all day sickened me. I felt so guilty, as if we were responsible.

Just across the street from the office, a lady lived in a two-room house with her five children. She supported them and her sick father on the five dollars that she earned doing domestic work. School had been open for two weeks and I noticed that the two girls were home every day. When I asked them the first week why they weren't in school, I was told that the younger girl had mumps. The older one said that she had to stay home with the younger. The second week of school I asked them again. This time they told me the truth. Their grandfather had been terribly sick during the summer. The mother, after buying medicine for her father all summer long, was unable to buy clothes for them to wear to school. The oldest boy, who was seventeen years old, had been able to buy clothes for himself and the other two boys, but not for his two sisters. With tears pouring down her cheeks, the oldest girl told me that they would be unable to go to school if they stayed out another week. My whole childhood came to life again. I thought of how my mother had suffered with us when we had been deserted by my father. How we went hungry all the time, never having anything to eat but bread and on rare occasions beans and bread. I was reminded of my sick grandfather who looked after my sister and brother while I was in school. I remembered how he used to fish a dollar out of his money sack and give it to my mother to buy food with. All that I had vowed to forget and overcome came back to me. The life these kids were leading was a replica of my own past.

When George returned from canvassing in the country with Mr. Chinn, we had a four-hour meeting trying to figure out how to get some clothes and food to needy families. After the meeting, Mr. Chinn and George went to Greenwood to talk with the SNCC workers. We knew they were getting clothes in the Delta. Maybe they would agree to have the next shipment sent to Canton. Anyway, if anyone could convince them how badly we needed those things, C.O. could.

The next day I received my first twenty-five dollars from CORE. Dave Dennis had been trying to get us on the payroll for about two months. George and I were finally being paid. There was also a twenty-five-dollar check for Mr. Chinn. Looking at my check, I thought, "You didn't get here when I needed you before, but now you're right on time." I kissed it and headed across the street. Standing before the two girls on the porch, waving my check, I said, "We're in business. Let's go shopping. Tomorrow, you two go to school."

"What?" the older one said. "Do you mean that?"

"You see this check here? It says"—and I pointed—"it says, 'Pay to the order of Anne Moody, twenty-five dollars'!"

"Twenty-five dollars!" the younger one said. It was as if this was more money than she ever hoped to have.

"That's right, and it's all ours," I said. "You two ready to go shopping?"

"Yes," they shouted simultaneously.

"First, you two watch the office until I get back. I'm going up to the Washingtons' to cash it."

The Washingtons were well-to-do Negroes who owned a grocery store. They also rented us the Freedom House we were now staying in. They were the only ones in Canton who would cash our checks. None of the white stores, or the Canton bank, would.

In minutes, I was back to the office, and our shopping tour began. Our first stop was the five-and-ten. We found some tennis shoes on sale for a dollar, and bought a pair for each girl. On another counter, we found some blouses for fifty cents. Then we picked up a dollar book sack for the younger girl, a ten-cent comb and fifty-cent brush for each and headed for the bargain store. There we found dresses on sale, two for five dollars. I bought each of them two. Then two pencils for five cents and two ten-cent tablets. It took only thirty-five minutes for us to do all this shopping. Realizing I still had money left, the younger girl said she was hungry. So our next stop was our favorite little restaurant where we could get baloney sandwiches for ten cents. We had two sandwiches apiece and went back to the office. They seemed like the two happiest girls in the world, but I think I was even happier.

When their mother got home, she came over and thanked me. She offered to pay me back when she got caught up. I told her to forget it, that people had done the same for me when I was small.

She looked at me as if to say, "I believe you, otherwise you wouldn't have understood."

The next day the girls stopped in on their way to school.

"Mama told us to let you see us and ask you if you want us to do anything for you when we get out of school," the older one said.

"Yes, there is something you can do for me," I said. "You can go home and study real hard. Then you might be able to make up for the two weeks you've missed. Now hurry on to school before you are late." I watched them out of the window until they were out of sight. They were beaming, and so was I.

Just as I was about to leave for the office, George and Mr. Chinn drove in from the Delta. They had enough canned food and peanut butter with them to last a month. As they put the food in the house, I said, "I have a surprise for you two."

George looked at me, puzzled. "If someone was shot, I don't wanta hear about it."

"It's good news."

"Did we have a fortune willed to us?" Mr. Chinn asked.

"Not exactly," I said, "but the three of us got our twenty-five dollar checks from CORE yesterday."

"That ain't exactly a fortune," Mr. Chinn said, "but right now it sounds like one."

"I have news for you, too," George said.

"Wait, let me brace myself." I backed against the wall. "Now, shoot."

"We might get some clothes in next week. SNCC has been getting quite a bit from the Delta. They have a big shipment coming in from a Jewish synagogue somewhere. We convinced them to send it straight to Canton."

"Are you kidding?" I said.

"I hope they ain't lying to us," Mr. Chinn said. "Anyway, they have enough food in Greenwood to keep us alive for a while. That I seen with my own eyes."

"In that case, we're in business," I said.

A few days later as George and I drove up to the office after a trip to Jackson, we found a big express truck outside. We jumped out of the car to see what it was. I had a feeling I knew, but I was afraid to find out it wasn't what I thought. As George got out of the car, the driver of the truck asked, "Are you George Raymond?"

"Yes," George answered.

"We have a shipment of clothes here for you."

As we unloaded the boxes of clothes, I realized there was much more than we had expected. The office got so crowded we could barely move around in it. Boxes were stacked from the floor to the ceiling with little space left for us. I was so happy that they had come. They would help a lot of people, I thought. Maybe they would also help encourage Negroes to get out and vote. That was what had happened in the Delta.

The rest of the week I worked on sorting out the clothes. It was hard work, but I was happy doing it. I was feeling great until the weekend, then all of a sudden I became so depressed that I didn't even feel like seeing or talking to anyone. When Dave and his wife Mattie came to Canton on Saturday afternoon for a weekend staff meeting, I excused myself and went for a walk alone. I was afraid someone would ask me what was wrong and I would burst into tears. I had cried lots of times when things weren't going well with the project, but no one had ever seen me crying. I wasn't about to let anyone see me now.

The others knew that I couldn't go home again, but no one knew of the agony I was going through because of it. I never told anyone about all the letters I was receiving from Mama, begging me to leave Mississippi and always telling me that my life was in danger. They all had their share of problems. They couldn't do anything about mine.

Now that I was walking, tears were running down my cheeks. Tomorrow I would be twenty-three years old, I thought. I had never failed before to get a birthday card from Adline or Mama. Mama was probably mad because I didn't answer her last letter. "Why should I keep encouraging her to write, anyway?" I thought. "She never writes me a cheerful letter. She couldn't possibly conceive of the things we're going through here." I knew she would never understand me if I tried to tell her why I felt I had to do the work I was doing. All she would say is what she always said: "Negroes are going to have troubles until they're dead, and after you are dead we'll still have the same problems."

Finally I headed back to the Freedom House. When I returned, I tried to be more cheerful, even though anyone could look at my eyes and tell I had been crying.

"Moody, come go shopping with me," Mattie said. "I'm not going to be long."

"O.K.," I said, knowing she wanted to talk with me and try to find out what was bothering me.

As we were walking to town she said, "What's wrong, Moody? Are you mad with us? It's not Dave's fault. He's tried to get someone to work in here with you all. People just don't want to come in here. Most of them are scared to work in Canton. You know that. Besides, Dave can't even get money to pay them. Dave thinks you're mad with him. You know how sensitive he is. He is trying, though, and he'll find somebody soon, I'm sure."

"That's not what's wrong, Mattie," I said. "I know Dave is trying."

"Then what is it?" she asked. "Did you get bad news from home? Are your people all right?"

"I guess they're O.K. It's just that tomorrow's my birthday and I was kinda looking for a card from them. When the mailman came and I didn't get one, I felt bad about it," I said.

"Why didn't you tell us? We could have planned something for you," she said.

"You all have enough problems without worrying about whether I'm happy on my birthday or not," I said.

COMING *of* AGE IN MISSISSIPPI

She seemed very glad to hear I wasn't mad at Dave and ready to jump up and leave the project. While we were shopping, she insisted on buying me two pairs of pajamas that were on sale for my birthday. When we got back to the Freedom House, she called Dave into the bedroom. "She's probably telling him I'm not angry at him," I thought. They were in there a long time. When Dave came out, he was smiling. He began twisting to a record that was playing on the radio.

"Come on, Anne, you ain't gonna let me finish this one by myself, are you?" he asked.

I was beginning to feel better.

"It's not that," I said. "I just don't want to show you up. My little brother twists better than that."

"Is that your excuse? I dare you to challenge me," he said.

I got up and began twisting with him. We were doing a a pretty nasty twist when Mattie came into the room.

"Anne Moody, how *dare* you dance with my husband like that!" she said.

"I think you're bitching at the wrong person. I'm not married to you, Dave is," I said.

"Dave, how dare you?" she scolded.

"Come on, George," Dave said, "let's go for a walk. Mattie is getting jealous."

When they were gone, Mattie and I sat down and talked for a while, and then I started cooking dinner. By the time I had finished, Dave and George were back carrying two large bags. "What have you two been buying?" I asked.

"Food, food, food," George said.

"Food! Where did you get the money? I thought you were broke."

"Mattie is calling you, Anne," Dave said, meanwhile looking at the plate of fried chicken on the stove.

"Did you call me, Mattie?" I yelled to her.

"Yes, come here, Moody. Come here a minute," she said.

"If you touch that chicken, Dave, I'll cut your hands off when I get back," I warned.

"I'm going with you," he said, "so if any's missing you know who did it." He looked at George, still standing there holding the two big bags.

"Do you want to go over to Henry Chinn's place tonight?" Mattie asked me. (Henry Chinn, C.O.'s brother, ran the biggest Negro nightclub in town.) "Dave, tomorrow is Annie's birthday."

"No kidding, how old are you, Anne? Nineteen?" he asked.

"Nineteen!" I said. "I'll be twenty-three and I look twice that old."

"Twenty-three," Dave said, "I thought you were going to say fifty, so I could be kissing you from now until tomorrow." Then he started kissing me.

"Dave Dennis, if you kiss Anne Moody again, I'll quit you," Mattie said. "Tomorrow is her birthday and then you better not kiss her no twenty-three times."

"You two are too damn jealous," I said. "Come on, let's eat."

As I was taking something out of the refrigerator, I noticed two gallons of ice cream and a large coconut cake in the box. "So this is what George had in the bag," I thought. "They're probably planning to give me a surprise birthday party."

We didn't go out that night, but we had so much fun just being together. We sat around the house and played cards half the night and cracked jokes. We used to sit around and play bid whist almost every Saturday night. Half of the time, though, we were just sitting up because we were afraid someone would try to kill us after we went to bed.

Sunday, September 15, 1963, was my twenty-third birthday. I got up about nine that morning feeling like one hundred and three. Everyone else was sleeping so I just decided to let them sleep. After a shower, I started to fix breakfast even though Mattie had promised to cook that morning. As soon as I finished, I got them up because we were supposed to have a staff meeting later.

"Breakfast is ready! Breakfast is ready!" I called.

Dave came running in the kitchen, yelling, "Mattie, shame on you. Today is Anne's birthday and here she is cooking breakfast while you sleep."

"Is today your birthday?" George asked, stumbling into the kitchen—as if he didn't know after buying two gallons of ice cream and a cake yesterday.

"I'm sorry, Moody," Mattie said. "I heard you cooking, but Dave wouldn't let me get up."

"You tell that on me, Mattie?" Dave said. "It was Mattie, Anne. She kept begging me, 'Just once more, Dave, Just once more.' Now who do you believe, Anne?" He was hugging Mattie and both of them were trying to look at me with a straight face.

We were all eating and listening to the radio when the music stopped abruptly in the middle of a record. "A special news bulletin just in from Birmingham," the DJ was saying. "A church was just bombed in Birmingham, Alabama. It is believed that several Sunday school students were killed." We all sat glued to our seats, avoiding each other's eyes. No one was eating now. Everyone was waiting for the next report on the bombing. The second report confirmed that four girls had been killed. I looked at George; he sat with his face buried in the palms of his hands. Dave sat motionless with tears in his eyes. Mattie looked at Dave as if she had been grounded by an electric shock. I put my hand up to my face. Tears were pouring out of my eyes, and I hadn't even known I was crying.

"Why! Why! Why! Oh, God, why? Why us? Why us?" I found myself asking. "I gotta find myself some woods, trees, or water— anything. I gotta talk to you, God, and you gotta answer. Please don't play Rip Van Winkle with me today."

I rushed out of the house and started walking aimlessly. I ran up a hill where there were trees. I found myself in a graveyard I didn't even know was there. I sat there looking up through the trees, trying to communicate with God. "Now talk to me, God. Come on down and talk to me.

"You know, I used to go to Sunday school when I was a little girl. I went to Sunday school, church, and B.T.U. every Sunday. We were taught how merciful and forgiving you are. Mama used to tell us that you would forgive us seventy-seven times a day, and I believed in you. I bet you those girls in Sunday school were being taught the same as I was when I was their age. It that teaching wrong? Are you going to forgive their killers? You not gonna answer me, God, hmm? Well, if you don't want to talk, then listen to me.

"As long as I live, I'll never be beaten by a white man again. Not like in Woolworth's. Not any more. That's out. You know something else, God? Nonviolence is out. I have a good idea Martin Luther King is talking to you, too. If he is, tell him that nonviolence has served its purpose. Tell him that for me, God, and for a lot of other Negroes who must be thinking it today. If you don't believe that, then I know you must be white, too. And if I ever find out you are white, then I'm through with you. And if I find out you are black, I'll try my best to kill you when I get to heaven.

"I'm through with you. Yes, I am going to put you down. From now on, I am my own God. I am going to live by the rules I set for myself. I'll discard everything I was once taught about you. Then I'll be you. I will be my own God, living my life as I see fit. Not as Mr. Charlie says I should live it, or Mama, or anybody else. I shall do as I want to in this society that apparently wasn't meant for me and my kind. If you are getting angry because I'm talking to you like this, then just kill me, leave me here in this graveyard dead. Maybe that's where all of us belong, anyway. Maybe then we wouldn't have to suffer so much. At the rate we are being killed now, we'll all soon be dead anyway."

When I got back to the Freedom House, Dave and Mattie were gone. I found George stretched out on his bed.

"What happened to Mattie and Dave?" I asked.

"Dave was called for a meeting in Jackson, and they had to leave. Where have you been all this time?"

"Walking," I said. "Was there any more news about the bombing?"

"No," he said, "except that the four girls were killed, and the city is getting pretty tense, the closer it gets to dark. They'll probably tear Birmingham to bits tonight. I pray that they don't have any violence."

"Pray! Pray, George! Why in the hell should we be praying all the time? Those white men who hurled that bomb into the church today weren't on their knees, were they? If those girls weren't at Sunday school today, maybe they would be alive. How do you know they weren't on their knees? That's what's wrong now. We've been praying too long. Yes, as a race all we've got is a lot of religion. And the white man's got everything else, including all the dynamite."

"Hold it—is that Miss Woolworth, the Nonviolent Miss Woolworth talking like that?" he asked.

"Let's face it, George. Nonviolence is through and you know it. Don't you think we've had enough of it? First of all we were only using it as a tactic to show, or rather dramatize, to the world how bad the situation is in the South. Well, I think we've had enough examples. I think we are overdoing it. After this bombing, if there are any more nonviolent demonstrations for the mere sake of proving what all the rest of them have, then I think we are over-dramatizing the issue."

"You feel like talking about anything else?" he asked.

"Yeah, let's talk about that beautiful march on Washington," I said, almost yelling. "It was just two weeks ago, believe it or not. And 250,000 people were there yelling, 'We want freedom.' Well, I guess this bombing is Birmingham's answer to the march. But what's gonna be our answer to the bombing? We're gonna send more of our children right back to Sunday school to be killed.

Then the President will probably issue a statement saying, 'We are doing Everything in our Power to apprehend the killers. And we are in close touch with the situation.' After which we will still run out in the streets and bow our heads and pray to be spat upon in the process. I call that real religion, real, honest-to-goodness nigger religion. If Martin Luther King thinks nonviolence is really going to work for the South as it did for India, then he is out of his mind."

On Monday, the day after the bombing, the Negroes in Canton were afraid to walk the streets. When they passed the office, they turned their heads to keep from looking in. Every time I passed one of them on the street, they looked at me and almost said, "Get out of here. You'll get us killed."

I left the office shortly after lunch. When I got to the Freedom House, I played freedom songs and tried to analyze what had happened thus far for us in the Movement. I discovered my mind was so warped and confused I couldn't think clearly. The church bombing had had a terrible effect on me. It had made me question everything I had ever believed in. "There has got to be another way for us," I thought. "If not, then there is no end to the misery we are now encountering."

I put a Ray Charles record on the box and he was saying, "Feeling sad all the time, that's because I got a worried mind. The world is in an uproar, the danger zone is everywhere. Read your paper, and you'll see just exactly what keep worryin' me." It seemed as though I had never listened to Ray before. For the first time he said something to me.

George came in later, bringing a girl with him. "Anne, I would like for you to meet Lenora. She might be working with us. She was kicked off her father's plantation."

"Why?" I asked.

"It seems as though she was thinking like you yesterday, after the bombing. Somehow it got back to her father's boss man, and she left running last night."

I knew that he brought her here because he wanted me to have some other person to talk to.

"If you can't go home, then don't go feeling like the Lone Ranger," I said. "I haven't been home since Thanksgiving of '61. I know a lot of other people that can't go home either. So you see, you have plenty of company."

She grinned like a silly little country girl.

"Where are you living now?" I asked. "Are you working?"

"In the project with an aunt," she answered. "I had a job, but..."

"Then why don't you move in with us?" I asked. "We need some help and maybe we can get you on the payroll. But you won't be making much money." I wondered, though, how long we could stay in the area ourselves, before the Negroes asked us to leave.

chapter

TWENTY-SIX

Lenora moved in the next day. The only thing she had to move was a shopping bag. She didn't come with any clothes, just Lenora.

That night she opened the icebox and found two gallons of ice cream. "Moody, what's the ice cream for? Can I have some?" she asked.

"Sure, Lenora, help yourself. It was for my birthday, which was Sunday," I said. "There's a coconut cake in there, too, if you'd like some."

"You want me to fix some for you?" she asked.

"No, thanks," I said. "I don't think I could eat it."

But suddenly I had an idea. We could use the ice cream and cake to give a party for the high school students. Maybe a party would stir up their enthusiasm again. I couldn't wait till George came in to ask him what he thought about it.

We gave the party Saturday night and it turned out to be a great success. There were so many high school students there that finally the party became a rally. We all went out in the yard and sat on the grass and sang freedom songs for hours. One of the students told me that the principal of the high school had forbidden anyone to come. I was glad he had—it seemed to have boosted attendance. Ten students volunteered to speak in church services throughout the county on Sunday and to spread the word about the clothes we were going to give out the following Wednesday. They did such a good job spreading the word that when Lenora and I turned the corner to the office early Wednesday morning, there were about two hundred Negroes already in line outside it.

The minute I saw them there, I got mad as hell. "Here they are," I thought, "all standing around waiting to be given something. Last week after the church bombing they turned their heads when they passed this office. Some even looked at me with hate in their eyes. Now they are smiling at me. After I give them the clothes, they probably won't even look at me next week, let alone go and register to vote."

As Lenora and I opened the door, the crowd almost trampled us in the rush to get inside. We told them nothing would be given out until Annie Devine, a Negro insurance lady, arrived. She knew most of the families, and we hoped her presence would help prevent people from taking things they could not use. While we all waited, the Negroes were making comments about the clothes. Some said things like, "Them white folks in the North is some good," or "Look at them clothes, just as brand new as they came outta the store."

When I told them that I would like to have their names and addresses so we could inform them of the next shipment, they all looked like they were ready to leave the office. I heard one lady whisper, "It's just a trick to get us to vote." I found myself wanting to deliver a sermon, but instead I left a pencil and paper on the back desk next to the door and asked them to put down their name and address as they left. After this, the tension eased. I knew they would not leave their names. Just in case, however, I stationed Mrs. Chinn at the back of the office. Over and over again I could hear her saying, "You people needn't be scared or ashamed to sign your names. We ain't gonna use them to get none of you in trouble. All Anne and the rest of these CORE workers are here to do is help you people. They have even been trying to get food to some of you."

It took us all day to give the clothes out. I had never in my life seen people who were so much in need. After we gave out most of the best coats and things, people started coming up to me telling me that they were desperate for a coat, a pair of shoes—anything. At five o'clock, I was exhausted. I looked at Mrs. Devine and Lenora and saw that their hair was white from the dust and the lint from the clothes. When I looked in the mirror, I discovered mine was too.

Around five-thirty, a group of people who had just gotten off work came to the office. I told them that everything was gone. A lady looked at a box of clothes in the corner and asked, "Can I look through these? I might find something I can use in there."

"If you would like to, yes. But these things aren't that good. Most of them are just rags," I told her.

Before I could finish answering her, she had begun to search through the things. About five other women and two men joined her. They turned the box over on the floor, pulling everything out. They were snatching for old rags and panties and bras. The men were taking shorts that didn't even have elastic in the waist or were without seats.

When they left, Lenora burst out laughing. "You see, Anne, I told you they weren't rags."

"I see that," I said, "and I don't think it's funny. It's a damn shame people have to be this poor in America—the land of plenty."

"Well, Anne, we've started them now. We have to get some more clothes, else a lot of Negroes will be plenty mad because they were left out," Mrs. Devine said.

"We'll never get enough clothes to supply all of the Negroes in Madison County," I answered. "I think we would do better trying to get them jobs so they can buy their own."

"I could sure use one," Mrs. Chinn sighed. "I ran out of food three days ago."

"How many signed their names, Mrs. Chinn?" I asked, deliberately changing the subject. Every time she talked about her financial condition she got terribly depressed. I not only got depressed, but felt guilty about the way she and C.O. exerted themselves to help us and how much they had suffered because of it.

"Only twenty," she said. "It's a shame. Some of them had the nerve to tell me, 'Minnie Lou, I can't sign my name, but you know me. Let me know when you people get some more clothes in.' I felt like killing them. If it was left up to me, I wouldn't give them anything. That's all Niggers is good for, looking for something for nothing."

When Lenora and I opened the office the following morning, people were constantly dropping by to see if we had any more clothes. However, when I asked if they were registered to vote, the answer was always no. And none of them had any intentions of trying to register in the immediate future. I began to have the feeling that either we came up with an idea or project better than voter registration or we would have to get out of Canton.

A few days later, A Negro high school girl, picking cotton after school out in the country, was raped by a white farmer. The news was whispered throughout Canton. All the Negroes thought it was horrible, but none of them stopped sending their children to pick cotton. They had no choice—the little money the teen-agers made from picking cotton kept them in school. In Madison County, the use of teen-aged labor during the cotton-picking season was an institution. The Negro schools actually closed at noon the first two months of the school year, so that the students would be available to work for the white farmers. Their own parents, who had almost as much land as the whites but received much smaller allotments from the government, practically starved. Most of them couldn't even afford to give their children lunch money and buy them school supplies.

This fall the cotton picking in Madison County continued as usual, and the man who had raped the girl went around talking about it and saying things like, "Them niggers even got the nerve to complain about getting rid of a little pussy since that damn organization [meaning CORE] moved in." One of his friends remarked, "I used to could pick up a nigger anytime; now they is all scared somebody might see them."

Because the girl came to the CORE office and filled out an affidavit, her father had to resort to packing a gun to protect his family. After that, several open assaults were made on young Negro girls by the white men in the area. The assaults provoked a lot of talk concerning other affairs. For about a week or so the talk went on and on about what white man was screwing which Negro woman. It came out in the open that some of the top officials of Madison County had Negro mistresses that they lived with almost full-time. It was Centreville all over again.

It was now three weeks since the Birmingham church bombing, and during this time the Klan had been extremely busy. What I feared most was that the threats would stop, and action would begin—that I would see a bunch of Klansmen riding through Canton. If this ever happened, I was sure the streets of Canton would flow with blood for days. We had been through enough to know that as long as the threats kept coming, nothing was immediately planned to terrorize the Negroes.

Out of compassion and sisterhood for me, Doris Erskine, my old jail buddy from Jackson, had finally consented to work with us in Canton. Once she arrived, there were four of us working in the area, and we again attempted to set up the nightly workshops. We also planned another Saturday night party for the high school students.

One day Doris and I went over to the high school campus to announce the party. The principal was one of the worst Toms in Canton. He had placed some informers on the school grounds to let him know if any CORE people came around. As Doris and I were making our way through a crowd of students, he came running up to us.

"May I speak to you two ladies in my office?" he said angrily.

"Oh! Mr. Principal," I said, as if I hadn't even noticed him before. "Why, we were just leaving. I would love to chat with you for a while, but I'm afraid I don't have the time. I have a meeting in about five minutes at the office. Maybe we can get together one day next week."

"Good evening, Mr. Principal. We'll be leaving now," Doris said.

As we walked away, he just stood there with his mouth wide open, not knowing what to say. Some of the students snickered at him. I thought it was pretty damn cool, the way we left him hanging there.

Many more high school students came to the second party than had come to the first. We sang freedom songs for four hours. I was told by one of the students that the principal again had threatened to expel any of the students that came to the party. He said that after this threat got around campus, some of the students formed a group to solicit for party participants.

Meanwhile the principal had asked the chief of police to have us arrested if we ever came on campus again. The chief agreed and also saw fit to promise that we would be arrested if we were ever caught trying to persuade the students to stay out of school. Every day the chief and his boys would hang around the high school at the lunch hour just in case we showed up; they would also be stationed there when school let out for the day.

The teen-agers seemed to be very aroused over the principal's actions. On Monday, they left school and held a rally in an open space behind the Boyd Street housing project. I wanted so badly to attend it, but I knew the teen-agers had to make their own decisions. I was glad that they had decided to act independently.

When the rally was over, the students marched in and around the Boyd Street projects, singing freedom songs, with the chief and two carloads of police driving alongside them. Lenora, Doris, and I sat watching from the steps of the Freedom House, guarded by two cops in a parked car. As we sat there, George came running up and told us that he had almost been arrested by the chief. He said that we had been accused of starting the demonstration.

Early that same evening, we were told that the police would raid the Freedom House late one night during the week. They evidently planned to frame Doris, Lenora, and me on some kind of prostitution charge, and hoped our arrest would cause so much public dissension that we would be forced to leave Canton. George, the only guy in the house, decided not to stay with us for a while in case the police went ahead with their plan.

All that first night police rode by shining flashlights on the Freedom House. Later on when they discovered that only girls were living in the House, they began to harass us every night of the week. We became afraid to stay there. Until dawn cars would pass by and bricks would be thrown at the windows. I was nervous, but I wasn't as bad as Doris when it came to nerves. She was afraid to sleep in a room alone. Some nights she and Lenora would both come in and sleep with me. Often we would talk all night to keep from falling asleep. After a week I was so tired I felt like I was dying on my feet. I felt as though I hadn't had a good night of sleep since coming to Canton.

We opened up two or three workshops in the county again, and that made things worse. We no longer had our protective guys riding around with us. Most of them had gone north or to California trying to find jobs. Now either George went with us, or we went alone. Doris and I were coming from a workshop twenty-six miles out in the country one night, when we were chased by a group of drunken whites. Doris panicked. She began driving like a crazy woman, making every curve on two wheels, sending rocks sailing everywhere. I just knew we would turn over in a ditch and be killed. I wondered whether it would be better to force Doris to stop, or to jump out of the car into a ditch, as Doris turned a curve, hoping the other car would pass without seeing me. If I forced Doris to stop the car, I thought, maybe we would just be beaten or raped by the drunks and not killed. Finally, I just closed my eyes and hoped that whatever would happen wouldn't take too long or be too painful. I must have blacked out, because when I opened my eyes we were at the Freedom House.

The next night George went with us but the fear was still there. All the jokes we were able to come up with couldn't erase the experience we had encountered on those long, dark, country roads.

I came to the Freedom House one evening and found Doris sitting in a chair with a rifle across her lap, and Lenora oiling a pistol.

"Hey, what in the hell is going on here?" I said. I stood there with my mouth wide open.

"I's a oilin' mah gun," said Lenora.

"This heah baby is a takin' a nap," said Doris.

"Come on, now, cut that shit out. Where did you two get those guns?" I asked.

"I've had this one a long time," Lenora said, in her normal voice.

"Where did you get the rifle, Doris?"

"Well, Moody, some nice colored man was kind enough to lend it to me," she said.

"Are we going to have a real shoot-it-out with the Klan tonight? If so, where is my piece?"

"No, we just kinda figured we needed some protection around the house. After all, three young women just don't live in Mississippi alone without any protection."

"Seriously, did we get a threat for tonight?"

"Don't we get them every night?" Doris asked.

I stood there looking at them, thinking, "These fools are out of their minds. What in the hell would we do with two guns against all the dynamite and ammunition the Klan has? I guess they are beginning to feel like a lot of other Negroes I know. If you can't beat them, join them. Matching fire with fire instead of kneeling and praying while some white cracker shoots you to death or throws a few sticks of dynamite on you and blows you to hell or somewhere. I figured if some Negro was kind enough to bring a gun to the Freedom House for us to protect ourselves with, then they must be gathering ammunition to protect the community."

Now that we had a gun around the house, my fear seemed to get worse. I was constantly wondering whether the man that brought the rifle was paid by the whites to bring it. If the cops caught us with guns in the Freedom House, they would surely have a perfect excuse to arrest us. I knew I couldn't talk Lenora and Doris into giving them back. In fact, I was not sure I wanted to. Just about every night cops were flashing lights on the house. If they weren't flashing lights, they were out there talking loud and laughing, trying to keep us awake. One night a man came by with a truck-load of big bloodhounds and K-9 police-type dogs. He let them out in front of the Freedom House and they ran all around scenting everything. He left them there a while and then drove back and whistled for them to jump up in the truck. This frightened the hell out of us. Night after night, the dogs were brought to the house, and Doris and Lenora would stay awake threatening to shoot them. I knew that this was the Klan's doing. I figured they were probably planning to burn down the house one night and run us out to be devoured by the dogs.

It had gotten to the point where my weight was going down to nothing. I was just skin and bones. My nerves were torn to shreds and I was losing my hair. I had been so happy when Doris first came to work with us, but now her presence only reminded me of what fear could do to a person. At this point, I would much rather have been in jail with her. When we were in jail, she had been one of the jolliest girls in my cell. She had been damn good at helping to keep up the morale of the high school girls when there were five hundred of us at the fairgrounds concentration camp. But so much had happened here in Canton that I guess the thought of working here had messed her up even before she came. Lenora was different. If she was really scared, she didn't show it very much. Anyway, she was born in Madison County and knew a lot about the white people there. Sometimes we would get a threat and she would say things like, "If they were gonna kill us they wouldn't do it like that." I was always interested in her comments about the threats. I actually wondered sometimes whether she had been placed in the Freedom House by the whites. "After all," I would think, "she is from this county and she doesn't seem to be upset over the threats and things." Whenever I found myself doubting one of the workers, I immediately dismissed the idea from my mind. I knew that kind of thinking could eventually destroy us. I knew the mind was tricky, and often the whites were smart enough to make our own minds work against each other to divide us. This I had learned from the Jackson movement, when they used the newspapers to play up a split in the organizations which did not exist.

In order to sleep at night, I finally had to resort to sleeping pills. Doris began sleeping in the same bed as me—her rifle standing in the corner right at her head. Lenora slept in the back room with her pistol on the nightstand. At the sound of anything, they were up peeping out of the window with the guns in their hands. It had gotten to the point we had to wake each other up when one of us needed to use the bathroom. Doris slept so lightly I would just touch her and she would jump up grabbing for the rifle. Then I would call Lenora until she answered. I was scared that if I had gone to the bathroom and stumbled over something and Doris and Lenora heard me, they would have shot the hell out of me.

In mid-October we attended a COFO meeting. COFO was a state-wide coalition of all the national civil rights groups in Mississippi. The meeting had been called to decide about running Aaron Henry, the state NAACP president and chairman of COFO, and Ed King of Tougaloo on a freedom ballot in the upcoming election for Governor and Lieutenant Governor of Mississippi. It was believed more Negroes would cast their votes in the freedom election than were registered already. COFO planned to rally up enough support so that thousands of Negroes in various counties might participate. This, they thought, would prove to the nation that Negroes wanted to vote and would vote if they were not afraid to do so.

I couldn't see us mobilizing the Negroes around a false campaign. We had enough problems getting them registered to vote period. As it was, they had shown very little interest in the gubernatorial election since Coleman, the liberal Democrat, had lost to Paul Johnson in the primary. Now that the only choice was between the Republican, Rubel Phillips, and Johnson, the Negroes just didn't give a damn.

At the COFO meeting Aaron Henry asked the workers for their opinions about the freedom vote. I voiced my opposition to the whole idea. Right after that, an NAACP member from Clarksdale got up and went on and on about how she thought it was such a good thing. She ended with, "I don't think the young lady (meaning me) has worked with Negroes in Mississippi. To my knowledge, most of the Negroes in Mississippi would participate in such an election." She made me so mad I was standing before she was seated.

"For your information, Mrs. P———, not only was I born in Mississippi, but I just happened to be born in Wilkinson County in southwest Mississippi, the toughest spot in the state. Because of my civil rights activities the last two years at Tougaloo, I have been barred from Wilkinson County. For the last five months, I have been working in Canton, another stronghold of the Klan. I think that should qualify me to have an opinion about the matter and a right to voice it." I took my seat and an old man got up.

"I think that young lady was right," he said. "We should be thinking of some other way to impress upon the people of the county the importance of the vote. If we hold this freedom vote, all the white folks is gonna say is that we want to take over everything, that we want to rule things. I just want to be represented and given the right to vote in all the official elections. If I am asked to vote in an unofficial election, then that right is taken away by my own people."

Aaron Henry decided to select a committee to settle the issue. As it turned out, I was the only person on the committee opposing the freedom election. However, once it was decided to hold it, I reluctantly agreed to try to get votes.

The following week, Dave came into Canton to move two of us out to work on the freedom vote in other areas. Doris volunteered to go to Natchez and Lenora was sent into Hattiesburg. Doris had only been in Canton a little over a month and she was glad to get away. I had become too valuable in Canton to be moved, since I was now well known by most of the Negroes. Besides that, I didn't have the energy to go into an entirely new area. I would not have been able to stand the strain.

We had only three weeks to rally up the Negro vote. Mrs. Devine and Mrs. Chinn helped me in Canton, while George, Mr. Chinn, and a few other men worked throughout the county. It was hard trying to explain the freedom election to the local Negroes. Most of them couldn't understand what we were trying to do—they thought we were trying to trick them in some way.

By this time, I had finally realized that the future of the Negroes in Mississippi didn't depend upon the older people. They were too scared and suspicious. It was almost hopeless to try and educate minds that had been closed for so long. All their lives their minds had been conditioned to Mr. Charlie's dos and don'ts. If we wanted to educate the vote, I thought, we should have been working with minds that were susceptible to change—ones that were open, inquisitive, and eager to learn. (I had a feeling that the whites in Canton knew that too. Why else had those five teen-agers been shot at the beginning of our work in the area?)

In addition to working on the election, we were planning to send five farmers from Madison County to the National Share-croppers Fund's conference in North Carolina. This project had my full support. Here were farmers with acres and acres of land who couldn't make a living off it. If they were able to get larger cotton allotments or find some other use for their land, perhaps get FHA loans to build up their farms, it would provide them with economic stability. This possibility really excited me. If there were 29,000 independent Negroes in Madison County instead of 29,000 starving Negroes I was sure things would be different.

We decided to call a meeting of the farmers. George and Mr. Chinn were in Greenwood the night it was scheduled, so Mrs. Chinn and I took charge of it. About thirty-five farmers and their wives showed up in the office. I was sitting by the window at a makeshift desk writing down names when I noticed that some of the farmers were shaking. They were facing the open door. I looked out of the window to discover about six cops standing out-side peeping at the meeting. The farmers kept shaking as I tried to get the information out of them. They just muttered their names. Finally I got up and closed the door. When I did that, the cops moved to the side of the building and began peeping in the win-dow. I immediately slammed it down. The panes in the window were painted black, but there was one missing pane. I covered the opening with one of the long sheets of paper I was writing on.

"That's a smart bitch," I heard one of the cops comment.

"Yeah, we gotta teach that black bitch a lesson," another one answered.

I got kind of worried about the lesson they might teach me, but I was pleased by the reaction of the farmers. The instant they could no longer see the cops staring them in the face, they relaxed. The names came through loud and clear now. To my surprise two or three of the farmers had already gotten FHA loans. Most of them, however, didn't know anything about them. They were all eager to go to the conference. When the meeting was over, one of the farmers gave Mrs. Chinn and me a ride home. I was staying at her house, since George was away.

As soon as we got to the office the next morning, a lady who lived across the street came running in.

"Anne! I was sitting on the porch and I saw what you did to them cops last night. Honey, you don't know these cops here in Canton. Last night after you slammed that window in their faces, they waited in the alley about two hours for you."

"Them dirty bastards," said Mrs. Chinn. "I wish they had come by my house looking for Anne. I would have blown their heads off."

"I'm going to show you the one that wanted to beat you up, Anne," said the lady. "You watch out for him. He's a mean thing."

Before she could finish telling me who to watch out for, two cops drove up outside and started parking their car.

"That's him that's driving, Anne," said the lady.

I looked them over. The one she referred to was slightly older than me. His general features were those of a pleasant person. However, those hating eyes of his were unbearable. I looked at him and wondered how a person that young could hate so much. Could he be so angry just because I slammed a window in his face? There was more to it than that. Maybe he was trying to prove a point. Maybe he was disturbed about something. He seemed more like the type that would rape me rather than beat me up, I thought.

Mrs. Chinn walked outside with the lady who had brought us the news. She went over to the car and I heard her say, "You cops don't have anything better to do than set in front of this office all the time? If you don't, I wish you would find something. I get tired of looking at you."

They looked at Mrs. Chinn and didn't say a word. Had any other Negro woman in Canton said that, they would have beaten her down to the ground. But they knew she was C. O. Chinn's wife, and no one, black or white, insulted C. O. Chinn's people and got away with it.

A few days later, Doris was back. She had tried to help get Negroes in Natchez organized and failed. From what she said, the Klan ruled the entire area. CORE didn't get enough cooperation from the Negroes to be able to stay. Doris seemed to have undergone quite a change. She was twice as scared as before. Now she was jumping in broad daylight. She still insisted on sleeping with me, with her rifle in the corner.

The county fair in Canton was the next coming attraction for Negroes in Madison County. Because the fair was segregated (a week for whites and a few days for Negroes), we thought at first of boycotting it. However, since we could use it as a means of contacting Negroes, we decided not to. Thousands of Negroes usually flocked to the fair from all over the county. We made special leaflets to pass out to them advertising the freedom vote.

The first day the fair was open to Negroes, Doris and I found hundreds of them, just as we expected. We ran into a group of high school students who had worked for us, and soon we had lots of help distributing the leaflets. I was feeling good at first but I soon became disheartened as time after time Negroes shook their heads and jerked back their hands when we offered leaflets to them. On top of this, I noticed that my favorite cop was there. When he saw me, his eyes lit up. Instantly he began to follow me around. He really puzzled me. I began wondering whether he was someone from my hometown. Maybe he had been sent from Centreville to bump me off, I thought. Whenever he noticed me looking at him, he would put his hand on his pistol and watch my reactions. A few of the high school boys volunteered to act as bodyguards for me. They had heard of his threat the night of the farmers' meeting. Until we finished distributing the leaflets, Doris and I were surrounded by these boys. The cop was only a few paces behind each step we made.

After handing out all the leaflets, we bought tickets to take a few rides. First, Doris and I decided to have a contest with the little race cars. We were surrounded by our group of high school students chanting to us. Since I couldn't drive, I just kept holding up traffic and slamming into people. Doris drove along smoothly, all the time laughing at me. The boys kept yelling, "Come on, Moody! Wheel, Moody! Come on, show Doris up!" Each time I crashed into someone, they cracked up laughing.

Next we played Pop the Whip. This game was on a wheel similar to a merry-go-round, but slanted to the sky. The person finishing up at the end of the whip seemingly would be thrown out of his seat. The wheel turned fast, and soon all the other passengers had had their turns at the end of the whip and were off the wheel. As Doris and I were about to come up to the end ourselves, all of a sudden the wheel stopped. We were now at the very top of the wheel. I looked down to see what was going on, to discover "my cop" talking to the man who operated it. My heart went blup, blup, blup, almost flooding on me. I couldn't open my mouth. Doris looked down and got hysterical. She started screaming, "Mister, please don't kill us! Oh, God help us! Please let us down." She was about to jump out of the seat and I had to wrestle her to hold her in. The high school boys were at this point surrounding the cop and the operator. We were up there for nearly ten minutes before they brought us down to the platform and released us. As we stepped out of the seat, the cop laughed and laughed. The crowd that had gathered around the wheel slowly walked away.

Back at the Freedom House that evening, I found another letter from Mama. As usual, it was full of pleas, begging me to leave Mississippi. I was mad with Mama and with Doris. Here was Doris driving me crazy and so was Mama. I took three sleeping pills and still was unable to sleep. I would have taken more, but I was afraid that one more would put me to sleep for good.

The next morning, I got up feeling awful. I could feel myself choking. It was like the choking feeling I'd had around the time I left home. "Maybe if I can just go out in the woods it will go away," I thought. I started thinking of how to get to the country and of a good excuse for going there.

Finally, I decided to go out to Mrs. Chinn's parents' farm. Mrs. Dearon, Mrs. Chinn's mother, had promised to organize the farmers in her area. It was just natural for one of us to stop in and see how everything was going. It always made me feel good to see Mrs. Dearon. She was the youngest, most energetic old woman I had ever known. When I suggested to Doris that we go out to the country to get some fresh air, she thought it was a great idea. After all, the Dearon farm was the most beautiful I had seen in Mississippi. It had huge cedar trees, a small lake and a lonely and delicious atmosphere. I was thinking that maybe a little fresh air might even cure Doris of the jibbies.

We dressed in blue jeans, long-sleeved shirts and wore long socks and boots to keep the briars from sticking so badly. I couldn't wait to get out in the woods and listen to the beautiful sound of the singing birds. As we were walking down the street to find someone who might drive us out to the Dearons', I noticed that Doris was carrying her rifle and Lenora's old pistol.

"Where in the hell do you think you are going with those guns?" I asked.

"We can do a little hunting while we are out there," she said.

"Hunting! Are you crazy?"

"You like to hunt. You told me yourself you did. What's wrong with us taking the guns out in the country with us? We might even kill a rabbit or something for dinner this evening."

"There's nothing wrong with carrying the guns out in the

country," I said. "However, there is something wrong with you walking around with them in Canton. If one of them stupid-ass cops or some white cracker saw us, we would be two dead fools lying in the streets. First thing they would say after killing us is that we went berserk and shot at them. Leave the guns here, and if we can find someone reliable to take us, then we can carry them."

"Let's find C.O.," she said. "He'll carry us."

"Yes, I know, and he's reliable too, hmm," I said sarcastically.

Now that Doris had suggested that we take the guns, I was not so sure that I wanted to go. Then it occurred to me they might prove helpful if we ran into some white crackers out there. If we threatened to shoot them, or maybe gave them a warning shot, we wouldn't be killed or beaten—or whatever they might do to us. "Maybe we just better take them," I thought.

We looked for Mr. Chinn for about an hour before we found him. After we told him we were going hunting, it took almost another hour to convince him that we could handle the guns. Finally, though, he agreed to drive us out to the country, and around noon we were walking up on the Dearons' porch, guns and all.

Mrs. Dearon greeted me with a hug and kiss, saying that she was glad we had decided to come out and pay them a visit. But then she just kept looking at me as though she knew something was wrong. It was not like me to run out in the country and take a whole day off from my work in Canton. After we told her why we were paying her an unexpected visit, she seemed to understand. Anyway, Doris and I were off in the woods before she got around to questions like could we use the guns. Just as we were running down the hill from the house, C.O. yelled, "Don't you all kill each other! I'll pick you up about five-thirty or six."

"O.K.," I answered, and we were on our way.

It was so peaceful walking through the woods. We walked for about an hour before realizing we were supposed to be looking for rabbits. We started looking, and soon enough we found them.

They were jumping up all around us. Every time one jumped, we jumped too—and here we were, dressed like men, with guns in our hands. I realized how nervous we actually were. Finally we gave up the idea of killing rabbits and just walked some more. We found all sorts of interesting things, an old graveyard, a running brook, and some bright yellow and red autumn leaves. When we could barely pick up our feet, we headed back to the Dearons' house.

As we came through the yard, we could smell the chicken frying, but we were too tired to walk up the steps. We just sat on the edge of the porch and fell back. I found myself falling asleep smelling that chicken. Suddenly I had the feeling someone was standing over me. As I opened my eyes, I heard Mrs. Dearon saying, "Well, you two look wore out. What did you kill?"

"Nothing," I said. "But we saw pretty near fifty rabbits, though."

"I didn't hear no shots. Then I started wondering what you all were doing."

"We just walked and walked until we couldn't walk any more," I said.

"You two come on inside," Mrs. Dearon said firmly. "You should be pretty hungry by now."

By the time I finished two or three hot pieces of chicken, some good collard greens, and homemade cornbread, I felt like a new person. Especially behind two good cups of coffee. I felt so good that I sat there and told Mrs. Dearon how good her chicken was, that I hadn't had a good home-cooked meal in years. I found myself flattering her just like one of those Baptist ministers would do. However, I really enjoyed that chicken dinner—unlike most ministers. With me it wasn't routine.

When Doris and I finished eating, we went outside and sat on the edge of the porch again. Then I discovered why Doris really wanted to bring the guns along. She suggested that we try some target practice.

"Come on, Moody, I bet I can outshoot you," she said.

"I don't feel up to it, Doris. But go ahead, let's see how good you are."

She picked up a can, placed it on a fence post, then backed away from it and fired.

As soon as Mrs. Dearon heard the shots, she came to the door to watch. Doris was good. She was cutting a round hole in the can with the rifle. "Can you beat that, Moody?" she asked. "I think so," I answered. Doris stepped back as I used the pistol to change the shape of the hole to the shape of an apple by adding a stem to it. "Want a bite?" I asked teasingly.

"You girls are real tomboys," Mrs. Dearon said. "There might be some good watermelons down in the patch. You wanta go see?"

"Which way is the patch?" I asked, running in the direction she pointed as Doris fell in at my side. We found watermelons, lots of them. They were good too. We just picked them up and dropped them letting them burst wide open as they hit the ground, and then we dug into them. On our way back up the hill with our watermelons, we saw Dave Dennis parked in the yard talking to Mr. Dearon. He looked as if he was as mad as hell with us, but I couldn't have cared less. I knew he wouldn't say anything to us. After all, he never spent all of his days cooped up in Canton. And he was well aware of the hell we were going through daily.

Now that I was on my way back to Canton, I began to feel choked up again. I hadn't been cured after all, and this meant something to me. Before, the woods had always done so much for me. Once I could actually go out into the woods and communicate with God, or Nature or something. Now that something didn't come through. It was just not there any more. More than ever I began to wonder whether God actually existed. Maybe God changed as the individual changed, or perhaps grew as one grew. Maybe my upbringing in Church had had a lot to do with the God I knew before. The God my Baptist training taught me about was a merciful and forgiving God, one that said Thou shalt not kill, Thou shalt not commit adultery, Thou shalt not steal, and a number of other shalt nots. Since I had been part of the Movement, I had witnessed killing, stealing, and adultery committed against Negroes by whites throughout the South. God didn't seem to be punishing anyone for these acts. On the other hand, most of the Negroes in the South were humble, peace-loving, religious people. Yet they were the ones doing all the suffering, as if they themselves were responsible for the killing and other acts committed against them. It seemed to me now that there must be two gods, many gods or no god at all.

That weekend I went to Jackson and stayed with Doris and her parents. While I was there, I stopped in to see Bobbie, one of the high school girls who had worked with us in Canton part of the summer. It was at Bobbie's house that I had one of the most horrible scares in my life. She showed me a Klan leaflet that she had gotten from a friend of hers who lived near a white neighborhood. (Often in Jackson, Klan leaflets were thrown up on Negro porches by mistake, because the lines between Negro and white neighborhoods were pretty confusing.) I couldn't believe it, but it was a Klan blacklist, with my picture on it. I guess I must have sat there for about an hour holding it. Bobbie told me that she had planned to come into Canton to tell me. There were pictures of Medgar Evers, James Meredith, John Salter, Bob Moses, Joan Trumpauer, Reverend Ed King, Emmett Till, and two Jackson ministers. There were also pictures of other Negroes who had been killed, with X's marked across their faces. Medgar's face was also marked out. This piece of paper shook me up worse than all of the letters Mama had sent me. She had been warning me, and I had ignored her. Not only that, I had even stopped answering her letters to discourage her from writing. The only reason I could see that I was singled out on this list was that I was the only one from my hometown working in the state. Perhaps they thought that I would somehow encourage the rest of the Negroes in Centreville to speak out. Now that I had stopped writing to Mama, I didn't even know exactly what was going on.

Most of the people on this blacklist were already out of the state. Medgar had been killed; James Meredith, Joan Trumpauer, and John Salter had left. One of the ministers was in Africa. He had made such a sudden exit that I had wondered at the time if he was running from a serious threat. Most of the people didn't worry about the daily threats, but making a Klan blacklist wasn't taken as lightly as that. This meant much more. In spite of the fact that I didn't want to worry about it, I did. I began to wonder even more about that cop in Canton, the one that looked at me so hard. I wondered how long the leaflet had been out. All that weekend I thought about it. I wanted to tell Doris about it, but I knew better. She was scared enough already. She would drive me crazy. "No, I just better keep it to myself," I thought. "It's better that way." These were my troubles, and each of us had our own load.

We headed back to Canton on Sunday evening. Next weekend would be spent on the freedom vote; therefore, we had plenty of work to do during the week. Monday we were up bright and early trying to rally up a little more support. The rest of the days we spent pushing and begging people to participate in the election. November 1, 2, and 3 were the three days delegated by COFO for casting freedom ballots. The state's gubernatorial election was to be held on November 4, a Tuesday. COFO held the freedom vote just prior to the state election so that the freedom votes could be tallied and publicized the day of the state gubernatorial election.

During the week leading up to the vote, there was too much confusion, too many threats, and too much work. The whites in Canton as well as throughout the state had, by this time, heard about the freedom vote. They were as confused about it as many of the Negroes were. However, they weren't so confused that they didn't try to counter it with violence. Twenty-five cops were added to the Canton police force. They were buzzing all over the place.

On Friday, I was walking around in a daze. I didn't only feel choked up, as I had been feeling for two weeks, I felt I was carrying the weight of the world on my shoulders. It was too much of a burden for me. I sat around in the office and made sealed boxes with holes in the tops to be used as ballot boxes at our polling places. I felt like a robot, and worked like one, too. We got everything set up for the voting and went back to the Freedom House.

Late that evening I tried to go for a walk and my feet felt as if heavy iron bars were attached to them. I could barely move them. I got a block away from the Freedom House and turned around. I went back and sat on the steps. It was there on the steps of the Freedom House that I decided to leave the project for a while. I sat there trying to analyze what was going on, and discovered that I couldn't even think any more. It was like my brains had gone to sleep on me or frozen.

On Saturday, the first day of the freedom vote, I volunteered to serve as a vote taker at a polling place. I was too tired to go out on the streets and canvass. Dave came into Canton and brought in a few more people to work during the vote. Several high school students volunteered to work also. There was lots of fresh young blood around to work. This pleased me. Dave had hoped that Madison County would get more votes than other counties participating. He felt as many of us once did, that perhaps one day Madison County would be looked upon and serve as a model for Negro progress in the state.

I sat there in the office all morning and only a few Negroes came in, although the teen-agers on the streets with ballot boxes were having better luck. Some of them came in a couple of times leaving a full ballot box and carrying out an empty one to fill up. The longer I sat there, the madder I got. I didn't feel as if we should be going out in the streets with ballot boxes. If Negroes truly wanted to vote, they would have come in the office and done so. "They know it's just a freedom vote," I thought. "They also know Aaron Henry is a Negro. After three weeks of walking and

talking until we were collapsing in the streets, these are the results we get. I knew it from the beginning. Until we can come up
with some good sound plans to help the Negroes solve their immediate problems—that is, a way to get a little food into their bel-
lies, a roof over their heads, and a few coins in their pockets—we
will be talking forever. They will never stop being scared of Mr.
Charlie until we are able to replace the crumbs that Mr. Charlie is
giving them. Until we can say, 'Here is a job, Sam. Work hard and
stand up to be a man.' Not until we can do that or find some way
for Sam to do that, will Sam stand up. If we don't, Sam will forever
be a boy, an uncle or just plain Sam, the recipient of crumbs."

I sat there on that stool until I couldn't take it any more. I
picked up one of the sealed ballot boxes and walked out in the
streets. Now the streets were completely saturated with cops.
They were following the workers everywhere. Some of the teen-
agers practically ignored them. But I could see their effort wasn't
helping much. The teen-agers might ignore the cops, but the Negroes whose votes they were soliciting weren't. In fact they were
so much aware of their presence that they almost ran when anyone held the ballot box before them, and asked had they voted. I
made several attempts to get people to vote and gave up. I went
over and sat on a bench in front of a grocery and just looked at all
those Negroes. I could estimate there were about five thousand in
the streets and maybe more. It was Saturday, and they were out,
almost all of them.

After three days of walking and pleading with Negroes to
demonstrate their desire to vote, our polls closed. Polling places
had been set up all over the county in churches, small Negro gro-
ceries, and even in some of the Negro homes. When all the results
were in and counted, to my surprise 2800 Madison County Negroes had cast votes in the election. The largest number of votes
came from polling places out in the country where voters were not
openly intimidated by the cops. However, several of the poll man-
agers reported incidents with local whites.

The total number of votes cast by Mississippi Negroes was 80,000. This was about 60,000 more than the number of Negroes officially registered in the state. But since there were more than 400,000 Negroes of voting age (twenty-one and older) in Mississippi, the 80,000 votes didn't greatly impress me—even though Negroes had not voted in Mississippi in significant numbers since Reconstruction. "If it took this much work to get 80,000 votes," I thought, "then we'll be working a lifetime to get the 400,000 and some registered."

The last evening of the freedom vote, I told George and Doris that I planned to leave the project for a while. They didn't take me seriously, though. They just sort of brushed me off. However, after I told Mrs. Chinn and a few other Negroes the next day, they believed I meant what I said. No one seemed to see that I was on the verge of a breakdown. I think the fact that I found myself on the Klan's blacklist brought it on faster. Had I stayed there another week, I would probably have died from lack of sleep and nervousness.

After George and Doris realized I was actually leaving, they tried to talk me out of it. The day before I was to go, I went to the office and found large posters on the wall saying, "Winners never quit and quitters never win," or "If a task is once begun, never leave it 'til it's done."

I had expected them to understand. Somehow I got the feeling that they thought I was leaving the Movement for good. I expected George to understand, because he knew I was always so serious and took things pretty hard. He was more philosophical. If things didn't go right, he would just say, "We have to try harder." And he had other things going for him. He mixed well with people in Canton. He had a lot of other men to hang out with. He had Mr. Chinn to rely upon. He could go out and drink beer with the men every night or so, and he had lots of girls. His life was pretty normal in many ways. With girls, things were different. We weren't allowed to go anywhere, and there wasn't anything we could do to relax. People were always overprotecting us. I knew Doris wouldn't stay long; she was too scared. She would leave soon after I did.

I was not sure myself that I was not leaving for good—and this really made me feel bad. I had gotten so tired of seeing people suffering, naked and hungry. It just seemed as if there was no end to it, or at least "the Vote" was not the way to end it.

Later on during the day, Dave Dennis came and talked to me. He started telling me about what a good worker I was, and all that shit. It added to the feeling George had caused me to have. But Dave knew that I had made up my mind, and he didn't really try to pressure me to stay. He said that he hoped that I would not leave the Movement for good, that he could tell I had a certain compassion for the work and these were the kind of people the Movement needed most. I found myself wishing I had just left without telling anyone that I was leaving.

The next morning George and Doris drove me to the train station in Jackson. Before the train pulled in, I found myself sitting in the white waiting room with a white civil rights worker I happened to meet. She was a fund raiser for CORE. Sitting there in the station, I got the same feeling I had in all the other sit-ins I had participated in. I remember getting up once, and going to the Negro section to ask the Negroes there if they knew the white section was desegregated. Then I knew that I would never really be leaving the Movement.

chapter

TWENTY-SEVEN

It was about 11 P.M. when I got off the train at the Carrollton Avenue Station in New Orleans. I was dead tired—too tired to be bothered with my luggage, a trunk of books and two boxes of clothes. I let it all go on to the main station with the intention of picking it up in a day or so.

Carrying only one small, light suitcase, I walked up Carrollton Avenue to Stroelitz. My Grandmother Winnie was now living in the second house on the corner of Stroelitz and Pine Street. Within a few minutes, I was knocking on her door and listening for her heavy footsteps.

"Who is it?" she called out.

"It's me, Essie Mae."

Winnie cracked the door and peeped out at me.

"What you want?" she asked as though she was talking to a complete stranger.

I just looked at her, not knowing what to do or say. It didn't seem as though she could have been talking to me—not Essie

Mae, her oldest grandchild. I had always stayed with her when I was in college and working at Maple Hill Restaurant.

"I am just in from Mississippi. I would like to stay with you a few days until I get straight," I finally said.

"I'm tired," Winnie said, her voice almost shaking. "And I don't want anybody staying with me."

I didn't say anything after that. I just turned and walked off her porch. She was scared of me, I thought. I knew it was because of my civil rights work. I hadn't seen her since I had become really active. She and my aunt and my other relatives probably had been thinking that if I came here, I would get involved with the Movement in New Orleans. "If so," I thought, "they are all too scared to take me in. Mama must have told them about all the threats and intimidations they were subjected to at home because of me."

I stood on the corner about fifteen minutes wondering where to go. It was now about eleven-thirty and I had to find a place to sleep. Then I remembered that my Uncle George Lee lived right around the corner in High Court and that Adline was now staying with him. She had written me a couple of letters from his place when I was in Canton. But I hated to go there. I had never forgotten the time George Lee set our house on fire when I was four years old and put the blame on me. I stood there with tears in my eyes and about seventy-five cents in my pockets. I had no place else to go. So I went. I was trembling as I walked up to his door. To my surprise he and his wife Etha seemed really glad to see me. They told me I could stay as long as I needed to, and wanted to know all about the Movement.

Adline wasn't in and I was relieved. She would have wanted to talk to me all night. Finally, as George Lee continued asking me questions, Etha realized how tired I was. She helped me let out the sofa which I would have to share with Adline. It was about two-thirty when I got to bed. I fell asleep with George Lee still talking.

I woke up about two the following afternoon. Adline had come in during the night, slept next to me, and had long since gone to the restaurant where she worked as a waitress. I got up, had a cup of coffee with Etha, and went back to bed. It was about nine that night when I awoke the second time. I opened my eyes and Adline was sitting in the chair opposite the sofa looking at me.

"Are you sick?" she asked. "Etha said that you had been sleeping all day."

"No," I said, staring at her. She looked different. "I guess it's because I haven't seen her in two years," I thought. Then I closed my eyes again.

"Didn't you sleep in Canton, Essie Mae?"

Half asleep again, I just shook my head. I could hear her rattling on and on about giving Mama a birthday party in a couple of weeks. She also told me that my brother Junior had come to New Orleans a few months ago and was working as a short order cook. He was staying with Winnie—which made me realize that my grandmother was really afraid to let me stay with her.

I woke up the next morning and it was Saturday. George Lee and Adline were both home from work. I had slept for two days and still hadn't gotten enough sleep. And I realized I wasn't about to get enough cooped up in George Lee's place. Two of his friends had come in and the three of them were now in the kitchen playing cards and laughing and talking. When I had lived with Winnie, I used to see people going into certain houses in High Court to gamble. But I didn't know George Lee's house was used to gamble in, too.

I decided to go to Maple Hill Restaurant that afternoon and see if I could get my old job. In spite of the fact that I had always been able to get a job there in the past, if only for a week, this time I was afraid to go back. I was sure that they'd heard of my civil rights work by now. The Woolworth's sit-in had been well publicized in all the papers throughout the country. Mr. Steve, the owner, might even worry about losing some of his customers if I began working there—I was sure most of the steady ones would remember me.

I needed a job badly. I didn't have any money. I needed a place to sleep—everything. And I really didn't have anywhere else to go for a job in New Orleans. With a college education, about the only thing you could do in Mississippi, Louisiana, and most of the South was teach. And I would not make the mistake of teaching in a Southern classroom. Most of the teachers were Uncle Toms. Those that weren't had to teach in awful, segregated, inferior Uncle Tom schools. The way I felt about teaching, I would much rather wash dishes with my degree—that is, if I weren't told how clean I should get them or where to stack them.

When I walked in the front door of Maple Hill, everything was the same. Joe, the short order cook, was serving the few customers at the counter. George, Mr. Steve's son, was going over the checks at the cash register, tapping his feet to some loud jazz tune that was playing on the juke-box. I must have stood there for about five minutes before he saw me. "Annie! Annie! Annie!" he shouted, as he greeted me with a hug. "Hey, Joe!" he called to the waiter serving the few customers at the counter. "Look who's here!" "Annie Moody! Annie Moody!" Joe yelled. "Come on, let's go to the pantry and see everyone," George said, almost running me in there.

"Look," he said as he opened the pantry doors. "None other than the rebel herself."

"The rebel! The rebel!" James shouted. "Them white folks finally got you out of Mississippi at last."

In no time I was feeling at home again. When George returned to the cash register, James said, "You know, Anne, we were so proud of you here after the sit-in and all. George even cut your picture out of the paper and showed it to us, and all of the new helpers. Then he even showed it to some of the students."

Just as I was leaving, Mr. Steve arrived. He was glad to see me, too. We stood in the street outside the restaurant and talked for about fifteen minutes. By this time, it began to seem as though I would never get away from talking about the Movement. Everyone I had talked to since being in New Orleans had talked me almost to death. Standing here in the street now, it seemed endless. Finally, we stopped talking about the Movement long enough for me to ask Mr. Steve if he could fit me in as a waitress for a while. "Yes, you know you are welcome at my place," he said in his heavy Greek accent. "Sure I make room for you. When do you want to come?" "Next week, if it's possible," I said. "I gotta find an apartment right away." "Sure me fix," he said, as we parted.

I started working on Tuesday of the following week. But once I had started, I really didn't want the job. I was working like a machine. My mind just wasn't on what I was doing. I found myself leaving the restaurant every day on my break. I would go home or for a walk for an hour or so. I just didn't feel like hanging around the place and joking with the other waiters like I used to when I was in college.

That weekend, between my salary and my tips, I had about sixty-five dollars, and Adline had about thirty. We put our salaries together and went out looking for an apartment. Within a couple of hours, we had found one. It was in a newly built, white, two-story apartment building in a quiet neighborhood. It was only fifty dollars a month, and had one large room, a kitchenette, and a bath.

After paying a month's rent and the security, we didn't have enough money left for a down payment on furniture. But we moved in anyway and slept on blankets on the floor until our next pay checks. Our apartment was only about five blocks from Winnie's house, so Junior came over to see us almost every night that first week. He and Adline would sit around on the floor and plan the birthday party they were going to give Mama when she came to town the following weekend. I dreaded the thought of that party. I hadn't seen Mama in two years and I had stopped writing her a couple of months ago.

The night before Mama was due to arrive, our new furniture was delivered. Adline and I were too tired to do anything but put the bed together, so we got up at seven the next morning, and rushed around trying to get everything arranged. We'd bought a mahogany bedroom set, a deep orange sofa, a small table for the kitchenette, and a couple of chairs.

Junior was knocking on the door within an hour. I knew Mama was with him, so I waited for Adline to go and open it. She pretended she didn't even hear the knock. Finally, I opened it myself—and there was Mama.

"Hi, come in," I said, trying to appear as cheerful as possible. She had brought my little sister Jennie Ann, and I turned to her immediately. "Goodness, Jennie Ann, you are almost as tall as me." I pulled her over to the mirror on the bathroom door and measured her height against mine.

"How are you, Mama?" I made myself say.

"O.K. and you?" she said as if she wanted to embrace me. Our family was not the embracing, hugging, and kissing kind, though. I can't even remember once that someone in my family embraced another. Mama turned away and started looking at the furniture, and I tried to think of something to talk about.

"I gotta go pick up some things that I left at work," Junior said.

"You coming back?" Mama asked him. "I want you to take me by Winnie."

"I'll be back later. But Essie Mae or Adline can take you there. It's just a few blocks from here," Junior said.

I wanted to answer him and say, "Maybe Adline but not me." But I kept my mouth closed. I didn't want Mama to start asking me why I didn't want to go to Winnie. What Winnie did to you?

"I will take Mama by there," Adline finally said after she realized I wasn't going to volunteer. Junior left, and Jennie Ann sat down and started looking through an old magazine.

"How do you like the apartment, Mama?" Adline said.

"It's nice, but ain't it too small?"

"For fifty dollars a month, it's plenty large, Mama."

Adline and Mama continued to make small conversation about the apartment. Then they talked about the children. I had been away from home for five years. And I had only been back once in that time. I felt so left out hearing about the children. Since I had been home last, Mama had had two more. They were complete strangers to me. All of a sudden I noticed Mama held a baby in her arms. She had walked in and been here for about thirty minutes and I hadn't even noticed the baby. "She must be feeling pretty bad that I didn't say anything about it," I thought. "That damn Adline is trying to be smart because she hasn't said anything at all about the baby either."

I sat there not knowing how to break the ice between Mama and me. I wanted to ask her a million questions about how they were treated in Centreville when I was going to jail and all. She had told me many times in her letters and Adline had told me even more since I had been in New Orleans. But it wasn't as if it had come from Mama herself. I wanted to hear it from her while she was sitting there but I thought she might start crying or something. So I didn't ask. I just sat and waited for her or Adline to start the talk again.

"Why don't you lay the baby down?" Adline said at last.

"Is it asleep?" I asked, taking advantage of my chance to talk about it.

"No, she ain't 'sleep. She is just a real good baby," Mama said.

"Then put her on the bed," I said. "I thought you were holding her because you didn't want to wake her."

"How old is she?" I asked as Mama walked over to the bed.

"Three months. And you ain't even looked at her."

I felt so bad when Mama said that. I got right up and went to look at the baby.

"She is cute. How old is she?" I said.

"I just told you, she is three months." Mama still sounded hurt.

"She is crazy, Mama. Don't pay her any attention," Adline said.

"She sit around and talk to people for hours and don't remember a word they say. Since she been back here from Canton, she sleeps and groans in her sleep. She is crazy."

"Mind your own business," I shouted to Adline. "I have more to do than talk all the time."

"Like what?" she asked me. "Like sleep all day?"

"Like think," I said. "Think. Something you are not capable of doing."

"Think, huh! Well, that's what's wrong with you now. If you don't stop so much thinking you are gonna end up in a nuthouse."

"When are you going back to Mississippi?" Mama asked.

"I don't know if I am going back," I answered her coldly to discourage her from talking further on the subject.

"Why don't you settle down and get a job?" she asked.

"I have a job," I said. "And at the moment I am settled."

"That's what you spend four years in college for—to wash dishes—to work in a restaurant? Why don't you get a job teaching in New Orleans?"

"Teaching!" I said. "I am not the teaching kind. Furthermore, I wouldn't teach in any of these schools here in New Orleans or in Mississippi if the job paid a million a year."

I noticed tears forming in Mama's eyes. But I couldn't stand her telling me what to do with my education. When I was sick and starving in college she couldn't get a dime from Raymond to send me to buy sardines or aspirins. I had finished only because of my own desire to do so without any encouragement at all from anyone. Now I felt as if I should please myself doing whatever pleased me.

Mama sat there for thirty minutes or so not saying another word to me. Then she and Adline left for Winnie's house.

I had only five dollars left after making the down payment on the furniture the day before. I took it and went out to buy Mama's birthday presents. I bought her a long flannel nightgown for $3.98 and invested another dollar in a bottle of sweet wine.

I was late getting to the party that night. It was at George Lee's place. When I walked in, there were about twelve people sitting around in the living room. Among them were Winnie and my Aunt Celia. All of them just sat there staring at me as though I were from Mars. I spoke, and they barely uttered a word. I went to the bedroom and put the presents I had for Mama on the bed where all the others were.

When I came back to the living room, I pulled a stool up to the bar where Jennie Ann was sitting and began talking to her. I asked her what grade she was in and a few general questions. She just answered them as though I were someone she didn't even know. I tried another approach. I started telling her how pretty she was, and asking her about boys making passes at her and all. Her eyes lit up then, and she started telling me things like "One boy in my class told me I was prettier than any brown doll he seen." Then I got a little mad because here she was eleven years old and the only thing she knew how to talk about was boys.

While sitting there I could see Mama in the mirror behind the bar. She was looking at me with her eyes full of water. I sat there talking to Jennie Ann for about an hour and all that time Mama never took her eyes off me. I could see that a thousand questions were going on in her mind. I looked at her and wondered how she had brought me into this world and did not understand me or it. Maybe she understood Adline better. I looked at Adline. She was running all around the place tonight acting as content as anyone. Sometimes I hated her because she was so content with nothing. I hated her now as I looked at her. We were sisters, but there was no likeness between us. Junior walked in and I directed my thoughts to him. We looked a little alike. And sometimes when I was with him, I could feel that he was just as rebellious and discontent as I was. But his discontent would come and go. I had never been able to do away with mine like that. It was always there. Sometimes I used to try to suppress it and it didn't show. Now it showed all the time.

I got tired of everyone staring at me so I decided to leave the party. I told Mama that I had a terrible headache, and that I had left a present on the bed for her. I wished her a happy birthday and left. On my way back to the apartment, I was almost blinded by tears running down my cheeks. I couldn't understand why I seemed so strange to everyone. At the party I felt like I had committed a crime and everyone was punishing me by not talking to me. All of a sudden, I found myself wishing I was in Canton again working in the Movement with people who understood me. Here among my own people, I seemed crazy because I was grieved over problems they didn't even think about.

I walked around most of the next week wondering what to do about the Movement. At one point, I made up my mind to go back to Canton. But then I couldn't think up any reasons for going. I had the feeling that I should be back in the Movement, but involved in some different way that I could not yet define. I decided to give up thinking about it for a while.

On Friday, November 22, 1963, I was headed for the pantry during the rush hour at the restaurant with a tray of dishes when Julian, the new cashier, a white Tulane Law student, walked up behind me and said, "President Kennedy was just shot!" Everything around me went black. When things were light again, I found myself sitting dazed in a chair with Julian holding my tray. Just that morning, I remembered, James had made a crack about President Kennedy coming to the South—I hadn't even given it much thought. Julian went out front to see if there was any further news. A short while later, he came back and said that President Kennedy was dead. For a while I just sat there staring at everyone and not seeing a thing. "So much killing," I thought, "so, so much killing. And when will it end? When?"

Miles away I could hear the other waiters talking:

"Where did it happen, Waite?"

"In Dallas."

"What? He should have known better than to come to Texas."

"Anne, there goes your civil rights," James said. "The Negroes may as well start packing. Yes, I think I'm going to haul ass back to Africa or somewhere."

All of us working there were Negro except Julian. I guess we were all afraid to even consider what his death meant to Negroes. I know I was.

After all the other waiters left the pantry, I somehow pulled myself together and walked slowly through the dining room. My customers were still there, all of them. I noticed how quiet it was. Usually during the rush hour it was so noisy. But right now no one was saying a word.

By the time I got to the front of the dining room, I was enraged. When I turned around and looked at all those white faces—all of those Southern white faces—fire was in my eyes. I felt like racing up and down between the tables, smashing food into their faces, breaking dishes over their heads, and all the time I would shout and yell MURDERERS! MURDERERS! MURDERERS! Then I wondered what was I doing in this segregated restaurant. What was I doing serving all of these evil-minded murderers? I stood there with blood gushing up to my brains, feeling the hot air as it came out of my nostrils. Tears were burning my cheeks. Mr. Steve noticed I was crying. He must have thought I was fainting or something. He walked me back to the pantry and asked me to take the rest of the day off. I looked at him and he had tears in his eyes, too. I wondered if he would be crying if he was a native white Southern American instead of a Greek. I didn't remember seeing a single tear when I was out there—no not one. All those stony faces were white as a sheet, but dry as a desert.

It took me about an hour to change my uniform and another hour to get enough nerve to leave the restaurant. It was as though I was afraid to go out into that world that was waiting outside, that cruel and evil world. I had the feeling that when I walked out on the street everything would be pitch black. "A world this evil," I thought, "should be black, blind, and deaf, and without any feelings at all. Then there won't be any color to be seen, no hatred to be heard, and no pain to be felt."

Stumbling up to the corner, I picked up a newspaper as I waited for the St. Charles streetcar. The headlines of the New Orleans *States Item* read PRESIDENT DEAD in the largest print I had ever seen.

On the streetcar, I tried to look at the faces of the people. All I could see was newspapers. Every head was buried behind one. I looked especially for the faces of Negroes who had so many hopes centered on the young President. I knew they must feel as though they had lost their best friend—one who was in a position to help determine their destiny. To most Negroes, especially to me, the President had made "Real Freedom" a hope.

chapter

TWENTY-EIGHT

Sometime during that next week, James said to me, "Annie, ever since Kennedy was killed you have been walking around here as though you were in outer space. Why don't you stop killing yourself over all these problems? You should never have come back to New Orleans. What you should have done was take a vacation from the States." I realized he was right. But I didn't even have money to cross the state line. I also realized that coming back to New Orleans was even worse than staying in Canton. Here I had nothing in common with the people around me except the color of my skin. Just to keep my sanity, I knew I had to get involved with the Movement again.

I called a girl I knew in the New Orleans CORE chapter, and the following week I went to my first meeting. I learned there that CORE had a voter registration drive going on in Orleans Parish and that teams were being organized to canvass on Saturdays and Sundays. I volunteered for one.

My canvassing partner was white—a quiet-spoken New York girl named Erika, who was managing editor of the *Tulane Drama*

Review. I brought her to my apartment several times and introduced her to Adline. Adline had never been introduced to whites before on a social level. She hated white people with a passion. Although she never did act up around Erika, I think Erika sensed how she felt. For a while Erika didn't act comfortable around her, but before long, she and Adline were cracking jokes with each other. I hadn't quite gotten Adline to canvass with us, but I could tell she was coming around.

After about two months, I found it as hard to persuade Negroes to register in New Orleans as it had been in Mississippi. In Orleans Parish the number of registered Negroes never exceeded 35,000—regardless of how many voters registered each year. To keep the number constant, a certain number of Negroes were purged annually from the voting list. The voting test was just as hard and the registrar flunked Negroes just as fast as in Mississippi. But most New Orleans Negroes were very content. The majority of them had come from rural Mississippi or rural Louisiana—in comparison, New Orleans seemed like a utopia; at least they were able to find work. The only big difference about canvassing in New Orleans was that here civil rights workers, Negro and white, could canvass together and not be threatened or openly assaulted.

The first weekend in March, Junior went home to Centreville. I was kind of sorry he was going. Everytime someone went home and returned, they always brought back bad news. If Negroes weren't being killed in Woodville or Centreville, the whites were beating them up or running them out of town. Late Sunday night, Adline and I had just gotten into bed when we heard someone knocking. Adline got up to see who it was. It was Junior.

"What are you doing coming by here this time of night?" Adline said.

"Mama sent y'all this," he said, giving Adline a package which consisted of two large feather pillows. "Essie Mae, you sleep?" he asked.

"No. Why?" I said, still in bed.

"Emma's brother was killed Friday night."

"What? Clift was killed?" I asked, almost daring him to repeat what he just said.

"You're kidding," Adline said.

"Why should I come by here at twelve at night to kid y'all," Junior said.

"How was he killed?" I asked him.

"He was coming from work Friday night. They say his whole face was almost shot off. I went to Woodville to see Daddy and Emma and they is almost crazy now. They don't know who did it."

"They know didn't nobody do it but them goddamn white crackers," Adline said. "They need to blow Woodville and Centreville off the map and kill all of them bastards."

"Essie Mae ought to see if she can get Martin Luther King or CORE or one of them organizations to go in there and help the Negroes," said Junior.

"What Essie Mae need to do," Adline said bitterly, "is try and get some of these organizations to take us back to Africa or somewhere. This government ain't no fuckin' good and ain't meant to protect us black folks. That's what she need to do while she is running around here trying to get the Negroes to vote. I'm goin' to save my money and get out of this fuckin' country."

"That's five Negroes been killed up there in three months," Junior said. "Them three killed in the car in Woodville in December, and some man in Liberty, Mississippi, last month. They say his head was almost shot off, too, just like Clift's."

Junior sat there on the sofa for almost an hour, without anyone saying much more. Finally he said, "I better go, I gotta go to work early tomorrow." After he left and Adline was getting into bed, I noticed tears in her eyes. She and Junior had never reacted to all the other killings in Woodville or Centreville. At least it had seemed that way to me. Now they were very concerned, for the killings were getting closer. All night I lay awake thinking about Clift, his beautiful young wife, Ruby, and their four children. I remembered how close I had felt to them all when I went with Daddy and Emma to visit them, and how much fun we'd had together. I had accepted Clift as one of my blood uncles.

Next morning, I realized that I hadn't shed one tear for Clift's death. I had cried so much for other people who had been killed—even people who were strangers to me. But now it was as though something had happened to me so that I couldn't cry. I just felt funny all over. I lay in bed and pretended I was asleep until Adline went to work about eight o'clock. As soon as she left, I got up. I felt so tired when I stepped out of bed, I could hardly move. I took a hot bath and went back to bed, setting the alarm clock for ten-thirty—I didn't have to be at work until eleven. Soon I was sleeping. When the alarm went off at ten-thirty, I tried to get up and couldn't move. There was what seemed like a heavy weight on my heart. I tried to breathe and couldn't. It seemed as if heavy weights also pressed against my diaphragm and kept it from moving. I felt like I had suddenly become paralyzed from my neck to my waist.

For almost three hours, I lay there unable to move. Then tears started running down my face. Slowly I began to breathe again. Slowly my heart began to beat. The more the tears came, the more I could breathe. Again I thought of Clift's death, his wife and children, and the tears wouldn't stop coming. I was glad—glad I was crying. Just a few minutes ago I'd thought I was going to die.

It was about three before I was able to get up and call the restaurant. Since we had no phone, I used a friend's phone across the street. Joe, the cook, answered.

"Joe, this is Anne," I said.

"What's wrong are you sick, honey?" he asked.

"Yes, let me speak to Waite," I said.

"Yes, Anne," Waite said when he came to the phone.

"I am sick, Waite," I said, "and I can't come in..." He cut me off. "If you are sick why didn't you call me earlier this morning?" he asked, almost yelling. "At least we could have gotten someone to work in your place. We got swamped in the dining room this morning."

"My uncle was killed in Mississippi, Waite. Now if I don't feel like coming in tomorrow I'll call you." Just as I was hanging up the phone, I blacked out. When I was conscious again, my friend was holding a wet towel to my forehead.

"You want me to get a doctor?" she asked.

"No, I'm all right," I said, "it's just that we had a death in the family."

But when I went back to the apartment, I started feeling tired again. I was afraid that if I got in bed again, this time I might not come out of it. I decided I'd better see a doctor after all.

I went to a doctor on Claiborne Avenue, one that Winnie went to all the time. He told me after checking my heart and blood pressure that I had a terrible strain on me, and that I was overexerting myself. He thought I had probably fainted because of anemia or overexertion. He gave me a prescription for iron tablets and tranquilizers and told me to stay in bed for a few days.

I stopped at a drugstore to have the prescription filled, and I bought some envelopes and writing paper. I was going to write Emma even though, after the Woolworth's sit-in, she had asked me not to write them. I was not sure I should write now, but I felt the need to express my feelings or at least let them know that I knew about Clift's death and that I cared.

On the bus back to the apartment I got that faint feeling again. I opened the window and the cool March wind made me feel much better. With the wind blowing into my face, I sat there trying to think of what I would write to Emma. This was the first time that someone had died in the family. I didn't know what to say. Everything seemed so inadequate. And perhaps in a sense I had caused Clift's death because I was the only one from that area who had actively participated in the Movement. In fact, every time anyone was beaten or killed in Wilkinson County, I had guilt feelings about it.

Back at the apartment, it took me about two hours to finish the letter to Emma. I read it, and reread it:

Dear Emma,

Junior told me about Clift's death Sunday night. It was a terrible shock to me. It has caused me much grief as I realized what it must have meant to you and the entire family. How are Ruby and the children taking it? When is the funeral? I am truly sorry that I cannot come. I would come in spite of the fact that it's not yet safe for me to come back. However, I have decided not to come because my presence might cause more trouble in the family. That is, if the whites found out that I attended the funeral.

I heard about the three people that were murdered in their car. I have also heard that nothing has been done about it yet and no arrests have been made. I personally would like to see these crimes solved. Have any officials from the Justice or FBI Departments been in to investigate the murders? From past experience, I know that even if there has been an investigation, as soon as the investigators leave nothing will be done; the murders will be forgotten and the killings resumed.

I know that Bob Moses, the SNCC director, is very much concerned about these murders. In fact, he has been making plans to move into southwest Mississippi (Natchez, Woodville, McComb, and Liberty). If you will find out all you can about the murder of those three people killed in the car and tell me what you know about Clift's murder, I will pass this information on to Bob. Perhaps there is some way that we can get some protection for Negroes in that area. I am sure that Bob will try to do what he can to see that something is done. I sincerely hope that this letter doesn't cause any trouble. And that it gets to you without being opened. Give my regards to Daddy with sympathy to Ruby and the children. Write as soon as you can.

Love,
Anne Moody

Finally I put it in the mail, and as soon as I had done so, I was sorry. I hadn't put my name on the envelope. However, I was thinking that after Clift's death the whites working at the post office in Woodville might open or censor all the mail to and from his immediate family. Because of this, I had not written Ruby directly, but had written Emma instead. Mama once told me that after I began to demonstrate in Jackson, all of the mail that she received at the post office in Centreville had been opened.

I went back to Maple Hill on Thursday and broke dishes all day. My mind wasn't on the work. I knew that I would be nervous until I received a letter from Emma. Two weeks passed and she still hadn't written. Another week and no letter. I was going out of my mind. Finally, I gave up hope of receiving one. I didn't know if the whites had received my letter or what had happened. I wanted to write Emma again, but decided not to. I was afraid that a second letter might cause trouble, even if the other one hadn't.

I worked about a month in the restaurant after my uncle's death and continued my voter registration work for CORE on weekends. During this time, Adline and I also moved to a larger and much nicer apartment. Then in mid-April I began to get restless again. The grass was beginning to get green, the trees were budding, sap was rising, and everyone seemed happy and pleasant. I had never been able to enjoy myself and feel relaxed like most people during this time of the year. Adline had bought all kinds of beautiful spring skirts and blouses. I hated to see people so content, especially Negroes. It made me mad every time I saw one smile. And it seemed as though every Negro in New Orleans was smiling but me.

I was down in the French Quarters at Erika's apartment for a party one weekend. A lot of the people there were students from Tulane who were members of CORE. When I noticed that even the Movement people were getting spring fever and talking about getting out of New Orleans, I knew that I couldn't remain there long myself. I also knew that I was more than likely headed back to Mississippi where the Negroes weren't laughing all the time. Where they knew, as I knew, the price you pay daily for being black. Where I felt I belonged. The weekend after the party, I quit my job at the restaurant and started canvassing full-time for CORE. But even that didn't help. I just had to get out of New Orleans.

When I came home one night from canvassing, I found that Emma had finally written me. I sat on the bed and read her letter over and over again.

> *Dear Anne,*
>
> *Only to let you know that I received your letter. We are O.K. only can't get over our grief over Clift's murder. Now the reason I was so long answering your letter, I was trying to get some information on the death of those three persons whom you asked about, but I can get only their names. Eli Jackson and Dennis Jones were the two men and Lula Mae Anderson the lady. The three of them were found dead in their car on old Highway 61 about ten (10) miles north of Woodville. The local paper stated they fell asleep with the heater on and motor running and was poisoned by the fumes from the gas. But it was revealed that two of them were shot and Eli's neck was broken. I don't know the exact date, but it was the last of '63. On Feb. 29, 1964, Clift was found riddle with buckshot on a local road on his way home from work. He was on the 3 to 11 P.M. shift and was supposed to have gotten home about 12 P.M. After he didn't Ruby thought he was*

working in someone's place which he had done before. So she didn't think too seriously about it.

About three o'clock the following day the sheriff and a highway man came out to her house and told her Clift was in a little trouble. They didn't even tell her he was dead or had been killed. So we all went to see what had happened. When we got in sight, we could see his car was riddled, his side glasses were shot out on both sides and his front ones. He was slumped over so we could see only a small portion of him. Later we discovered most of his face was shot off and all of his teeth shot out. As of now as to who or why we don't know and haven't heard anything and if any arrests have been made, we haven't heard of it yet. So you see it's not much information I can give. Of course, the FBI's visited his wife asking a lot of questions a number of times. Such as, was he a member of any Organization, and what he had to say about those three people that were murdered in their car.

Whoever it was ambushed him it appeared to have been well planned from every angle. I am sorry that this is all I know, but I hope that you all will be able to help uncover it and we will know who did it and why.

Daddy is well sends love also the rest of the family.

Love,
Emma and Dad

I sat there with tears in my eyes and again read, "I am sorry that this is all I know, but I hope that you all will be able to uncover it." Then I got mad because I felt so helpless. They were expecting me to do something and I was all too aware of how little Bob Moses or I, or anyone could do. As for myself, I couldn't even go back to Woodville or Centreville again.

The second week in May, I received a letter from the registrar at Tougaloo College. My credits had at last been cleared from

Natchez. I was asked to come back to Tougaloo the last week in May to take part in the graduation exercises and to receive my diploma. As I looked at the letter, I realized that the last week of May was only one week off. I had to buy a white dress and black shoes for the graduation exercises. And I couldn't really afford either. "All the time and money you put into college," I thought, "and then you gotta put out more time and money to get that little piece of paper."

Since I had quit my job and had only enough money to pay rent until the first of June, I decided that I wasn't going to spend a dime on graduation. I went through my old college clothes and found an old white dress I had worn as a junior in college. I bleached it up and it looked almost like new. Then I found some old black shoes that Adline had packed away in the closet. They were good enough to use for two days. I polished them and was surprised at how good they looked. Now I was ready to participate in the exercises. I had just bus fare enough to get to Mississippi. I didn't know how I would get back. In fact, I don't think I really wanted to come back. However, I hated to run out on Adline. We had just moved into that apartment, we owed at least one hundred dollars on the furniture, and she couldn't take care of those bills alone.

As I packed my suitcase on Tuesday night, Adline stood looking at me with tears in her eyes. I knew she was feeling bad because here I was graduating from college and no one in my family really cared. As I put the old white dress and her old shoes into the suitcase, she walked out of the apartment. She was like me. She didn't like people to see her cry or know her emotions when they were too deep to talk about.

About a half hour later, she walked back into the apartment with two big red apples in her hands. I was washing dishes. "Want one?" she asked. "Yes, thanks," I said. She put my apple on the table and walked over to the sofa and sat down. As I continued to wash the dishes, she sat there watching me. She looked as though she wanted to say something and didn't know how. Finally, as I finished the dishes, she asked, "What time is your graduation?"

"The baccalaureate sermon is at ten-thirty Sunday morning, and the commencement is at five," I said. "Why?"

"Nothing." Then she said, "I was thinking about coming. I think Junior might wanta come too."

Now Adline looked as though she felt much better. She wasn't crying any more. I didn't think that she would really come to Tougaloo on Saturday but I felt better knowing that at least she cared, that someone in the family cared.

The next morning I was once again on Greyhound headed for Jackson, Mississippi. I arrived at Tougaloo just in time to eat in the cafeteria. I was glad because I didn't have money to buy food or anything else. As soon as I finished dinner, I headed for the Kings' place to find out what was going on in the Movement. I had lost all contact with the Movement people in Mississippi, when I was in New Orleans. But I knew Reverend King would be part of everything that was going on.

When I walked up on his porch, his door was open as usual—always open to students and Movement people. I knocked and walked right in. The Kings were just finishing dinner. A couple of other students were having dinner with them. I sat at the table and had coffee with everyone and the talk went on for two hours about the Movement and what was going on in Mississippi and on campus.

"Don't forget we have an occasion to celebrate tomorrow," Reverend King said to me as I was leaving.

"Tomorrow?" I asked blankly.

"Don't tell me you've forgotten. To be honest with you I had too, until you came."

"I'm afraid I don't remember," I said.

"Come on, Anne. The Woolworth's sit-in. It will be a year tomorrow."

"My goodness! That's right!" I said. "But it seems to me like it was years ago."

"It's only that you have done so much since then," Reverend King said.

At eleven the next morning, I was on my way with some other students to celebrate my "anniversary" by participating in another sit-in. This time our target was Morrison's Cafeteria. A dignitary from India who was visiting Tougaloo at the time was part of our group. Reverend King had invited him to join in our celebration.

A couple of white students had been sent to the cafeteria ahead of us. They were to be inside the cafeteria when we arrived so they could keep an eye on what was going on as we attempted the sit-in. Our timing was off and the sit-in didn't go as we had planned. We all arrived at different times and minutes too late. The cops were there waiting for us when we arrived and had barred the entrance to the cafeteria. By the time the car I was riding in pulled up, the dignitary from India had been arrested—a short time later, when his identity was discovered, they immediately released him. The rest of us gathered around Reverend King's station wagon to decide whether or not to try the sit-in again. Finally we agreed to call it off. There was no bail money available for us if we were arrested and five of us were to take part in the graduation exercises on Sunday. So we all piled into Reverend King's station wagon just as we had on May 28 a year before. However, there were no fresh ketchup and mustard stains to add to the old ones still in the car from last year's sit-in.

The night before, when I was talking to Reverend King, I had become excited over what he told me about the Mississippi Summer Project. I was convinced that it was the best project yet proposed or introduced by the organizations. The Summer Project, which was sponsored by COFO, was a statewide program designed primarily to encourage qualified Negroes to register and vote. However, in addition to the voter registration drive, Freedom Schools and community centers were to be set up to teach courses in remedial reading, government, humanities, and other scholastic and vocational subjects. To assist the Summer Project, COFO was expecting about one thousand college students from all over the country. I was told by Reverend King that many ministers, lawyers, and other skilled persons had already volunteered their services.

Since Reverend King had to drop some of the students off in Jackson, I decided to stop in at the COFO headquarters and see for myself what was going on. When I walked in the office my head began to spin, there were so many people there. And everyone in the place seemed to be doing three things at once. The office was a total mess. Night riders had thrown bricks through the glass window that had previously covered the front of the office. There were fragments of glass littering the sidewalk and the entrance. A shipment of clothes had arrived, but there was nowhere to store them, so they were just left all over the place. Right outside the office, five or six boys were unloading a shipment of books that had just come. The books added to the clothes hardly left standing room. Behind a partition, two old dirty mattresses lay on the floor. This was where two of the new arrivals slept. Typewriters were going at full speed. Mimeograph machines were turning out stencils as soon as they were taken off the typewriters. Five or six telephones were being installed. FBI men were running around all over the place as though they were lost. "So this is the beginning of the Long Hot Summer," I thought.

According to one of my old Movement friends, white Mississippians were really preparing for it. The state was in the process of tightening legislative screws to try and outlaw practically all phases of the project. Six new laws had already been enacted in the state legislature, authorizing cities to pool manpower, personnel, and equipment to assist each other in riot control. I learned from my friend that an anti-invasion bill had also been introduced to prohibit entry into the state. Besides all the bills being passed, the state police force had been doubled and armed to the teeth. Among Mississippi Negroes, however, I had never witnessed such anticipation in all my life. It seemed that for once in the history of civil rights work in Mississippi something was actually going to be accomplished. I was so carried away that until Bob Moses came walking through the door, I had almost forgotten that I planned to see him to talk with him about the killings in Woodville. Somehow, with all of the excitement going on about the Summer Project and Bob directing it, I had expected a change in him, but I could see he was still the same quiet, slow-walking, eye-glasses-wearing Bob. I quickly cornered him and we talked for about an hour. He had been well aware of the killings. However, he hadn't known that my family was involved.

From Bob, I learned that the man who had been killed in Liberty, Mississippi, was Louis Allen. Mr. Allen had witnessed the 1961 slaying of Herbert Lee, a voter registration worker, by E. H. Hurst, a member of the Mississippi legislature. Hurst told a grand jury that Lee had threatened him with a tire iron, and Allen, fearing for his life at the time, identified the weapon at the hearing. But when Hurst was freed, Allen signed an affidavit stating that Hurst had killed Lee "without provocation." After this, Allen's life was threatened many times and once the sheriff of Liberty beat him up and broke his jaw. Bob said that Allen had asked the Justice Department for protection several times. However, the reply had always been, "We can't protect every individual Negro in Mississippi." At last Allen gave up and decided to move to Milwaukee. Less than twelve hours before his departure, he was struck down in his front yard. Half of his head was blown off by a shotgun blast as he crawled under his truck to escape the assassin. Inside the house, his family heard the shots, but because shots had been heard several times outside the house at night, at first no one bothered to see what had happened. Later, during the night, noticing that the truck lights were still burning, one of Allen's children went outside and discovered his body. The way Bob sighed after he finished telling me about Allen's murder, I could detect in him a feeling of guilt, disgust, and helplessness. I also knew he could tell that I, too, felt guilty about my uncle's death.

Bob's theory was that the murder of my uncle and the other three persons in Woodville were just "terror killings." That is, they were murdered to keep Negroes in their place and to keep civil rights workers out of the southwest during the summer. Some people had already been sent into Woodville to try and find out something about the killings but they weren't able to get the Negroes to talk. Bob said that plans had been made to send civil rights workers in there to work, but they couldn't find anyone willing to risk putting the workers up. However, the surrounding areas (Natchez, McComb, and Liberty) would be worked during the summer. This way he thought that the attention drawn to the other areas would make it possible to move into Woodville and Centreville later in the year.

After talking to Bob, I was really upset. He only confirmed what I had been thinking—that beyond focusing attention on the area, we, the civil rights organizations, were powerless when it came to trying to do something about the murders. Yet the United States could afford to maintain the Peace Corps to protect and assist the underprivileged of other countries while native-born American citizens were murdered and brutalized daily and nothing was done. "I guess Negroes aren't even considered human," I thought. "They're just shot and butchered like hogs."

I was so mad after talking to Bob, that I walked the three and a half miles to the Maple Street apartments to see Dave and Mattie Dennis. From Dave I learned that the following day Canton was having a big "Freedom Day." He said that he would pick me up at eight o'clock the next morning. Then I left and went back to the

COFO's office to try and bum a ride back to Tougaloo. I got back to campus about twelve-thirty that night. I was so tired that I just made it to the bed and fell across it. Then I was dreaming down about being back in Canton and seeing Mrs. Chinn and George and all of the teen-agers again.

chapter

TWENTY-NINE

On Friday, May 29, 1964, I was again headed for Canton, Mississippi. When Dave drove up in front of the Freedom House, the first person I saw was Mrs. Chinn. I jumped out of the car before it came to a complete stop and ran to her. "Anne! Anne! Anne!" she kept saying as we hugged each other. A minute later, I was hugging Mrs. Devine, then George, and it went on and on from one to the other for about thirty minutes. It was like I had come home to a family that I hadn't seen in a long time. Actually it was only six months ago that I'd left Canton. As soon as I walked into the Freedom House, I was thrown a magic marker and was asked to help write freedom slogans. Within an hour, we had turned out about three hundred posters.

Mrs. Devine told me that they were expecting about five hundred adults to march. If the adults were not allowed to march, they had about eight hundred high school students ready to demonstrate at the courthouse. It was hard for me to believe that this was the same Canton, Mississippi.

After we talked a while, Mrs. Devine and I walked down to the church. We got there just as the march started. I stood in the street and watched as three hundred adults piled out of the church. I just didn't believe it. I felt like running up to them and touching them to see if they were real.

The entire street was lined with cops. Just about every hick in the county had been deputized. Some of them wore faded-out jeans and guns hanging off their hips like cowboys. The marchers were allowed to go about a block before they were stopped by a barricade of armed policemen, and asked to turn around or they would be arrested. Reverend Cox, a CORE field secretary who was the leader of the march, led the group in a silent prayer and then they all returned to the church.

Just as I watched the first marchers enter, all of a sudden I realized which church they were returning to. It was the church of that big number one Uncle Tom. So, finally he had given in, I thought. I hurried inside myself to see how many of the other big-shot ministers were around. As I walked in, Reverend Cox was leading the adults in "Oh, Freedom." It was so moving that I forgot about the ministers and joined in the singing. I stood there singing with tears in my eyes as I listened to those old wrinkled-faced adults. Everytime I heard them sing, they brought tears to my eyes. Then I knew that there was something to singing, suffering, and Soul.

> *Oh, Freedom, Oh, Freedom,*
> *Oh, Freedom over me.*
> *And before I'll be a slave*
> *I'll be buried in my grave*
> *And go home to my Lord and be free.*
> *No more lynchings, no more lynchings,*
> *No more lynchings over me.*
> *And before I'll be a slave*
> *I'll be buried in my grave*
> *And go home to my Lord and be free....*

"All right! Sisters and brothers! I can just listen to y'all sing twenty-four hours a day," Reverend Cox said. "We are goin' to sing our way to freedom yet. Let's sing a few more verses and decide if we are goin' to jail or not."

I went outside to see if the high school students were going to demonstrate at the courthouse. I passed Mrs. Devine on the church lawn and asked her about the teen-agers. "Oh, I'm on my way over to Asbury now to deliver a message," she said. "Why don't you go with me? They have lots of kids over there."

On our way to the church where the teen-agers were, a police car drove up behind us. I spotted my pet cop. The one that wanted to beat me up so bad. The car followed behind us slowly. Mrs. Devine and I acted as though we didn't even know it was there.

As Mrs. Devine and I walked into the church, the high school students were ending a song. It seemed as though everyone was in a singing mood. Sometimes it seemed that, without the songs, the Negroes didn't have the courage to move. When I listened to the older Negroes sing, I knew that it was the idea of heaven that kept them going. To them heaven would end their troubles. But listening to the teen-agers, I got an entirely different feeling. They felt that the power to change things was in themselves. More so than in God or anything else. Their way of thinking seemed to have been "God helps those that help themselves" instead of "When we get to heaven things will be different, there won't be no black or white," which was what my grandmother thought.

There were about three hundred teen-agers in the church. I saw all those that had been on my canvassing teams and many more. After they finished the song, the room swelled with noise. I found myself carried away just being in their presence. Standing there looking at them, all of my hopes in the future came to life again. I could see them as men and women living a normal life as a real part of this world, as a group of people that belonged—belonged because they had fought the battle and won. My thoughts were interrupted as some of the teen-agers recognized me stand-ing in the back of the church. "Annie Moody!" They sang my name out and ran to me. Several of the girls swung around my neck almost pulling me down to the floor of the church. By this time the place was so full of noise that the sound waves rang like bells in my ears.

Just as we were about to leave the church, some flashbulbs went off. As the teen-agers began to thin out, I looked around and saw my favorite cop taking pictures of me and the teen-agers. As the teen-agers noticed him, they began to pose before the camera. They were putting on all kinds of monkey faces. They embar-rassed the cop, posing and carrying on so. "I don't want y'all's pic-ture," he said. "I want that gal's there," pointing to me.

"What gal?" one of the teen-agers asked.

"Oh! You mean Miss Moody, huh?" another one said.

"Go on, Miss Moody, pose for him," one of the teen-aged boys yelled as all of them stepped back leaving me in front of the cam-era alone. And that stupid cop went click, click, click until he was out of film. He finished his roll of film and said, "Much obliged."

One of the boys asked, "What are you going to do with them— sell 'em or put them up in your room?" At that point, I too began to wonder what he was going to do with them. Again I thought he must be from Centreville.

Mrs. Devine called me and I fell in by her side but I did not say a word to her as we walked back to the church where the adults were gathered. She had seen what happened, and I sensed she too was wondering about the cop.

Getting back to the church, we discovered that the adults had been granted permission to march to the courthouse. However, they could march only under the condition that they did so two at a time with ten minutes' walking time between each couple. It was after one o'clock now and it was really hot. Those country cops were standing in the streets lined up all the way from the church to the courthouse. Now that it was hot, they looked like they were mad as hell having to stand sweating out in the boiling sun to "guard a bunch of niggers." Slowly the adults began moving down the road. They too looked like the heat was getting next to them. They were walking so slow it would have taken two months for them to get to the courthouse two at a time and ten minutes apart.

There were now about two hundred people sitting around on the church lawn. Most of them were teen-agers watching the adults march. I noticed Mrs. Chinn talking to some men and I went over to where she was standing.

"Where've you been, Anne?" she asked.

"I went over to Asbury with Mrs. Devine. They got about three hundred screaming teen-agers over there in the church. When are *they* going to demonstrate at the courthouse?" I asked her.

"They can't," she said. "Most of these kids here have already tried to get there. But they can't get near the place. Those country bastards have formed a solid wall around it."

As we stood there talking we were interrupted by a conversation between the teen-agers and two of the cops in the street.

"What y'all niggers marching for anyway?" one of the cops asked.

"Niggers? Niggers? Niggers? You don't see no niggers out here," one of the teen-agers said. "If you mean us *Negroes*, then we are marching because we are aiming to taste a bit of that freedom you white people are enjoying."

"Freedom?" one of the cops asked.

"Y'all wouldn't even know what to do with it," the other cop said.

"Well, we are on the road to getting it. When we do, we'll show you all what we'll do with it," another teen-ager said.

"That's telling him, man," someone shouted as others pitched in.

"Yes, we gonna eat in your restaurant, drive your police cars, vote and everything else," they were saying.

All of a sudden, the air was filled with laughter from the teen-agers on the church lawn. At that moment, the two cops jumped the little ditch between the street and the church lawn and began pulling a young man named McKinley Hamilton toward the street by both arms. When they made it as far as the ditch, they jumped it again, still dragging McKinley, who was stumbling along behind. They thought he was resisting them. One of the cops cracked him across the head with his billy stick, and the other one joined in. The licks were hitting hard and sounded loud against McKinley's head. Two more cops joined in. The Negroes on the lawn began to move slowly toward the street.

"Stop beating that boy!" Mrs. Chinn yelled.

"We ain't gonna take that!" someone yelled as every Negro on the church lawn began to move faster.

McKinley was down on the pavement in a pool of blood. By the time the Negroes reached the ditch, a jeep driven by a cop had pulled up. As McKinley was picked up bodily and thrown into it, big clots of blood dripped from his head and you could only see the whites of his eyes.

"They killed him!" some old Negro screamed.

"Jesus, they've killed the boy," cried another.

I don't know how I got there but I found myself standing on the edge of the ditch with the other Negroes. I realized that within a second or so all hell was going to break loose and that I, too, was going to be a part of it. I turned and looked at the rest of the crowd. Everyone in the church was now standing on the church lawn—about six hundred Negroes. They were all raging with anger.

"Come on, let's get back inside!" Reverend Cox was yelling over the noise that filled the air. Almost everyone ignored him and continued talking. "We can't handle this out here this way! Let's go inside and discuss it."

Suddenly there was a new commotion as I started back toward the church. Two white men were standing in the street. Negroes were shouting at them. "What happened? What happened? You men are crazy," a teen-ager yelled.

"Weren't you sitting over there in that car?" shouted another teen-ager. "We saw you. And you saw what happened just like we did!"

Angry shouts from other teen-agers and adults forced the two white men to retreat to a red car that had been parked at the intersection by the church all morning. "Who are they?" I asked Mrs. Chinn, who was standing just outside the church door.

"FBI's," she said. "They were sitting over there and they saw it all just as we did, and them bastards had the nerve to ask what happened."

Reverend Cox was praying and all the Negroes stood with their heads bowed as Mrs. Chinn and I entered the church. "I hope all of you realize what just happened out there," Reverend Cox said to the crowd. "At any minute, violence could have broken out. And I stand here as a minister in the house of God and wonder if I would have actually taken part."

Someone yelled, "We should all go to jail and stay there until something is done. For all we know that boy is dead."

After this statement, everything really roared. It took about an hour to decide what to do. Many of these people couldn't go to jail. Some had small children to look after, others had jobs. In fact I don't think anyone had any idea of going to jail that day. Finally, Reverend Cox asked for volunteers. About eighty volunteered to go for no more than a week. After this a march was organized by the volunteers. An eighty-six-year-old man was chosen to lead it.

A short while later, the marchers filed out. I was now standing in the street across from the church. As I watched that eighty-six-year-old man leading the line walk, I could taste hot tears running down my face. He walked with the aid of a cane because of a limp in one leg. His head was held high and he was chewing tobacco and spitting every few minutes or so. About a block and a half from the church, just in front of the railroad tracks, the cops had formed a solid wall along the entire street. They wore helmets and were armed with rifles, pistols, and billy sticks. As the old man got within a few yards of the wall of cops, he picked up his cane and seemed to walk straight up to them without a limp at all. I think every Negro who saw this happen was toughened by the way that old man faced those cops. I felt something and I knew that I was not the only one who did. All the marchers were stopped and made to wait in line until two large city trucks arrived. Then they were taken off to jail. We all went back inside the church, and Reverend Cox called for a moment of silent prayer for those eighty volunteers. Then we were dismissed.

Because of the tension that had built up around the Freedom Day, Canton had been placed under a 9 P.M. curfew, two weeks prior to the march. Dave's car had been used to carry home some of the Negroes who lived far out in the country after they had participated in the march. Now we sat around the Freedom House and waited for news on McKinley's condition. As soon as we had gotten news that he was unconscious but alive and the car was returned, we got out of Canton. Everything was so tense now that the whole town might go up in smoke after dark. The Negroes were still angry because of the cops beating McKinley. And the whites were mad because the Negroes were trying to get together at last.

When Dave dropped me off at Tougaloo it was after six o'clock. I was so tired. I hadn't eaten anything all day and I was extremely hungry. Since they had already served dinner in the dining room, I decided to go to Reverend King's for a bite to eat. Reverend King and a group of students were getting ready to go to Canton when I walked into his house. They had heard the news of McKinley's beating on the radio along with an announcement of a mass meeting that night. I told them about the curfew and tried to persuade them not to go. However, they went anyway with the intention of getting out of town before nine.

After I had helped myself to a sandwich and coffee, I went to the dormitory to get to bed early. I was just getting into bed an hour later when someone knocked on my door.

"Moody, did you hear the news?" one of the girls said as she peeped in the door.

"What news?" I asked.

"Reverend King them have just been beaten up in Canton. Someone just called. They are at the hospital in Jackson."

I sat there for a while with my face buried in my hands. I was too tired to even think. Finally, I pulled myself off the bed and went back to the Kings' house. Three other students were already there. I was told that no one was hurt except Hamid Kisenbasch, a Pakistani assistant professor of sociology at Tougaloo. They said that Reverend King had called and said that they would be back to the house soon.

It was about 11:45 when they came and told us what had happened. "Well, Anne, you were right," Reverend King confessed. "We were on our way back. And just as we got on 55 headed back to Tougaloo, a truck and two cars came up from somewhere. We hadn't noticed anyone following us when we left. Anyway, one of the cars swung around in front of us forcing us to stop. We quickly locked the car doors. Almost before we could get them locked, about fifteen white men were surrounding the car. They had clubs, guns of all sorts, and one had a large can. I think it was filled with kerosene or gasoline. When they were about to break the windows out of the car, Mr. Kisenbasch rolled his window halfway down to try and reason with them. He was hit on the side of the head at the same time two other men reached in to open the car door. When I realized they must have thought he was Negro because he was dark, I yelled to them, 'He's not Negro, he is Indian.' Blood was now spurting out of his head. They let him go and talked among themselves for a while. I think they thought he was the Indian that participated in the sit-in with us yesterday. Anyway, they let us go, warning us never to come back to Canton again."

"If I have ever been close to death it was tonight," Joan Trumpauer added.

"I think everyone in the car thought so too. I know I sure did," Mrs. King said.

Then Reverend King told us how he had gone to the highway patrol headquarters to report the incident. He said they were handled like they had committed the crime.

I just didn't feel like wasting any breath on Mississippi law officials. I had done it a million times before anyway, and I was exhausted. I said goodnight and headed back to the dorm, dreading the thought of practice marching tomorrow for the graduation exercises.

At ten o'clock on Sunday morning, I found myself standing in line in front of the college chapel. It was hard for me to believe, but within thirty minutes I would be marching through that door to listen to a college baccalaureate sermon as a member of the graduating class. Standing there at that moment, the whole campus looked different. The wind was blowing, and it was very humid. The moss hanging from the trees swayed back and forth with the breeze. The students in the line weren't talking very much at all. In fact, there was a sense of sadness in the air. As we slowly began to move, the only thing that could be heard was the sound of marching feet.

Inside the chapel, everyone was standing and music saturated the air. The audience remained standing until the last graduate in line was seated. When I sat, I breathed for what seemed like the first time in years.

I didn't realize that the audience consisted of parents of the graduates until the minister delivering the sermon addressed them. "Yes, parents," I thought. And then I realized that not a single member of my family was present. Adline and Junior had said that they would come, but they hadn't. "Here I am," I thought, "alone, all alone as I have been for a long time." Then I had the feeling that now that I was out of college and couldn't go home, I would be even more alone than in the past. Graduating, I thought, and I had no idea of where I was going or how I would get there. The only thing I knew was what I would have to face as a Negro trying.

After the sermon was over, we were asked to line up in the front of Galloway Hall for pictures. When all the pictures were taken, I went inside and went to bed. I couldn't stand the sight of the other graduating seniors showing their parents around the campus. It made me feel funny—sort of like an orphan.

I got up about 4:20, put on my cap and gown, and went running outside to go to the graduation ceremony. When I got to the door, I discovered it was pouring down rain. "Just my luck," I thought. "Here I am late and don't even have an umbrella." It seemed as though I was the only person left in the dormitory. Any other time it was raining, a couple of dozen people would be walking out of this dorm, I thought. I stood there looking at the rain for about ten minutes. Then I realized I would have to get wet. I just walked out and headed for the gym. I found the rest of the students lined up there ready to march. "Moody, you're gonna be sick," a couple of them said as I passed them in line. My face was dripping with water, and I was glad that it was. Because of that, they couldn't tell that I was crying.

When I found my place, Memphis Norman and Joan Trumpauer, my Woolworth's sit-in buddies, came up to me.

"There you are," Memphis said. "We been looking for you ever since the baccalaureate sermon. What happen to you?"

"I went to bed. I didn't feel very well," I said.

"Did your parents come?" he asked.

I shook my head.

"Well, whatta you know," Joan said sadly. "The three Woolworth's orphans."

"Reverend King would like to adopt us this evening and take us out to dinner," said Memphis.

The line started moving and they ran to get in their places.

When I walked in chapel, I almost fainted it was so hot. It seemed as though everyone in the chapel was fanning with hand fans. The electric fan in the chapel only circulated hot air, and the open windows brought in the warm dampness from the rain.

I felt so bad sitting there. I was dripping with water, and my hair was as nappy as it could possibly get. I was completely soaked from my head to my waist. After a while I started sneezing and couldn't stop. The guy sitting next to me gave me his handkerchief. I was embarrassed. All of the other students were constantly turning and looking at me. Some looked mad and some of them thought it was funny. The worst moment in the whole episode came when my name was called to receive my diploma. I walked up to the platform and just as I was about to change my tassel from one side to the other, and at the same time take the diploma, I sneezed three or four times. I stood there sneezing with both hands up to my face as President Beittel stood waiting. The graduates laughed for about five minutes. Instead of showing my discomfort, I smiled slightly, bowed my head to the audience, turned up my lips and walked off the platform. The students really roared after this.

By the time the commencement exercises were over, it had stopped raining. I went to the dorm, changed clothes, and then went over to the Kings'. Joan and Memphis were already there. I was still sneezing when I walked in and everyone broke up. Mrs. King gave me a hot cup of tea and a couple of aspirins before we left. Then Reverend King carried us to Steven's Kitchenette and ordered five of the biggest steaks in the house.

As we were all sitting there eating, I looked at Reverend King. And silently, I asked him to forgive—forgive me for doubting him when he first came to Tougaloo. I think because he was a white native Mississippian almost every student at Tougaloo doubted him at that time. We had never before had a white Southerner on the faculty. His wife, Jeanette, was from Jackson. I remember, I used to look at her going in and out of the chapel after visiting Reverend King there and just hate the thought of a white Southern minister and his wife taking over the most beautiful and cherished building on campus. Now sitting across the table from them I realized I had more respect for them than any of the white Northern teachers on campus. And for that matter, any white persons I had ever known.

The next day Joan and I were, as usual, the only students left on campus with nowhere in particular to go, but the matron of Galloway Hall asked us to leave the dorm by noon. We headed to the Kings' again, this time to see if they would put us up for a few days. Joan's train fare hadn't come and I didn't have any coming. I thought of borrowing my fare from Reverend King, but I would have felt bad asking him for the money, although I was sure he would have given it to me. My intention was to go into Jackson on Tuesday and see if I could bum a ride to New Orleans. When Joan and I got to the Kings', we found Ed and Jeanette packing to go to the Gulf Coast for a week. They said we could stay in their house while they were gone if we liked, and eat all the food in the refrigerator too, before it spoiled. So were were set up for a week.

The next day, Joan and I caught a ride into Jackson with one of the teachers that was on campus for the summer. We went straight to the COFO headquarters on Lynch Street. When we walked in, I was again overwhelmed by all the excitement going on in the office. There were now about thirty white students standing around who had just arrived for the Summer Project. Joan and I walked around and talked with a few of the students for a while. Then the two of us had a conference—we decided that instead of sticking around for a week we would both go home immediately and come back within two weeks to work on the Summer Project.

It seemed as though I had become a professional bum. Before I left the office, I had found a ride all the way to New Orleans the very next morning with Richard Haley, the new CORE Southern Project Director who was in Jackson to see Dave Dennis.

It was about five-thirty the following afternoon when Richard Haley stopped in front of my house. Adline was just getting off work when I got out of the car. She came running down the sidewalk to greet me and peep in at Richard Haley. "Where did you find him?" she asked teasingly. "So I see why you didn't come back on Sunday night. Where is your diploma?" I looked at her and wondered what she was happy about. She had lied and said that she would come to the graduation on Sunday. Now she was asking me for my diploma as if she doubted that I really had one. I didn't answer her, I just walked up the steps and opened the door.

When we got in the apartment, I went to the refrigerator for some water, and Adline went to the bedroom. When I came out of the little kitchenette, she was standing in the living room with a box in her hands. "Here, it's for you," she said. I took the box and opened it. Inside was a green two-piece dress—one of the prettiest dresses I had laid my eyes on. I just stood there holding it against me, with my mouth wide open not knowing what to say. "I decided I wouldn't come to the graduation but use the money to get you something real nice," she said. "Now can I see your diploma?" I opened the suitcase and gave it to her. She stood there a long time just looking at it. And I knew exactly what she was thinking, because at that moment, I thought it too. Here I was, the first person in my entire family to graduate from college. "It's just like high school diplomas," Adline said. "Did you expect it to be any different?" I asked. "No, it's just that I was thinking one day I may get mine since it looks just like a high school one," she said and smiled.

chapter

| THIRTY |

I didn't stay long in New Orleans—just a couple of days—because I realized I had no way of making any money during the next two weeks. I was a little sorry I had quit my job at the restaurant so soon. The evening after I got back, Tim and Carol, a white married couple from California working with New Orleans CORE, stopped by the apartment and asked if I wanted to ride into Mississippi with them the following morning. They were going to visit a friend of theirs who had been arrested in the Canton Freedom Day march. I just couldn't resist that free ride to Mississippi.

The following morning I was back in Canton, ready to start work on the Summer Project. As soon as I had left my suitcase at the Freedom House, I went to see Mrs. Chinn. I found her looking terribly depressed.

"Anne," she said, "if I were you and didn't have no ties to Canton, I wouldn't waste no time here. Looka here, alla that work we put into that march and McKinley almost beaten to death and things are even worse than they were before. These niggers done went into hiding again, scared to stick their heads outta the door.

C.O.'s in jail, them goddamn cops coming by my house every night, just about to drive me crazy. This ain't the way, Anne. This just ain't the way. We ain't big enough to do it by ourselves."

I had never seen Mrs. Chinn that depressed. What she said got me to thinking real hard. I walked around Canton for hours looking at the familiar streets. There were hardly any Negroes to be seen. The whole place looked dead. Walking past the jail, I saw C.O. Chinn coming in with the chain gang. They had been out digging ditches all day and he was filthy from head to toe. When he saw me, he waved trying to look happy. I couldn't hardly bring myself to wave back. I walked away as quickly as I could. I couldn't get that picture of C.O. out of my mind. A year ago when I first came to Canton, C.O. was a big man in town, one of Canton's wealthiest Negroes. He had opened up Canton for the Movement. He had sacrificed and lost all he had trying to get the Negroes moving. Now he was trying to look happy on a chain gang!

I felt worse about everything than I had ever felt before. Mrs. Chinn's words kept pounding through my head: "We ain't big enough to do it by ourselves." My head began to ache. I found myself running. I was trying to get away. I felt like the walls of Mississippi were closing in on me and Mrs. Chinn and C.O. and all the other Negroes in the state, crushing us. I had to get out and let the world know what was happening to us. I ran faster, and faster. I soon got back to the Freedom House out of breath, just in time to stumble into Dave Dennis' car and head for Jackson. About twenty minutes later, Dave was parking in front of the COFO headquarters on Lynch Street. Parked right in front of us was a Greyhound bus. The motor was running and smoke was shooting out of its exhaust pipe. It looked and sounded like it was about to pull off. Getting out of the car, I saw Bob Moses holding the door open waving goodbye to the people inside. I ran up to him and asked:

"Hey Bob, where's this bus going?"

"Oh! Moody, I'm glad you came. Can you go? We need you to testify," he said.

"Testify? What do you . . . ?"

"Hey Moody! C'mon get on, we're going to Washington!" It was little twelve-year-old Gene Young, leaning his head out of the window. As the bus began to pull out, Bob grabbed the door and held it for me. I just managed to squeeze in. The bus was packed. To avoid the staring, smiling faces I knew, I just bopped down between Gene and his friend. As soon as the bus was really moving, everybody began singing "We Shall Overcome." I closed my eyes and leaned back in the seat listening to them.

> *We shall overcome, We shall overcome*
> *We shall overcome some day.*
> *Oh, deep in my heart I do believe*
> *We shall overcome some day.*

"C'mon, Annie Moody, wake up! Get the Spirit on!" little Gene yelled right in my ear. I opened my eyes and looked at him.

"We're gonna go up there to Washington and we're gonna *tell* 'em somethin' at those COFO hearings. We're gonna tell 'em what Mississippi is all *about*," Gene said excitedly, joining in the singing. His eyes were gleaming with life and he clapped his hands in time with the song. Watching him, I felt very old.

> *The truth will make us free,*
> *The truth will make us free,*
> *The truth will make us free some day.*
> *Oh, deep in my heart I do believe*
> *The truth will make us free some day.*

Suddenly he looked at me again and saw that I still wasn't singing.

"Moody, what's wrong? What's the matter with you? You cracking up or something?" he asked, looking worried for the first time. When I didn't answer, he gave me a puzzled look and joined the singing again, but this time he was not so lively.

I sat there listening to "We Shall Overcome," looking out of the window at the passing Mississippi landscape. Images of all that had happened kept crossing my mind: the Taplin burning, the Birmingham church bombing, Medgar Evers' murder, the blood gushing out of McKinley's head, and all the other murders. I saw the face of Mrs. Chinn as she said, "We ain't big enough to do it by ourselves," C.O.'s face when he gave me that pitiful wave from the chain gang. I could feel the tears welling up in my eyes.

"Moody..." it was little Gene again interrupting his singing. "Moody, we're gonna git things straight in Washington, huh?"

I didn't answer him. I knew I didn't have to. He looked as if he knew exactly what I was thinking.

"I wonder. I wonder."

> *We shall overcome, We shall overcome*
> *We shall overcome some day.*

I WONDER. I really WONDER.